I0022775

UNDERSTANDING RURAL AND COMMUNITY DEVELOPMENT IN NIGERIA
THEORY AND PRACTICE

UNDERSTANDING RURAL AND COMMUNITY DEVELOPMENT IN NIGERIA
THEORY AND PRACTICE

OJUKWU UCHECHUKWU G.

Rex Charles & Patrick Limited

Copyright © Ojukwu Uche, 2013

All Rights Reserved: This publication or any part of it MUST not be copied or reproduced or repackaged or stored in any retrieval system and sold; or used to develop another publication by anybody without the signified consent of the author.

ISBN: 978-978- 51963-5-1

Printed and Published by:
Rex Charles & Patrick Limited,
Booksmith House, Harmony Place,
P. O. Box 575, Nimo,
Anambra State, Nigeria.
08023182425, 08080608127

DEDICATION

This book is dedicated to God Almighty

CONTENTS

Chapter Eight
DEVELOPMENT PLANNING   **158**

Chapter Nine
COMMUNITY DEVELOPMENT RESOURCES   **184**

ACKNOWLEDGEMENT

I am grateful to God for the privilege to write this book and for other blessings too numerous to count.

My appreciation will go to all the people who have touched my life. Significantly, my heartfelt appreciation goes to my lecturers: Prof. Nduba Echezona (late), Prof. Ezeani E., Prof. Obasi, Igwe, Chukwu C. C., Prof. Okorie A. and Prof. Ifesinachi Ken.

I will not forget to mention my amiable colleagues in the Department of Political Science, Anambra State University, Igbariam such as Dr. O.B.C. Nwankwo, Barr. Chidozie Ezeozue, Dr. Chubah Ezeh, Mr. Agbata Ifeanyi, Mr. Ikenna Alumona and Mr. Maduekwe Vincent, especially Mazi Mbah C. C., who wholeheartedly reviewed this book, I say thank you. Special thanks to Barr. Okeke Vincent Obiajulu Sunday, who has actually came up with the perfect title for this book.

Essentially, I remain grateful to Prof. Obikeze Sunday Obiajulu A. who in spite of his busy schedule agreed to review this book and write the foreword.

Also, I am not forgetting my good friends who in their own little way assisted me in this book, Mrs. Ify Ekwueme, Mrs. Maudlyn Ohuoha and Adaobi Chrishel Okonkwo and all the students of the Department of Political Science, Anambra State University, Igbariam from where I garnered inspiration, knowledge and support, you are all very wonderful and great to the fulfillment of this book.

My hearty gratitude goes to my Parents, Chief and Mrs. N. M. Okpalaume for the role they played in making sure that this book is a successful one. Also to my siblings especially my beloved eldest brother, Mr. Wilson Ogochukwu Okpalaume as well as members of my husband family, they were all instrumental to the success of this book.

At this point, I am very much grateful to my Darling husband, Comrade Ojukwu John Ugochukwu Chibusom for his fatherly advice to me and his encouragement in the course of writing this book. I pray that God will bless him abundantly in every of his endeavours in life.

Finally, I am grateful to Rex Charles and Patrick Publishing Company Ltd.

Ojukwu Uchechukwu G.

PREFACE

Community development is a dynamic process by which local citizens develop capacity to help improve and control their local area. The community development process is one that requires an understanding of the nature of community groups, the function of nonprofit organizations, the ways services are provided, and the networks that tie community groups to each other in the area and region. Community development functions to help community participants influence the direction of important public tasks including planning, governance, economic development, health and social service provision, responses to poverty, effective transportation, housing for all groups, and improved education and human resources. Changes in community practices over the last few decades have given increasing importance to community-wide collaboration, partnerships, and new forms of public-private organization. Similarly, the projects that community organizations are involved in are vastly more complex than those of even a few years ago, requiring inputs of technical, financial, legal, and social service expertise.

It is my sincere desire to present a textbook on Rural and Community Development in Nigeria that provides an up-to-date material arranged in a systematic and comprehensive manner. Steps have been taken to discuss fully all the topics of vital importance. This book is designed to provide an overview of the theory and practice of community development, including an historical review, an examination of contemporary issues, debates and challenges faced by communities in Nigeria and other countries, particularly those in rural areas. Key concepts to be explored are the important definitions of communities, community development, the characteristics of rural, and urban communities, community development theories and policies: principles, processes and programmes of community development, the issues confronting communities, such as insecurity, poverty, conflict, to name but a few. The book explores various approaches of community development in relation to their goals, processes and outcomes and the challenges of community development in the context of the current socio-economic realities in Nigeria.

The objectives of this book are to offer the knowledge and skills you will need to: Understand and think critically about the core elements of substantive issues in community development; Understand and apply the basic elements of a community development process to encourage participation and decision-making informed by multiple perspectives and sources of information; Identify and evaluate available resources related to community development practice and the wide range of topics that may be addressed by those working in areas linking community, environment, and development. Again, the book is to help students develop an appreciation of the main approaches, theoretical debates, experiences and research findings in community development both as a change process and as an interdisciplinary field. Students will be able to relate these theories and concepts to an analysis of how communities work for positive and comprehensive development. It is hoped that this book shall be of immense value to Practitioners of Rural and Community Development, Policy makers, Scholars and Students of Political Science, Public Administration, Local Government, Social Work and the entire general public who must be interested in how the society can be developed through joint efforts of the people and Governmental and Non-Governmental Agencies.

Accordingly, the discussion in this book reflects the views of a range of disciplines. The word limit necessitates a generic discussion rather than a detailed assessment of perceptions of distinct disciplines. It is also important to remember that this collection is not intended to be comprehensive. Although quite detailed in parts, it is intended to complement other sources. To this end, suggestions for improvement of the book will be thankfully received and incorporated in the subsequent editions.

Ojukwu Uchechukwu G.
Department of Political Science
Anambra State University, Igbariam, Campus
July, 2013
07033331344

FOREWORD

Rural and Community Development is an aspect of knowledge which scholars in the past did not give much attention. Scholars in Political Science and Public Administration were much more concerned with areas that enticed their ideological interests. Rural and Community Development was therefore explored mostly by sociologists and others in Urban, and Regional administration.

It is therefore heartwarming to observe that Political Scientists are now beginning to show interest in the area of community development. This is encouraging, especially, when we consider the emerging global issues and the need for researchers to pay attention to matters of rural and community development.

The attempt by Uche Ojukwu, in this area, is therefore, highly commendable. Rural and Community Development is an area that requires scholarly and intellectual investment especially when we consider the fact that more than 70% of Nigerians still live in the rural areas. These areas, therefore, require that considerable and conscious efforts should be made in creating some theoretical and practical approaches to enhance the development of these areas. With the dwindling economic and financial fortunes of states and central governments, the need for rural and community development has become both important and inevitable. Community development which conscious, concerted, co-ordinated and co-operative efforts of people who live within a given geographical area and who feel that their energy, finance and cognition are vital and should be pulled together to enhance their well-being, should be encouraged.

Mrs. Ojukwu has, therefore, courageously and painstakingly put together this comprehensive scholarly work to enable students, scholars, policy makers and administrators have a document that will be of immense help as they strive to ensure positive change in their environment. She has carefully combined effective classroom experience and field studies to come out with this very interesting and captivating book.

All the chapters have been tailored to capture the interest of general readership as they are written in simple but alluring language. The practical nature of the book makes it novel, couched in practical issues rather abstract concepts and theories.

The book starts with an introduction which effectively documented a number of basic issues in community, development, rural community, community development and others. Chapter Three and Four looked at, the history, origin, and dynamics of rural and community development. Chapter Fifteen - deals with conflict resolution at community level and causes of conflicts were well treated as well as the management of conflicts. This chapter is significant for dealing mostly with rural and community development initiatives and efforts which are deterred by conflicts. The concise attention given, by the author in all the chapters of the book makes it outstanding and of high quality. I, therefore, very warmly recommend this book for all.

Prof. Obikeze O.S.A.
Professor of Political Science and
Deputy Vice Chancellor,
Anambra State University, Uli

Chapter One

INTRODUCTION

1.1   Meaning of Community

A critical examination of the theory and practice of community development depends upon an understanding of the concept of community. The term "community" is used extensively in almost all areas of our lives. It is used in both our common, everyday language and also by professionals, politicians and corporations. We frequently hear about "community care", "community revitalization", "community service" and many other references to community. Yet, while everyone seems to have a fairly common understanding of what is meant by "community" it eludes a clear and comprehensive definition. The first step in considering the meaning of community is to understand that, fundamentally, it is a fluid concept. What one person calls a community may not match another person's definition. The evolving sociological debates surrounding the term, community, have been well documented (Black, 1998; Clark, 1983; Fraser, 1987; Pahl, 1966; Stacey, 1969; Thorns, 1976). For instance, Bell and Newby (1971) found that there were 98 definitions of the term. While there is a problem of securing an agreed definition of the term community, Williams (1976) claims that the term is rarely used disparagingly: "Community can be the warmly persuasive word to describe an existing set of relationships, or the warmly persuasive word to describe an alternative set of relationships. What is most important, perhaps, is that unlike all other terms of social organization (state, nation, society, etc.) it never seems to be used unfavourably and never to be given any positive opposing or distinguishing term" (Williams, 1976: 66).

The word "community" is derived from Latin and has been used in the English language since the 14th century. It refers to both the development of a social grouping and also the nature of the relationship among the members. The concept of community was further developed in the 19th century to contrast the dynamics and relationships of residents within a local setting to that of larger and more complex industrial societies. It is related to the terms **Commune** (French) and **Gemeinshaft** (German), in terms of denoting particular kind of relationships. Relationships within a community were thought to be more direct, holistic and significant than the more formal and abstract relationships with the larger society (Bakardjieva, http://www.ucalgary.ca/~bakardji/community/definition.html accessed January 17/2012). It was Aristotle who first defined the word "community" as a group established by men having shared values. That initial definition has been refined and expanded through the years. Also, we have come, for example, to recognize that people can belong to a number of different "communities" simultaneously--communities of place; cultural communities; communities of memory, in which people who may be strangers share "a morally significant history"; and psychological communities "of face-to-face personal interaction governed by sentiments of trust, co-operation, and altruism" (Baha'i, 1996).

Since the late nineteenth century, 'the use of the term community has remained to some extent associated with the hope and the wish of reviving once more the closer, warmer, more harmonious type of bonds between people vaguely attributed to past ages' (Hoggett 1997: 5). Before 1910 there was little social science literature concerning 'community' and it was really only in 1915 that the first clear sociological definition emerged. This was coined by C. J. Galpin in relation to delineating rural communities in terms of the trade and service areas surrounding a central village (Harper and Dunham 1959: 19). A number of competing definitions of community quickly followed. Some focused on community as a geographical area; some on a group of people living in a particular place; and others which looked to community as an area of common life. Thus, other than elucidating the concept through its examination, one operational definition may be that community exists in three broad categories as discussed by Wilmot (1989). One is defined in terms of locality or territory; another as a community of interest or interest group, such as the Black community or Jewish community; and thirdly, a community composed of people sharing a common condition or problem, such as alcohol dependency or cancer, or sharing a common bond like working for the same employer. Although this is a useful categorization, community must remain an essentially contested concept.

How, then, can community be defined? Community is defined according to Webster dictionary as a group of people residing in the same region and under the same government. A community can be defined as a conscious organization of individuals within a geographical area with definite and legal boundaries which support primary institution and use some common facilities within the area; hence, a community can be found in both urban and rural areas. It is also defined as a class or group with common interests. The community is the most important framework in which an individual learns to grow and develop socially. It is the centre of activities which contribute significantly to the development of human values. A community may be defined as a group of people sharing a common geographic area, a common value system, common needs and interests and who have had similar or shared experiences (Taken from Community Rights and Responsibilities, an original publication of the Social Development Commission for the Government of Jamaica, October 1975). Research on the definition of community has three elements in common:

- ✓ Community as a Place
- ✓ Community as an Institutional Structure
- ✓ Community as a Process

Community as a place: refers to that aspect of community which denotes the territorial location of people, or where people have something in common which is understood geographically. Another way of naming this place is "locality". There is a sense of attachment to a place, which has distinct geographic boundaries. This concept of community as a place is seen as being the first and most common element on which the community is based. For example, the Igbo community, the Yoruba community, the Nigerian community etc.

Community as an institutional structure: Community is also defined by the institutions that serve its residents many needs. They may have similar socio-cultural institutions like religious institutions, political institutions economic institutions and educational institutions, etc. These include health centres, schools, churches etc. One characteristic of a community is that people share these institutions. For example, **Academic Communities-** in an academic community, we have such examples as boarding schools, colleges, universities, research laboratries, or corporate training organizations. An illustration here is Anambra State University, (ANSU) Igbariam. These academic institutions attract people from other regions, bringing new capital into the area. Academic institutions in rural areas are very much like factories in that the economic success of the community depends upon the success of the institution. However, academic institutions primarily offer medium-skilled or professional jobs, while factories tend toward low-skilled work.

Community as a process: This refers to the interaction and socialization among people in a community – their interests, common objectives and needs. This element implies a "spirit of community" a sense of attachment with each other which forms the basis for their interaction in a variety of social groupings. These interactions offer a sense of "belonging" among people. Social networks/groups are developed to ensure connectedness and interaction among people. For instance here, we have the Ohaneze Ndi Igbo, the Arewa Forum, the Catholic community, Gay community etc.

World Health Organization (WHO), (1978) stated that a community consists of people living together in some form of social organization and cohesion. Its members share in varying degree political, economic, social and cultural characteristics, as well as interests and aspirations including health. Sociologically, community is defined as a group of people who live in a geographically defined territory and share common socio-cultural attributes with similar socio-cultural institutions-political, economic, cultural and social. These may be common businesses; common methods of education, common world-view, common religious beliefs and practices etc. Communities vary widely in size and socio-economic profile, ranging from clusters of isolated homesteads to more organized villages, towns and cities, for instance; we have the Nigerian community, the African Union, the Economic Community of West Africa (ECOWAS) and the global community. Sometimes communities are formed by self-identified members of a reference group based on characteristics outside of their control, e.g. a disability, ethnic group, or low income, which give them a sense of common identity and shared concerns. Thus, today we have what we refer as "an Online Community"- If the mechanism is a computer network, it is called an Online Community. Online communities are "social aggregations that emerge from the Net when people carry on those public discussions long enough, with sufficient human feeling, to form webs of personal relationships" (Rheingold, Howard, The Virtual Community http://www.rheingold.com/vc/book/intro.html (Accessed Jan. 11/2012).

In the light of the above Olise (2007) defined a community as a group of people living in a defined area and sharing some common interest; examples are towns and villages. A community can be homogenous that is consisting of people sharing the same culture e.g. villages or heterogeneous that is consisting of people sharing different culture e.g. urban cities. An individual can belong to several different communities at the same time; e.g. a faith community, a business community and a neighborhood community. Communities can be healthy or unhealthy, with most being somewhere in the middle. In an unhealthy community there may be an environmental disaster, such as the contamination of the water supply, a high level of poverty due to a major industry closing, or entrenched conflict over a divisive community issue. The path to becoming a healthy community starts with broad community engagement, leadership, the development of a shared vision and community goals, effective planning, local government commitment and collaborative use of internal and external resources. You can see the different ways a community is defined. Each of these definitions expresses the idea of living together in an area. As a result, individuals may belong to multiple communities at any one time. In simple terms a community may be said to be a group of people living within specified area and sharing things in common. Needless to say, the interests of the community pertaining to their means of livelihood, health, education, infrastructures and national resources are at their disposal. The term is most often associated with one or more of the following characteristics:

- common people, as distinguished from those of rank or authority;
- a relatively small society
- the people of a district;
- the quality of holding something in common
- a sense of common identity and characteristics.

1.1.1 Types of Communities

From the foregoing definition there are different types of communities depending on the size, origin, make-up and activities of each community. To this end, these paired major types of communities are easily identifiable. These are: Traditional (Primary) community and Secondary (Adopted) community, Rural community and Urban community, Open (Public) and Closed (Private) community, Homogeneous community and Heterogeneous community etc.

❖ Traditional (Primary) Community versus Secondary (Adopted) Community

1. **Traditional (Primary) Community:** A traditional community (Gemeinschaft) is one which is usually small and the inhabitants can easily trace their origin to a common ancestor or community. The people of traditional communities are usually emotional and sentimental, which may be as a result of their common origin with everyone looking and perceiving one another as brothers and sisters, no matter the size of their community. Such communities usually have a common world view with common aspirations. The people from such communities are relatively equal in terms of achievements and progress in life. By the reason of folklore, and in some cases, actual history, most communities in Nigeria belong to the primary or traditional type (Aliyu 1982). Examples here are Nnewi community,

Igbariam community, Adazi – Ani community, Adazi – Enu community etc.

2. **Secondary (Adopted) Community:** Secondary or adopted communities (Gesellschaft) are usually communities with people of diverse background that is different ancestors, different cultures, different world view etc. the people are usually outgoing, less sensitive and less emotional. They aspire differently and engage in what fancies anyone's attention. They are very progressive and achievement minded. This type of community is usually associated with urban areas or large areas where it is usually difficult to establish the identity of those who make up, live or work in such communities. There is no common culture in such secondary communities for instance, the Nigerian community in USA, the Nigerian community in France and the Igbo community in Kano State etc.

❖ Rural Community versus Urban Community
3. **Rural Community:** Rural areas are defined/characterized by small-tight knit communities, with lack of technology and resources. Ever seen those shows where everyone knows everyone else? Well that's a rural community. Villages or small towns are considered to be rural areas. People know each other and are neighbours, friends, etc. Rural areas are classified according to their small population and having farming abilities. Many people in rural areas are considered to be farmers. Rural areas are more dependent on natural resources and organic materials. They have small stores and family run businesses, compared to the big supermarkets in urban areas. Many governments have also taken an active part in trying to further urbanize more rural areas and provide extra help in forms of technology, medical and other resources. Rural areas are more community based people and depend on social gatherings and other similar events. Rural places also have pollution due to lack of large factories.

4. **Urban Community:** Urban areas are defined by faster lifestyle, increased technology and high population density. Urban areas are characterized by having higher population density and vast human features compared to the surrounding areas. Cities, towns are commonly referred to as urban areas. It must also have ongoing urbanization for further development. Metropolitan cities, which include satellite cities, are also considered as urban places. Urban areas have also been characterized by high amounts of pollution

(noise and air), large-scale industrialization and faster lifestyles. Pollution in urban areas are high due to the large amount of people, cars, buses, train, factories etc. Industrialization includes factories, machines and offices. It also has higher employment rate compared to rural areas. Lifestyle in urban areas is considered to be fast paced, where time for little things are not enjoyed. People are often depicted as workaholics or having an active social life. Urbanization also includes having more advance technology and science, where hospitals have more advanced machinery and people have smart-phones, tablets, laptops, desktops, etc.

❖ Open (Public) Community versus Closed (Private) Community

5. **Open (Public) Community:** An open community maintains social relations with other communities. According to Obikeze (2002), an open community or society is one in which the inhabitants are free in all the ramifications of freedom – freedom of movement to wherever they desire to go; freedom to engage in whatever activity they choose; freedom to live their lives the way they choose. The government has control over the activities of individuals which deviate from the legally approved standards. Wilcox and Shepherd (1975) maintained that open communities are competitive, fair, equitable, efficient and inclusive. Such communities include countries in Western Europe, Canada and United States of America.

6. **Closed (Private) Community:** A closed community intentionally limits links with other communities (Raymond, 2012). Closed societies or communities are the ones in which the opposite of the life in open societies are attained. The people have their lives, regulated by the government or other overseeing agencies. Wilcox and Shepherd (1975) also, have identified closed communities as monopolistic, exclusive, rigid and unequal. In some cases, the people's choice of work to do, their lifestyle and their world-view is dictated by the government as was the case in the former communist bloc of the defunct Soviet Union and their allies.

❖ Homogeneous Community versus Heterogeneous Community

7. **Homogeneous Community:** A homogeneous community is a group of people who are all of the same culture, race, or ethnicity living within a community or area for instance the traditional Igbo community or Yoruba community, the Black community etc. Homogeneity occurs in

many human communities because human beings as a whole like to be surrounded by familiar things and people, given the choice. Therefore, many communities are homogeneous in the sense that they speak the same language, value the same things and have the same beliefs. These people, therefore, have a lot in common. However, "sameness" can also fall into other categories such as, age, academic abilities, or gender. A homogeneous community can also be defined as a group of people who meet on a regular basis for a particular reason or who live near each other. For example, a community of musicians, a community of activists.

8. **Heterogeneous Community:** Heterogeneous community may refer to a society or group that includes individuals of differing ethnicities, cultural backgrounds, sexes, or ages for instances, the Global Community, the Economic Community of West African States (ECOWAS), the Nigerian community. In Nigeria for example, there are not less than 250 different ethnic groups having their different cultural and social issues yet they all inhabit the Nigerian community.

   ❖ Intentional Community versus Natural Community
9. **Intentional Community:** In the context of community development, it is important to realize that we are not dealing with intentional communities that are communities built around an intention where their members become members of this community as they share this specific intention. Examples of intentional communities are a company, cooperative, club, or interest group such as Amnesty International.

10. **Natural Community:** Rural communities are natural communities, as the members are part of the community, just as they are born in this community. The members of a village community may have different intentions or differing opinions, but they are bound through a common history, shared culture and values, and are part of a community. Community development of such natural communities faces challenges that are distinct from those of organizational development or the development processes of a cooperative. Community, in general, means a network of people shaped by joint experiences, sharing certain common values, having specific concerns, feeling bonded to each other, and often living in a particular geographical area.

1.1.2 Differences between Rural and Urban Communities

Rural areas are usually referred to as small, inward looking, idyllic communities held together by kinship relations and supporting basic agricultural occupations. While urban areas on the other hand are dynamic, ever-changing, and commercial centers (Ekong, 2003). The major differences between rural settings and urban centers and cities are given below:

Table: 1.1: **Differences between Rural and Urban Communities**

Serial No.	Rural Community	Urban Community
1.	**Environment:** Close / direct contact with nature. Preliminaries influenced by natural environmental elements like rain, heat, drought, frost, snow etc. over which there is no control.	Greater isolation from nature. Predominance of manmade (artificial environment).
2.	**Occupation:** Agriculture is the fundamental occupation. Majority of the population are engaged in agriculture. Neighbours of Agriculturist are also agriculturist	No fundamental occupation. Most people engage in manufacturing, mechanical pursuits, trade, commerce, professions and other non-agricultural occupations.
3.	**Size of Community:** Size of community is small. Agriculturalism and size of community are negatively co-related.	Size of community is large. Urbanity and size of community are positively co-related.
4.	**Density of Population:** Density of population is lower. Density and rurality are negatively co-related.	Size of community is large. Urbanity and size of community are positively co-related.
5.	**Homogeneity and heterogeneity of population:** More homogenous in social, racial and psychological traits. Negative co-relation with heterogeneity. (Most as agriculturists are directly connected with agriculture).	More heterogeneous than rural. Urbanity and heterogeneity are positively co-related (Different types of population are seen in cities, different places, religions, caste, class race, community, economic and cultural differences, occupations and behavioural pattern also differ).
6.	**Social Differentiations:** Low	High degree of social differentiation.

		degree of social differentiation.	
7.	**Social Stratification:** More rigid, Fewer economic, occupational, and sociopolitical classes. Less social stratification than urban.		Less rigid Urban community is much more strategic than the rural, having much more economic, occupational and social political classes.
8.	**Social Mobility:** Mobility is less intensive. Territorial, occupational and other forms of social mobility of the population are less intensive. They pursue same occupation and stay in the same village		Social mobility is more intensive. People change occupation and even leave places in search of new and better occupation.
9.	**Social Interaction:** Less numerous contacts. The area of interaction system is narrower. More professional, simple, face to face. Informal, sincere relations.		More numerous contacts. Area of interactions are wider, the relation are superficial and short-lived. The popular are more formal and showy.
10.	**Social Solidarity:** Social solidarity or cohesiveness and unity are stronger / greater than urban. Common traits, similarity of experiences, common aims and purposes, common customs and traditions are the basis of unity in the village. Strong sense of belonging and unity.		Social solidarity is less strong than rural, dissimilarities, division of labour, interdependence, specialization, impersonal, strictly formal relationships results to comparatively less sense of belonging and unity.
11.	**Social Control:** Social pressure by community is strong. Conformity of norms is more by informal social pressure.		Control is more by formal impersonal means of laws, prescribed rules and regulations.
12.	**Social Change:** Rural social life is relatively static and stable.		Urban social life is under constant and rapid social change.
13.	**Culture:** Sacred (Religious) culture.		Secular (Non-religious) culture.

14.	**Leadership Pattern:** Choice of leadership more on the basis of known personal qualities of individual, due to greater face to face contacts and more intimate knowledge of individual.	Choice of leadership is comparatively less on the basis of known personal qualities of the individual.
15.	**Group:** Rural society is simple unit-group society.	Urban society is a complex multi-group society.
16.	**Social Institutions:** Most of the institutions are natural outgrowth of rural social life. Less enacted institutions.	Numerous enacted institutions.
17.	**Standard of Living:** Home conveniences, public utilities, educational recreational religious, medical, communication and other facilities for living can be provided if supported by sufficient population base.	In urban areas such conveniences and facilities are provided due to greater density of population.
18.	Standard of living is low	Standard of living is high
19.	**Political Inclination:** Political awareness and or political consciousness are very low.	Political awareness and or political consciousness are very high.

1.2 CONCEPTUALIZING DEVELOPMENT
Definition of Development

Development is a complex issue, with many different and sometimes contentious definitions. Desai (2008) submits that development is a generic term. This means that it has many uses and variants; which variety is clarified in the context of the definition of the usage. Development is the process of enlarging people's choices (UNDP, 1990: 1). Development consists of the removal of various types of un-freedom that leave people with little opportunity of exercising their reasoned agency... ... Development can be seen... ... as a process of expanding the real freedoms that people enjoy... ... the expansion of the 'capabilities' of persons to lead the kind of lives they value - and have reason to value (Sen, 1999: xii, 1, 18). In the view of Long John (1998), development is induced. It has to be worked to be attained. For the purpose of this work;

development is defined as a permanent condition of positive growth, resulting in a higher level or condition, which is better than the previous stage or position (Iheanacho, 2012). This is more apt for community development which is desired for the transformation of such places to become better and more conducive and more hospitable than they previously were. As a desired stage, the attainment of any stage in community development has to be planned, programmed, and the process towards development implemented, evaluated, reviewed and ascertained.

1.2.1 Dimensions of Development

Even if the development of a socio-economic system can be viewed as a holistic exercise, i.e. as an all-encompassing endeavour; for practical purposes, in particular for policy making and development management, the focus of the agents aiming at development is almost always on selected parts of the system or on specific features. To this end, "development" is qualified and specified in different ways. A summary (non-exhaustive) list of possible qualifications comprises:

- **Economic Development:** i.e., improvement of the way endowments and goods and services are used within (or by) the system to generate new goods and services in order to provide additional consumption and/or investment possibilities to the members of the system. Economic development has traditionally been seen as the first form of development. It has often been strictly associated with the concept of economic growth, in turn defined as an increase in the per capita income of the economic system. Indeed, growth defined in this way can be seen more as the result of an economic development process, i.e. the transformation of the structure of an economic system, rather than as a development process per se. Countless economists provided insights and proposed models to explain how economic systems develop (or should develop) to generate growth. Just to mention some milestones, it is worth mentioning the contributions of Shumpeter (1911), who suggested that economic systems evolve through subsequent disequilibria due to agents which introduce innovations, more than "developing" according to a pre-determined path.
- **Human Development:** People-centred development, where the focus is put on the improvement of the various dimensions affecting the well-being of individuals and their relationships with the society (health, education, entitlements, capabilities, empowerment etc.) Nowadays the concept of development encompasses a set of elements comprised in more than one of the above-mentioned

qualifications. UNDP (2010) for instance, provides an aggregate concept of human development on the basis of three criteria: (i) "Long and healthy life", (ii) "knowledge" and (iii) "A decent standard of living", respectively measured by life expectancy at birth, mean years and expected years of schooling and gross national income per capita at purchasing parity. The associated Human Development Index (HDI) is then adjusted on the basis of (iv) the inequality in the distribution of the specific features within countries, assuming that the unequal distribution of wealth is an undesirable feature of the development processes.

- **Political Development:** Political development is the ability to enhance the capacity of the political system. Political systems may be conceived in dynamic terms as active agents which have capabilities, perform functions, influence their environment and are in turn influenced by it. Political development takes place when there is democratization of political process: pluralism, competiveness, equalization of power, and similar qualities. It also promotes a high level of political mobilization and participation. Political development occurs when the political system is compelled to respond to certain types of problems or crises like national identity, political legitimacy, integration and distribution etc.

- **Sustainable Development:** The concept of "sustainable development" was first introduced by Brundtland (1987), who defines development as "sustainable" if it "meets the needs of the present without compromising the ability of future generations to meet their own needs". The current UNDP definition of sustainable development is: "The process of enlarging people's choices and freedoms so that they may lead long, healthy and secure life, acquire knowledge, and have equal access to the resources needed for a decent standard of living without compromising the prospects of future generations" (UNDP 1998). Development which considers the long term perspectives of the socio-economic system, to ensure that improvements occurring in the short term will not be detrimental to the future status or development potential of the system, i.e. development will be "sustainable" on environmental, social, financial and other grounds. Sustainable development implies minimizing the use of exhaustible resources, or at least, ensuring that revenues obtained from them are used to create a constant flow of income across generations, and making an appropriate use of renewable resources. This applies to energy (oil and oil products in particular) but also to fish stock, wildlife, forests, water, land and air. Land degradation, due to soil erosion and salinisation, persistent water and air pollution, depletion of fish stock and deforestation are all examples of consequences of non-sustainable activities. Soil conservation practices; Good Agricultural Practices (GAP) based on reduced use of energy, pesticides and chemicals; waste management and recycling, waste water treatment, use of renewable energy sources such as biomasses and solar panels, are frequently cited as techniques for sustainable development. The concept of sustainability has also been extended beyond environmental concerns, to include social sustainability, i.e. long term acceptance and ownership of development changes by the citizens, their organizations and associations (civil society), and financial and economic sustainability. According the World Bank Report (1997) "Sustainable Rural Development can make a powerful contribution to four critical goals of poverty reduction: wider shared growth, household, national, and global food security and sustainable natural resource management."

- **Territorial Development:** Territorial development is the development of a specific region (space) achievable by exploiting the specific socio-economic, environmental and institutional potential of the area, and its relationships with external subjects. This dimension of development refers to a territorial system, intended as a set of interrelationships between rural and urban areas, in a space characterized by the existence of poles of attraction for human activities (production and consumption of goods and services, but also culture and social life), and connected by information systems and transport infrastructures. When referring to production activities, poles of attraction can be characterized as "Clusters" where, for various reasons, homogeneous or closely interlinked activities are implemented. Territorial systems are open to influences from the national and supra-national contexts and from the interrelationships between territories. Territorial development implies focusing on the assets of the territory, its potential and constraints (FAO, 2005). Polices to exploit and enhance this potential, play an important role in the development process.

Three Core Values of Development
Three core values serve as standards of development.
- a. **Sustenance:** This refers to the capacity to meet basic necessities such as food, clothing, and shelter. The lack of even one of these basic needs means that a person's life is not progressive. A country

develops if its citizens have enough or more than enough for their basic necessities, there is growth of income, extreme poverty is addressed, and there is equality among members of society.

b. **Self-esteem:** The quality of life is good when there is respect, trust, and self-value. Each person has needs which can be achieved through the presence of respect, dignity, and a good reputation in society. A person's worth as an individual cannot simply be measured by the ownership of material things which is often given emphasis by progressive capitalist countries such as the United States. In the Philippines, material wealth is not the only important thing but the love for one's family, the family's reputation, and a person's dignity and self-esteem. A country is developed if this unique need of the people is addressed.

c. **Freedom from Servitude:** This freedom is drawn from liberation from oppressive systems in society, poverty and abuse, slavery, ignorance, and the absence of the freedom to choose one's culture or religion. This freedom can be seen in the range of choices in a society. What is good about development is not only the joy of being free from poverty but also the availability of a wide range of choices. In general, freedom prevails if people live a comfortable life, if they have the freedom to choose their religion, to vote and to express their opinion about administration and governance, and if they enjoy equal opportunities for education and employment.

1.2.2 Development Indicator

A development indicator is often understood as an easily presented index that represents data on a multi-dimensional concept that is being measured. Indicators are measured for a specific place and time and are typically used to represent, compare and monitor complex development issues such as poverty over time and between countries and regions. Indicators are therefore a key mechanism for measuring progress toward development objectives. To be effective they must communicate useful information - enabling situations to be understood and decisions made. Indicators must be both meaningful - accurately portraying what is happening - and resonant - allowing people to grasp the relevance to their own lives. Here, Human Development Index (HDI) and Millennium Development Goals (MDGs) have been highlighted on.

Human Development Index

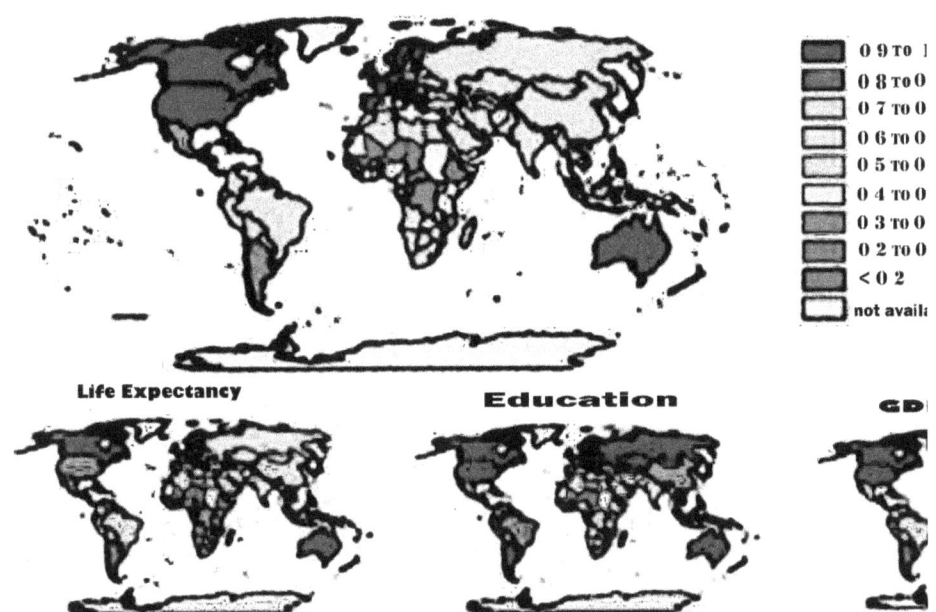

Figure 1.1: The Human Development Index of 2006 and its three components.

The Human Development Index (HDI) is a creation of the United Nations Development Programme and represents the practical embodiment of their vision of human development as an alternative vision to what they perceive as the dominance of economic indicators in development. Economic development had the gross domestic product (GDP) so human development had to have the HDI. In essence the HDI represents a measure of the 'quality of life'. A tool developed by the United Nations to measure and rank countries' levels of social and economic development based on certain criteria. The HDI makes it possible to track changes in development levels over time and to compare development levels in different countries. Since its appearance in 1990 the HDI comprises three components:

I.   Life expectancy (a proxy indicator for healthcare and living conditions).
II. Adult literacy combined with years of schooling or enrollment in primary, secondary and tertiary education.
III. Real GDP/capita ($ PPP; a proxy indicator for disposable income).

According to the World Bank, almost one-half of the world's 6.5 billion inhabitants live on the equivalent of less than two dollars a day, and about one-fourth of the world live on the equivalent of less than $1.25 a day (Chen and Ravallion, 2008).Meanwhile, people in the 20-richest countries on average earn 39 times more than people in the poorest 20 (Milanovi, 2007). At the same time, the extent of poverty has declined significantly. For example, the World Bank estimates that from 1981-2005 the percentage of people living on less than $1 per day was halved. The amount decreased from 52 percent to 26 percent in this period (Chen & Ravallion, 2008). These contrasts highlight both the problem and the progress of what is known in the international community as "development." Large numbers of the world's inhabitants are mired in poverty, especially in Africa, while inhabitants of the world's richest countries live in both relative and absolute luxury. But people in poor countries are getting wealthier over time—a process linked to globalization because poorer countries can raise their standards of living by integrating with rich countries. The term "development" in international parlance therefore encompasses the need and the means by which to provide better lives for people in poor countries. It includes not only economic growth, although that is crucial, but also human development—providing for health, nutrition, education, and a clean environment.

The choice of these three components for the HDI is not surprising, and they can be found in many lists of development indicators. It can certainly be argued that the selection of only three components for human development is problematic. Income inequality, for example, is not included alongside GDP/capita and neither are there any elements of 'consumption'. The UNDP have argued that these three can act as proxy indicators for many others. For example, provision of a clean water supply and/or adequate nutrition would be reflected in life expectancy. Indeed, given that the UNDP wanted an index that was relatively transparent and simple to understand it is also not surprising that they decided to include only three components.

Sadly, and perhaps unsurprising, large swathes of Africa have low values for the HDI (orange and yellow), implying that the level of human development for the continent is poor. The preponderance of dark green and blue across the globe (higher values of the HDI) paint a more positive picture, but its still Africa which stands out. But that just gives the overall picture, and how does this breakdown in terms of the three components of the HDI? Well the story is not all that different whichever component is looked at. The three 'bits' of the HDI are also presented in Figure 1.1. The GDP/capita (income) component almost exactly mirrors the coloring for the HDI. The two other components – life expectancy and education – do show some nuanced differences. Life expectancy is particularly poor in the southern African countries, a reflection of the preponderance of HIV/AIDS, while education is especially poor in West Africa. However, looking at the maps for the three components it is easy to see how they merge into the map of the HDI. Neither is it hard to appreciate how the three components may be related – higher income per capita could mean greater expenditure on education and health care for example. In that sense even though the three components are quite different (a heterogeneous index) the HDI does have an internal consistency.

The Millennium Development Goals (MDGs) Indicator

Table 1.2: The United Nations Millennium Development Goals (MDGs)
❖ **MDG 1. Eradicate extreme poverty and hunger.** **Target 1.A:** Halve, between 1990 and 2015, the proportion of people whose income is less than one dollar a day. **Target 1.B:** Achieve full and productive employment and decent work for all, including women and young people. **Target 1.C:** Halve, between 1990 and 2015, the proportion of people who suffer from hunger. ❖ **MDG 2. Achieve universal primary education.** **Target 2.A:** Ensure that, by 2015, children everywhere, boys and girls alike, will be able to complete a full course of primary schooling. ❖ **MDG 3. Promote gender equality and empower women.** **Target 3.A:** Eliminate gender disparity in primary and secondary education, preferably by 2005, and in all levels of education no later than 2015. ❖ **MDG 4. Reduce child mortality.**

Target 4.A: Reduce by two thirds, between 1990 and 2015, the under-five mortality rate

❖ **MDG 5. Improve maternal health.**

Target 5.A: Reduce by three quarters, between 1990 and 2015, the maternal mortality ratio.

Target 5.B: Achieve, by 2015, universal access to reproductive health.

❖ **MDG 6. Combat HIV/AIDS, malaria, and other diseases.**

Target 6.A: Halt and begin to reverse, by 2015, the spread of HIV/AIDS.

Target 6.B: Achieve, by 2010, universal access to treatment for HIV/AIDS for all those who need it.

Target 6.C: Halt and begin to reverse, by 2015, the incidence of malaria and other major diseases.

❖ **MDG 7. Ensure environmental sustainability.**

Target 7.A: Integrate the principles of sustainable development into country policies and programmes and reverse the loss of environmental resources.

Target 7.B: Reduce biodiversity loss, achieving, by 2010, a significant reduction in the rate of loss.

Target 7.C: Halve, by 2015, the proportion of people without sustainable access to safe drinking water and basic sanitation.

Target 7.D: Achieve, by 2020, a significant improvement in the lives of at least 100 million slum dwellers.

❖ **MDG 8. Develop a global partnership for development.**

Target 8.A: Develop further an open, rule-based, predictable, non-discriminatory trading and financial system. Includes a commitment to good governance, development and poverty reduction — both nationally and internationally.

Target 8.B: Address the special needs of the least developed countries. This includes: tariff- and quota-free access for the least developed countries' exports; enhanced programme of debt relief for heavily indebted poor countries (HIPC) and cancellation of official bilateral debt; and more generous ODA for countries committed to poverty reduction.

Target 8.C: Address the special needs of landlocked developing countries and small island developing States (through the Programme of Action for the Sustainable Development of Small Island Developing States and the outcome of the twenty-second special session of the General Assembly).

Target 8.D: Deal comprehensively with the debt problems of developing countries through national and international measures in order to make debt sustainable in the long term.

Target 8.E: In cooperation with pharmaceutical companies, provide access to affordable essential drugs in developing countries.

Target 8.F: In cooperation with the private sector, make available the benefits of new technologies, especially information and communications technologies.

Source: UN (2007); Green Facts, based on the Millennium Ecosystem Assessment; see: www.un.org/millenniumgoals/

The Millennium Development Goals (MDG) Indicators are widely used examples of development indicators. Since the late 1990s MDGs has been one of the internationally agreed set of development indicators in the form of the United Nations MDGs (see 1.2). The MDGs are the product of agreements at international conferences led by UN agencies, giving them some legitimacy as desirable development outcomes or targets. The signing of the Millennium Declaration (United Nations, 2000) by UN members at the UN Millennium Assembly in New York, on 18 September, 2000 was the basis for a 'road map' – the MDGs – prepared for the UN General Secretary by a Working Group including the UNDP, other UN-specialized agencies, the IMF, the World Bank and the OECD (Poston et al., 2004). The MDGs themselves comprise eight goals with 18 targets and 47 indicators (refer to Table 1:2 and United Nations, 2007).

The MDGs are, of course, not without critics. Saith (2007: 1184) has argued strongly that the MDG 'scaffolding' 'ghettoizes' the problem of development by locating it exclusively in the 'third world' with an agenda created almost exclusively by industrialized countries without adequate consultation and based entirely on absolute standards of living. As well as a trenchant methodological critique, Saith argues, that there is a potential distortionary MDG effect through a diversionary impact on the orientation of the social science research agendas – which are themselves largely dependent upon funds provided by government-funded research councils or from development agencies which are 'MDG driven'. He also argues that there is a potential distortion of practice through the behaviour of international aid agencies and government bureaucracies which tend towards the 'misuse and manipulation of statistics and the misrepresentation of outcomes... [so that] perverse incentives and behaviour can result' (Saith, 2007: 1174). He continues with the points that data availability and quality are very uneven or weak and that many of the MDGs fail to capture dimensions of wellbeing adequately (for example, what do primary enrolment/completion rates really say about educational achievement?). He suggests that the MDGs significantly understate the new dimensions of development (i.e. participation, democracy, sustainable livelihoods, vulnerability and risk).

1.3 CONCEPTUAL EXPLANATIONS OF COMMUNITY AND RURAL DEVELOPMENT

1.3.1 The Concept of community Development

The concept of Community Development (CD) occupies a pivot position around which all the socio political thought of twentieth century revolves. The term is so vast, in its scopes and application that, it is quite difficult to put it within the framework of a comprehensive and adequate logical definition. Again, the changes in emphasis on different aspects of it, at various points in time have complicated it for a text book definition. Several thinkers, committees, international organisation have defined it in varying ways. Some definitions have emphasised on material progress. Many have described it as a movement; others see it as an aspect of administration, a process of development technique of bringing people and local resources together for development. The meaning of the term will become clearer as we will go on analysing its various aspects in ensuing pages. However, to start with, we can consider some of the important definitions already put forth.

In attempt to give a definition to this concept, the Cambridge summary conference of (1948) in Hanachor (2009:5) opined that:

> Community development is a movement designed to promote better living for the whole community with the active participation and if possible, on the initiative and if not forth coming spontaneously, by the use of techniques for arousing and stimulating it in order to ensure it's active enthusiastic response to the movement.

In the same direction, the Ashridge Conference of (1954) presented community development as "a movement designed to promote better living for the whole of the community with the active participation and on the initiative of the community". The United States International co-operation administration (1956) defines community development as a "method by which national government reaches out to people at the village level and helps them use local initiative and resources to achieve increased production and higher standard of living". This contribution presents community development as a social process within the community which gives room to community members not only to identify their areas of need (felt needs) but also go on to offer solutions from within their local resources.

In the same direction, the United Nations in 1948 viewed "Community Development as a process designed to create conditions of economic and social progress for the whole community with its active participation and fullest possible reliance upon the community's initiative" (Head, 1979:101). Subsequently, the United Nations Organizations (1978) quoted in Anyanwu (1992:3) viewed community development as: A process by which the efforts of the people themselves are united with those of governmental authorities to improve the economic, social and cultural conditions of communities, to integrate these communities into the life of the nation and enable them contribute fully to national progress. The definition of the United Nations stresses on the need for local effort, involvement in form of active participation and self help in initiation, planning and execution of projects in communities with much reliance on their local resources, and the vital role of governmental and non-governmental sources of assistance in the areas of technical and financial services to encourage communities in the achievement of specific goals. In its contribution, the Economic Commission of Africa (ECA) as reported in Hanachor (2005:7), defined community development as: The outcome of a series of quantitative change occurring among rural population. It is a process by which a set of institutional measures are implemented with and for the inhabitants of rural areas, with the aim of improving the socio-economic condition of the rural populace. Since community development implies change for better, the concept suggests that people are not committed in whatever circumstance dictates for them. They have the capacity to make creative input to the improvement of their situation and the mastery of their environment.

In addition to the contributions of conferences and organizations, individuals also took positions in the attempt to define community development. One of the early contributors in this area was Baker (1950). He presented community development as an educational process and said: "It is not better roads, better bridges, pure water nor better sanitation. It is something of the spirit more than something of material. It must reach deep into cultural patterns of the people, examining them and testing them as principles of faith. It is not a temporary, physical construction; it is a building with the heart and minds of men, not a recreation centre in the middle of the field". Baker in his definition emphasized on the conscious involvement of members of the community. This fact tallies with the idea of the Ministry of National Planning on true development as the development of man, the unfolding and realization of his creative potentials (see fig 1.2). Community development is seen as a move by the people (community members) to provide their basic needs through their own efforts and sometimes with external assistance (where necessary and possible). He asserted that though this external assistance may come or not, it is believed by professionals in community development that adequate injection of external assistance in self help endeavours by the communities reinforce local development actions.

Figure 1.2

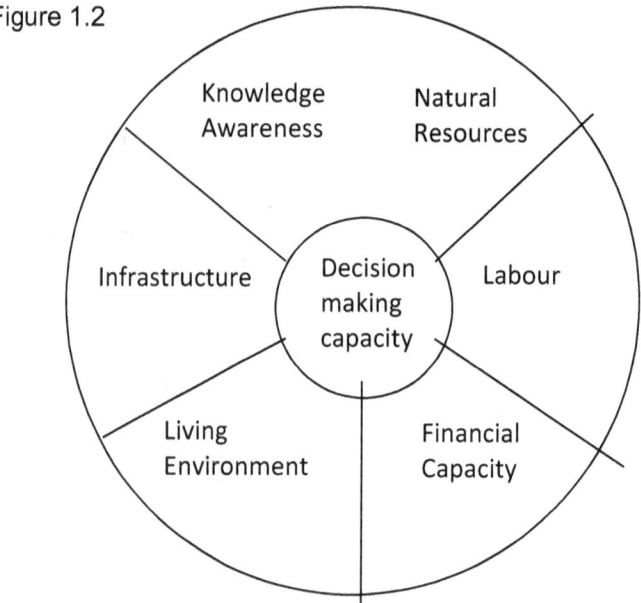

Source: Understanding   Community   Development. www.communitydevelopment.com,au/DOC. (Cavaye, 2000).

Community development as reported by Hillman (1960) in Bello I.O. and Bola Oni S (1987:2) is: A method of helping local communities to become aware of their needs, to assess their resources more realistically, to organize themselves and their resources in such a way as to satisfy some of their needs and in so doing acquire the attitude, experience and co-operative skills for repeating this process again and again on their own initiative. In his definition, Hillman presented a process approach to community development as involving dynamic sequence which sets in motion people's effort in the realization of their goals in which ever direction. Still revolving around the process of educating the members of the community for change, community development also has been defined as the process involved in the education of members to take deliberate action for community change, the nature of which is determined by them in terms of their own valued system.

To Nelson and Lowry, social change should be man's cherished aspiration. In a related view, Anyanwu (1992:2) defined community development as: A process of social action in which the people of a community, organized themselves for planning and action, define their common and individual needs and problems..., execute these plans with maximum reliance upon community resources and supplement these resources when necessary with services and materials from government and non–government agencies outside the country. Community development is seen as a process when individuals are assisted through organized effort, to acquire the attitudes, skills and orientation required for effective and meaningful participation in programmes designed to improve their standard of living. Mexiro (1967) had earlier argued that community development is "a planned and organized effort to assist individuals to acquire the attitudes, skills and concepts, required for their democratic participation in the effective solution of a wide range of community problems in order of priority".

Community development when viewed in the light of educational process manifests in behavioural change and acquisition of new skills and confidence as a result of repetition or practice and co-operation. Murry (1966) in Bello I.O. and Bola Oni S (1987:1) took another dimension (programme approach) thus; 'The utilization under a single programme of approaches and techniques which rely upon local communities as units of action which attempts to combine outside assistance with organized local self determination and effort which correspondingly seek to stimulate local initiative and leadership as the primary instrument of change. Murry's definition like others emphasized on the importance of participation by the people of a community in the improvement of their living condition and physical environment. It also brought in the element of external assistance for successful community development. Thus community development is positive change in the social, economic, organizational, or physical structures of a community that improves both the welfare of community members and the community's ability to control its future. It entails a variety of citizen-led efforts, carried out within or on behalf of a community, to define problems, develop solutions, and attract the resources necessary to implement activities that address the identified problems.

1.3.2 Assumptions of Community Development

The assumptions, upon which the concept of community development is based, are very similar to those upon which community organization is based. This is because of the interrelatedness of the two processes. More specifically, the concept of community development assumes that:

I. The local community has been overshadowed by the larger society as a result of long isolation, colonial domination (external and internal) and consequent decline in community spirit.

II. The local people are poor owing to an underdevelopment of both the available resources in their environment, and their own individual potentialities.

III. People everywhere want better conditions of living and a richer economy and can develop the capacity to improve these things by themselves.

IV. Many problems besetting rural populations can be solved at the community level with local community resources and with outside intervention limited to education and technical aid.

V. Participation of people in decision making on major changes taking place in their communities is desirable and functional; and

VI. Local people do not see their problems in isolated packages but as a complex whole, hence community development must be multipurpose in nature, touching all aspects of community life.

1.3.3 What is Rural?

The rural community is predominated by a natural environment having a direct relationship to the size of the place, with a general low density of population. The rural society characterized by the village communities and the urban society characterized by towns and cities have a number of contrasting features (Chaudhuri, 2012). Within a rural society the population is more homogeneous with less sociological differentiation. Rural societies tend to exhibit low territorial and social-strata mobility's and the relationships among the rural inhabitants are through direct and primary contacts. Their social relationships tend to be personal and relatively durable over time. In fact, some of these characteristics can be better understood on a comparative basis, in contrast to urban society. In addition to social indicators, demographic indicators also distinguish rural society from urban society. In general, demographers tend to classify a settlement with a population greater than 5000 as urban. In terms of occupations, and settlements where more than 75% of the populations depend on agriculture are considered to be rural.

According to Ekong (1988), in the strictly traditional sense, various parts of Nigeria had their own conception of the rural area referring to the farm and farming settlements while the town referred to the seat of an important chief or ruler. Among the traditional Yoruba, Nupe, Hausa and Fulani, the rural area was more or less a temporary farming settlement, while the town was the place where the permanent family house was located, where the dead were buried, where marriages and other feasts were celebrated. In the Eastern part of Nigeria, among the Igbos, the people traditionally lived in villages surrounded by farms and virgin forests, hence most large towns in the present eastern Nigeria are of recent emergence. By now you should be able to identify your home place as a town or a rural area. Olawoye (1987) posited that, the concept of rurality is dependent upon its relationship with urbanity for its meaning. A community that is not rural is by definition urban. Historically, rural referred to areas with low population density, small size; relative isolation, where one major economic activity was agricultural production, and where the people were relatively homogenous in their values, attitudes and behaviour (Bealer et.al; 1965). In general, a place that is "not declared urban" based on the above conditions is said to be a rural area.

1.3.4   Characteristics of Rural Areas

i.   **Poor Road Network:** If you are from a rural area or if you have ever visited one, you would have observed that the road network cannot in anyway be compared with that of the urban area in terms of good quality. Both inter and intra road - networks are bad. The gutters are not dug; the roads are not tarred and therefore predisposed to erosion. Most roads to the farms are mere footpaths. Bad road network in the area is one of the factors that increases cost of food production, hence, increase in prices of farm products.

ii.   **Large Dependence on Agriculture:** Another characteristic of rural area is that, a large percentage of the adults are engaged in agriculture or other agriculture-related activities. The term "rural" can as well be defined as an area or settlement in which half or more of the adult male working populations are engaged in farming.

According to Imoudu (1986), while urban dwellers are generally non-agricultural, ruralites are essentially agricultural. Consequently, the word 'rural' can be equated to agriculture and other agriculture-related occupations carried on in the rural areas.

iii. **Large Percentage of Illiterates:** Have you ever noticed that a large percentage of people in the rural areas are illiterate? There are more elderly people than youths? Yes, these elder people did not have the opportunity for western education and that is why a larger percentage of them are farmers, since they cannot do other jobs which may demand some levels of literacy. The educated ones are found in the towns and cities striving for survival.

iv. **Larger Number of Old People than Youths:** Rural areas usually have larger number of old people than youths. This is because youths often migrate to urban areas in search of work, higher education, apprenticeship to a trade or other engagements for survival.

v. **Large Dependence on Local Farm Tools:** Can you mention some local farm tools used in the rural areas? Yes, if you mention hoe, cutlass, knife then you are correct. The rural people cannot afford mechanized farming because of its need for high capital outlay. So, rural farmers are into subsistence farming.

vi. **Minimal Capital Investment:** Rural area is also identified with minimal capital investment. The rhythm of poverty prevailing in rural settings does not afford the rural dwellers the opportunity for high capital investment. Their source of income is mainly from the savings from the sale of their farm products. Strict collateral security, often demanded by credit institutions, does not equally afford the rural dwellers the opportunity for loans as obtained in urban areas.

vii. **Dependence on Household Labour:** Another characteristic of rural areas is that, the main source of their labour is by the household. Can you define a household? What is the difference between a household and a family? Labour supply for the various farming activities is mainly from the household family. Though hired labour or cooperative labour is also available, the unpaid and cheap labour force from the household family is most prevalent.

viii. **Absence of Large/Good Markets:** Have you been to any market in the rural area? If you have, you would have observed that, the markets often don't have lock-up shops but in the open and usually no standard of measurement but on the bargaining ability of the buyer. Again, farm products usually predominate in rural markets.

ix. **Lack of Portable Water and Electricity:** Not until recently that the government administrations and other international donor agencies began to give consideration to the provision of portable water and electricity, typical rural areas have been associated with the lack of them. In fact, lack of these and some other social amenities have been the reason why youths often migrate to the urban areas in search of better living standards. The absence of these necessary amenities is also the reason why cottage industries such as farm product processing facilities cannot be provided. So, while the rural areas produce the farm products the processing is mainly done in the urban areas.

x. **Poor Communication Facilities:** Rural areas are also characterized by poor communication facilities. Rural areas lack postal services, telephones, fax and electronic mails (e-mail). Television and radio are scarcely used due to lack of electricity. Village criers normally convey information from the ruler to the subjects.

xi. **Smallness of Farm Holdings:** Earlier you have learnt that the rural settlers have minimal capital investment; they use local farm tools and depend mostly on household labour supply. All these are the factors militating against big farm enterprise resulting in the smallness of holdings among rural farmers. Olajide (1980) had earlier classified small farmers as people having less than two hectares of farm size. Not only that the farms are small, they are equally scattered over distant areas.

1.3.5 Meaning of Rural Development
Figure 1.3

There is no universally acceptable definition of rural development; the term is used in different ways and in many divergent contexts. Rural development can also be viewed in terms of concept, a phenomenon, a strategy and a discipline. As a concept, it involves overall development of rural areas with a view to improving the quality of life of rural people. In this sense, it is a multi-dimensional concept and it includes the development of agriculture and allied activities such as the cottage industries and craft, socio-economic infrastructure, community services and facilities, and above all, human resources in the rural areas. As a phenomenon, it utilizes the interaction of various physical, technological, economic, socio-cultural and institutional factors. As a strategy, it is designed to improve the economic and social well being of a specific group of people in the rural area. As a discipline, it is multidisciplinary in nature representing an integration of engineering and management sciences.

According to Lele (1975:20), rural development means improving the living standards of the masses of low income residing in rural areas, and making the process of their development self-sustaining. It can also be defined as the articulation, provision and stimulation of economic activities, health and educational advancement facilities, and utilities for rural dwellers (Ugwu, 2009:130). Furthermore, Ugwu claimed that, rural development is a venture towards urbanizing the rural environment by way of encouraging rural dwellers to participate in activities that will promote economic and social development and enhance their living standards. On its own part, the World Bank (1973:3), defined rural development as a strategy designed to improve the economic and social lives of a specific group of people. According to the financial body, it involves extending the benefit of development to the poorest among those who seek a livelihood in the rural areas (Ujo, 1994:111). But Basu (2006:470), in a contrary opinion, stated that the essence of rural development is the all round development of the rural areas or villages with the efforts of the people. He contended that the need for citizen participation in plan formulation and implementation processes has been repeatedly stated as the gateway to bringing about social, economic and political development in the rural areas.

The definition of rural development has evolved through time as a result of changes in the perceived mechanisms and/or goals of development. A reasonable definition of rural development would be: development that benefits rural populations; where development is understood as the sustained improvement of the population's standards of living or welfare.

Rural development can be seen as not an outside intervention, but the aspiration of local people living in rural areas for taking the challenge themselves and improving their life circumstances and their immediate environment. Olayide et al. (1981) see rural development as a process whereby concerted efforts are made in order to facilitate significant increase in rural resources productivity with the central objective of enhancing rural income and creating employment opportunities in rural communities for rural dwellers to remain in the area. It is also an integrated approach to food production, provision of physical, social and institutional infrastructures with an ultimate goal of bringing about good healthcare delivery system, affordable and quality education, improved and sustainable agriculture etc. According to Van der Ploeg et al. (2000), rural development is reconstructing the eroded economic base of both the rural economy and the farm enterprise... (and) represents the well understood self-interest of increasing sections of rural population.

Rural development ensures the modernization of the rural society and the transition from its traditional isolation to integration with the national economy. It is essential so as to generate foreign exchange, and to attract revenue to finance public and private consumption and investment. Rural development may also be seen as an ideology and a practice. It may mean planned change by public agencies based outside the rural areas such as the National Government and International organizations. It may also be the bringing of the countryside into an active state, as well as the transformation of the inferior nature of the country side into something more superior in terms of activities. According to the World Bank (1975); rural development must be clearly designed to increase production. It recognizes that improved food supplies and nutrition, together with basic services, such as health and education, not only directly improve the physical well-being and quality of life of the rural poor, but can also indirectly enhance their productivity and their ability to contribute to the national economy.

From the foregoing, the above definitions have salient points which are common to most of them. The writers are interested in the welfare of the rural populace. They are worried on how to improve their living standards from their low per capita income and their participation in the policy formulation and implementation of their own areas. With these, rural development can be comprehensively defined as a strategy for improving the living standards of the rural people from their low per capita income, through the active participation of these rural dwellers themselves in the formulation and implementation of all rural developmental programmes. Rural development, therefore, implies the transformation of rural community into a socially, economically, politically, educationally, orderly and materially desirable condition, with the purpose of improving the quality of life of the rural populace. Rural development must be clearly designed to increase production. It recognizes that improved food supplies and nutrition together with basic services, such as health and education, not only directly improve the physical well being and quality of life of the rural people, but can also enhance their productivities and their ability to contribute to the national economy.

1.3.6 Objectives of Rural and Community Development
The following are the main aims and objectives of rural and community development:

1. **To create awareness:** The main objective of rural and community development is working to make the people aware of various problems in a community. It helps them to provide knowledge and to know about the main causes and affects of their social life.
2. **All sided development:** Community programme is interested in all aspects of a community. The development is necessary in these places as a whole in education, health, recreation and employment. It seeks the opportunities for the better living standard of the community people. Development is required in all sectors of the community.
3. **To motivate people:** Programmes are adopted for the motivation of community people. Social organizers are employed in various sectors for their arousal and working for community welfare and betterment of humanity.
4. **Provide equality:** It gives equality to all people living in a territory. It gives equal chances and opportunities to bring the resources for their utility. So it provides equality in education, health and also other facilities provided to them.
5. **Help the people to motivate themselves:** Such programmes have the interest of the people at heart enable them to help one another and themselves. It helps them to stand on their own feet. They have to use their resources to make their lives comfortable.
6. **Change thinking:** One of the objectives of rural and community development programmes are changing of pattern and style of community people. It gives new directions to changing life styles. It

helps create acquaintances among them, to following the positive thinking of the people.

7. **To bring reforms:** Such programmes aim at bringing social reforms in a community. It helps them in eradication of social evils which are at the grass roots, which bring social disorder in communities. So one of the aims of rural and community development is to provide them with better opportunities to solve the problematic situation through reforms.

8. **Social Justice:** Social justice is another objective of community development. It provides justice to all types of people. There would be no concept of rich and poor, thus, the programmes would be for the utilization of all.

9. **Solve community problems:** Different problems faced by community people may be solved due to the start of such programmes in the effected areas. The community also assists the government in development and growth.

10. **To create interest:** These programmes are adopted to create the interest of community welfare among the people. It mobilizes the attitude of people to participate in the collective work for the community development. The motivation of these people depends on the skill of social organizers working in the areas.

1.3.7 Importance of Rural and Community Development

There are lots of reasons why we need community development now more than ever. Expectations are increasing for communities to take on roles in service design and delivery, planning and budgets for their local neighbourhoods. Accounting for differing and minority voices in the process will be a challenge for diverse and rapidly changing communities. Thus, importance of rural and community development include:

➢ By encouraging local people to get involved in activities, people are empowered to start to come up with their own solutions to problems and issues.

➢ Bringing people together around common themes or problems helps to build communities, improve community cohesion, and to make connections between different communities.

➢ The many opportunities that community groups provide for people to take part in activities together not only benefit the community as a whole, but also allow people to develop skills and abilities to make improvements in their individual home lives.

> ➢ Involving local people in improvements to health, security and prosperity will give them a sense of ownership, which means the improvements are more likely to be effective and long-lasting.
> ➢ By listening to people, sharing good ideas and learning from past experiences we can spread good ideas, and avoid wasting time and money on 'reinventing the wheel' too many times.
> ➢ Community group activities help build good quality environments to live in. This then helps improve local health and education, and contributes to safer and stronger communities overall.

Ekong (2003) identifies the importance of the rural area to include:

a) The rural area is the predominant food and fiber producing sector of the society. Apart from food and fiber, it can be observed that nearly all natural resources which constitute the wealth of a nation are obtained from the rural areas. This makes development of the rural sector the best interest of national development agenda.

b) The rural area is the seed bed of national population and serves to replenish the human resources of the urban centres.

c) In times of national emergencies and crises, the rural areas constitute the place of refuge and also a huge reservoir of national patriotism and manpower owing to the fact that rural people are relatively unaffected by international threats and aggression flourishing among the multi ethnic mix of people in the urban centres.

d) The relative conservativeness of rural dwellers and apparent natural resistance of rural cultures to rapid change make rural areas the conservatory of pristine cultures and traditions of the people which are often quickly discarded in urban areas. In other words, the sector plays an important role in cultural heritage.

e) The rural population is equally a source of stability or neutralizing influence on the urban population in many ways. Also the rural environment provides a necessary break to the urban from the hectic activities and tempo of urban living. In other words, the rural area serves as a resting place.

f) In Nigeria, the importance of the rural areas also lies in the mere fact that over 70 per cent of the people live and derive their livelihood from there.

From the above discussion, the necessity of developing the rural areas becomes evident. In a developing society like Nigeria with infant industries, weak industrial base and overwhelming neo-colonial influence, it is imperative to develop the rural areas for that sector to continue to perform the above enumerated functions more efficiently and effectively.

1.3.8 Rationale for Rural - Community Development in Nigeria

The development of the rural communities in Nigeria is cardinal for, but certainly not limited to, the following reasons:

a) No country is completely urbanized.

b) They form the most important sector of the economy. This is because; they supply the entire country with its food needs, raw materials for industries, employment generation and foreign exchange earnings.

c) Urban populations are serviced by the rural population as they replenish urban population.

d) Lack of development activities characterizing the rural areas has led to sharp development difference existing between the urban and rural areas and has contributed to youth exodus from rural to urban centres. Rural development can reduce this exodus.

e) Lack of development of secondary and tertiary infrastructures entails concentration of manpower in the urban centres. In order to reverse this trend, rural community infrastructural development becomes an imperative.

f) There is the humanitarian reason why policy makers should give attention to the rural areas. This is because; the human beings in the rural settings deserve the good things of life, having contributed so much to the entire system.

g) Economic development is a process which requires the growth and modernization of both the rural and urban sectors.

1.4 COMMUNITY AND RURAL DEVELOPMENT AS A SUB-FIELD OF PUBLIC ADMINISTRATION

Community development as a field of study draws from diverse academic disciplines, including: Political Science, Sociology, Urban Planning, Anthropology, Cultural Studies, Environmental Studies, Geography, History, Social Psychology, Communication, and Urban Design among many others. Wikipedia (2009) sees Community Development (CD) as a broad term applied to the practices and academic disciplines of civic leaders, activists, involved citizens and professionals to improve various aspects of local communities. Community development is eclectic, integrating specialized knowledge from Education, Public Health, Economic Development and Politics. Community development is a set of approaches undertaken by individuals, informal groups and organizations.

People have been making careers of stimulating improvement or development of communities for generations. There is no clear point at which a type of approach directed toward this end became identified as "community development".

Community development can be regarded as both old and new. Its roots are deep in the past, i.e. some of its essential features and some aspects of its practice are as old as community life. Community development in its essential aspects is not a new idea, but its application to problems of the underdeveloped areas; there have been some rather original adaptations. Batten (1957) is very vivid on the subject when he says "I must make another preliminary point. Enthusiasts for community development sometimes speak or write about it as if it was something entirely new, and they irritate the very many who feel that community development is not new, but that its principles were in fact applied by a multitude of individual government offices and missionaries long before anyone had thought of such a term as community development. This is true and in every sense of the word, community development, as we recognize today is based on, and has grown out of, the experiences of the past. What is new is that these principles are becoming more widely recognized than ever before and more consciously and the more purposely applied by the many agencies, which are basing their policies upon them. It is the emphasis that is new, rather than the principles.

However, we cannot overlook the fact that community development in its new dimension, as a tool in large scale social planning has been recognized not far long ago (Dwarakinath, 1967). Interest in community organization and community development appeared to originate in the period following World War I (Sanders, 1958: 32) and developed more conspicuously after World War II (Sanders, 1958: 389-391). Sander is very emphatic when he says, community development is the brain child of our generation. The antecedents are many, tracking back into history, but it was in the post World War II period that the term gained popularity. Activity under this banner, much of it in the then colonial world, was enough that by the 1950s, sections of the United Nations felt compelled to attempt to define it (United Nations, 1955). From then on, agencies, associations and scholars have been proposing and promoting definitions for community development with abandon (Sanders, 1958; Ad Hoc Group, 1963; Lotz, 1970; Warren, 1978; Christenson and Robinson, 1980). Community development is a discipline unto itself, with a body of theory, standards of practice and professional associations. In general, community development is regarded as a domain of less developed countries, but since 1990 many developed countries such as Japan, England, Germany, Australia, and the U.S. have been trying to stimulate community engagement in public affairs as well as support local development through a wide variety of policies. It may be necessary here to re-state that the major goals of community development include to induce social change for balanced human and material betterment; to strengthen the institutional structure in such a way as to facilitate social change and the process of growth and to promote social justice by permitting less privileged groups to give expression to their aspirations and to participate in development activities. Community development professionals work on a wide variety of issues, including: housing, transportation, economic development, environmental conservation, and empowerment.

In order to understand community development it is important to understand that it means different things to different people in different places — and that our understanding about what constitutes effective or appropriate community development has expanded considerably in the past few years. What we do know is that it is found on voluntary and healthy interdependence, mutual benefit and shared responsibility. In recent years, more often than not, community development has involved local people seeking and taking advantage of opportunities or working together to solve problems. Community development is a conscious and deliberate effort aimed at helping community to recognize the needs and to assume responsibility for solving their problems, thereby increasing their capacity to fully participate in the life of the nation. It is a process by which the effort of the people are united with that of governmental authority to improve the economic, social and cultural condition of community, thereby integrating the people in the life of the nation which in turn enable them to contribute fully to the national progress. Good community development helps people to recognize and develop their ability and potential and organize themselves to respond to problems and needs which they share. It can – and should – be practiced in all sectors, whether public, private or voluntary. Community development can be paid or unpaid, qualified or simply experienced.

i. **Community Development as a Process:** Community development as a process has the focus on the changes through which a community passes. It is a process from one condition to another. "It involves a progression of changes in terms of specialized criteria. It is an evolutionary state of change from lower point to the upper. It is a neutral scientific term ... emphasis is on what happens to people, socially and psychologically (Sanders, 1958: 31). It is the process of total development of man in a community. It is the motivation of people towards change in their behaviour and mental growth.

ii.   **Community Development as a Method:** Community development as a method is more an action oriented approach. That is, a method of practical work in the community; people are involved in it to bring change and development in the community. It is a method of improvement and progress in which the social organizer play an important role. Here, community development is looked upon as "a means to an end; a way of working for, that some goal is attained... the processes are guided for a particular purpose (Sanders, 1958: 31).

iii. **Community Development as a Programme:** Community development as a programme amounts to a set of activities that have been carefully considered as to the contents and procedures. The importance here is given to the activities and the objective. The method is taken as a set of procedures and the content as a list of activities. By carrying out the procedures, the activities are supposedly accomplished (Sanders, 1958). The community programme tries to meet the basic needs and requirements of the people. Basically community development programme activities are as under:
- Physical improvements, such as roads, housing, sanitation, drainage system and farming etc.
- Functional activities are health, education, protection, recreation etc.
- Social activities including group discussion cooperation, work together, self reliance etc.

iv.   **Community Development as a Movement:** Community development as a movement is considered to be something more than a programme. It is the gradual change in behaviour, belief, mental horizon and motivation towards change in human life. Community development is viewed here as "crusade, a cause to which people become committed. It is not neutral ...but carries an emotional charge. It is dedicated to progress... Community development as a movement tend to become institutionalized (Sanders, 1958). As a movement, it is the persuasion of masses to become self reliance and work for the betterment of community. This movement is impossible without the help, cooperation and coordination and also active participation of the people in community programmes.

Community development is generally considered as a process. Defining community development as a process puts the emphasis on the manner of proceeding. This implies that it is possible to follow an orderly progression from exploration and initiation through study and discussion to action and evaluation. It puts the emphasis on the local group, on local initiative, on local participation. Finally, it puts the emphasis on full responsible participation and the action by all the people affected (Curtiers, 1958).

Community development seeks to empower individuals and groups of people by providing these groups with the skills they need to affect change in their own communities. Community Development therefore is the total efforts or strategies adopted by any group of people of a geographical area to positively raise and uplift the standard of their existence. In other words, Community Development (CD) may be simply rendered as the process of helping a community strengthen itself and develop towards its full potential. A number of different approaches to community development can be recognized, including:

- Community Economic Development (CED);
- Community Capacity Building;
- Social Capital Formation;
- Political Participatory Development;
- Nonviolent Direct Action;
- Ecologically Sustainable Development;
- Asset-based Community Development;
- Faith-based Community Development;
- Community Practice Social Work;
- Community-based Participatory Research (CBPR);
- Community Mobilization;
- Community Empowerement;
- Community Participation;
- Partcipatory Planning including Community-Based Planning (CBP);
- Community-Driven Development (CDD); and Approaches to Funding Communities.

Chapter Two

PRINCIPLES OF COMMUNITY AND RURAL DEVELOPMENT

2.1 PRINCIPLES OF COMMUNITY AND RURAL DEVELOPMENT

The principles of Community Development include:

a) **Principle of Felt Needs: -** Felt needs are problems/issues the people recognized. They are conditions which disturb people and are causing general discontent. These are differentiated from needs which service providers and do-gooder groups or agencies have determined based on their perceptions. The community organizer's task is therefore to discover what these felt needs are and to channel these and the people's discontent into organization and action. It is also easier to organize and mobilize people for addressing felt needs which are widely shared.

b) **Principle of Leadership: -** Leadership is a key to successful community organizing. It is important that the leader is: accepted, well respected, has a charisma or influence to a number of people, is democratic, has a track record of working for the common good, and demonstrated capability of making things work. One must therefore be careful in the selection of leaders in the community organizing process.

c) **Principle of Self-Help: -** The idea of self-help is one of several distinguishing features of community development theory, practice, and ideology. Self-help is based on the premise that people can, will, and should collaborate to solve community problems. In addition to the practical problem-solving utility of this perspective, self-help builds a stronger sense of community and a foundation for future collaboration. Self-help is emphasized not only as a goal to be achieved in and out of it, but also as a strategy for the accomplishment of broader development objectives. Helping communities achieve a capacity for self-help is fundamental to both the theory and practice of community development. Self-help embodies two interrelated features: (1) it is expected to produce improvements of people's living conditions, facilities, and/or services); and (2) it emphasizes that the process by which these improvements are achieved is essential to development of the community. The "developed community" is both improved and empowered as a result. Thus, a self-help approach not only emphasizes what a community achieves, but more importantly, how it achieves it. Another way of stating this is to distinguish between development in the community (the improvements) and development of the community (how these improvements are achieved) (Christenson & Robinson, 1989).

d) **Principle of Effective Participation:** People affected by the problems must be actively involved in all phases of the organizing process: needs identification, capability building, resource identification and utilization, other decisive actions to solve the problems, and evaluation. Genuine community development aims to enable people to be in control in management of projects or programmes designed to address their problems in which they were involved in the decision-making process. Community organizers must veer away from token participation such as information giving, consultation and placation efforts.

e) **Principle of Communication:** Open lines of communication must be established and maintained among community organizers, local leaders and community members. Individual and group deed backing is an important communication process. In addition to verbal communication, the community organizers can utilize mass media such as printed and broadcast media. People are motivated when they hear or know that development is taking place in their community.

f) **Principle of Structure:** Community development should develop an organizational structure that is simple and functional based on the needs of the people. It need not follow the structure of formal organizations. Instead, the community organizers may set up working committees, education, research; ways and means of logistics; membership and mobilization; and liaison/negotiations.

g) **Principle of Self Determination, Working and Learning Together:** Individuals and groups have the right to identify shared issues and concerns as the starting point for collective action. Valuing and using the skills, knowledge, experience and diversity within communities to bring about changes.

h) **Principle of Social Justice:** Working towards a fairer society that respects civil and human rights and challenges oppression.

i) **Principle of Evaluation:** Assessment is an on-going process in community development. Efforts should be made to assess the gains of any mobilization or social action, its strengths and weaknesses and to sum-up the lesson learned. This process is also referred to as ARA, or Action, Reflection, Action.

2.2   COMMUNITY DEVELOPMENT VALUES

The theory and practice of rural and community development has always been informed by a set of values. This value base is important in defining the people and places where its efforts are concentrated, the way it works with people, and the sort of outcomes that it seeks. The value of community development can be considered with fewer than three broad headings: the things it challenges; the ideas it promotes, and the thinking it influences.

Community Development Challenges Exclusion

Community development is committed to combating social exclusion, poverty, disadvantage, and discrimination. As such, it should not be considered as a value-free or universal approach. It is based on recognition that some people, some groups and some communities are excluded from social, economic and political opportunities for reasons of lack of wealth, cultural oppression, physical obstacles or prejudicial attitudes. Its focus is with groups and communities that are excluded due to one or more of these causes, and its role is to work with such groups to achieve change. Thus, community development promotes social inclusion. In emphasizing the need to tackle the consequences of poverty, disadvantage and discrimination and to promote social justice and participation, social inclusion expresses ideas that have long been shared with community development. Social inclusion can be promoted through the activities of providing support to the development of individual capacity, and building community capacity to generate social, economic and democratic activity and opportunities. Achieving social inclusion is therefore an active process of people participation. It is not something that can be done to people but must be done with and by them. It is a participative and dynamic process of learning, action and reflection.

Community Development Promotes Strong Communities

The second set of values informs the way such change is understood. Community development reflects and promotes a number of ideas. These include:

- **Full Citizenship:** Many groups are effectively disenfranchised through the lack of opportunity to participate in decision making, or the failure of decision makers to recognize or respond to excluded voices. The idea of full or active citizenship recognizes that the health of communities, and society as a whole, is enhanced when people are motivated and able to participate in meeting their needs. Active citizenship is not based on the idea of do-gooding or benevolent philanthropy but ideas of mutuality and reciprocity which are the "glue" that binds people together and underpins the very idea of society. The expression of shared responsibility evidenced in practical action is to be found in all dimensions of community life - politics, sport and recreation, care, art and culture, religion, the environment, health, economic development - and, at its best, involves participation across boundaries of race, age, gender and disability.

- **Community Led Collective Action:** Community development is an approach to change that depends on building solidarity and support through emphasizing the common aspects of individual problems, and the capacity of people to work together in their common interest. The worker supports the development of community leadership and encourages the building of a collective, accountable approach. Collective action in communities includes small-scale and large-scale activities to meet local needs, as well as action to lobby for change.

- **Participative Democracy:** The will of the majority must be carried out, but only after all voices are heard and considered and minority rights are protected. Widespread, active participation in public affairs is good in itself, as well as a means to achieving best value and effectiveness in administration of public services. A participative approach can lead to a better understanding of needs and issues, clarity about who benefits from, and who is excluded from services, and can develop better ways of targeting scarce resources. It can also lead to innovative ways of meeting needs, including partnership arrangements through which communities can develop, administer and benefit from running services.

- **Inclusive:** There are many barriers to participation in society; poverty, disability, age, race and ethnicity and some other characteristics that often marginalize people. A healthy community embraces diversity and recognizes that all community members have a right to be heard and participate in processes that affect their lives.
- **Non-authoritarian:** Organizational structures are as flat as possible, with all participants being seen as equally important and having equal input.

- **Community Self Determination:** Community members come together to discuss their concerns, assess options and arrive at their own conclusions. They may seek advice from 'experts', but consider it along with other sources of information and their own experience and make their own decisions that are right for them.

- **Community Ownership:** Communities thrive when they develop their own assets, but also when they "own" their problems and issues. When communities accept that it is 'their' problem, then they are more likely to work together to develop a solution, thus, the solution will be better than one provided solely by an external 'expert'.

- **Enhance Natural Capacities and Networks:** There are sources of strength in every community; for example, informal networks and social support systems, or certain individuals that have particular talents or are able to help others in need. A community developer identifies these existing community assets and works with them. It is important not to duplicate existing structures and functions as that may weaken rather than strengthen the community.

- **Empowerment:** Most forms of exclusion are based on lack of power and influence, and imposed solutions are at best paternalistic and at worst oppressive. Community development has at its heart a commitment to empowerment: encouraging communities and groups to learn how power relationships operate, and to develop their ability to deal with the problems.

- **Problem Focused Learning:** This is the core approach taken to empowerment. Community development is based on the idea that people learn from the experience of tackling their own problems. It seeks to encourage people to think about the causes of problems, act on those causes, and learn from the outcome. Similarly policy on lifelong learning recognizes that developing skill and understanding needs to be a continuing process. Fact this reflects the value of continuous individual and community self-development and improvement. Equally it recognizes that technological, social, economic, environmental and other forms of change require new skills and understanding. Hence lifelong learning is functional to the employability of individuals and the needs of the labour market and the national economy. It is also a source of personal fulfillment, achievement and self-realization, and as such, a basis for building strong communities.

- **Preventative Action:** Much public service provision is based on dealing with problems after they have occurred. While recognizing the importance of this, community development seeks to identify the underlying causes of problems and to deal with these, rather than with their manifestations. Strong communities have capacity to identify potential problems and take preventative action.

- **Collaboration:** Community development involves collaboration between interest groups, government and citizens. Some approaches to work in communities only emphasize self-help: things they can do themselves in their own interest. Others seek to confront and challenge power holders directly. Neither of these approaches led to partnership or collaboration. Community development emphasizes collaboration. Communities may be forced to adopt a confrontational position to get an issue recognized. Once it has been, it is usually in the interest of both the community and the decision maker to identify and implement solutions. Similarly, many activities that start out as self-help will begin to engage with public agencies for funding or other forms of support. Once this happens some form of collaboration is almost inevitable. It is important to understand the strengths and weaknesses of communities (and other collaborators) in such relationships.

Community Development Influences Policy
Finally, community development seeks to identify and define issues of public concern, and influence public policy in relation to those issues. It is a value in itself that it seeks to inform and influence public policy in this way. It has a particular role in making the connections between private troubles and public issues. In doing so, it reflects all the values discussed above, but seeks to reflect them in the way that public issues are identified, and in the way the formulation of policy is influenced.

- **Social Justice and Equity:** This is fundamental to community development and is at least implicit in all community development work, if not an explicit goal of a community development programme.

- **Universality:** Services are available to everyone, without requiring means or needs testing.

- **Service Integration:** Often services provided to persons in need are fragmented, so that one service provider doesn't know what other services are available or being used, resulting in gaps, duplications and sometimes conflicting advice or treatments. A community development approach would ensure that services are coordinated, that they enhance and strengthen natural community and family supports, that effective communication among all involved, and that services are directed by the individual receiving them, to the extent possible.

- **Upstream:** The distinction between upstream vs. downstream approaches uses a river as a metaphor for the increasing impact of conditions and events which affect health over time and space, and relates to the point of intervention. For example, if there is a toxic spill upstream, it will affect the quality of the water in the river for everyone living downstream. You can focus either on dealing with the illnesses that are experience by the downstream people (downstream approach) or you can stop the spill and prevent others from happening in the future (upstream approach).

Chapter Three

HISTORY OF RURAL AND COMMUNITY DEVELOPMENT

3.1 THE HISTORY OF RURAL AND COMMUNITY DEVELOPMENT: A GLOBAL VIEW-POINT

Community development practice has arisen from a variety of sources and settings. Community development according to Wikipedia (2009) has been at sometimes explicit, sometimes implicit goal of community people, aiming to achieve, through collective effort, a better life, and has occurred throughout history. From the Wikipedia account therefore, the 18th century's work of the early socialist thinker Robert Owen (1771–1851), sought to create a more perfect community. At New Lanark and at later communities such as Oneida in the USA and the New Australia Movement in Australia, groups of people came together to create utopian or international utopian communities, with mixed success. Such community planning techniques became important in the 1920s and 1930s in East Africa, where Community Development proposals were seen as a way of helping local people improve their own lives with indirect assistance from colonial authorities.

In the 1960s, the term "community development" began to complement and generally replace the idea of urban renewal in the United States, which typically focused on physical development projects often at the expense of working-class communities. In a capitalist system, certain groups are relatively excluded from taking part in the economic, political and social systems and from getting their due share of the benefits that derive from these systems. As a result, capital is accumulated within the hands of minority groups. In the underdeveloped countries it was also the result of colonialism and neo-colonialism leading to urbanization without attention to rural areas. In the late 1960s, philanthropies such as the Ford Foundation and government officials such as Senator Robert F. Kenndy took an interest in local nonprofit organizations—a pioneer was the Bedford-Stuyvesant Restoration Corporation in Brooklyn—that attempted to apply business and management skills to the social mission of uplifting low-income residents and their neighbourhoods. Eventually such groups became known as "Community Development Corporations" or CDCs. In the 50's and 60's community development or community organization, as it came to be called, was used in deprived or underdeveloped urban and rural settings in North America (Smith, 1979: 52). Community development was a response to the perceived disintegration of society due to rapid technological change, economic dislocations, disruption in traditional family and community structures and the extension of government and commercial services into personal and family life, with negative impacts on personal effectiveness and community ties.

Federal laws beginning with the 1974 Housing and Community Development Act provided a way for state and municipal governments to channel funds to CDCs and other nonprofit organizations. National organizations such as the Neighbourhood Reinvestment Corporation (founded in 1978 and now known as Neighbour Works America), the Local Initiatives Support Corporation (founded in 1980 and known as LISC), and the Enterprise Foundation (founded in 1981) have built extensive networks of affiliated local nonprofit organizations to which they help provide financing for countless physical and social development programmes in urban and rural communities. The CDCs and similar organizations have been credited with starting the process that stabilized and revived seemingly hopeless inner city areas such as the South Bronx in New York City.

Furthermore, Wikipedia (2009) observed that community planning techniques drawing on the history of utopian movements became important in the 1920s and 1930s in East Africa, where Community Development proposals were seen as a way of helping local people improve their own lives with indirect assistance from colonial authorities. Mohondas K. Gandhi adopted African community development ideals as a basis of his South Africa Ashram, and then introduced it as a part of the Indian Swaraj movement, aiming at establishing economic interdependence at village level throughout India. With Indian independence, despite the continuing work of Vinoba Bhave in encouraging grassroots land reform, India under its first Prime Minister Jawaharlal Nehru adopted a mixed-economy approach, mixing elements of socialism and capitalism. During the fifties and sixties, India ran a massive community development programme with focus on rural development activities through government support. This was later expanded in scope and was called Integrated Rural Development Scheme (IRDS). A large number of initiatives that can come under the community development umbrella have come up in recent years. Community development became a part of the Ujamaa Villages established in

Tanzania by Julius Nyerere, where it had some success in assisting with the delivery of education services throughout rural areas, but has elsewhere met with mixed success. In the 1970s and 1980s, Community Development became a part of "Integrated Rural Development", a strategy promoted by United Nations Agencies and the World Bank (Wikipedia, 2009). Central to these policies of community development were

- Adult Literacy Programmes, drawing on the work of Brazilian educator Paulo Freire and the "Each One Teach One" adult literacy teaching method conceived by Frank Laubach.
- Youth and Women's Groups, following the work of the Serowe Brigades of Botswana, of Patrick Van Rensburg.
- Development of Community Business Ventures and particularly cooperatives, drawn on the examples of Jose Maria Arizmendiarrieta and the Mondragon Cooperatives of the Basque Region of Spain.
- Compensatory Education for those missing out in the formal education system, drawing on the work of Open Education as pioneered by Michael Young.
- Dissemination of Alternative Technologies, based upon the work of E. F. Schumacher as advocated in his book Small is Beautiful: Economics as if people really mattered.
- Village Nutrition Programmes and Permaculture projects, based upon the work of Australians Bill Mollison and David Holmgren.
- Village Water Supply Programmes (Wikipedia, 2009).

Community Development in Canadahas roots in the development of co-operatives, credit unions and caisses populaires. The Antigonish Movement which started in the 1920s in Nova Scotia, through the work of Doctor Moses Coady and Father James Tompkins, has been particularly influential in the subsequent expansion of community economic development work across Canada. In the 1990s, following critiques of the mixed success of "top down" government programmes and drawing on the work of Robert Putnam, in the rediscovery of Social Capital, community development internationally became concerned with social capital formation. In particular, the outstanding success of the work of Muhammad Yunus in Bangladesh with the Grameen Bank, has led to the attempts to spread microenterprise credit schemes around the world. This work was honoured by the 2006 Nobel Peace Prize (Wikipedia, 2009).

The "Human Scale Development" work of Right Livelihood Award winning Chilean Economist Manfred Max Neef promotes the idea of development based upon fundamental human needs, which are considered to be limited, universal and invariant to all human beings (being a part of our human condition). He considers that poverty results from the failure to satisfy a particular human need, it is not just an absence of money. On the account of Wikipedia (2009) whilst human needs are limited, Max Neef shows that the ways of satisfying human needs are potentially unlimited. Satisfiers also have different characteristics: they can be violators or destroyers, pseudo-satisfiers, inhibiting satisfiers, singular satisfiers, or synergic satisfiers. Max-Neef shows that certain satisfiers, promoted as satisfying a particular need, in fact inhibit or destroy the possibility of satisfying other needs: e.g. the arms race, while ostensibly satisfying the need for protection, in fact then destroys subsistence, participation, affection and freedom; formal democracy, which is supposed to meet the need for participation often disempowers and alienates; commercial television, while used to satisfy the need for recreation, interferes with understanding, creativity and identity. Synergic satisfiers, on the other hand, not only satisfy one particular need, but also lead to satisfaction in other areas: some examples are breast-feeding; self-managed production; popular education; democratic community organizations; preventive medicine; meditation; educational games.

In tropical Africa, nevertheless, the motion of community development was pursued vigorously in Ghana where the national organization for community development and social welfare was first fully developed. In 1945, the Ashridge Conference on social development redefined community development as a movement designed to promote better living for the whole community with the active participation and on the initiative of the community. This redefinition came when it became obvious that the concept of mass education, though served a particular phase, could not be the sole orientation of community development. In 1951, Ghana launched a five-year programme for mass literacy and mass education comprising literacy campaigns, home economics, extension work for women. The programme was meant to aid self-help and provide for starting a common service organization for extension activities. In 1948, community development was further redefined by Cambridge Summer Conference on African Administration under the sponsorship of the Colonial Office as a movement to promote better living for the whole community with the active participation and if possible on the initiative of the community, but if this initiative is not forthcoming spontaneously, by use of techniques arousing and stimulating it in order to secure its active and the postive responses to the movement.

Again, community development principles were formulated and applied in third world development efforts following decolonization. In an effort to save rural communities from disintegration, to rescue them from the vicious cycle of stagnation, to enable them meet the needs of the wider community, national governments in a number of low – income countries instituted community development programmes. Communities were to be improved to enable them contribute fully to national progress and to be integrated into the national life. Nevertheless, community development is a discipline unto itself, with a body of theory, standards of practice and professional associations. Masters and doctoral programmes in community development are usually associated with either a school of social work or rural development. Community development is eclectic, integrating specialized knowledge from education, public health, economic development and politics. It may be necessary here to re-state that the major goals of community development include; to induce social change for balanced human and material betterment; to strengthen the institutional structure in such a way as to facilitate social change and the process of growth and to promote social justice by permitting less privileged groups to give expression to their aspirations and to participate in development activities.

However, in 1956, the United Nations adopted the following definition: Community development is the process by which the effort of the people themselves are united with those of the governmental authorities to improve the economic, social and cultural conditions of communities, to integrate these communities into the life of the nation, and to enable them contribute fully to national progress. This process is made up of two elements: the participation by the people themselves in efforts to improve their level of living with as much reliance as possible on their own initiative; and the provision of technical and other services in ways which encourage initiative, self-help and mutual help and make these more effective.

From these various definitions, it is clear that community development emphasizes:
- Community self-help
- Attention to community's felt needs
- The development of the community as an integrated whole, and
- Technical assistance.

3.2 EVOLUTION OF RURAL - COMMUNITY DEVELOPMENT ACTIVITIES IN NIGERIA

The art of community development is not new to the history of mankind. As a basic fact, the transition of mankind from the simple to the complex is in part shrouded in the exercise of community development. The evolution of the practice of self-help development activities has the following periodic dimensions; the pre-colonial period, the colonial period and the post colonial experience. Before the onset of colonial administration, communities across Nigeria had employed communal efforts as the mechanism for mobilizing community resources to provide physical improvement and functional facilities in the social, political and economic aspects of their lives. Communal labour was employed in constructing homesteads, clearing farm lands, roads or pathways, construction of bridges and for the provision of other social infrastructural facilities required by the people. Some of the relevant institutions were the age-grades and the village councils. Though some of these institutions have persisted, the difference between self-help activities undertaken in the past and those prosecuted today are not hard to find, hence the widening and complexing modern society and its complex web.

3.2.1 The Pre - Colonial Experience

In pre-colonial times, Nigeria was almost entirely rural; City-States existed in parts of the Muslim North and in Yoruba-land, but the centre was only weakly integrated with the periphery limited flow of goods and services between rural areas and towns. Chronic warfare between many ethnic groups was a major disincentive to trade. Urbanization took off very slowly in the early period and was undoubtedly more rapid along the coast, because of the higher volumes of trade. The intensive slave-raiding characteristic of the nineteenth century had earlier created an opposition between the walled towns of the north and the scattered settlements of the Middle Belt, often located in inaccessible areas for defense. Historically, at very local levels, the family, inter-family and village settings, the pre-colonial trappings of mutual assistance through self-help persisted for the construction of homesteads, clearing farmlands, clearing water points and for providing other socially felt needs. Church organizations were also able to cooperate with members for the building of schools. Nonetheless, rural areas have been partly defined by inaccessibility and pre-colonial communications were largely dependent on foot and horse traffic between major urban centres.

Nevertheless, the dynamics of pre–colonial history in Nigeria has unfolded various forms and manifestations of community development practices. For example, based on the warrior tradition, every male child was a potential warrior and part of the invisible army that rose in defense of the motherland whenever it was threatened. At the same time, the distinction between the military, economic, political, social and religious spheres were blurred (Elaigwu, 1990). This same person as an individual was deeply engaged in the affairs of his community as they relate to the various spheres. These were neatly woven into the fabric of the value system, which nurtured a 'we' feeling in the community. Theoretically, different scholars have identified various forms of community development exercises namely: - Communal Crisis Task Force, Citizen Succor, Communal Tribute and Development Landmarks. The first three fall within the classified period of pre – colonial Nigeria (Gofwen, 1999).

i.   **The Communal Crisis Task – Force:** This is regarded as the oldest manifestation of community co–operation. It is characterized by a spontaneous action by members of community especially able-bodied men who respond to tackle an emergency problem. Examples abound in addressing natural disasters as floods, unusual pests (like locust, army birds etc.) and combating external aggression.

ii. **Citizen Succor:** This form of community cooperation practice has the members voluntarily contributing materials or money, labour or any artifact. This is to be used by an individual member or family in need with the expectation that another member will so benefit in the same manner based on the principle of rotation. Examples include large scale assistance in a short time on a farm, harvest, building or fencing a house or compound etc.

iii. **Communal Tribute:** As part of the benefits of royalty are some special services. As pre- requisites of traditional royal institutions are farms and residential quarters, the functioning and maintenance of these were the collective responsibility of the subjects as their tribute. These were evident in the cultivation of royal farms, estates, road etc. (Gofwen, 1999).

3.2.2   The Colonial Experience

Within the colonial context, community development was conceived as a pathfinder to the socio- economic transformation of the colonies. In this regard, a comprehensive operational guide on the concept became necessary. It was in response to this quest that the Cambridge Summer

Conference on African Administration held in 1948, came out with a definition that was adopted as the working formula for British Colonies. The Conference viewed community development as:

> *A movement designed to promote better living for the whole community with the active participation and if possible on the initiative of the community, but if this initiative was not forthcoming spontaneously, by the use of techniques for arousing and stimulating it in order to secure its active and enthusiastic response to the movement. It includes the whole range of development activities in the district whether these are undertaken by government or un-official bodies; in the field of agriculture by securing the adoption of better methods of soil conservation, better methods of farming and better cares of livestock; in the field of health by promoting better sanitation and water supplies, proper measures of hygiene, infant and maternity welfare; in the field of education by spreading literacy and adult education as well as by the extension and improvement of schools for children. Community development must make use of the cooperative movement and must be put into effect in the closet association with local government bodies (Nweze, 1988: 21).*

Historically, community development gained utmost popularity in the colonial period. It was within this context that the modern conception of the term assumed its definite character. As aptly noted by Coombs, et al (1974: 66) "the term community development gained currency in pre–independence British Africa when Colonial Social Welfare Officers and later designated Community Development Officers – sought to stimulate self–help actions in selected rural areas to improve health, nutrition, adult Education and general community welfare". Social development was the main objective not economic development. Hence, after the Second World War the British Colonial Office became concerned with 'community development'. Mayo (1975: 130) suggests that administrators 'concocted' the term out of their attempts at developing 'basic education' and social welfare in the UK colonies. For example, a 1944 report, Mass education in the colonies, placed an emphasis on literacy training and advocated the promotion of agriculture, health and other social services through local self help (Midgley et al, 1986: 17). This was a set of concerns similar to those surrounding the interest in rural development and educational 'extension' in North America in the first two decades of the century. Community development was defined in one UK government publication as: active participation, and if possible on the initiative of the community, but if this initiative is not forthcoming spontaneously, by the use of techniques for arousing and stimulating it in order to achieve its active and enthusiastic response to the movement (Colonial Office 1958: 2). The concern with community development was, in part, a response to the growth of nationalism, and, in part an outcome of a desire to increase the rate of industrial and economic development. The notion began to feature strongly in United Nations documents during the 1950s - and these drew extensively on the British literature and experiences in Africa and India (Midgley et al 1986: 18). Three important elements were identified:

➢ A concern with social and economic development.
➢ The fostering and capacity of local co-operation and self-help.
➢ The use of expertise and methods drawn from outside the local community.

Within this spectrum, there does appear to be a certain contradiction hence community development emphasizes participation, initiative and self help by local communities but is usually sponsored by national governments as part of a national plan. While from one side it can be seen as the encouragement of local initiative and decision making, from the other it is a means of implementing and expediting national policies at the local level and is a substitute for, or the beginning of, local government (Jones, 1977). These contradictions are what prompted Okoli (1985) to assert "there have been various concepts of community development based on ideological orientation and the key concepts have not been well explicated and operationalized". Among the British Colonial Office, community development meant a movement to promote better living for the whole community, with the active participation and if possible on the initiative of the community, but if this initiative is not forthcoming, by the use of techniques for arousing and stimulating it in order to secure its active and enthusiastic response to the development. It includes the whole range of development activities in the districts, whether they are undertaken by government or unofficial bodies (1985). The International Co-operation Administration sees it as a process of social actions in which the people of a community organize themselves for planning and action and the individual plans with a maximum reliance upon community resources and supplemented these resources when necessary with services and materials from government and non-governmental agencies outside the community.

Evidently, a form of participation can be traced back at least to colonial times- In Eastern Nigeria in the late 1940s and early 1950s British colonial officials pursued a policy with many similarities to participatory development. The chief propagandist of this policy was E.R. Chadwick, the Senior District Officer in charge of community development. The earliest record of the colonial development fund for development purposes was that made by Chadwick, the district officer in Udi about 1945-1949. He used the fund to encourage communities to carry out community development. He documented his community development activities in film known as "Day-Break-in-Udi". The film shows how the district officer used equipment and materials to assist communities. Following the "Day-Break-in-Udi", government gradually became seriously involved in community development. In 1952, community development Training Centre Awgu was established for training Administrative Officers and Local Government Staff; and Community Leaders by Chadwick. By 1956, Major Riggs became the first Resident principal of the CDTC, Agwu. Administrative Officers and Local Government Officers all over the country were sent for training at the CDTC, Awgu to make them conscious of community development.

From 1952 the government of Eastern Nigeria made it a policy to contribute 50% of the cost of community projects carried out by any community. This policy 50/50 was continued until 1963. During this period, apart from contribution of their labour, communities contributed 50% of the cost of materials of the projects undertaken by them while the government matched this with 50% in addition, supplied technical staff and equipment for the projects. This policy brought healthy competitions among communities and was responsible for a lot of development projects like road, bridges, cottage hospitals, healthcentres, schools etc. During this period, competition among communities was so much that each community tried to get her due share of the government match grant. By 1963 government found it difficult to raise enough fund to match the contributions of the communities towards community development projects. Some communities were depositing millions of pounds for projects like bridges and water supplies. Government became indebted to many communities.

As a result, in 1964, the government of Eastern Nigeria decided to change the policy. Instead of 50% matching grant to infrastructural projects, it shifted emphasis from infrastructural development to economic projects like agriculture, small scale industries etc. Government provided technical assistance, subsidies and loans while the communities provided land, labour and money for community development. Instead of 50% matching grants, government established works units which provided the communities with technical equipment and technical staff. The communities had to hire equipment at very low rates for the projects. During this period, 1964-1967 when the civil war broke out, numerous community farms, rural industries like weaving and community link-road were established. Chadwick wrote frequently about how self-help development could transform the capacity of Nigerians (as individuals and communities) to identify their own needs and strengthen their abilities to improve their own conditions. He was puritanical in his refusal to 'deliver' development since this undermined the very transformation that the policy sought to achieve. This surprisingly modern view already contains many of the central themes that are still present in current approaches: self-help, the community as well as the individual, transformation and capacity building and, at least by implication, a limited form of empowerment.

Perceptibly, differences exist in the mode and scope of the operations, equipment utilized and the extent of government involvement. As Idode (1989) observed:

> In the past, self help efforts in Nigeria particularly in Bendel State now Edo and Delta States mainly related to the construction of footpaths or roads, dredging of rivers and streams, clearing of public land and market places. Later, Idode further observed, the scope of operation included the building of schools and market stalls. Projects such as pipe-borne water, road tarring, dispensaries, and cottage hospitals and so on, were not usually attempted. Furthermore equipment simple used were hoes, cutlasses, diggers and shovels were generally utilized. The construction of walls did not follow any standard measurements as the people used their imagination to plan and construct such projects. At this stage, there was little or no government involvement as the planning and execution of these self-help projects was the sole responsibility of the people. Where the government was involved at all, was for the purposes of taking over completed projects for operation or maintenance. But where neither the State Government nor the Local Government Councils were interested in such projects, the missionaries took over.

During the colonial period, community development efforts took a compulsive and coercive turn. The alien governmental apparatus with its clientele (Warrant Chief) arrangement heavily extorted taxes and compulsory labour from the people. Taxation by itself questioned the rationality of further labour conscription for road and other infrastructural development at the instance of the District Commissioner. The contradictions in the new development effort, therefore, did not the corporate imagination of the people and this was given expression by the tax debacle of 1929, popularly known as the Aba women riot. It questions the whole essence of the tax laws as established then, the imposition of the Roads and River Ordinance and the apparent shirking of development responsibility by a government that had already extorted taxes for this purpose. Apart from the establishment of governmental exploitative infrastructural apparatus, linking the major seats of government through forced labour, no serious self-help programmes eliciting popular participation was encouraged. Any development that occurred was a by-product of profit (Hancock, 1942).

By the late 1940s however, an element of modern community concept in rural development was introduced in the form of mass mobilization for self-help activities. This was heralded by the abrogation in Britain of the Colonial Development Act which was replaced by the Development and Welfare Act in 1939. As rightly noted by Arndt, (1981), this gave a positive economic and social content to the philosophy of colonial trusteeship by affirming the need for minimum standards of nutrition, health and education. At the local level, the earlier Native Authority Councils were replaced by the Country Council. Suffice it to say that this development led to the establishment of Community Development Division at the local level and thus became an important organ of government, charged with the responsibility of channeling and coordinating the efforts of the people towards promoting social and economic development (Onwuzuluike, 1987). The Development and Welfare Fund provided for the colonies by the British Government was thus able to permeate to the grassroots level through this third tier of government.

3.2.3   The Post Colonial Experience
Today, the term community development has come to assume a broader meaning with a more encompassing one as it embraces both the social and economic objectives of development packaged in various forms of activities as catalysts. However, the practice today is aptly for state and local governments, in their efforts to encourage community development,

to place more emphasis on the promotion of physical projects. For this reason, community development in form of major "landmarks" projects such as schools, clinics or dispensaries, rural roads and bridges, electricity, pipe-borne water, market stalls etc. were executed through communal efforts. Even the Governor's Trophy for community development introduced by the defunct military government of Northern Nigeria in January 1967 was based on this pre-occupation (Nweze, 1988: 23).

By the beginning of the war in 1967, the observations of Sir James Robertson, aptly typified the state of development needs and awareness and the immense role the governments expected self-help activities were to play to compliment their efforts. After the Nigerian Civil War (1967-1970), the need for massive reconstruction work further aroused the people to a revival of the spirit of self-help which is deeply rooted in their rich traditions. Most communities realized that the only way for immediate reconstruction of the war ravaged facilities was through self-help. This period also marked the evolution of a multiplicity of social clubs with aims consonant with social insurance and self-help. Further efforts by government, to motivate development at the grassroots, led to the enactment of the 1976 Local Government Reform, to create new growth centres in order to facilitate spatial spread of development. In addition is the creation of the local government service commission, the conferment of wider powers and functions to the Local Governments by the 1979 Constitution and the enactment of the Special Development Fund Law, aimed at generating more funds for community development at the local level. Thus, deliberate government support became necessary to increase the spate of development activities by the various communities (Akpomivie, 2010).

The focus on the social and economic, local and global also helps to situate debates about community development - and the disillusionment with its achievements that was widespread in many Southern countries by the 1970s. Many governments, particularly in Africa, failed to provide adequate financial support but nevertheless extolled the virtues of self-help. Community development was soon recognized by the people to amount to little more than a slogan which brought few tangible benefits (Midgley et al 1986:18). People's participation as a concept was formulated – or rediscovered – in the 1970s, in response to the growing awareness that the various approaches then employed for rural development, such as community development, integrated rural development or basic needs did not often lead to significant rural development and especially poverty reduction, largely, as was then thought, because there was little involvement in development projects of those undergoing 'development', and particularly the poor.

An important milestone in people's participation in rural development was the World Conference on Agrarian Reform and Rural Development (WCARRD – Rome, 1979). After WCARRD, and throughout the 1980s and 90s, participation in rural development – as well as in development at large – gradually became more established among governments, donors and international organizations, to such an extent indeed that, as Stirrat (1996) put it:

> It is now difficult to find a rurally based development project which does not in one way or another claim to adopt a participatory approach involving bottom-up planning, acknowledging the importance of indigenous knowledge, and claiming to empower local people'. Inevitably, at the same time as participation became a 'good thing', there was also a trend towards greater diversity in the interpretations of what it really means and in the forms of its application in practice, as the various actors involved – ranging from consultants and academics to developing country governments, NGOs, bilateral donors and international organizations – chose from the different approaches, principles, methods or simply emphases available, to fit their own missions or interests. Participation thus became what some describe as a 'new orthodoxy of development', but one lacking an ideology (Henkel and Stirrat, 2001).

The period between 1973 and 2007 marked a watershed in rural development efforts in Nigeria. The period witnessed deliberate government efforts at mobilizing the people for rural development. A number of task forces and bodies were set up to oversee, organize and to direct partnership with the people on self-help activities. They include: Directorate of Food, Roads and Rural Infrastructure (DFRRI), Rural Electrification Schemes; Credit Schemes to small holders through various specialized institutions such as Peoples Bank, Agricultural and Cooperative Development Bank, Community Banks, NERFUND, SME Credit Schemes, the Family Economic Advancement Programme (FEAP), Universal Primary Education Schemes and Low Cost Housing Schemes, Health Scheme as the Primary HealthCare Programme, National Directorate of Employment (NDE), Better Life for Rural Women

Programme as well as the Family Support Programme (FSP). More recent programmes include the National Poverty Eradication Programme (NAPEP), as well as the Small and Medium Industries Equity Investment Schemes (SMIEIS). The various state governments had also articulated blueprints on rural development, adopting the Integrated Rural Development Strategy as their strategic option of motivating development to the masses. From the foregoing historical analysis, two principles underlying rural community development activities have emerged. These are (a) the principle of individual and corporate survival and (b) the principle of societal felt need. These two principles have variously acted as the caring force in organizing and mobilizing the people in their pursuit of self development.

Chapter Four

DYNAMICS OF RURAL AND COMMUNITY DEVELOPMENT

4.1 LOCATING COMMUNITY DEVELOPMENT IN WIDER DEVELOPMENT DISCOURSE ON EVOLVING IDEAS AND APPROACHES TO RURAL DEVELOPMENT INTERNATIONALLY

The history of community development globally articulates closely with the different approaches to development briefly, and somewhat crudely, outlined below. Community development has to be located within a context of extremely rapid urbanization and economic change, including powerful trends towards market fundamentalism and global economic integration driven by trade liberalization. This has resulted in increased economic interdependence among nation states and reductions in national economic sovereignty. At the same time, the disparity between the rich and poor continues to grow, both within countries and between them.

The literature on community development is characterized by a mix of theory and practice: "that is, both ideas about how 'development' should or might occur, and real world efforts to put various aspects of development into practice." (Potter, 2002: 61). The vision and priorities for rural development closely reflect changing global development trends and relations of power and influence. Yet investment in and support for a broadly 'pro-poor' rural development can be a useful indicator reflecting the extent to which the governments and international institutions are serious about reducing poverty and inequality. Cousins & Lahiff (2005) has highlighted how there has been constant debate about the relationship between the state and the market and between the productive and social sectors with respect to rural development (Phuhlisani and PLAAS, 2009).

Histories of thinking about community development often attempt to periodise different approaches and key ideas by decades. In fact, these reflect the preoccupations of the four UN development decades which commenced in the 1960s. Hence it is often said that the:

- 1950's - 60's are associated with modernization approaches emphasizing technological transfer
- 1970's are associated with large scale state development interventions and integrated rural development programmes.

- 1980's are associated with market liberalization and attempts to roll back the state.
- 1990's are characterized as being strongly process focused with an emphasis on participation and empowerment within a context of diversifying rural livelihood opportunities. By end of the 1990s a more balanced approach had started to emerge but there remains no agreement worldwide on how to get the right mix.
- 2000's have a focus on poverty eradication, reinvigoration of small holder agriculture, sustainable farming systems and the location of producers within global value chains.

However Ellis and Biggs caution that community policies have not evolved in such a neat, linear and schematic manner and that "there are leads and lags in the transmission of new ideas across space and time" (Ellis & Biggs, 2001).

Figure 4.1: Rural development ideas timeline, (Ellis & Biggs, 2001).

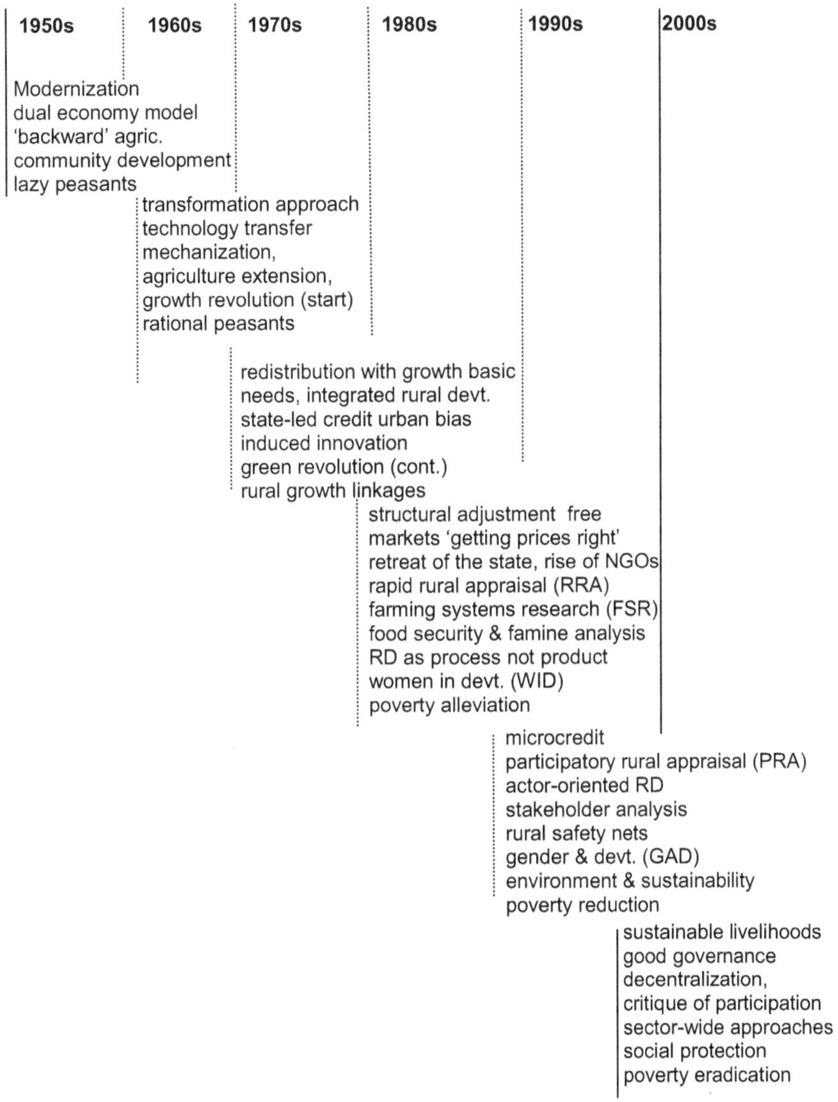

1950s	1960s	1970s	1980s	1990s	2000s

Modernization
dual economy model
'backward' agric.
community development
lazy peasants

transformation approach
technology transfer
mechanization,
agriculture extension,
growth revolution (start)
rational peasants

redistribution with growth basic
needs, integrated rural devt.
state-led credit urban bias
induced innovation
green revolution (cont.)
rural growth linkages

structural adjustment free
markets 'getting prices right'
retreat of the state, rise of NGOs
rapid rural appraisal (RRA)
farming systems research (FSR)
food security & famine analysis
RD as process not product
women in devt. (WID)
poverty alleviation

microcredit
participatory rural appraisal (PRA)
actor-oriented RD
stakeholder analysis
rural safety nets
gender & devt. (GAD)
environment & sustainability
poverty reduction

sustainable livelihoods
good governance
decentralization,
critique of participation
sector-wide approaches
social protection
poverty eradication

The table below (has been adapted from Ellis and Biggs, 2001) an analysis of the Rural Development timeline ideas as it provided an annotated chronology of the changing thought and approaches internationally to community development.

Table: 4.1
1950's

Changing ideas informing approaches to rural development	Commentary
• Modernization	Modernization theory held that the small scale subsistence sector had little potential for improved productivity or growth. The development of agriculture could only be stimulated by investment in large scale mono-crop estates and plantations. Large farms were perceived to be more efficient than small farms as a consequence of economies of scale. Rural development was implicitly associated with scaling up.
• Dual economy	Dual economy models posited the parallel operations of a relatively advanced sector and a relatively backward sector alternatively characterized as capitalist and subsistence, formal and informal, modern and traditional. (Fields, 2007)
• Community development	Community development approaches were dominant in this decade. These aimed to mobilize rural communities for development. They rested on the placement of multipurpose village level workers in rural communities to catalyze and co-ordinate local development initiatives. However, at the time this approach was primarily fuelled by US foreign policy priorities and became regarded as an intervention to counter the spread of communism (Holdcroft, 1976). There has been renewed interest in this approach subsequently. The training and placement of Community Development Workers in South Africa is a contemporary example.
• Perceptions that peasant producers were 'lazy' and required motivation	Much rural development thinking was premised on the notion of the need to

| | change the work ethic of the small peasant whose 'backward attitudes' were regarded as the primary obstacle to rural development. This narrative has been a constant feature of South African development discourse – both pre and post 1994. |

1960's

Changing ideas informing approaches to rural development	Commentary
• 'Green Revolution" Technology transfer	This decade is characterized by high expectations of the promise of technology. Technology transfer focused on large scale input intensive agriculture based on packages of higher yielding hybrid seeds, fertilisers, pesticides, mechanization and post harvest technologies which came to be known as the Green Revolution. There are different perspectives on the success and sustainability of this 'revolution' as well as concerns about its impact on smallholder farmers – many of whom were displaced by larger and wealthier producers in the process. Ironically the Green Revolution had significant environmental impacts including a dramatic rise in pesticide and chemical fertiliser use, stalinization of soils and pressure on groundwater resources. Patel et al observe that: "from 1970 to 1990 the amount of food available per person rose by 11 percent, and more than 150 million people were lifted from the ranks of the world's hungry. However, they caution that "most of that rise was driven by transformations inside China. Subtract China from the picture and the heyday of the Green Revolution saw global hunger increase by 11 percent".(Patel, Holt-Gimenez, & Shattuck, 2009).
• Agricultural extension	The origins of agricultural extension were based on methods to try to get rural farmers to adopt new technologies and farming practices. In this period extension largely ignored local and indigenous

	knowledge, farming systems and tenure arrangements. It also targeted men overlooking that much agricultural work was done by women.
• The contribution of agriculture to economic growth/small farm efficiency	During this decade there was a re-evaluation of the contribution of small scale agriculture to economic growth. A new perspective held that small scale agriculture could in fact be the engine for economic development in developing countries. An argument developed that there was an inverse relationship between farm size and economic efficiency and that in fact smaller farmers were more efficient than large farmers (Berry & Cline, 1979). However advocates of both small and large farm focus remain deadlocked throughout this period and these differences in approach extend into the subsequent decades.
• The changing perception of rural people as rational managers of risk and change.	Research into farming systems changed the perception of rural people who had been characterized as 'incurably lazy' and resistant to change. Small farmers were now seen to be behaving in an economically rational way when they rejected improvements which they perceived to be too risky. This highlighted the need to properly assess and develop ways to manage and minimize risk as part of the process of innovation.

1970's

Changing ideas informing approaches to rural development	Commentary
• Redistribution with growth	A joint IDS/World Bank study in 1972 entitled Redistribution with Growth conceded that, "It is now clear that more than a decade of rapid growth in underdeveloped countries has been of little or no benefit to perhaps a third of their population." It examined ways in which resources could be transferred from wealthy groups to poorer groups in society by means of: • direct transfer of income from richer to poorer groups

	• taxation resulting in income transfers to benefit poor people directly • targeted investments in agriculture, education and health which would increase the productive capacity, production and incomes of the poorer groups. • redistributing land or other assets in favour of poorer groups (Jolly, 2006).
• Promotion of a basic needs approach	Basic needs approaches to 'Third World' development gained ascendance as the new approach which represented "a shift of emphasis towards social services and transfer payments, designed to help the poor, and an extension of "new style" projects in nutrition, health and education". (Streeten, 1984)
• Large scale integrated rural development programmes,	The 1970's was also characterized by large scale, complex, state led, top down, blueprint approaches to rural development. These placed emphasis on the development of interlocking national policies and institutions to guide and regulate development planning and support. However integrated rural development projects were often too complex and overwhelmed the management capacity of state institutions. Many became technocratic and remote from local people's needs. Programmes became dependent on external expertise from donor countries for their design and management. Much of the money invested through aid programmes ended up being captured by Northern consultants and experts and not finding its way to meet needs on the ground. The effectiveness of such programmes was limited as a result the approach became discredited. This approach however is making a come back in South Africa where there is a risk of repeating the same mistakes.
• State driven agricultural policies	Rural farmers got a lot of support through parastatals in the form of controlled floor prices and subsidized inputs which protected local producers and stimulated

	production. Extension services during this period continued to be provided by government agencies, but now started to embrace new approaches which were more gender sensitive and which built on local knowledge.
• Limits to growth – World Conservation Strategy	The limits to growth debate began in the 1970's. This assumed that there were direct linkages between population growth, poverty and environmental degradation. The debate promoted 'disaster narratives' which cast the poor as destroying the environment while ignoring the disproportionately large, wasteful and unsustainable use of resources by industrialized countries. This gave rise to the World Conservation Strategy driven by the conservation concerns of ecologists which contributed to an era of largely coercive natural resource management strategies which prioritized protection of biodiversity, often at the expense of poor people and their needs.
• Focus on the role of women in development.	The Women in Development approach (WID) approach had its roots in United Nations programmes of the 1970s which aimed at reversing the exclusion of women from development process. These promoted women's projects with a view to increasing women's productivity and income and their ability to manage their households.

1980's

Changing ideas informing approaches to rural development	Commentary
• The advent of World Bank led economic structural adjustment and market liberalization. • Emphasis on 'getting the prices right' of inputs and outputs,	The quadrupling of oil prices between 1973 and 1974 and further steep rises in 1979/1980 were the primary external factors in creating an international debt crisis. After the first oil shock developing countries were encouraged to take loans to pay their energy bills from financial institutions keen on capitalizing on their vast reserves of petrodollars. The second oil shock forced countries to

	borrow again, this time to pay off their initial loans. This resulted in an exponential debt spiral where countries borrowings continued to escalate with no prospect of repayment. This coincided with the emergence of neo–liberal economic policies and created the impetus for the emergence of Structural Adjustment Programmes (SAP). "As of the late 1970s, the WB began to lend money conditional upon economic reforms referred to as the Washington Consensus, and other donors followed its lead soon after" (Aubut, 2004). These reforms based on deregulation, liberalization and fiscal discipline, were designed to engineer a policy environment which would be conducive to market liberalization, economic growth and development. SAPs advocated the progressive removal of price and wage controls and the reduction in government expenditure on social services. This had significant impacts on the rural economies and poor households in the South. Farmers lost access to input subsidies. Extension services which had been free were either cut back or provided by government agencies and consultancies which recovered a portion of their costs from their rural clients. People had to pay for education and heathcare. The progressive withdrawal of the state and a scaling down of financial and technical support to farmers created great hardships and certain countries like Malawi experienced famines as a result.
• The shrinking state and the rise of international development NGOs.	In the context of a shrinking state, international development NGOs started to play a major role in countries of the South. At the United Nations, from 41 NGOs granted consultative status by the Economic and Social Council (ECOSOC) in 1948, and 377 in 1968, the number of NGOs in consultative status has now expanded to over 1,550. The significant rise of non-state actors in development

	has its roots here and in the process of 'neoliberal destatisation' and accelerated globalization associated with the rise of neoliberalism in subsequent decades (McArthur, 2008)
• Initial emphasis on participatory research methods in the form of Rapid Rural Appraisal.	During the late 1970's and 1980's there was an increasing focus on approaches and methods to enable outside professionals to better understand rural realities. This saw a shift to qualitative and participatory research methods and an increasing awareness of the value of Indigenous Technical Knowledge. (ITK) (Robert Chambers, 1997).
• Focus on understanding the functioning of existing farming systems.	Field research on mixed farming systems practiced by rural people highlighted their interdependence and complexity. This assisted in the provision of more appropriate support measures.
• Gender and development	Gender and development (GAD) emerged as an alternative to the WID approach in the previous decade. This sought to empower women and transform unequal gender and power relations that prevented equitable access to resources.
• Interventions to promote drought mitigation and household food security.	Drought was perceived to be the primary cause of African food insecurity in the early 1970's (the Sahelian drought) and the mid 1980's. Between 1980 and 1985, drought was estimated to have affected around 150 million people in Africa (FAO). A food crisis was experienced in several parts of the continent during the 1980s. Most of the solutions proposed were purely technological, stressing production rather than equitable distribution of food, where an abundance of food can and does exist alongside famine (Clover, 2003).
• Policies and strategies to alleviate poverty	Poverty alleviation measures focused on interventions which would reduce the impact of poverty on poor households.
• Environment and sustainability	The publication of the Brundtland report in 1987 reframed the emphasis from purely ecological dimensions environment to a more holistic, if vague concept of sustainable development. However

	received wisdom on supposed population – poverty environmental degradation spirals remained difficult to shift.

1990's

Changing ideas informing approaches to rural development	Commentary
• Structural adjustment	The 1990's saw the peaking of SAPs with a particular focus on former communist bloc countries in 'transition'. These programmes were increasingly associated with high social and environmental costs and have been criticized for turning "developing countries into amenable players in the globalizing system of free trade and TNC dominated investment."(Carley & Christie, 2000: 107).
• Good governance	In combination with the post-Washington Consensus and the focus on institutions and public sector management in the 1990s, a new policy agenda was formulated focusing on a more selective allocation of aid based on the quality of governance. The WB characterized good governance as: "the manner in which power is exercised in the management of a country's economic and social resources for development." OECD countries prioritized four elements: the rule of law, public sector management, control of corruption, and reduction of military spending.
• Micro credit	The success of the Grameen Bank in Bangladesh prompted a global reappraisal of approaches to microcredit for poverty reduction. Grameen Bank started from the premise of credit as a human right which could be extended only to members of groups, and for the purposes of enabling self employment as opposed to financing consumption. The lending programme targeted poor women, provided service to the users where they stayed, and depended on collateral of trust and member responsibility. Extension of credit was always accompanied by involvement

	in voluntary or compulsory savings programmes. This model was taken up and adapted in a variety of different settings around the globe (Grameen Foundation, 2009).
• Poverty reduction	Poverty Reduction Strategy Papers (PRSPs) were introduced in 1999 by the World Bank and the IMF as a new framework (the successor to SAPs) to enhance domestic accountability for poverty reduction reform efforts; a means to enhance the coordination of development assistance between governments and development partners; and a precondition or access to debt relief and concessional financing from both institutions' (World Bank).
• Participatory rural appraisal	Participatory approaches placed new emphasis on how rural people compare options, minimize risk, adapt practices and seek information (Garforth & Harford, 1997). There was increasing recognition of local knowledge and agency through processes of participatory research and planning (Robert Chambers, 1997).
• Actor oriented rural development	Actor oriented approaches were based on the mapping of relationships and flows of information to provide a basis for reflection, planning and action. They have their roots in anthropological and social network research techniques. (Biggs & Matsaert, 2004). There was a shift in emphasis to an 'endogenous development paradigm' which was premised on development originating from within a social system as opposed to modernization with its emphasis on imported models and expertise. Actor oriented approaches emphasized the importance of participation, the empowerment of local actors and unlocking of local resources (Nemes, 2005).
• Stakeholder analysis	With renewed focus on projects, rural development planners started to focus more on assumptions and risks which would impact on design and

	implementation. As part of the actor oriented development and participation paradigms was the recognition of different interests, institutions and local power relations. There was an increasing awareness that development projects could create winners and losers and have unintended consequences which impacted on the interests of particular stakeholders.
• Environment and sustainability	There was increasing recognition of the contribution that environmental goods and services make to livelihoods of poor rural households and the rise of triple bottom line environmental accounting. Emphasis shifted to improved management of the ecosystems that produce these goods and services to increase household incomes of the poor. Community based natural resource management and co-management of environmental resources gained ascendance. However, there was a realization that this required a change in natural resource governance to improve access and control to key resources by the poor. This in turn required a focus on the development and strengthening of institutions.

2000's

The current decade has been characterized by flux and fragmentation in development thinking and rural development policy despite the overarching focus of attaining the Millennium Development Goals. This has been accompanied by increasing concern about the de-politicization of issues inherent in policy development processes. It has been argued that rationalist models tend to depoliticize the issues which are the focus of policy through the use of neutral scientific language. "Thus, the masking of policy under the cloak of neutrality is a key feature of modern power", Strong critiques of the "rationalist model of a …linear policy development sequence" have emerged which are characterized as "simplistic and reductionist" (Dhunpath & Paterson, 2004: 126).

The start of the decade was marked by the dominance of broader livelihoods approaches which replaced a more conventional and narrow *sectoral foci* on small farmers, agriculture and the non farm economy.

However, people have experienced difficulties in practically applying livelihoods thinking on the design of rural development programmes and currently there appears to be a refocusing on the potential of agriculture and natural resources to make a contribution to economic growth and household livelihood security. This has been accompanied by an increasing emphasis on decentralization and the principle of subsidiarity which holds that decisions need to be taken as close to the citizenry and the local level as possible.

There remains a tension between more trans-disciplinary thinking and the reassertion of sector wide development approaches. Issues of good governance and decentralization remain important, but at the same time there has been critique of what passes for participation and the lack of meaningful downward accountability in the decentralization process. Environmental issues, vulnerability reduction and disaster risk mitigation measures are increasingly taking centre stage as there is increasing recognition of the severity and speed of climate change and its impacts on the poor.

Changing ideas informing approaches to rural development	Commentary
• Sustainable livelihoods	The emergence of sustainable livelihoods framework (Carney, 1999) (R Chambers & Conway, 1992). Drew on much of the development theory and approaches summarized above and is explicitly trans-disciplinary. Its focus on an asset vulnerability framework draws on the famine and food security literature. (Ellis & Biggs, 2001). Many earlier development approaches downplayed differentiation between households in rural areas and assumed that rural households had single-purpose economies (in other words, that they only had one way of making a living). As a result, development planners tended to focus on narrow, sectoral, production-orientated strategies that often bypassed those most at risk and failed to recognize that poor households have multiple livelihood strategies. (de Satge, Holloway, Mullins, Nchabaleng, & Ward, 2002). The approach "cuts across the boundaries of more conventional approaches to looking at rural development which focus on defined activities: agriculture, wage employment, farm labour, small-scale enterprise". (Scoones, 2009). The SL

	approach recognizes the different livelihood sources of the poor, highlights shocks and stresses which impact on these and the enabling factors which enhance them. It does not automatically cast rural people in the role of farmers. "Diversity is the watchword, and livelihoods approaches have challenged fundamentally single-sector approaches to solving complex rural development problems. The appeal is simple: look at the real world, and try and understand things from local perspectives" (Scoones, 2009).
• Millennium Development Goals, country ownership and good governance	The Millennium Declaration in 2000 set 2015 as the target date for achieving most of the Millennium Development Goals (MDGs), which aim to halve extreme poverty in all its forms. Given the failure of prescriptive and one size fits all SAP programmes, the WB and Northern donors sought a new approach to lending and aid agreements. This approach continued to emphasize the good governance agenda which had been prominent in the 1990s. However the 2005 Paris Declaration on Aid Effectiveness proposed that effective aid must be aligned with recipient countries' own policies and systems and be country owned rather than externally imposed. In this context, development aid should help strengthen the capacity of recipient country's to make and effectively implement policy while financing programmes that benefit poor people. However, there remains the challenge of what should be done when the "institutional set-up in an aid-recipient country is profoundly unfavourable to providing honest and effective leadership of development efforts?" (Booth, 2008). From a rural development perspective this approach requires that recipient countries are able to develop a coherent rural development vision and build the institutions which can give effect to it.
• Decentralization	Linked with the good governance agenda has been the concept of democratic decentralization. This involves the restructuring of authority so that there is a system of co-responsibility between institutions of governance at the central, regional and local levels according to the principle of subsidiarity" (UNDP). Democratic decentralization is premised on new local institutions being representative and accountable to local populations and having a secure and autonomous domain of powers to make

	and implement meaningful decisions. The intended benefits of decentralization include: • Improved quality of public decision making at local authority levels • Integration of local knowledge • Improved targeting of programmes • Downward accountability to local populations However political decentralization is not always accompanied by fiscal decentralization and it will not be successful unless adequate provision is made to finance the devolved or decentralized responsibilities (Larson & Ribot, 2005).
• Critique of participation	While there has been an emphasis on democratic decentralization there has been a simultaneous critique of what passes for participation in planning and development processes. Participation has been increasingly 'cast in the market idiom' – with people conceptualized as consumers – users and choosers of services (Cornwall: 2002). Critics assert that participation has degenerated into what Foucault termed a 'political technology' – where participatory methods could suit any agenda. They highlight the co-option of participatory approaches by existing power structures (Cooke & Kathari, 2001).
• Sector wide development approaches	The appearance of sector wide approaches is closely linked with recent shifts in donor thinking, emphasizing the importance of 'country ownership of donor' programmes. It also marks a shift from project funding to the development of sectoral policy and strategy. However the focus on sectoral approaches is limited in its ability to deal with the cross sectoral nature of rural development. Sector programme has six components. 1. A clear sector policy and strategy; 2. A sectoral medium term expenditure programme, based on a comprehensive action plan; 3. A performance monitoring system; 4. A formalized process of donor co-ordination; 5. An agreed process for moving towards harmonized systems for reporting, budgeting, financial management and procurement; 6. A systematic mechanism of consultation with clients and beneficiaries of government services and with non-government providers of those services (HLSP Institute, 2005).

• Social protection	In previous decades development initiatives were often predicated on an assumption that incomes could be generated through production projects of one kind or another. However, the record of such interventions is generally poor as projects survive while there is donor support, and then fold when it is withdrawn. The focus on Social Protection (SP) and direct cash transfers is about putting money directly in the pockets of the poor to invest and use at their discretion. This helps people to manage risk and vulnerability and "enables the very poor to share in the benefits of economic growth since many will not be reached by "trickle-down"." Direct cash transfers are starting to replace traditional food aid and famine relief measures (Peppiatt, Mitchell, & Holzmann, 2001). Social protection can also involve other protective or enabling measures in such setting and enforcing of workplace employment and safety standards, enabling access to land and water etc. Public work programmes also form part of social protection measures. However, they have limitations when attempting to tackle chronic poverty as the many very poor families often lack the labour capacity to take up the jobs on offer (Department for International Development, 2006).
• Poverty eradication	The World Social Summit (1995) which followed three years after Rio prioritized poverty, calling on governments to address the root causes of poverty. However, progress in addressing poverty has been slow. This resulted in the 24th special session of the General Assembly setting targets to halve the number of people living in extreme poverty by one half by 2015. This target has been endorsed by the Millennium Summit as Millennium Development Goal 1. These goals are receiving international attention as part of the Second United Nations Decade for the Eradication of Poverty (2008-2017).
• Revitalizing small holder farming	This is closely linked to MDG 1 in Chapter one above. Over the past thirty years, agriculture's share of foreign aid has dropped from 17% to 3% of total spend. The reinvigoration of smallholder agriculture, which is once again attaining prominence, assumes that improving the productivity of agriculture in general and the competitiveness of smallholders and marginalized groups in the expanding global,

	national and local markets in particular, as well as by creating employment among poor rural people and making food available to consumers everywhere, can make meaningful impact on poverty (McIntyre, Herren, Wakhungu, & Watson, 2009). However there are fundamentally differing approaches on how to do this. Patel et al caution that "Conventional wisdom suggests that if people are hungry, there must be a shortage of food, and all we need do is figure out how to grow more. This logic turns hunger into a symptom of a technological deficit, telling a story in which a little agricultural know-how can feed the world. But there's a problem: the conventional wisdom is wrong. Food output per person is as high as it has ever been, suggesting that hunger isn't a problem of production so much as one of distribution" (Patel et al., 2009). Farming and food security debates take place against a backdrop of a threatened food deficit in rapidly growing economies like China which has led to a search for land to purchase on lease in the South for large scale industrial agriculture. According to IFPRI these land acquisitions have the potential to inject much needed investment into agriculture and rural areas in poor developing countries, but they also raise concerns about the impacts on poor local people, who risk losing access to and control over land on which they depend (Von Braun & Meinzen-Dick, 2009). The energy crisis has also led to a search for land on which to grow crops intended for the production of bio-fuels. Rapidly rising international consumption of meat and associated changes in livestock farming methods have potential negative impacts on small scale livestock producers. At the same time the rise of biotechnology and particularly GMOs has been the site of a fierce debate. Supporters argue that genetic engineering is a key technology to address food insecurity and malnutrition. Opponents highlight potential impacts on the environment, and "a corporate takeover of traditional agriculture and the global food supply" (Food and Agriculture Organization, 2004) which will exacerbate poverty and hunger.
• ICTs for development	There has been a growing emphasis on the potential of Information and Communication Technologies (ICTs) for pro-poor development. Much of the debate

	has focused on the so called digital divide and overcoming the problems that the rural poor have in accessing information for innovation and improved competitiveness in the market place. Reviews of ICT projects in rural areas indicate measurable impacts from ICT projects focusing on price information and market access (IICD, 2006). However, they also caution that ICTs are no panacea for development problems and that projects which focus on technological solutions in isolation are doomed to failure in the same way that mechanization and large scale infrastructure development schemes are associated with failure in development practice.
• Climate change	During this decade there has been a mounting awareness of the challenges posed by climate change and its impacts on poor and vulnerable households.
• Fair trade	The increasing dominance of global supermarket chains over the world food economy has been highlighted as one of the main consequences of a globalizing agriculture. Efforts have been made to secure *niche* markets for producers of particular commodities such as coffee and fruit. These initiatives aim at ensuring a fair return to the producers. Fair-trade really took off in the late 1980's with the launch of the first Fair-trade label in Holland marketing coffee from small growers in Mexico. This concept spread to other countries in Europe and North America in the 1990s before all the different labels were brought under Fair-trade Labeling Organizations International (FLO). This was followed by the launch of an International Fair-trade Certification Mark in 2002. FLO then split into two organizations – one to set standards and provide business support and the other which is an inspection and certification body (Fair-trade Foundation, 2009).

Source: Phuhlisani and PLAAS (2009). International and local approaches to rural development Key issues and questions: A review of the literature for the Drakenstein Municipality Phuhlisani Solutions: September 2009; Adapted from Ellis & Biggs, 2001.

The chronology above highlights the breadth and diversity of elements associated with the rural development agenda. The chronology excludes changing approaches to rural service provision, primary healthcare,

HIV/AIDs and malaria mitigation, education and transport – all key components of rural development initiatives. The inclusive, complex and crosscutting character of rural development is both the source of its strength and the fundamental challenge implicit in the design, implementation and monitoring of rural development programmes. The concept has strength because of its ability to connect different sectors and disciplines, synthesize professional and local knowledge and make micro-macro linkages. However, it presents significant obstacles in that effective rural development initiatives and programmes depend heavily on shared institutional ownership and knowledge systems; and require programmematic alignment and harmonization across different spatial scales which are notoriously difficult to manage and achieve.

Chapter Five

THEORIES AND APPROACHES TO RURAL AND COMMUNITY DEVELOPMENT

5.1 THEORIES OF RURAL AND COMMUNITY DEVELOPMENT

Community development theory is committed to the service of the people: through service to people's organizations and communities. It supports the people's economic and political resistance as the people strive for structural social transformation and the pursuit of human rights. It combines support for the people's initiatives towards immediate economic survival with support for their efforts at empowerment and self-organization. It is committed and is in solidarity with the people's struggle for genuine agrarian reform, national sovereignty, and respect for human rights, female empowerment, and the right to self-determination among indigenous peoples. While the social sciences identify different concepts of theory, it is taken here to mean generalizations about, and classifications of, the social world. It is a method of linking a set of ideas in order to help us understand a particular issue or set of issues. This network of ideas provides us with a theoretical framework (or conceptual framework). Theory—interrelated sets of concepts and propositions, organized into a deductive system to explain relationships about certain aspects of the world (e.g., the theories listed below). A theory differs from a model in that the latter is what Thomson describes as, "an intermediate step in the process of theory building. A model seeks to describe, for example, by mapping a set of interrelationships. This may show how certain factors interrelate but it will not show why they do so--that is where theory comes in. A model is a framework for practice.

5.1.1 Rural Development Theory

The concept of rural development has changed significantly during the last three decades. Until the 1970s, rural development was synonymous with agricultural development and, hence, focused on increasing agricultural production (Harris, 1982; Chambers, 1983; Asian Development Bank, 2000a). By the early 1980s, according to Harris (1982: 15), the World Bank defined it as "...a strategy designed to improve the economic and social life of a specific group of people – the rural poor." Four major factors appear to have influenced the change: increased concerns about the persistent and deepening of rural poverty, changing views on the meaning of the concept of development itself, emergence of a more diversified rural economy in which rural non-farm enterprises play an increasingly important role, and increased recognition of the importance of reducing the non-income dimensions of poverty to achieve sustainable improvements in the socio-economic well-being of the poor. Chino (2000: xiii) added that today's concept of rural development is fundamentally different from that used three or four decades ago. The concept now encompasses "concerns that go well beyond improvements in growth, income, and output. The concerns include an assessment of changes in the quality of life, broadly defined to include improvement in health and nutrition, education, environmentally safe living conditions, and reduction in gender and income inequalities." Fernando (2008) points to inclusive rural development which covers three different but interrelated dimensions (Figure 5.1): economic, social, and political.

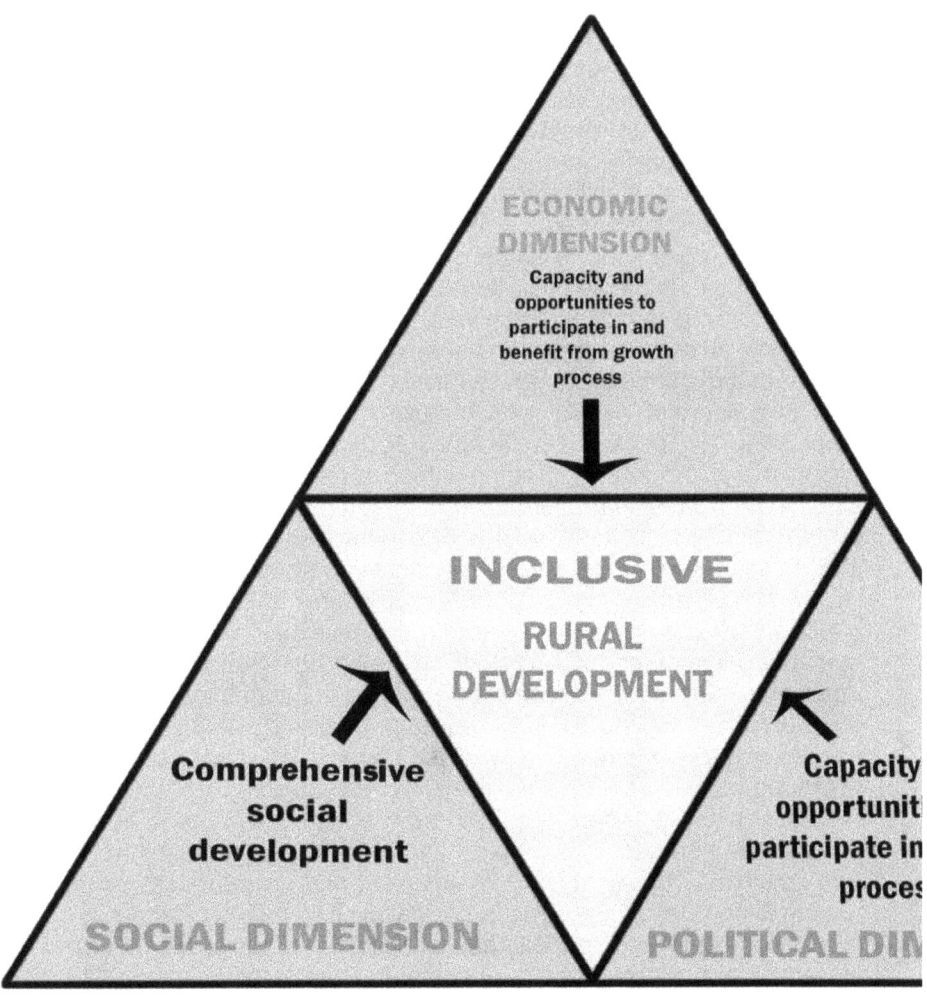

Figure 5.1: Three dimensions of inclusive rural development (Fernando, 2008). (Adapted from Cheam, Phan Viriya; Cambodian Institute for Cooperation and Peace, (CICP): http://www.cicp.org.kh. October 2009)

This figure illustrates the elements necessary for empowerment programmes which engage in growth, capacity enhancement, competency improvement, and opportunities. It also distinguishes approaches from the developing world to promote rural development. China, for example, attempts to identify farmer innovation and self-organization as an approach to sustainability (Wu, 2003: 7). It refers to Sustainable Rural Livelihoods (SRL) precisely. According to Wu (2003: 24), the term farmer innovation here is used to emphasize the nature of the farmer as the first actor of rural technological and social change. Bearing in mind the interrelationship between technical and institutional changes, farmer innovation is defined narrowly as a technological change selected and determined by farmers per se. Wu asserted that the term self-organization is a concept that usually encompasses not only organizational forms dominated by farmers themselves, but also an organizational (or evolutionary) process from simple to complex, from informal to formal. Originating from Nobel Laureate Ilya Prigogine's work on thermodynamic system and complexity (Nicolis & Prigogine, 1977; Prigogine & Stengers, 1985), self-organization has been increasingly fashionable in systems research (Silverberg et al, 1988; Krugman, 1996). Defined as "the capability of some systems to reorder themselves into ever more complex structure" (Rycroft and Kash, 1999: 61), self-organization has been widely applied to interpreting the complexity related to information technology and the economy. Linking to Wu's strategy, Carney (1998: 4) agrees that instead of a single dimension, what is needed is an integrated approach: A livelihood comprises the capabilities, assets (including material and social resources) and activities required for a means of living. A livelihood is sustainable when it can cope with and recover from stresses and shocks and maintain or enhance its assets and capabilities, whilst not undermining the natural resource base. It is widely recognized that livelihoods comprise five basic capital assets that serve different functions in satisfying basic needs (Carney, 1998; Pretty and Ward, 2001). They are:

- Natural capital: various natural resources or processes that can be used for food, wood, clean water, recreation and leisure.
- Social capital: trust, reciprocity and obligation, norms and sanctions that encourage people working together.

- Human capital: related to individual capability, health, nutrition, education, skills and knowledge.
- Physical capital: for example, local infrastructure, road and irrigation systems, and farm machines.
- Financial capital: for example, savings, credit and subsidies.

Integrating the five capitals together, Pretty and Hine (2001) established an asset based model for sustainable rural livelihood, showing that these five assets are transformed by policies, processes and institutions to give desirable outcomes such as food, job, welfare, economic growth, and a clean environment.

Regarding China's both technological applications and development potential in the rural Shaanxi area, the government has highlighted agricultural innovation as the core of its poverty-alleviation programme (Wu, 2003). Accordingly, Wu added the government innovation strategy which contains many objectives related to grain and income growth and improvement of the ecological environment. It reveals a concentration on innovation strategy for farmer participation. In contrast to the traditional Farmland Extensive Agriculture (FEA) in the north, the rural innovation strategy comprises the following elements: infrastructure development, high-yield agriculture and pillar industry (Wu, 2003: 70). It is widely recognized that poor infrastructure is a bottleneck against technological diffusion and applications. A good example is the construction of terraces, which has been listed as a main target of the poverty alleviation programme. Associated with improvement of cropland quality, the transformation of the traditional farming system is equally important because the outputs and effect of high-quality land are largely dependent on the inputs of production elements. Instead of low labour and external element inputs in the traditional FEA, Highly Efficient Agriculture (HEA) emphasizes intensive element inputs and cropping management through a package of wide-furrows, high-yield seeds, fertilizers, plastic sheet and subsidized credit (Cheam, Phan Viriya; Cambodian Institute for Cooperation and Peace, (CICP): http://www.cicp.org.kh. October 2009).

The theory of rural development "asserts that community change can best be brought about through broad participation of a wide spectrum of people at the local community level" (Zastrow, 2006: 299). This theory surmises that change efforts at the community level are most achievable with the cooperation of the local citizens, as they should be involved in the problem-solving process. In community development, the practitioner's role is to be that of a catalyst within the change effort due to the fact that residents and citizens are responsible for the contribution of various ideas in the problem-solving process. This is evident as many organizers are challenged in allowing the community members complete objectives, as they could readily be accomplished by the organizer. However, there is a blatant necessity in this theory for organizers to encourage community participation, because residents should be responsible for obtaining, maintaining, or securing their own interest, rather than the organizer. In doing so, the outcome is greater cohesiveness, pride, confidence, and problem-solving capabilities within the community. The basis of this theory is that individuals are stronger together than they are separately, and therefore collectively they may be able to resolve issues and challenges.

5.1.2   Community Development Theory

In some situations development is used as a synonym for growth. When used without reference to quality or consequences, development may be good or bad. However, Cook (1994) argued that, "in the context of community development, development is a concept associated with improvement and it is a certain type of change in a positive direction" (para. 2). Though, he said the consequences of efforts to bring about development might not be positive, the objective is always positive. He added that development's distinguishing characteristic is that it focuses on a unit called 'community' and induce non-reversible structural change. To stabilize preferred situation of structural change, he suggested the use of paid professionals/workers, initiation by groups, agencies or institutions external to the community unit, emphasize public participation, participation for the purpose of self-help, increasing dependence on participatory democracy as the mode for community (public) decision making, and use a holistic approach (Cheam Phan Viriya, Cambodian Institute for Cooperation and Peace, (CICP): http://www.cicp.org.kh. October 2009).

As an emerging profession, community development is distinguished from social work and allied welfare professions through its commitment to collective ways of addressing problems (Gilchrist, 2004). That is, community development helps community members to identify unmet needs and to undertake research on the problem and present possible solutions. Initially, this may be on a self-help basis (relating to one sense of empowerment), pioneering different ways of addressing a particular issue. As Gilchrist continued, if this is successful and demand grows, the community worker would assist group members to establish the initiative on a more secure footing, with a formal management committee, constitution, funding arrangements and paid staff. It will involve direct support of individuals as well as help with managing group dynamics and developing appropriate organizational structures. Overall, community development is primarily concerned with meeting the needs and aspirations of community members whose circumstances have left them poorly provided for, often without adequate services, with limited means to organize and exclusion from mainstream opportunities to participate in activities or decision making (Gilchrist, 2004: 21). Community development seeks to build collective capacity by improving skills, confidence and knowledge for individuals and the community as a whole. It urges use of evolving approaches through time to deal with the needs of the community, sometimes by supporting informal networks as well as formal organizations.

In the UK, there are three different models of community development, each related to contrasting political analyses of society and the state (Gilchrist, 2004: 23). The first approach assumes that there is a broad consensus about social issues, how they can be tackled and how society in general should be organized. Within this model, state-sponsored community development projects have been devised to encourage local responsibility for self-help activities, to facilitate the delivery of welfare services particularly to marginalized section of the population, and to support community 'user' involvement in democratic processes or consultation and project management. Second, the pluralist or liberal model contains a stronger sense that society consists of different interest groups and that these compete to influence decision making. This approach acknowledges that some sections of the population are disadvantaged in this struggle and community development is seen as enhancing public decision making by enabling them to be heard. Lastly, the more radical version of community development explicitly identifies conflicts of interest within society and aligns itself with the poor and other oppressed groups (Baldock, 1977; Cooke & Shaw, 1996). It argues that the causes of poverty and disadvantage are to be found in the economic system and reflect historical patterns of exploitation embedded in social and political institutions. In addition, the Federation of Community Work Training Groups (FCWTGs) based in the United Kingdom has been working for some years on the national occupational standard for community development work. Recently, it identified the key purpose of community development work as "collectively to bring about social change and justice, by working with communities to:

- identify needs, opportunities, rights and responsibilities,
- plan, organize and take action,
- evaluate the effectiveness and impact of the action, all in ways that challenge oppression and tackle inequalities" (FCWTGs, 2002: 1).

What is more, Green and Haines (2002) refer to community development as a planned effort to produce assets that increase the capacity of communities to improve their quality of life. They argue that there are five forms of community capital to focus on: human, social, physical, financial, and environmental capital. Their idea is to use this capital in the process of defined community development comprising of four stages: community organizing, visioning, planning, and implementation/evaluation. This approach is called 'asset building' for community development. Community capital is being used in different aspects to improve each element accordingly (Cheam, Phan Viriya, Cambodian Institute for Cooperation and Peace, (CICP): http://www.cicp.org.kh. October 2009).

5.1.3 Systems Theory

Community Development is a very complex activity. There are so many elements involved that it seems almost impossible to describe development in a clear and organized manner. Although it is indeed a very complex field, there is a method which can be used to identify many of the components and processes involved in this work. This way of organizing information has been called System Theory. A system can be viewed as a whole and its interrelated parts. Its guiding principle is organization. The main assumption underlying systems theory is that a well-integrated, smoothly functioning system is both possible and desirable. General System Theory, which was developed by Ludwig Von Bertalanffy (1969) and others, provides an analytical framework which can be used to describe some of the many factors involved in community development. Weber (1947) defines a system as "A set or arrangement of things so related or connected as to form a unity or organic whole" while the concept of administrative system originated from the theoretical work that is most frequently cited in Political Science – System Analysis by Easton (1965). A system is thus a unified whole having a number of interdependent parts or sub- systems and it have identifiable boundaries that distinguish it from its surrounding environment in which it is embedded, and with which it interacts.

Some of the key concerns in community development, such as assessing power and influence, understanding the dynamics of inter-group relationships, and considering the changes involved in planning development activities, can be understood and described using System theory. Terms such as systems and sub-systems, closed and open systems, system boundaries, the transfer of energy or influence across boundaries, feedback and system balance (or homeostasis) can be used to clarify what sometimes seems to be a bewildering array of information involved in community development work. Other System theory concepts, such as the description of various environments related to a system, and the very important notion of entropy, can also be used in community development. This book will describe these basic System theory concepts in a way which will relate them directly to community development.

These basic concepts form the foundation of System theory as applied to community development. Most community development work usually involves the following steps:

1. Assessing the community;
2. Selecting development goals;
3. Planning a strategy to reach those goals;
4. Carrying out activities to achieve goals, and;
5. Evaluating progress and including the results of evaluation in subsequent activities.

The use of these System theory concepts can help workers organize information and see the patterns in complex community processes as they plan and carry out development activities with their communities.

5.1.4 Empowerment Theory

Empowerment Theory refers to the experience of personal growth and an improvement in self-definition that occurs as a result of the development of capabilities and proficiencies (Staples 1998). Another definition suggests that empowerment is a combination of personal strengths, initiative, and natural helping systems to bring about change (Perkins & Zimmerman, 1995). According to Ledwith (2005), "Empowerment is not an alternative solution to the redistribution of unequally divided resources." Empowerment is more than providing the resources for one to help themselves out of poverty, it is the act of providing the necessary tools to shape the whole person and promote a critical way of thinking and consciousness (Ledwith, 2005). Parpart et al (2002), cited Amartya Sen's work (1995, 1990) on human capabilities, which stress empowerment as both a means and an end. It is a process of developing individual capacities through gaining education and skills in order to empower individuals to fight for a better quality of life. Sen sees poverty as an indication of the inability of people to meet their basic needs, whether physical or more intangible, through participation, empowerment and community life (Dreze and Sen, 1989).

This theory can be applied to community development by empowering the people within the community to develop their own community. This theory can be applied to development work through the action of going to a community and waiting on the outside to be invited in. The idea of "treading lightly" is to work alongside individuals and not possess an overarching power. Action needs to be taken through advocating for change on an individual, community, and policy level. Empowerment can be attained through working together and forming a collective state of consciousness that promotes and encourages change. Empowerment can be used in community organizing when developing new initiatives in a specific community. By empowering the citizens, the community organizer can instill a sense of pride and ownership that the citizens may not have had. Empowering citizens can help them understand they have strengths to offer the community and that their community belongs to them and not someone else. Empowerment theory can also be applied in community development by involving members of the community in organizational planning processes. In this way, community organizers can engage community members and provide an opportunity for members to take ownership of the direction and future of their own community during transitional times.

This theory could be adapted into an office business amongst the employment team. Instead of the leadership exerting power over their "trainees," the empowerment theory could be used to promote a collective voice in the work environment. This theory, when executed correctly and collectively, has the potential to change the face of business centers and the ways in which people of power interact with people of lesser power in the business world. However, Staudt et al (2002: 240) concluded that the empowerment serves as a local grassroots catalyst creating dreams among poor people. In international organizations, "empowerment has become the new adjective that embellishes many education, income generation, and service projects".

5.1.5   **Partnership (Government, NGO, Donors) Theory**

According to Pieterse (2001a), after development thinking has been more or less successively, state-led, market-led and society-led, it is increasingly understood that development action needs all of these in new combinations. New perspectives and problems (such as complex emergencies, humanitarian action) increasingly involve cooperation among government, civic and international organizations, and market forces. Human development, social choice, public action, and urban/rural development all involve such inter-sectoral partnerships. For government at local and national levels, this increasingly involves a coordinating role facilitator and enabler of inter-sectoral cooperation. Much of the interest in partnership in development circles since the 1990s has been aimed at seeking to build links between the work of government agencies and NGOs in development projects (Farrington & Bebbington, 1993). Brown & Ashman (1996) also suggest that cooperation between government and NGOs needs to span gaps of culture, power, resources and perspective if they are to be successful. In broad terms, the creation of partnerships is seen as a way of making more efficient use of scarce resources, increasing institutional sustainability and improving beneficiary participation. Lewis (2007: 93) added that, at a more general level, creating links between government agencies and NGOs may have implications for strengthening transparency in administration and challenging prevailing top-down institutional culture, both of which may contribute to the strengthening of the wider 'civil society'. Both NGOs and government tend to cooperate and support each other in the context of local rural community projects, though there is a concept of efficiency which argues that NGOs provide services more effectively than government agencies can (Smith, 1987) and, intensiveness, that NGOs are able to generate self-sufficient, self-reliant and sustainable interventions for local communities. There are many arguments regarding the NGO-government partnership; However, local authority has been playing facilitating and supporting roles for the NGO projects in the community. The NGO is project-based, implementing interactions with the community without having to overcome positions or policies taken by the authority, thus helping to smooth the way for development.

NGOs in Development Theory

This section focuses on what development NGOs actually do, and argues that what they do can be summarized broadly in terms of three main overlapping sets of roles: those of implementers, catalysts and partners (Lewis, 2007: 88). Kilby (2000) agrees NGOs pursue a wide range of objectives (relief, development, advocacy, and empowerment) through a variety of methods (direct action, funding, lobbying, and networking). Of course, each role is not confined to a single organization, since an NGO may engage in all three groups of activities at once, or it may shift its emphasis from one to the other over time or as contexts and opportunities change.

The implementer role is defined as the mobilization of resources to provide goods and services, either as part of the NGO's own project or programme or that of a government or donor agency (Carroll, 1992; Chambers, 1987; Bebbington, 1991; Kaimowitz, 1993). It covers many of the best known tasks carried out by NGOs and includes the programmes and projects which NGOs establish to provide services to people (such as healthcare, credit, agricultural extension, legal advice or emergency relief) and react quickly to local demand (Green and Matthias, 1995) as well as the growth of 'contracting', in which NGOs are engaged by government or donors to carry out specific tasks in return for payment. The role of catalyst is defined as an NGO's ability to inspire, facilitate or contribute towards developmental change among other actors at the organizational or the community level. This includes grassroots organizing and group formation (and building 'social capital') (Thomas, 1992; Putnam, 1993), empowerment approaches to development (Rowlands, 1995; Friedmann, 1992), lobbying and advocacy work (Korten, 1990; Covey, 1995; Rooy, 1997), innovation in which NGOs seek to influence wider policy processes, and general campaigning work. The role of partner encompasses the growing trend for NGOs to work with government, donors and the private sector on joint activities (DFID, 1997; World Bank, 1996; Farrington & Bebbington, 1993), as well as the complex relationships which have emerged among NGOs, such as 'capacity building'. The new rhetoric of partnership now poses a challenge for NGOs to build meaningful partnership relationships and avoid dependency, co-optation and goal displacement. All in all, NGOs in rural communities operate with a distinguished (clear, focused) viewpoint. They study the areas, tradition, situation, and need of the people so that they can formulate goals which find a way out of poverty and offer lasting self-help approaches even without further assistance of NGOs in the future. Additionally, in reality, most governments of less developed countries seemed stuck in long-term power-holding relationships with dictators and corrupt officials. The rise of NGOs to help the people is a good start in development locally, and in offering alternatives to unresponsive governments.

5.1.6 **Conflict Theory**

The several social theories that emphasize social conflict have roots in the ideas of Karl Marx (1818-1883), the great German theorist and Political activist. Conflict theorist's sees society as an arena of inequality that generates conflict and change. They see society less as a cohesive system and more as an arena of conflict and power struggle, instead of people working together to further the goals of the "social system." He further argued that the struggle between social classes was the major cause of change in society. Marx is a conflict theorist. Not all conflict theorists are Marxists. Weber is also a conflict theorist whereas Karl Marx focused on class conflict as the "engine" of historic change others see conflict among groups and individuals as a fact of life in any society. Conflict can occur over many other aspects of society unrelated to class.

According to Phillips and Pittman (2009); "Conflict theory suggests that conflict is an integral part of social life. There are conflicts between economic classes, ethnic groups, young and old, male and female, or among races". It is argued that conflicts between these people result because power, wealth, and prestige (are in short supply) not available to everyone. Therefore, one party has power over the other and it is assumed that whoever holds this power will protect their own interests at the expense of others causing conflict. One should realize that conflict is not intrinsically bad. Conflict provides grounds where people unite in order that they may act on their common interests. Conflict is the motor for desirable change.

Community organizers can use conflict theory in different ways. According to Phillips and Pittman (2009), it helps them to gain insight into why specific differences and competition have developed among groups and organizations in the community. The transformation of an aggregate of individuals who share a set of common, oppressive conditions into an interest group that will engage in conflict to change the situation is critical for conflict theorists and has relevance for social work advocates and community practitioners. A main ingredient of that transformation seems to be the development of an awareness or consciousness of one's relative state of deprivation and the illegitimate positions of those in power. Community organizers can use it to understand the distribution of power in a community, and upon doing so, can upset the status quo. Community organizers can determine if the amount of power in a community is too one sided and use different methods such as protests or boycotts to shift the power to be more equal. Conflict theory is essentially the basis or foundation for the social work practice, particularly for macro work with communities. Leaders, organizers, and planners recognize that there is a need to organize, because their interests may be overlooked because they do not align with dominant thinking. Moreover, communities may also organize to protect their interest, even if they do represent a dominant portion of society. This can be attributed to the fact that conflict is prevalent in our society and community, and conflict will occur because people are seeking to protect their varying interests that may place another social group at a disadvantage. Thus, as community organizers, it may be fundamental to bridge the division found within communities due to the occurrence of conflict among citizens. Nevertheless, this may not always be possible or feasible because social groups may not be willing to communicate or interact due to their differences.

Conflict theory can be found within every aspect of society. Conflict can happen in a multitude of different arenas such as businesses, schools or even families. Conflict theory can be used to help people resolve their differences. Once the competing interests of groups are identified, the said groups can come up with ways to solve their issues. If a business seems to be making decisions only benefiting certain people the other's can identify the problems and bring it up to everyone so the problems are resolved and everyone can benefit from them. In the medical field, there is a conflict concerning the implications of universal medical care, which illustrates the power struggle between those who have power (or insurance) and those who do not have power (or insurance). In the educational setting, conflict can be found between privileged counties and districts and those, who lack adequate resources for their educational institutions. In almost every field and discipline there will be a conflict because individuals appear to be naturally driven to protect their own interests, while overlooking the impact that it may have on the opposing group or party.

5.1.7 Social Exchange Theory

In as much as people act in their own interests, whether economic, social, or psychological, exchange is the act of obtaining a desired commodity from someone by offering something valued by the other party. Commodities exchanged can include adoration and praise for job security, information for status, sexual favours for protection, and influence for political donations. Whether exchange actually takes place depends on whether the two parties can arrive at terms that will leave each of them better off or at least not worse off, in their own estimation, after the exchange, compared with alternative exchanges possible and available to them.

Social exchange theory, associated with theorists such as George C. Homans (1974), Peter M. Blau (1964), and Richard Emerson (1962), forms another conceptual building block for community practice. Built on the operant conditioning aspects of social learning theory and an economic view of human relationships as concerned with maximization of rewards or profits and minimization of punishments or costs, exchange theory underlies such skills as bargaining, negotiating, advocating, networking, and marketing. The part of exchange theory that deals with power and dependency is especially pertinent to community practice. Community practice takes place in an action or exchange field. In terms of exchange theory, the exchange field represents a market consisting of two or more parties who interact with each other, at different times and in various combinations, to exchange desired resources or products. These resources can be tangible or intangible. They can include counseling and community organization services, money (a proxy for other products), information, ideas, political influence, goodwill, compliant behaviour, meanings, and energy. For transactions to occur, the involved parties require information about the products to be exchanged and a desire for the exchange product(s). Given relevant information and desire, ex-change theory holds that parties in a transaction select from all possible exchanges those that have the greatest ratio of benefits or rewards to costs. In social exchanges, this calculus is seldom as precise as in economic exchanges. For example, in a contribution to a United Way campaign, the donor is giving dollars (an easily measurable unit), but the products received in return—say, social status, community improvement, and assistance to people in need—are not easily measurable or readily comparable with alternative products for the donor's money.

All of the parties in an exchange field do not necessarily have relationships with each other at any given point in time. Two agencies, for example, might not have any transactions, but both might transact business with the same third organization. When Party A in an exchange field (be it an individual, a group, or an organization) can accomplish its goals without relating to Party B, and vice versa, these parties can be said to be independent of each other. However, as soon as either party cannot achieve its ends without obtaining some needed product or resource from the other and exchanges begin to occur, they can be considered interdependent. Usually, interdependent relationships are not perfectly balanced; that is, Party A may need the resources that Party B controls much more than B needs what A has to offer. In fact, B may not need what A can offer at all. In this extremely imbalanced situation, A may be said to be dependent on B. This imbalance in exchange relationships sets the stage for relations of power or influence among the members of an exchange field.

5.1.8 Ecological Theory

Ecological theory draws on environmental, biological, and anthropological precepts to highlight interconnections between the social surround and geographic and other factors. Numerous illustrations make the point. Rainforests are destroyed and humans are hurt as an incidental repercussion. Diseases are exchanged between England and France, and between Africa and the United States. U.S. movies and music influence cultures around the globe. Spicy foods from Third-World countries replace more bland food in Western diets. An ecological framework underscores such transactions, adaptations, and shaping (Kuper & Kuper, 1993). This theory reminds us that human beings have ever-changing physical and cultural environments. Suppose that within 50 years, as some have predicted, a third of the earth's people live in areas of earthquake and volcanic activity. How might this change in physical environment affect our grandchildren and the relationships between nations? Cultural environments also shape things as they change. For instance, a statue of President Franklin Roosevelt, seated in a wheelchair, was recently erected. It took group advocacy to create a new cultural perspective on a bygone leader who—because of the mores of his era—never let the public know how dependent he was on a wheelchair. Ideas about ecology and ecosystems of human groups have influenced helping professions (Germain & Gittelman, 1995; Pardeck, 1996). Factors that affect social functioning and a new orientation for intervention include the following:

- Viewing context to be as important as the immediate situation
- Seeing how mutuality and interdependence suggest values and obligations beyond family, neighborhood or nation.
- Examining ways communities organize to maintain themselves in given areas.
- Looking for ecological, natural, and impersonal influences in addition to personal causes of human problems.

To date, social work has highlighted primarily the immediate environment rather than community groups or societal forces; for a critique of this emphasis, Beckett and Johnson, 1995; Elizur, 1995; and Gardella, 2000.

5.1.9   Feminist Social Theory

The differentiation of people, at home and abroad, that sometimes leads to "honour killings" of women and girls and increased use of date-rape drugs has traditionally been discussed in terms of biology, customs, and atrocities. Like many theories, feminist theory explains, "why things are the way they are, how they got that way and what needs to be done to change them" (Ryan, 1992: 60). Growing out of a social movement, feminist theory remains critical and activist, seeking world betterment, and may be the only theory in which those who developed it benefit so directly from the insights it provokes (Tong, 1992). Yet, it shares much with other multidisciplinary, contemporary theories because it asks us to:

- relinquish conventional wisdom, thought categories, and dichotomies or binaries;
- interrogate traditional beliefs about roles, behaviour, socialization, work, conception; and
- discern absences.

"Where are the women?" While Marxism encourages us to see the world from the perspective of workers rather than bosses, feminism asks us to consider the vantage point of what traditionally was the invisible half of humanity. For instance, "feminist scholars reveal how gendered assumptions help to determine whose voices are privileged in ethnographic accounts" (Naples, 2000: 196). Among others, Nancy Hartsock (1998) introduced the idea of standpoint theory and feminist epistemology (ways of knowing). Feminist theory suggests that we question formal knowledge and core assumptions (Hyde, 1996; Kemp, 2001), since so much emanates from male-dominated scholarship.

For decades, the woman-focused perspective was considered more ideological than theoretical. Then, scholars began to realize how much had been missing from their usual scope of inquiry because women were seldom the objects of study, and their day-and-night experiences were so often ignored (Smith, 1999). Many fields have changed since addressing the question: "And what about the women?" (Lengermann & Niebrugge-Brantley: 1990). "The struggle against misogyny and for equality led to a broad array of social concerns: Social hierarchy, racism, warfare, violence [sports, domestic violence, pornography, and rape] and environmental destruction were seen to be the effects of men's psychological need for domination and the social organization of patriarchy" (Abercrombie, Hill, & Turner, 1994:162-163).

Insights about the role of gender have led social work to take a closer look at identity, difference, domination, and oppression. Concepts from feminist theory also have furthered an interest in experiential knowledge, personal narrative (telling your story), the actualities of people's living, and bodily being (Harris, Bridger, Sachs, & Tallichet, 1995; Tangenberg: 2000). Feminist theory is sometimes subsumed under the heading of empowerment, justice, liberation, emancipation, and Queer theory. Such theory has the goal of recognition, an emphasis on how categories shape the way we see the world, insights regarding privilege, and an affirmation of resiliency. All of these features are common to new frameworks about race, ethnicity, disability, and sexual orientation as well as gender (Weed & Shor, 1997). Academics have begun to join activists in naming what contributes to marginalization. Empowerment theories may motivate social workers to take a critical look at processes of paternalism, silencing, and societal denial (Lamb, 1991; Profit, 2000). In community practice, we aspire to give voice in societal discourse to previously silenced persons.

5.1.10 **Social Action Model**
This theory asserts that "there is a disadvantaged (often oppressed) segment of the population that needs to be organized" (Zastrow, 2006:298). Therefore, social justice needs to be employed in order to assist the community system in challenging the power structure. Social action brings about the question of ethics and morality and determining whether there is an unjust action taking place for which social action needs to take place. While not every party has the same ethics and morals when there is a marginalized community that is being taken advantage of, social action is the key to ending discriminatory policies. Regardless of where everyone stands, social action brings people with the mindset together to fight for a common cause.
Communities may experience various sources of oppression; in which case, it is the role of the worker to function as an activist, advocate, or broker in order to determine the appropriate services or intervention. It is important to understand what the community needs, rather than what leaders promote as their agenda. Communities are in various stages, and may need different strategies in order to best assist them. Maybe

members in the community may find that their concerns are not heard, and thus social justice may be more effective than trying to build a unified community. This may be significant as hearing the community's concerns and mobilizing them into action may result in building community interaction.

This is also evident when working with abused clients on an interpersonal level (micro), such as counseling. A worker's first notion may be to begin counselling or discuss personal information pertaining to the client's pressing problem and history, rather than ensuring that the client has had his or her basic needs met, such as safety, shelter, food, or clothing. Therefore, case management services are more likely to be necessary first, instead of intervention. Case managers will act as advocates and broker services for the client relating to their basic needs to ensure that her or his holistic needs are met. Maybe members in the community may find that their concerns are not heard, and thus social justice may be more effective than trying to build a unified community. This may be significant as hearing the community's concerns and mobilizing them into action may result in building community interaction.

5.2   APPROACHES TO RURAL AND COMMUNITY DEVELOPMENT
Rural and community development approach is referred to as a systematic, comprehensive and reliable tool aimed at bringing about desirable rural transformation. An approach for community development is expected to produce results, hence it has been tested and found effective under certain circumstances and can be replicated under similar circumstances in another setting. It is a campaign plan indicating the main lines of action to be adopted in pursuit of a given set of objectives. The people whose development is at stake must decide what the specific content, objectives and means of attaining the objectives should be. Community development in a contemporary context of deliberate policy action is essentially a transition of a rural society from an existing state to a desired state. There are many different approaches used in community development which have been identified as follows:

5.2.1 The Top-Down Approach
The top-down community development approach has roots in the early British settlement movement of the Victorian/Edwardian period--late 19th Century and early 20th Century--which was overlaid with Christian and moral values. Unlike the work of the Charity Organization Society, which centered on an individual casework approach and was the forerunner of social work, pioneers of the settlement movement argued it was necessary

for those who gave charity to become more familiar with the reasons for poverty. As well as observing and attempting to analyze people's experiences, concerned leaders, usually linked to the Anglican Church and universities, established centers (i.e., settlements) in poor neighborhoods and offered educational and recreational opportunities for local communities (Parry and Parry, 1979).

A major theme of the Top-Down community approach, therefore, is to integrate individuals and groups into mainstream society and to make services and resources more sensitive to their needs, usually in running and organizing the projects.

Most European countries adopted a top-down approach to their rural areas, but it was particularly strongly pursued in France, Ireland, UK and Scandinavia. By the late 1970s, there was growing evidence that the model had not worked (and indeed had been to the detriment of many rural areas). Top-down development was criticized as 'dependent development', reliant on continued subsidies and the policy decisions of distant agencies or boardrooms. It was seen as 'distorted development', which boosted single sectors, selected settlements and certain types of business (e.g. progressive farmers) but left others behind and neglected the non-economic aspects of rural life. It was cast as 'destructive development', which erased the cultural and environmental differences of rural areas and was unresponsive to the local knowledge held within these localities, and 'dictated development' devised by experts and planners from outside local rural areas (Lowe and Ward, 1995).

In Africa, especially at independence, the state inherited a Top-down development approach in which it played dominant role in the provision of amenities and infrastructure. This approach is reflected in National Development Plans and characterized by the establishment of the State hospitals, pipe borne water schemes, schools, farm settlements etc. this is usually done without due consultation with the people who incidentally are the end users of the projects or facilities. The result is usually the lack of commitment of the people to the maintenance and eventual collapse of these facilities and infrastructure (Osegbue, 2003). Ake (2001) averred that the ideology of development was exploited as a means for reproducing political hegemony. Osegbue (2003) maintained that this approach was politically motivated and was aimed at ensuring the maintenance and exploitation of power and paucity of social transformation. Thus, it received limited attention and served hardly any purpose as a framework for meaningful economic transformation.

5.2.2. **The Bottom-Up Approach**

The Bottom-up approach is the second method of developing the rural areas known as 'development from below'. This implies mounting development agencies in the rural areas, making use of local leaders in decision-making over their own affairs, with limited assistance from government. This is exemplified in the concept of community development by which the human and material resources are mobilized under government direction for specific and general developmental purposes. Village councils, autonomous communities and country or local government councils became the political arrangements for carrying this theory into practice. While it raised the hopes of the affected people, and brought them on the verge of realizing the set objectives, the plans usually failed for lack of sustenance. There was not enough money to finance even the smallest projects. The carefully drawn development plans became a dead letter, while the basic needs of the people remained unattended to. With this state of affairs, the rural communities were made to look up to, and rely on, the state and central governments for the solution of their ills rather than rise by their own efforts.

The Bottom-Up approach to community development could be traced to the United Kingdom in the 20th century. One of the earliest forms of UK community action occurred in the City of Glasgow in Scotland. During the early part of the 20th Century, there were a number of struggles in the city against the Munitions Act and for the campaign demanding a 40-hour work week. In 1915, both working class and lower middle class communities demonstrated against increases in rents and the lack of attention to the problems of slum housing. Thousands of Glasgow tenants were involved in a rent strike, with protests spreading to other British cities, leading to rent strikes and calls for lower rents and improved housing (Damer, 1980). Working class collective action was also prevalent in the 1920s and 1930s with the growth of the national unemployed workers movement (Hannington, 1967; 1977). Craig (1989) argues that this was the first attempt to link struggles in the home with those in the workplace.

In more recent times, examples of community action have been varied and include the squatters' movement, the welfare rights movement, and different forms of resistance against planning and redevelopment. In the last two decades, thousands of people mobilized, protested, and acted against the nuclear arms race, particularly the women's peace movement at Greenham Common in Southern England, and in widespread objection to the Poll Tax introduced by the Conservative government in the 1980s (Hoggett and Burns 1992). The role of women, central in the majority of community action, reflects the different experience of community for women and for men (Dominelli, 1990). Cornell (1984) has argued that women appear more active in community life and occupy greater range of communal spaces than men do. For example, whereas many men can derive a sense of community from the local pub, women have wider networks, including schools, shops, and neighbours. The fact that women are key actors in informal community networks has led to the observation by Bornat, et al. (1993), that women are at the front line of negotiations over nurseries, schools, housing, health, and other welfare agencies. Not surprisingly, then, women have also been central in community-based actions to organize, defend, or protest about such services. Similarly, minority ethnic communities have used community work both to confront racism and discrimination and to forge alliances to protect and support cultural, religious, and national groups.

5.2.3. **Community Driven Development (CDD) Approach**
The World Bank defines CDD as 'a development approach that gives control over planning decisions and investment resources to community groups and local governments' (Dongier et al 2003). The World Bank together with client countries promotes CDD as the empowerment of communities and local governments, often phasing in empowerment by starting with communities. Experience has shown that given clear rules of the game, access to information and appropriate capacity and financial support, poor men and women can effectively organize to identify community priorities and address local problems by working in partnership with local governments and other supportive institutions. The World Bank recognizes that CDD approaches and actions are important elements of an effective poverty reduction and sustainable development strategy. Over the last decade, the World Bank has increasingly focused on lending to CDD programmes in order to reach local communities directly. The Bank has used the CDD approach across a range of countries to support a variety of urgent needs: water supply and sewerage rehabilitation; school and health post construction, nutrition programmes for mothers and infants; building of rural access roads and support for micro-enterprise.

CDD programmes operate on the principles of local empowerment, participatory governance, demand-responsiveness, administrative autonomy, greater downward accountability and enhanced local capacity. With a view to sustainable and wide ranging impacts, CDD operations and regional strategies have increasingly embraced two important pillars of sustainability and scale: linking communities to the private sector and to local governments. Because CDD provides communities with a voice and control over all project stages, it is believed to 1) Enhance sustainability; 2) Improve efficiency and effectiveness; 3) Allow poverty reduction efforts to be taken to scale; 4) Make development more inclusive; 5) Empower poor people, build social capital, and strengthen governance; 6) Complement market and public sector activities (Dongier et al., 2003; Van Domelen, 2007, 2008; Baird et al. 2009; Binswanger et al., 2010).

Figure 5.2:

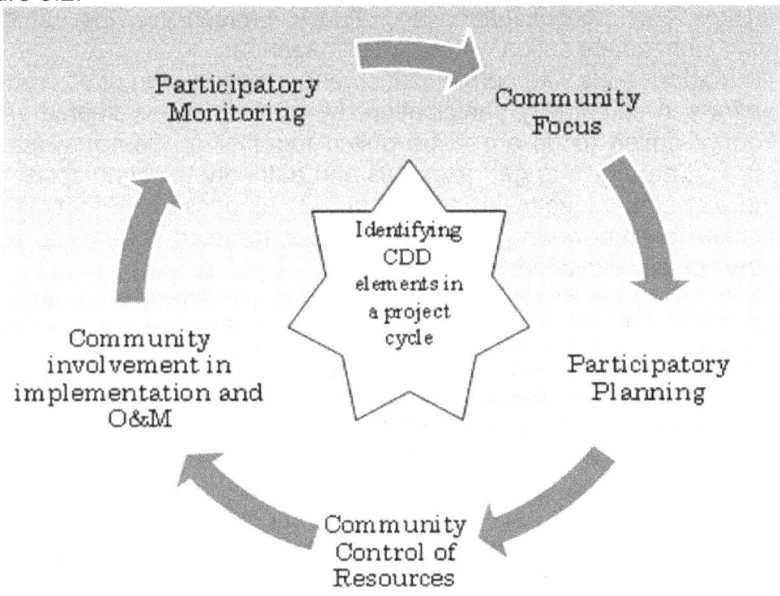

Source: World Bank Report on CDD, (2000).

Since the last two decades the concept of community driven approach has gained currency within the African development community. The goal is to move political, administrative and fiscal power from top to bottom. Using a CDD approach is warranted in cases of 'local institutional failure' - e.g. market institutions, public services, or local governments, where local institutions are absent or non-existent, or non-functional. The problems lay in the inability of central government agencies and donors to respond to local priorities or take advantage of local skills. The result is that poverty remained deep although countries of Africa got some of the largest flows of net aid per capita in the world (the World Bank, 2000). CDD aims at building social capital by harnessing community participation and also to improve social capital by strengthening incentives for participatory development. This approach to rural development is targeted at poverty alleviation or reduction and currently gaining popularity and application in Africa. This approach has five key elements: empowering communities, empowering local governments, re-aligning the centre, improving accountability and capacity building. While it is suggested that each country/community may have to fashion its own CDD process, three stages are conceptually relevant. They are decentralization – initiation, scaling up and consolidation, and finally sequencing that involves combining immediate action with long-term agenda.

- **Initiation** deals with harmonization and strengthening of all on-going efforts in community participation. All existing uncoordinated efforts donor driven funds are to be pulled together to create investment fund. The aim is to get resources and authority to spend social fund to as many communities and as quickly as possible. Priority is also given to empowering communities over targeted scheme to reach the socially excluded.
- **In scaling up stage**, efforts are made to make local government assume full responsibility for frontlines services delivery. This is achieved by strengthening their capacity and accountability mechanism. This stage is built around the principle of transferring responsibilities in stages from a social fund to local governments, and local government which performs well advances faster along the path of additional resources and responsibilities.
- **Consolidation** is a stage for functioning political, administrative and fiscal arrangements and for further upgrading of local skills. In this stage, decentralization becomes fully operational where local governments are already functioning well; donors try to switch their strategy from direct funding of communities to providing budgetary support to the central government for onward disbursement to local communities through various local governments.

5.2.4 The Directive Approach (DA)
The greatest hallmark of directive approach to community development is the involvement of the external body or outsiders in promoting community developmental efforts. Here, an outside influence or agency like Local Government department, philanthropic organization and other community based organizations (CBOs), taken direct initiative to identify the needs of

a community, plans for action, organizes and provides resources to meet the needs. In this case, the only contribution of the benefitting community is to participate actively in the project implementation through direct labour or encouraging of the initiators (Obodoechi, 2006). The main objective of this approach is that over time, the people themselves will be able to learn and be in a position to do things by themselves. It is also assumed that the provision of their needs by the external body will stimulate them to take action in future for other needs. However, this approach has some set backs, in that inhabitant tend to shy away from the responsibility of proper safeguarding and caring for their projects. This is the problem with the rural electrification project of the 1980's in Nigeria, where the host communities could not safeguard the lines and poles of electricity, believing it is a government property not theirs.

Nevertheless, situations under which the directive approach can obtain are spelt out in Ogili (2004) as follows:

> ➢ When a community lacks the human and material resources to identify, plan for action and provide certain needs. This can happen in primitive or backward societies, which may sometimes resist change.
> ➢ Provision of certain services that require technical know-how and sophisticated equipment, which the community does not possess.
> ➢ Introduction of new methods of carrying out some occupations such as farming, fishing and carving.

The directive approach is expected to be a temporary measure, over time. The people are supposed to be able to identify, plan, organize and take action on their own with little or no interference from any external body.

5.2. 5. **The Non-Directive Approach (N-DA)**
Under the non - directive approach, the people of a community are expected to be able to identify their felt needs, plan for action, provide their own resources and execute projects or provide services all on their own. This approach is the opposite of the directive approach. All that the community requires from an external body is technical advice in planning and in designing some projects like buildings, bridges and roads. In non – directive approach, what is pertinent is for the people to initiate a process by which a community seeks to identify and take action in respect to its own problems. The main objective is to encourage the community to identify what it considers to be its problems and to work systematically on these problems, in the belief that such an experience will increase the

capacity of the community to deal with problems which will confront it in future.

5.2.6 Match-Grant Approach

A matching grant is a one-off, non-reimbursable transfer to project beneficiaries. It is based on a specific project rationale for particular purposes and on condition that the recipient makes a specified contribution for the same purpose or subproject. Grants and matching contributions can be either in cash or in kind, or a combination of both. They may or may not be provided together with other financial services, such as loans, or linked to them. As one-off transfers, matching grants differ from permanent public transfers, such as subsidies for inputs and services (e.g. fertilizer or interest rate subsidies) or safety nets (e.g. cash transfers, food for work). Matching Grant is a grant or gift made with the specification that the amount donated must be matched from other sources on a one-for-one or some other prescribed basis. A good example of Match Grant approach is the Joint Action on Development (JAD) that was adopted during the Administration of former Governor Mbadinuju of Anambra State in Nigeria.

Within community-driven development projects, matching grants are typically used to finance social and economic infrastructure, productive assets and income generating and livelihood-diversification activities by groups, and sometimes by individuals. Within rural and agricultural business development projects, they are used to develop agricultural value chains, promote innovation and technology, enhance access to extension and support services, and support farm diversification. They can be classified by purpose (type of goods and services financed), by the public or private nature of these goods and services, by type of recipient, by allocation mechanism and by type of resources provided see (Table 5.1).

Table 5.1: **Types of Matching Grants according to key criteria**

Criteria	Categories	Examples
By characteristics of goods/services	• Public goods/services	• Social infrastructure (schools, clinics, goods and services water supply and sanitation), productive infrastructure (roads) • Inputs, machinery, business

	• Private goods	development or engineering services to individuals or companies
	• Impure public and private goods	• Goods and services targeting individuals, groups within a community (irrigation, storage, group-based processing) or entire communities
By purpose (type of capital)	• Working capital • Investment capital	• Seeds, fertilizer, fuel, etc. • Equipment, vehicles, land, related technical services
By recipient	• Suppliers of goods • Users of goods and services	• Financial institutions, researchers, technology providers and services Farmers and farmer groups, rural and services micro-, small and medium-sized enterprises
By allocation mechanism	• Entitlement based • Competitive • Through financial Institutions	• Community-driven development • Some value chain, research and technology generation • Linked to a complementary loan from a financial institution

Source: (IFAD) International Fund for Agricultural Development Report on Matching Grant (2012).

An illustration using Integrating Matching Grants and Bank lending: The case of the Rural Enterprise Programme in Ghana (IFAD, 2012).
Phase II of the IFAD-funded Rural Enterprise Programme in Ghana financed production and processing equipment using matching grants: 30 per cent of investment costs were grant funded, 10 per cent was funded by the beneficiary and the remaining 60 per cent was covered by a loan provided by a participating financial institution. Financial institutions bore the full credit risk of the loan component. Ceilings per client for total investment cost of equipment were fixed in terms of the level of enterprise development for micro- and small enterprises:

- At start-up stage: maximum investment of US $500 and maximum grant of US $150

- At survival stage: maximum investment of US $1,000 and maximum grant of US $300
- At high-performing and growth stage: maximum investment of US$ 3,000 and maximum grant of US $900.

An investment cost higher than the ceiling had to be met by the client. No systematic evaluation of the results has been undertaken so far. However, portfolio quality data for 21 rural and community banks and three branches of the Sinapi Aba Trust participating in the programme show a portfolio at risk (PAR > 30 days) of 6 per cent and an overall recovery rate of 98 per cent. This compares favourably with data from a survey of portfolio quality among rural and community banks carried out in 2007, which reported a PAR of 22.7 per cent, versus 7.3 per cent for financial NGOs and 5.3 per cent for savings and loan companies. One reason for the good repayment performance might be that clients are selected among trainees of Business Advisory Centres supported by the project.

There are no comprehensive data showing repayment rates for loans granted by participating financial institutions that are co-funded by matching grants. However, selected evidence shows that the repayment rate over such loans is about 20 percentage points below that for loans funded purely from own resources without a matching grant component. Most practitioners and analysts apparently agree that this has less to do with confusion between grants and loans and more with (a) the fact that decisions on matching grants often experienced lengthy delays and (b) the involvement of government funds, which seems to entice borrowers to escape from repayment.

5.2.7 The Integrated Rural Development (IRD) Approach
Integrated rural development can be defined as area development schemes which involve a broad range of activities designed to improve production, infrastructure, services and living standards in line with the objectives, and with emphasis on the linkages between the various components and geographical areas internal and external to the area. The Integrated Rural Development (IRD) approach became popular in the 1970s and was fuelled by substantial donor allocations during the 1970s and 1980s. IRD was a holistic way to improve well-being in a community unit along social, economic and environmental dimensions. The approach drew on systems thinking, an emphasis on local participation and community ownership, and on observations that economic growth was not necessarily benefiting the rural poor directly. It recognized the

complementarity of, and interconnections between, different development objectives.

This approach was based on the premise that a combination of factors not only the right technology and education but also access to physical inputs and attractive markets will get agriculture moving. Integrated rural development is multipurpose in nature because it entails inter-connectivity of programme on education, health, agriculture, nutrition, cooperatives and the like and no one is treated in isolation but together. The strategy contends that the key to improving the productivity of small scale farmers and the promotion of more effective government support is a package of reinforcing activities. These activities include the provision of farm credit, extension agricultural inputs, reliable marketing facilities, assured agricultural product prices, rural public works and stronger village institution. It becomes popular in the 70s because of the realization that rapid economic growth does not guarantee availability or equitable access to social services and amenities. The aim of the programmes carried out under IRD was to assist small and medium level farmers to produce marketable goods that were non-agricultural and moved farmers beyond the level of subsistence farming. At the same time, in some contexts, a parallel move was made to encourage investment and support for agricultural exports to increase returns to farmers (Brohman, 1996). The approach apart from increasing agricultural production, also addresses the basic needs of the population. It helps in modernization of agriculture and also improves the quality of life through formation of farmer's cooperative society. Increase in agricultural productivity is dependent on rapid technological change and since agricultural technology is location specific, it cannot just be transferred from area where it is developed to another area without being adapted to local ecological conditions. Research and extension that will make this adaptation possible are required. It helps in the mobilization of human and materials resources for the creation of a healthy national economy whose benefit will be shared by all the rural people.

The Integrated Rural Development (IRD) approach was officially introduced in Nigeria during the Third National Development Plan, 1975-1980. It was regarded, within the official circles, as an entirely new dimension to rural development and constituting a multi-dimensional, multi-disciplinary and multi-sectoral approach, which is deeply rooted in the understanding of the realities of the rural life. This approach had come to operate under the auspices of Agricultural Development Programmes (ADPs) sponsored by the World Bank, which brought about a set of programmes ostensibly to improve the lots of the rural folks. The central focus of this approach is people and their social and physical environments. Thus, people have to actively participate in the social, political and economic affairs that affect them through Community Development (CD) efforts. In essence, the main features of Integrated Rural Development indicate that: the primary target for identification is the rural poor, the objectives of the programme range from agricultural productivity, equitable distribution of income to agrarian reform, popular peoples' participation and employments. Other features include the holistic conceptualization of development as well as the recognition of local initiatives to expand the scope of the programme. Typically IRD programmes included activities such as increasing agricultural productivity, farm and non-farm employment and income generation, physical and social infrastructure development (schools, clinics, and road), social and food security, drought and floods mitigation. An example of an Integrated Rural Development Scheme is the Farm Settlement Scheme of the Eastern and Western Regions of Nigeria in the First Republic. They were conceived largely as a means of reducing urban unemployment, increasing food production and decentralizing amenities. Other examples of integrated development approach are Integrated Rural Development Scheme (IRD), in Nigeria the Agricultural Development Projects (ADPs), including the on-going National Fadama Development Project (NFDP). It has now clearly appeared that there exists no categorically stated and people oriented National Policy on Integrated Rural Development in Nigeria based explicitly on Community Development (CD). Notwithstanding the transient fragments of some policy statements by different regimes on Integrated Rural Development, these policy statements should not be considered as National Policies.

While there were some outstanding IRD successes, the barrier seemed to be their scaling up. Too little was invested in the managerial and institutional development, hence project evaluations reported unsustainable and unsatisfactory performance of IRD efforts. While contextual features varied widely, the main shortfalls drawn from IRD experiences in various parts of the world were (USAID, 2005):

- IRD approaches tended to become supply-driven because of the top down method of implementation.
- IRD projects by-passed official agencies to set up their own units for efficiency purposes, but this negatively affected sustainability of the programme beyond the donor's involvement, and did not build local institutions.

- There was little interaction, evaluation and training of the social and institutional capital existing in the community, therefore negatively affecting operational issues once donor involvement with the project ended.
- The projects allowed state intervention in all sectors of agricultural farming from circulation to distribution while avoiding the vital issue of land distribution, thus, allowing paternalistic relations to emerge and impeding the sustainability of the exercise.

5.2.8 Extension Approach

The extension approach focuses on the teaching of local people, the improved methods and techniques of farming, healthcare, or reading and writing (agriculture, health and adult education). It is used to transfer recommended practices from research and other knowledge-based bodies to client groups such as farmers, fisher-folks, nursing mothers, the poor, the aged or physically challenged. It is based on the assumption that if the information is available, these clients will make informed decisions.

Agricultural Extension Strategy: Agricultural extension strategy was based on the premise that the cheapest materials in the rural areas are land and these resources can be developed through effective agriculture extension services. This strategy aims at increasing agricultural productivity and welfare of rural farmers. It helps farmers to increase their production by persuading them to adopt improved technical practices. Agricultural extension develops skills, knowledge and attitudes in farmers and their families. It finds solutions to the problems of the farmers by taking the problems into research for solution and the solutions back to the farmers. It utilizes various methods in teaching the farmers such as demonstration farm visits, group meeting and mass method through audio visual and printed materials.

Figure 5.3

Source: (IFAD, 2012)

Since most families farm are closely linked together, agricultural extension incorporates programmes on home economics and in youth development using individual, group and mass methods. There is a little difference between agricultural extension and community development both of them are educational programme and aims at developing people. Agricultural extension concentrated only on agricultural development but indirectly concerned with rural problems such as health, nutrition and cooperatives. It encourages related agencies to extend their services in rural areas while community development agencies endeavour to provide some of these services to the rural areas. The training received by the agents enables them to perform their different roles. Agricultural extension as a strategy to rural development helps in improving the farmer's productivity and changing the outlook of farmers towards their problems while its shortcoming as a strategy lies in its ineffectiveness in promoting agricultural development. The main reasons for this are:

> ➢ Low ratio of extension agents to farmers who are to teach the farmers improved farm practices.
> ➢ Inadequate credit facilities to purchase farm inputs
> ➢ Inadequate use of local leaders to assist extension agents in teaching farmers
> ➢ Inadequate motivation of extension on workers
> ➢ Inadequate funding of extension services by the government.

5.2.9 Basic Needs Approach

Historically, the Basic Needs approach to development planning and mobilization has many early "fathers". One was Mahatma Gandhi. His approach may be described as action oriented (the environment of domination and oppression was his laboratory), normative (the welfare of the poorest of the poor was his standard) and global (a non-violent world society was his ultimate goal). Another contributor was a humanistic psychology and the human potential movement, Abraham Maslow, who died in 1970. His book: "Toward a Psychology of Being and his later The Farther Reaches of Human Nature" develop his concept of the hierarchy of needs, "self-actualization", and "peak experiences". More significantly is the contribution by the American "structural-functionalist" school of sociology with Talcott Parsons, Robert Merton, Marion J. Levy and David Apter as the leaders. For an analysis of structural functionalism's contribution to development approaches, see Ankie Hoogvelt (1976) "The Sociology of Developing Societies".

In the modern times, the basic needs approach was first put forth in an international forum by the International Labour Office (ILO), at its 1976 World Employment Conference, and was subsequently elaborated by others at the World Bank, the OECD and within A.I.D. It was the 1976 World Employment Conference of the International Labour Office which placed basic needs directly on the governmental world agenda. In the ILO presentation, basic needs were defined in terms of food, housing, clothing, and public services, like education, healthcare and transport. Employment was both a means and an end, and participation in decision-making was included. The conclusions of the 1976 World Employment Conference state some of the requirements for satisfying human needs within one generation: "Strategies and national development plans and policies should include explicitly as a priority objective the promotion of employment and the satisfaction of the basic needs of each country's population...Often these measures will require a transformation of social structures including an initial redistribution of assets. "The Programme of Action puts emphasis on the participation of the people, through organizations of their own choice in making the decisions which affect them... In view of the highly hierarchical social and economic structures of agrarian societies in some developing countries, measures of redistributive justice are likely to be thwarted unless backed by organizations of rural workers."

The ILO report goes on to indicate two crucial elements in the Basic Needs approach: "First, they include certain minimum requirements of a family for private consumption: adequate food, shelter and clothing, as well as certain household equipment and furniture. Second, they include essential services provided by and for the community at large, such as safe drinking water, sanitation, public transport and health, education and cultural facilities." The Basic Needs approach constitutes an attempt to come to grips directly with poverty in the fields of food, nutrition, health, education, and housing. It is predicated on a policy consisting of relatively high growth rates, redistribution of income, reorientation of investment and a review and modification of consumption and production patterns. A Basic Needs approach stresses the importance of the household as a basic institution. It is the household which allocates among its members incomes earned by members who are employed for wages, and it produces goods and services for its own use. Moreover, household activities play a crucial role in converting education, health and nutrition into improvements in the quality of life of individuals. By stressing the household, the Basic Needs approach comes close to reality and focuses on the family which has often been overlooked in development planning.

The ILO report stresses the importance of popular participation in development policies, especially of rural populations which are the least organized of workers. The report goes on to state: "It is imperative for rural workers to be given every encouragement to develop free and viable organizations capable of protecting and furthering the interests of their members and ensuring their effective contribution to economic and social development." The world employment programme built upon an increasingly sophisticated understanding of what employment is by better analysis of the role of the informal sector in employment. In addition to the informal sector, the World Employment Conference stressed rural employment and the role of rural workers associations, subjects, more often considered in the UN Food and Agriculture Organization. Rural workers' organizations should represent the workers' interests by engaging in planning development programmes at local and national levels, providing an educational base for workers and in general mobilizing to improve the resources and services available to the workers as well as ensuring that social and economic development is responsive to the workers' needs. Such groups of popular participation must not only breakdown old ways of doing things but must group human beings around new ways of doing them. Popular participation and the mobilization of the disadvantaged is an essential requirement of a Basic Needs approach to development. It is this requirement of popular participation that distinguishes a Basic Needs model of development from other kindred poverty eradication models.

The UN emphasis on basic needs is a good example of the role of the UN system in highlighting ideas and placing them on the agenda for action. The basic needs approach per se does not purport to cover all aspects of development planning. However, it does provide a suitable basis for planning framework institutions where a high priority is placed on achieving a pattern of growth that results in alleviation of absolute poverty on a sustainable basis. Such a priority is appropriate and plausible not only on the grounds that the needs of those in poverty are relatively urgent, but also on the basis that poverty is widespread. However the approach did not specify a priori how they were to be chosen or the way in which they were to be weighted. Structural criticisms leveled against BNA were largely conceptual:

- Basic needs are difficult to quantify, and the trade-offs between improving income equality and reducing savings for investment were not considered sufficiently (Bagolin, 2004).
- BNA incorporated arbitrary assumptions about human nature (assuming particular western cultural values) and about social change following a universal, linear pattern of development (Gough and Thomas, 1994).
- Some operational forms of BNA were exclusively focused on resources and inputs, and this particular form overlooked people's varying abilities to convert resources into what Sen. later called 'functioning's'.

- It was not quite clear how the BNA included participation and freedom (Streeten 1984, Sen 1984).

5.2.10. Asset Based Community Development (ABCD) Approach

In recent years, Asset-based Community Development (ABCD) approach has caught the attention of numerous community development practitioners. As an alternative to the more commonly practiced needs-based approach, ABCD shifts the focus of community development from "problem solving" to "asset building". ABCD takes a "grassroots" approach to community development, drawing upon the best of what a community has to offer. Asset-Based and Citizen-Led Development is an approach that recognizes the strengths, gifts, talents and resources of individuals and communities, and helps communities to mobilize and build on these for sustainable development (Coady, 2002). According to Braithwaite (2005) Asset-based community development is based on the principle of community-driven development rather than development driven by external agencies, where communities, public and private sectors work in closer partnership. Also, Green, Moore and O'Brien (2006) defined Asset-based Community Development (ABCD) as a powerful approach that focused on discovering and mobilizing the resources that are already present in a community. The ABCD approach provides a way for citizens to find and mobilize what they have in order to build a stronger community.

Leading the ABCD movement are John Kretzmann and John McNight of the Northwestern University Asset-based Community Development Institute. The Institute's numerous publications on the topic have received attention both nationally and abroad. Asset building following the ABCD approach involves identifying and tapping all of the potential assets in a community. Community assets include the talents and skills of individuals, organizational capacities, political connections, buildings, facilities, and financial resources (Adams and Sherraden, 1997). According to Mathie and Cunningham (2005), Kretzmann and McKnight's ABCD approach operates under the premise that community's can drive the development process themselves by identifying and mobilizing existing (but often unrecognized) assets, thereby responding to and creating local opportunity for positive changes. Such unrealized assets include not only personal attributes and skills, but also the relationships among people that help local associations and informal networks. Mobilizing social assets can activate more formal institutional resources such as local government, formal community-based organizations, and private enterprise. In this way, the community development process is sustained and scaled up while it continues to recognize local associations as the driving force – the vehicles through which all the community's assets can be identified and then connected to one another in ways that multiply their power and effectiveness.

It is an approach to community-based development, based on the principles of:
- Appreciating and mobilizing individual and community talents, skills and assets (rather than focusing on problems and needs).
- Community-driven development rather than development driven by external agencies.

It builds on:
- Appreciative inquiry which identifies and analyses the community's past successes. This strengthens people's confidence in their own capacities and inspires them to take action.
- The recognition of social capital and its importance as an asset. This is why ABCD focuses on the power of associations and informal linkages within the community, and the relationships built over time between community associations and external institutions.
- Participatory approaches to development, which are based on principles of empowerment and ownership of the development process.
- Community economic development models that place priority on collaborative efforts for economic development that makes best use of its own resource base.
- Efforts to strengthen civil society: These efforts have focused on how to engage people as citizens (rather than clients) in development, and how to make local governance more effective and responsive (Mathie and Cunningham 2003).

ABCD is a process of self-mobilization and organizing for change. This process has happened spontaneously in many communities. The challenge for an external agency, such as an NGO, is to stimulate this process in other communities without having the opposite effect of creating dependency. There are a set of methods that can be used, but it is important not to consider this a blue-print, but more as guidelines for achieving community-driven development. We are already seeing variations in how ABCD is facilitated by different NGOs.
1. Collecting stories.

2. Organizing a core group.
3. Mapping the capacities and assets of individuals, associations and local institutions.
4. Building a community vision and plan.
5. Mobilizing and linking assets for economic development.
6. Leveraging activities, investments and resources from outside the community (Mathie and Cunningham 2003).

1. **Collecting Stories:** - To begin building confidence in the community, informal discussions and interviews that draw out people's experience of successful activities and projects will help to uncover the gifts, skills, talents and assets people have. Not only does this uncover assets that people have not recognized before, but it also strengthens people's pride in their achievements. This celebration of achievement and realization of what they have to contribute builds confidence in their abilities to be producers, not recipients, of development.

2. **Organizing a Core Group:** - In the process of collecting stories, particular people will emerge as leaders in the community -- people who have shown commitment and leadership in the past or who are currently taking a leadership role. The next step is to organize a group of such committed individuals who are interested in exploring further the community's assets and acting on the opportunities identified. Each of these individuals will have a network of relationships inside the community whom they can draw into the process. Each of these individuals will have a personal interest -- something that motivates him or her to act.

3. **Mapping Completely the Capacities and Assets of Individuals, Associations, and Local Institutions:** - Mapping is more than gathering data. It is very important that citizens and their associations do the asset mapping themselves so that they themselves build new relationships, learn more about the contributions and talents of community members, and identify potential linkages between different assets.
    a) Identifying associations - The starting point of this exercise is to identify associations in the community. These relationships are the engines of community action, and are therefore essential (and often unrecognized) as assets. One way to do this is to start with the core group and ask them what associations and informal

groups they belong to. Once these have been listed, ask the core group to expand the list to include associations they know about. This longer list of associations can then be clustered by type and those associations most likely to participate in working together for a common purpose can be identified. In the process of identifying associations, the list of leaders in the community also expands.

b) Identifying individual gifts, skills, and capacities - There are many ways of trying to elicit individual gifts, skills and capacities. The important thing is to ensure that this is not just a data gathering exercise, but a way in which people feel that their abilities and contributions are appreciated. Eventually a "capacity inventory" is developed, listing these capacities in categories such as "community-building skills", "enterprise skills", "teaching skills", and "artistic skills". A simpler approach might be to divide them into skills of the heart, head, and hand.

c) Identifying the assets of local institutions - This would include government agencies, non government agencies and private sector businesses. The assets of these institutions could be the services and programmes they provide, the meeting places they offer, the equipment and other supplies they may have, or the communications links they may have. They also have paid or unpaid staff who may be important links in the community

d) Identifying physical assets and natural resources - Assets such as land, water, mineral or other resources can be listed here, identifying those which are communally owned and managed and those which are individually owned and managed.

e) Mapping the local economy - This exercise helps people in the community understand how the local economy works, showing how well local resources are maximized for local economic benefit. Are products and services imported that could be produced locally?

4. **Convening a Broad Representative Group to Build a Community Vision and Plan: -** During this part of the process, assets are matched with opportunities around an "organizing theme" -- a vision for community development. An activity is selected within that organizing theme for the community to begin working on right away. It needs to be concrete (people know what to do to succeed, and what success will look like), immediate, achievable with community resources, unifying (it brings people together), and strengthening

(people's skills are used and valued). How is this process managed? It is important that the representative group that is convened reflects the energy that has been identified at the associational level. Institutions take a back seat role, leaving decision-making to those who have been identified as leaders in the community with key links to associational networks.

5. **Mobilizing Assets for Community Development: -** The process continues as ongoing mobilization of community assets for economic development and information sharing purposes, initiated by the associational base. Associations are encouraged to engage by appealing to their interests, finding common ground and ensuring that they are contributing on their own terms. Eventually, an "association of associations" emerges.

6. **Leveraging Activities, Investments and Resources from Outside the Community to Support Asset-Based, Locally Defined Development: -** The process of realizing the community vision begins with associations asking themselves "What can we do to make this vision happen?" External resources are not tapped until local resources have been utilized. This puts the community in a position of strength in dealing with outside institutions.

However, it's almost impossible to find a single definition of asset based community development approaches – one that will sit comfortably across many spaces and different traditions. However, what we can do is to try to piece together some of the common themes so that we have a starting point from which to begin to discuss such approaches. The approaches are frameworks – maps or conceptual scaffolds that help us to understand how local development can be initiated and driven by the communities themselves. Such approaches:

> ➢ Begin from and focus on the strengths of a community.
> ➢ Suggest that development can be community or outsider initiated as long as it is 'by the community, for the community'.
> ➢ Seek to build or release the capacity of community members to continue to drive their own development by starting with what already exists in the community.
> ➢ Build on a social justice approach by seeking to build inclusive and resilient communities Carnegie UK Trust (2009).
> www.carnegieuktrust.org.uk

An example of Asset-based Approach Implementation: - At the center of the ABCD movement is the Asset-Based Community Development Institute at Northwestern University in Evanston, IL, a northern suburban district of Chicago. In 1996, the Institutes' co-directors John Kretzmann and John McKnight visited Chicago's Grand Boulevard Neighbourhood. The neighborhood holds the dubious distinction of being the fourth-poorest neighborhood in the United States, where 82% of the children live below the poverty level (Marshall 1997). During their visit, Kretzmann and McKnight identified 319 active groups ranging from church choirs to political clubs. (Marshall 1997). They discovered that a majority of these groups were willing to work on projects such as attracting new business to the community and creating job-training programmes. Kretzmann and McKnight have since continued to work with the neighbourhood applying ABCD strategies. Carnegie UK Trust (2009). What Are Asset-Based Approaches to Community Development? Adapted from International Association for Community Development (IACD), November 2009 www.carnegieuktrust.org.uk

Chapter Six

THE PROCESSES OF RURAL AND COMMUNITY DEVELOPMENT

6.1 STEPS IN RURAL AND COMMUNITY DEVELOPMENT

Community development as a process usually follows certain identifiable steps. Since community development is a problem-solving process, there is an identification of a problem or need. What a community needs is usually determined by the condition it wants and how the existing condition differs from that which is desired. "Wants" therefore refer to desired state of affairs whereas "needs" refer to the effective means of achieving such desired state or maintaining it. For instance, if a community wants constant and reliable water supply, then it needs a well, or reservoir and all those things required for the construction of any of these facilities. Apart from identifying the desired state of affairs or the ideal condition, the citizens must also identify the alternatives which exist before fully deciding on what actions they will embark upon to attain what they desire. Although, the entire process may vary from community to community and from one situation to another, some basic steps are crucial to the success of community development. These steps are itemized as follows:

1. **Learn about the Community:** - Whether you want to be an active member of the community, an effective service provider or a community leader, you will have to be familiar with its issues, resources, needs, power structure and decision-making processes. Your initial orientation could include reading your local newspaper regularly, attending community events, reading reports and familiarizing with available services as well as community projects and activities. Close observation of the community as you interact with it will also provide significant insights into the strengths and weaknesses of the community.

2. **Listen to Community Members:** - You won't be able to learn everything you need to know by reading and observation. You will need to talk to others about their interests and perceptions to put it into context. You can contact community members through formal channels, such as joining a local organization, or informally by

chatting with people that visit the library or that you encounter in other situations, such as shopping at local stores or attending school activities. By listening to the community you may identify an area in which there seems to be a common interest in making a change. For instance, health organization staff should maintain regular contact with the community to collect enough information to make sound recommendations and decisions on health services and priorities and to identify important community issues.

3. **Bring People Together to Develop a Shared Vision: -** Once you have identified that there are some common interests among community members and you have identified a few individuals who seem willing to work on a community development initiative, the next step is to hold a community gathering. In some circumstances it may be appropriate to invite representatives of specific organizations or communities to attend, but more often it would be a public event for a neighbourhood or, for other types of communities, for all the identified members. The purpose of this gathering would be to develop a shared "community vision"; i.e., through imagining their ideal community and discussing their ideas together they will determine or arrive at a common vision and some broad strategic directions that all are committed to working towards. You may also use this gathering to ask for support for the initiative, elicit community input or invite members to join a steering committee or help in other ways.

4. **Assess Community Assets and Resources, Needs and Issues: -** To be able to work effectively in a community development context, you will need to gather some information about your community. It is extremely helpful to undertake a comprehensive community assessment which will collect both **qualitative** and **quantitative** data on a wide range of community features. Unfortunately, time and budget restraints will necessitate choosing between methods and limiting the assessment to particular areas of interest. Deciding what and how much information to collect may be aided by a SWOT (Strengths, Weaknesses, Opportunities and Threats) analysis of the community, which may point to particular areas being higher priorities for action. Compiling a community demographic profile is an excellent start. It is helpful to update the profile periodically so you will be able to track changes that occur within your community and respond accordingly. A demographic profile includes statistical

information about age, gender, language, visible minority status, education, and family income. Other community statistics may also be of interest to you, such as crime rates, morbidity and mortality rates, or availability of affordable housing. Some of these are available from Statistics Nigeria, but local data may be obtained from local agencies; e.g. the local police service will have crime statistics. However, simply collecting information is not sufficient; it must be analyzed in order for it to be meaningful. For example, you might be interested in the relative proportion of adults/elders to youths in your community, or the proportion of the population for whom Ibo is a first language. You may want to compare the most recent data available with previous years; perhaps to identify the rate of growth of the population, changes in ethno-cultural patterns or age distribution. Statistical information isn't the only type of information that is important to collect. Finding out how residents perceive their community is also essential to effective community development practice. Community surveys, community asset mapping, environmental scans, focus groups and key informant interviews are other methods of obtaining community data.

5.   **Help Community Members to Recognize and Articulate Areas of Concern and Their Causes:** - In any community development process, it is the community that is in the driver's seat. Community members will define the issues and the process for resolving them, which might be quite different than what would be proposed by an external "expert". However, it is the community members that are most familiar with the situation and, in many cases, have knowledge and wisdom that an external "expert" lacks. By providing tools, resources, meeting space and facilitation, community developers empower the community to start to take ownership of the issues and the development of solutions. If we genuinely want to empower [communities], we must do it in such a way that they become independent of our charity, that they become self reliant, that they can sustain their own development without our help.

6.   **Create Vehicle for Change:** - In most circumstances it will be necessary to create a "vehicle for change" for an organizational change, which in most cases will start as a steering committee. Depending on the circumstances, this nature of the group could range from a few unaffiliated individuals or a coalition of organizations and institutions. In time, the steering committee may

evolve into or be adopted by a community organization. There is a wide range of activities that the steering committee will need to undertake to ensure that it will be able to plan, organize, implement and evaluate the initiative effectively, including developing a charter or terms of reference, establishing governance policies, obtaining sufficient resources to carry out the work and identifying potential partners who can contribute to its success.

7. **Develop an Action Plan: -** Assuming that the community as a whole has set the strategic directions for the initiative, the steering committee will now develop the action plan. Depending on the size of the group and the complexity of the initiative, there may be other steps between setting the strategic directions and the action plan. You may want to create a comprehensive strategic plan containing long, mid and short-term objectives, and mid-level plans for communications, resource development or human resources. In addition, if there are a number of activities or events to plan, you will need a separate action plan for each one. The point you need to arrive at is a well thought out plan that is easily comprehended by community members, clearly links activities with objectives and indicates responsibilities, time frames and resources required.

8. **Implement Action Plan: -** This is the heart of the initiative, in which financial and human resources, including volunteers and community members, are mobilized to take action. This may take many different forms. Perhaps the community has decided to establish a coalition against homelessness and is working to ensure all organizations that come into contact with homeless persons are able to provide referrals to appropriate sources of assistance. The actions might consist of:

- working with community workers to identify needs and appropriate services;
- developing informational brochures;
- eliciting support from targeted organizations;
- distributing the brochures to the organizations; and
- meeting with organizational representatives to provide further information.

In addition to implementing the various action steps, it is important to ensure that the factors that are required for the success of any community initiative are in place, such as:

- shared vision and purpose.
- concrete, attainable goals and objectives.
- sufficient funds, staff, materials and time.
- skilled, participatory leadership.
- clear roles and policy guidelines.
- mutual respect.
- open communications, including both formal and informal methods.
- recognition that there are "process" people and there are "action" people; ensure there is a variety of ways of participating in or contributing to the initiative.
- time and resources management; don't take on more than you can handle at one time; set priorities.
- conflict management; don't let problems slide - address them in an open, honest and timely manner.
- good record-keeping; e.g. financial reports, minutes of the meeting.
- celebration of successes- don't forget to celebrate your successes - even small ones.

9. **Evaluate Results of Actions:** - Traditionally, community development workers have relied more on their own experience, anecdotal evidence from others to guide their practice rather than formal evaluation procedures. Often it is difficult to find reasonable and appropriate measures in terms of the cost and time involved, especially when the desired outcomes, as is often the case with prevention and capacity-building initiatives, may not be seen for several years. However, there are many reasons why it is important to evaluate your work. Most importantly, you may need to demonstrate that you have not caused any harm to others through your actions. Other reasons to evaluate may be to demonstrate the effectiveness of the initiative so that it will be continued, to satisfy funder requirements and to provide information that will be useful to others or to subsequent initiatives. Evaluation plans may be formal or informal and tailored to the needs and resources of the group. In community development, a participatory evaluation method is usually conducted in addition to

or sometimes in place of more traditional method. Participatory evaluation involves programme participants and/or community members in the evaluation design, data collection, and the analysis and interpretation of results. "If one is concerned with increasing people's capacity to participate fully and gain some degree of control over their lives, then research methods themselves can be part of this method."

10. **Reflect and Regroup:** - Allow time for the group to catch its breath before embarking on the next initiative. Thank everyone that contributed and make sure there is good follow up communication with media, partner and funders. Celebrate your successes and reflect on any disappointments that might have occurred. Discuss how well the developmental processes and structures worked and identify areas that need some attention before the next rush of activity occurs. Also, it is important to provide a space for participants to reflect on their personal development as a result of being part of the group. When the group is ready to tackle a new initiative, they might want to revisit the community assessment information and the strategic directions and decide whether either of those steps should be repeated.

6.2   RURAL AND COMMUNITY DEVELOPMENT PROCESS

The community development process is an action learning guide fundamental to community development. In community development, there is emphasis on broad based participation of community members in all phases of the programme. This is because the development of a sense of belonging or identification is a major aspect of the community development effort. Although community development programmes generally tend to emphasize the construction of infrastructure and economic revitalization, the ideal goals of community development are not economic or physical structural changes. The goal of community development is to achieve the pre-conditions to economic growth which include bringing about change in the attitudes and beliefs of the people and the organization of learning experiences to enhance individual growth It contains identifiable steps from developing an understanding of the problem, through careful planning stages to implementation, evaluation, and reconsideration of the problems being tackled.

A. **Analysis of Prevailing Situation** - This is the first stage in the community development process. It is the stage to obtain a clear understanding of "what is", "what is not" and "why is it so" in the community. This may involve the conduct of informal surveys, fact-finding exercises and identification of community concerns needs and problems. The aim of this stage is not to be judgmental, but to provide the baseline information for subsequent stages in the process. If a clear understanding of the prevailing situation is not obtained, then it will be impossible to do a good job in all subsequent stages of the community development process. It is important therefore, that the utmost care be taken at this early stage to ensure that the best and factual information are gathered, properly analyzed and validated to ensure that mistakes are clearly avoided early in the process.

B. **Identification of Group Leaders and Interest Groups -** The second step in the development process is the identification of group leaders and interest groups that can be used as a facilitator in the community development. Existing leadership, if identified and engaged early in the development process is usually an asset to community development efforts.

C. **Identification of Immediate Problems and Needs -** The problem in any particular community is the difference between the desired situation and the existing one. If the prevailing situation is effectively analyzed, one of the main outputs should be a clear identification of the problem as well as the requirements to solve the identified problem. In this stage, the problem should be captured in a way that is presentable to the community.

D. **Discussing and Sharing the Problems Identified -** The first point of call for sharing the problem is with community leaders, first for their own understanding and then for legitimization. That is, the leadership of the community should be made to agree that the identified problem is a "real" problem of the community and that it is necessary to commit community resources to addressing it. Legitimization is the factor that makes it a "community issue". Legitimization confers on the problem, the status of one that all members of the community who recognize the authority of the leader should cooperate to address. This is desirable, especially when the problem had been identified by persons other than the leader.

E. **Diffusion of Problem and Definition of Needs -** Unless the problem is known to a good number of the people in the community, it will get at best a lukewarm attention from community members, despite its legitimization. Appropriate channels of communication should be employed to popularize the problem, its nature and what needs to be done to address it in the community.

F. **Securing Citizen Commitment to Act and Participate** - The success of the preceding step will ensure that members of the community become committed to addressing the problem. It is also important to ensure that commitment needs to be backed up by willingness and ability to act.

G. **Identification of Needed Resources** - No problem can be tackled if the material and human efforts required to do so are not known. The resources required to address a problem will be determined by the nature of the problem, its coverage, its impact and the ramifications of solving or not solving the problem.

H. **Appraisal of Available Internal Resources and Invitation of External Aid** - Having identified the resources needed to address a problem, the next stage is that of determining the quantity of each item required. A decision also needs to be made as to the quantity and quality of resources that can be obtained locally, and where necessary the quantity and type of resources is to be obtained from outside the community. It is also important to determine the relative ease of obtaining the needed resources and consider all alternative means of getting the needed resources.

I. **Formulation of Detailed Plan of Action** - This is the stage where an intensive thought process is given to physical implementation of the problem solving approach identified. This is the stage to propose "what should be done", "by whom", "with what resources" and "at what time". This is also to decide on a timetable and think of which activities overlap and which needs to be synchronized to achieve the best result.

Figure 6.1

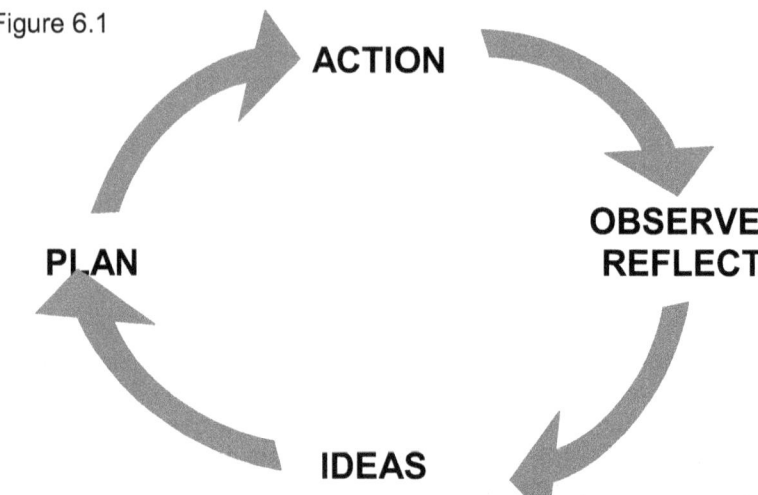

Figure 6.1: The action learning cycle – fundamental to processes of community development (Source: Building Rural Leaders, Dept. of Primary Industries in Cavaye, J., (2000) Understanding Community Development. www.communitydevelopment.com,au/ DOC.

The crux is that community development is more than a planning process. It is an ongoing learning process where new attitudes and networks develop from action and reflection (Figure 6.1). The appropriate use of the principles of community development guides the process rather than a recipe or prescription.

J. **Implementation of Planned Action or Programme -** The success of implementation is heavily dependent on how well all the earlier stages were carried out. Despite this, there is a need for care and dedication during implementation. There is also the need for patience and foresight. Patience is required to ensure that every essential detail is taken care of without undue delays in the schedule. Foresight is required to envisage any implementation problems that may arise and address them before they cause greater damage.

K. **Evaluation of Implementation, Procedures and Results Achieved -** Evaluation is the periodic examination of the implementation of an activity to determine how it conforms to the original plan. It is necessary on an on-going basis to redress any errors observed during implementation. It is also of value after the completion of implementation to draw out lessons learnt in the process of solving a particular community problem. This way, future community projects stand a better chance of success and actors in the implementation process can be properly acknowledged and rewarded for their efforts in the project implementation stage. It is important to evaluate both procedures and results. If a particular method was found useful, it can be duly documented and replicated and a poor method can be avoided in future. The evaluation of results, also known as impact evaluation, allows the community to recognize what has been achieved and serves as a driver in subsequent community mobilization efforts.

L. **Outcomes:** The outcome of successful community development would give rise to communities that are more able to generate wealth, maintain or improve their competitive position, preserve and use community resources and adapt to change (Shaffer, 1989).
Specific outcomes are:
  - An expanded, diverse, inclusive citizen participation base,
  - An expanded leadership base,
  - Strengthened individual skills,
  - A widely shared, understood and agreed local or regional vision for the future,
  - A strategic community agenda (i.e. a widely agreed strategic plan),
  - Consistent, tangible progress toward community goals,
  - More effective community organizations,
  - Better use of resources (adapted from Aspen Institute, 1996).

M. **Identification of Derived Problems or Needs and Planning for the Continuation of the Process -** Derived problems are those unanticipated effects of the change implemented. This unanticipated effect may be positive or negative. Whichever happens, they may be the basis for reconsideration, and possibly another situation analysis. This final step can lead to the institutionalization of the entire community development process as it infuses value into the change effected.

6.3   COMMUNITY DEVELOPMENT ROLES

The role of community development is to support people and community groups to identify and articulate their needs, and to take practical, collective action to address them. It works with communities of place, interest and identity, helping diverse and competing community voices to be heard. By addressing issues of power, inequality and social justice, it aims to bring about change that is empowering, fair and inclusive. Community development is both a practice and an occupation. Individuals, informal groups and organizations can all practice community development, whether in paid or unpaid roles. Those who practice community development come from a range of backgrounds and gain their skills and knowledge both from formal qualifications and through practice. Community development can – and should – be practiced in all sectors, whether public, private or voluntary.

A community developer may take on a variety of different roles and he/she works with the community. However, in all the roles, the worker always respects the autonomy and self-determination of the community members and does not impose an externally directed agenda upon them. Their work conforms to professional standards and ethics and is comprehensive and systematic in its approach.

Currently, there are few positions that are explicitly named "Community Developer" and it is increasingly more common for managers and employees in a variety of settings to be expected to take a community development approach to their work. There are many opportunities for anyone who is involved with community members to incorporate a community development role into their practice. In community development literature, the roles commonly ascribed to community development workers are enabler, guide, technical expert and liaison.

a)   **Guide:** As a guide, the worker helps the community identify their goals and find the means of achieving them.

b)   **Enabler:** The worker can enable the community in a variety of ways. He/she might facilitate a problem solving process with the community, which could include helping them to articulate dissatisfactions and identify their causes. The worker could also help them to organize and plan their activities and encourage positive interpersonal relationships. The enabler role is most associated with locality development strategies.

c)   **Technical Assistant:** This "expert" role is most associated with social planning. However, in all forms of community development there is usually some need by the community to access technical support, in areas such as community assessment, media relations, accessing information or project development.

d)   **Liaison/Advocate:** Depending on the nature of the community and the type of community development initiative it has taken on, there may be a need for the worker to assume a liaison or advocacy role. He/she may be the intermediary between the community and other bodies such as government, institutions or other community factions. The worker may be asked by the community to present their views, access information or negotiate an agreement.

Chapter Seven

TRADITIONAL SOCIAL INSTITUTIONS AND MOBILIZATION IN RURAL AND COMMUNITY DEVELOPMENT IN NIGERIA

7.1 TRADITIONAL SOCIAL INSTITUTIONS

Various group efforts are oftentimes involved in the process of rural and community development in separate Nigeria. These groups, according to Chukwuezi (2000), combine the efforts of their members in pulling resources together to attain one form of development or the other within the various communities. There are various groups within the Nigerian communities that engage in the development of their immediate communities. The issue of associational group was quite common in various parts of Nigeria and they are widely regarded as veritable tools for rural and community development. This associational spirit and orientation was relatively popular in traditional Igbo society of Nigeria and the modern society of the Igbos has witnessed invigorated form of associational life, hence there are elements of dynamism in self-help group relations. A handful of writers commented on this dynamics. Scholars such as Wallenstein opined that these modern associational structures were as a result of European civilization. Onwuejeogwu (1981), noted that the Igbo society was (and is still) characterized by various forms of associations, which formed part of Igbo traditional governance. The various associations found among the Igbos were part of Igbo traditional lives and the modernized forms of these earlier associations are being put in place to suit the modern times. They have equally encouraged development efforts in the community through awareness and sensitization of the community members. Some of these groups include:

7.1.1 Town Unions

This is an agency of the community through which innovations and development purposes are achieved for the community. The term "Town Union" dates back to antiquity. Town unions are organizations of people from the same town or community formed for the purposes of developing their various towns socially, culturally, physically, economically, and politically. The town unions embrace people from all works of life in the community such as civil servants, businessmen, farmers, academics, politicians, etc. It is made up of the executive body that deliberates, presides and oversees the activities of the unions. Town unions have been existing in Nigeria before 1940s. For example, Awka Town Union was formed in 1948, Obollo Progressive Union came into existence in the 1950s, Mgbowo Progressive Union was established in 1938, and Ikem Improvement Union was formed in 1952.

The town unions represent an association formed by the people of the same town, local government or even district as the case may be. The modern face of town union emerged during colonial rule especially after people have migrated to the colonial cities. The colonial government had no well-designed welfare for the teeming migrants that were flocking to the city and the city proved a difficult sphere of survival and a place of strangeness. The idea of having a union to look after the welfare of their members far from home was not new, as could be deduced from the Igbo axiom, "Nwanne di na Mba", which denotes the significance of town unionism especially in a foreign land. In the spirit of the above stated axiom, many African migrants carried the various forms of social relations in their traditional societies into new areas in which they moved to. They also had attachment to their homes and felt that they will come back to it. Further, the various social amenities and services they enjoyed in the city, they would want to have and enjoy in their home towns. This nostalgic feeling may be regarded as the magic wand that rural and community development have utilized in making Town union a veritable tool of self-help approach of rural and community development in Nigeria since inception. Today, Town unions are perceived as veritable instrument and catalyst for community development. They are seen as an agency through which a community could facilitate and achieve socio-economic, cultural and political objectives. While they have been useful in some communities, in some other communities they have suffered the problem of under utilization. In recent times, most town unions have championed rural development. Interestingly enough every community has a town union, referred to as Development Union.

7.1.2 Age Grade Associations

Age grade is a social institution which constitutes vital system in the social structures of any given society. An age grade is an association of persons who were born within a period of time. However, the age brackets of the age grades may vary from one community to the other. In some communities, persons born within a specific period of three, four or five years usually form an age grade. But the most important thing is that each age grade is clearly distinguished from one another. It then means that a man can only belong to one age grade at a time and each is usually associated with specific roles. More significantly, age grade as an organized group of people born within a given period and whose activities are centered on a set of common goals and a set of code which regulates their conduct. Apart from a high degree of personal intimacy and informal conduct, members are bound together by common challenges such as marriages, burial of parents building of houses etc. Over the years, age grade in different communities have distinguished themselves in the performance of such roles that aim at enhancing the socio-economic life of the people.

According to Akude (1992), age grade is a very vital organ of social structure especially in our traditional Nigerian communities. For example, amongst the Igbo in Anambra, Imo and Edo and Delta States), the Tiv in Benue State, the Ibibio in Cross River State and so on, the formation and membership of an age grade is much revered. He continued further that age grades, are characterized by the events that occurred during the period members were born or when each age grade becomes officially recognized in the community. In essence, the names of the various age grades in the different communities are often drawn from the historical events that took place when the age grade was initially formed, age or condition of members and their activities in the area. For example, in Onitsha Inland Town, all those who were born between 1960 and 1962, formed a group which they called 'independence' (in commemoration of the year 1960) when Nigeria gained her independence from the British. In addition, Onitsha has about seventy-three recognized age grades, the oldest (represents people born between 1886 and 1888) known as 'Ekwueme'. Similarly in Njikoka Local Government Area in Abagana, there is an age grade known as 'Oganiru', meaning development or progress. This group represents all males born between 1945 and 1949. Historically, the period 1945-1949 marked the return of war veterans of the Second World War (1939-1945).

Age Grade Associations exists in many African communities in general and Nigeria in particular especially among the Igbos in the South-Eastern part of the country. Among the Igbos, the traditional age grade organization has been transformed into modern age grade associations. The Igbos has elaborate age sets that are graded according to the periods of births of its male members. In Adazi-ani, we have the Igwebuike, Chinemerem, Ifeadigo, Umuoma age grades to mention but a few. The various age grade sets obtained are graded within the interval of three years; these age grades include the women folk of the same age range. In the traditional Igbo society, the age grades perform various tasks depending on what was assigned to them. They had in the pre-colonial and colonial periods concerned themselves with traditional functions such as the maintenance of law and order, settlement of disputes between warring members, construction and maintenance of roads and markets, maintaining the cleanliness of local streams and above all, protecting their communities from external aggression.

In recent times, however, age grades have diversified their roles to include newer activities which aid development. They have contributed immensely to the educational, political and social development of their various communities. Today, in many Igbo societies, the age grades have accomplished important tasks and are still accomplishing various strides in community development. For instance, in Adazi-ani town, the Igwebuike age grade built an ultra modern two storey-building school hall, situated in the community. This, they accomplished alone as the other age grades have their own assigned tasks to carry out. In Adazi-ani, age grades engage in competitive activities to see who builds more for the community. With varying age grades struggling to register its mark, community development have become more popular thereby improving the welfare of members of the host community. In many Igbo areas, the age grade organizations have built schools, hospitals, post offices, etc. Others have formed transport companies and other valuable commercial ventures.

7.1.3 Youth Associations
The development of community is a dynamic process involving all segments of the locality, including the often-overlooked youth population. Youth is generally the time of life between childhood and adulthood (maturity), (Macmillan Dictionary, 1981: 1151). Youth is a term used for people of both sexes, male and female, of a young age. Experiences of different countries reflect the fact that broad participation of different age groups, especially youths, plays an effective role in the development of rural community. Youths represent a vast and often untapped resource for immediate and long-term community development efforts. Thus, the youths in Anambra State for instance, comprise about 42.9% of the population and also about 92.7% of the working population. The youths and some Non Governmental Organizations act as watch dogs to government policies and programmes. In Anambra State, they have been very useful in the provision and maintenance of security especially since

January 2004 when the Nigerian Police unjustifiably withdrew the Security guards of the State Governor. The youth of any Society is a serious factor for consideration in the supply of Labour, Production and Productivity in that Society. Hence the physical well being of the youths, their education and training are required for good Supply of labour. The problems of the youth are acute unemployment, vulnerability to the savaging scourge of HIV/AIDS, and non-participation in Policy formulation and Programme implementation on issues concerning them. The youth in Anambra State require mobilization into useful social and economic force capacity building and Social re-orientation in the light of Nigeria's embrace of free market economy and the march to globalization.

7.1.4 Social Clubs

A social club may refer to a group of people or the place where they meet, generally formed around a common interest, occupation or activity (e.g. hunting, fishing, science, politics or charity work). Social clubs also helps in community development. Membership can be limited or open to the general public, as can their events. Most clubs have a limited membership based upon specific criteria, and restrict the events to members to increase their feeling of security, creating an increased sense of affection and belonging. The Social clubs were quite popular even before the Civil War in Nigeria. There were traditional clubs which participated in community development. Such traditional clubs included, hunters club, titled men clubs, i.e. Nze, Ozo title holders, Masquerade group, musical groups and so on (Obikeze, 2002). In the Igbo area of Nigeria, the Civil War, among other things caused various forms of dislocation in terms of losing political, economic and social positions in the Nigerian societies. The people were desirous to improve their lots, personally and collectively after the Civil War. Various associations of common interests were formed for one form of goal or the other. Some of these associations metamorphosed into social clubs. However, the end of the Civil War saw the upsurge of what could be regarded as modern social clubs (Obikeze, 2002). Some of these social clubs draw their members from a particular town or local government areas while others draw their members from various sections of Nigerian society. These social clubs protect the interest of their members and also serve as forms of social security for its members. The social clubs especially those from the local government or town try to improve the area. They could contribute towards erecting certain social amenities in the host communities. They also award scholarships to some of the vulnerable and less privileged and disadvantaged, yet deserving individuals of the communities. In Igbo land for instance, many of the social clubs built bus stops, motor parks, Markets etc. Even though of late, social clubs in Nigeria are no longer as viable as they were in the 1970s, however, they are still veritable instruments of self-help approach of rural and community development.

7.1.5 **Traditional Rulers**
It is no longer a secret to know that certain persons, for example the traditional rulers possess and exercise great influence on the masses. Anambra State is made up of 177 autonomous communities which are distributed into 21 Local Government Areas. The traditional Kingship system historically, was first identified with the Onitsha Igbo across the River Niger; however it has now been adopted by all the communities. Currently, there is in existence the Anambra State Council of Traditional Rulers with Igwe, Obi Gibson Nwosu Eze Uzu Awka as the President. Traditional rulers have been very useful in giving publicity to government policies and programmes at the grass-root level. They have also helped in mobilizing their Subjects for support to government policies and programmes and also in Joint Venture Programmes with Donor Agencies and Civil Society Organizations (CSOs). Somehow, traditional rulers still enjoy the confidence and great respect of the greater part of Nigeria's population, to such a degree that they still remain an undisputable force to reckoned with for effective and successful mobilization of efforts. This statement is true in the South Western part of Nigeria, especially among the Yorubas and Benins, truer in the Northern part of the country where the Emirs, to a large extent, hold sway over the lives and activities of those in their domain; but less true in the South Eastern part of the country, especially among the Ibos, the Ibibios and the Ijaws whose egalitarian and republican way of life make them less amenable to unalloyed loyalty and unresolved obeisance to their traditional rulers. However, in these days of Naira Chiefs (most of the traditional stools are keenly contested by various wealthy aspirants and since these traditional rulers are in charge of various villages or communities, the views and status of the victor, after the usual life and death contest, may hardly be respected outside his own immediate village within the town). Therefore, excessive reliance on the so-called traditional rulers especially in the eastern part of the country for purposes of mass mobilization may boomerang especially if they are at logger heads with the people-oriented and people-elected interest groups such as town unions, social clubs, etc. Therefore, in the Eastern part of Nigeria as opposed to those States in the West and in the North, there should be a cautious use of agents of mass mobilization for self-help efforts in rural development.

7.1.6 Occupational Associations

Occupational associations are formed by the coming together of people of the same occupation with the aim of promoting and protecting the occupation. The associations seeks to improve technical skills of members, assist members in times of need, procure loans as a group as well as ensure quality delivery and protect customers from fraud and excessive charges. Examples of such association in agriculture are; The Cocoa Farmers Association, Cassava Farmers Union, and Association of Cashew Farmers etc. Before the period of colonial rule in Africa in general and Nigeria in particular, there were indigenous professional groups like the Guilds of Native doctors and Guilds of Black smiths etc. These associations were collectively concerned with the welfare of their members and that of the community. In modern times, professional associations have tried to improve the community in one way or the other. Members of a professional association, who are united by the fact that they are of the same community, think of impacting development activities through such forum. This kind of association might set target for themselves and find ways and means of achieving such targets. Some have built schools, roads, brought electricity and other amenities through their influence.

Trade and Commercial Associations: Trade and commercial associations are established mainly for assisting members in all aspects of life and in particular in areas of price regulation, addition of value to goods and services, standardization of goods and capital investment. They also help members to secure loan from financial institutions. Trade and commercial associations can be of benefit to the community in which they are located by giving scholarship to the indigene students. Examples of such association are; Cocoa Marketers Association, Plank sellers as well as food vendors.

7.1.7 Women Associations

In Igboland, the women have various forms of associations that aid community development. There are two types of women groups especially in Igbo communities. These are women who are married from other communities into a town known as "Otu Alutaradi" and the second group, very influential and strong known as "Umuada". The Umuadas are daughters of the community who have married into other villages but retain their ties with their community of birth. Otu Alutaradi are wives of the men of the village who have come from diverse socio-cultural backgrounds. Both groups maintain order, promote life and create consolidation, joy and solidarity for themselves and for the village community. The month of August every year witnesses a massive homecoming from different towns and cities across the world of "Igbo women" groups to their matrimonial rural hometowns, where they unite with their rural-based colleagues for what is now popularly known as the "August Meetings." These "mothers' congresses," as they truly are, were originally often geared towards self-help rural community development, but have in recent times delved into conflict management, peace-building and human development in rural societies. They organize meeting periodically where they discuss various self-help-based rural community developmental projects. The women association contributes to various development projects in their home communities. These women involve themselves in resolution of conflicts, fighting injustice and protecting womanhood. They use their association to assist the men in their various developmental projects. It is worthy of note that towns Women association have initiated and completed various community developmental projects such as town halls, school blocks, markets, post offices, etc.

7.1.8 Individual Efforts

Community development, in the words of Chukwuezi (2000), has always been described as a group activity organized by the people or the people in co-operation of government. The essence of group action is always emphasized. One could equally and aptly also argue that some individuals, singularly contributes to community development. They may be solely responsible for the resources; however, their activities benefit the community. In this light, it might be logical to hypothesize that even though, individuals singularly provide the resources, but since their activities are geared towards the development of the group, it is seen as community development. Some wealthy individuals make enormous contributions towards the development of their communities by way of providing resources both human and resources for certain development a projects. Some of them singularly sponsor a number of scholarships to their kith and kin to ensure their academic development. Some of them have donated the stated amount of money for which a launching was slated.

7.2 MOBILIZATION IN RURAL COMMUNITY DEVELOPMENT IN NIGERIA

The following institutions can serve and has always served as agencies of mobilization at the local communities;

7.2.1 The Local Government

The roles and involvement of local communities in local government administration in Nigeria can never be over-emphasized. The United Nations' Office for Public Administration defines Local Government as a political sub-division of a nation or (in a federal system) state, which is constituted by law and has substantial control of local affairs, including the powers to impose taxes or to exact labour for prescribed purposes. The governing body of such an entity is elected or otherwise locally selected (UNO Summer Conference on Local Government in Africa, 1961). Local Government refers to a system of governance at the grassroots level. The 1976 Reform firmly established Local Governments throughout the federation as the third-tier of government. The structure and functions of the local government are contained in Section 7 of the Fourth Schedule of the Constitution of the Federal Republic of Nigeria. Accordingly, Local Government is seen as the first level in the national rural development process. Any rural development activity that ignores the first level (local government) is doomed to failure. From the provision in the Constitution, it can be seen that local government is assigned wide ranging responsibilities in the areas of Education (UBE), Healthcare (PHC, NPI), Social and Community Development, Sanitation, Agriculture, Rural Water Supply and Economic Development. Today, it is estimated that more than 70% of Nigerians live below poverty level; the local government being the government nearest to the populace, is one of the best mobilizations for generating motivations and encouraging mobilization for self-help, as well as including the much needed wider participation of the local population in the decision making process at the local level. Nigeria is in a third world country where any meaningful discussion of rural development really means not only talking of overall national development, but because it is in the rural areas that the problems of inequitable distribution of resources or a marked lack of purchasing power and of grinding poverty in which the wretched members of society stagnate and stare one in the face with brutal clarity. The raison d"etre of the Local Government in Nigeria is to, at least halt the deteriorating living conditions in the rural areas. An effective Local Government will be better disposed than the state or Federal Government, not only to stem the grim reality of the rising tide of rural poverty but also be able to evoke the spirit of locality corporation thereby being more able to galvanize and mobilize the support of local citizenry in participating in all the programmes that may affect them.

7.2.2   State Government

Community development is very wide in scope as it cuts across all sectors that affect the livelihoods of the people of the State as a whole, albeit on a smaller scale. Such sectors include health, education, skills acquisition and training, micro-credit, natural resources and environmental management, women and youth empowerment, provision for basic infrastructure including roads, transportation, water and sanitation, housing etc. Using Anambra State as an example, it will be difficult to look at the entire state to measure the impact of the community development of this current administration of Governor Peter Obi through ANIDS Programme, on each community. Thus, among Anambra State Government projects to boast rural community developments include: Orient Refinery Aguleri – Umuleri, State Secretariat, General Hospitals Umuchu, Enugwu-ukwu and Ekwulobia, Kenneth Dike Library to mention but a few. Some of the road constructed by the State Government in various communities for instance are Old – Onitsha road and New – Onitsha, Nkwo Nnewi to Nkwo Orafite road, Amuko – Nnobi road, Izundu road Nnewi, Iyiowa/Odekpe road and Awkuzu – Igbariam road, Achalla – Ebenebe road etc. But general observations can be made on the physical expansion of each community, the enrolment of students in their secondary schools since inception, the number of patients that attended the rural hospitals. All these can be looked at in contributing in no small way to the social and economic development of a community.

7.2.3   Federal Government

Governments at all levels can only be relevant to the people if the people are positively affected by the policies and programmes of such government; Nigerian Federal Government is not an exception. The place of Federal Government in community development in Nigeria is very glaring. Thus, certain projects are capital intensive, so communities cannot carry them out, yet they are needed for the welfare of the people. Some projects have long gestation period that the community will not be willing to carry them through. Besides, the presence of Federal Government will improve the quality of some services they render which private individuals or communities may not worry about, for instance a project may involve resettlement of people, of which community cannot handle, including full exploitation of the nation's mineral and other resources for the overall benefit of the economy and creation of new jobs for the unemployed ones. With the renewed emphasis on rural poverty reduction in Nigeria and the acceptance that projects are "the cutting edge of development" (Gittinger,

1972), many rural projects have been conceived and executed by the Federal Government of Nigeria, in particular, rural poverty alleviation through agricultural transformation. There are programmes inspired by the economic planners of Federal Government with the objectives of achieving employment generation, enhancing of agricultural output and income and reversing the strong trend of rural migration. These range in scale from the Agricultural Development Programmes (ADPs), the Agricultural Credit Guarantee Scheme (ACGS,) Rural Banking Scheme (RBS) to the River Basin Development Authorities (RBDAs), the Directorate of Food, Roads and Rural Infrastructure (DFRRI) among others. For instance, most poverty alleviation programmes are intended to salvage the individuals at the community level.

7.2.4 Multinational Corporations

A Multinational Corporation is an enterprise operating in several countries but managed from one (home) country. Generally, any company or group that derives a quarter of its revenue from operations outside of its home country is considered a multinational corporation. Multinational corporations are adjudged as corporations that transcends countries of the world (Boarman & Schollerhammer, 1977). They serve as vehicles through which the national resources particularly petroleum, bauxite, iron, ore, copper and uranium of developing countries are developed (Behrman & Gross, 1999). They aid the transfer of technology and managerial skills from developed world to developing countries. They created employment in host countries (Agba & Ushie, 2005).

Multinational companies performed a number of socio–economic functions aimed at enhancing the welfare of society. They work with the government of host countries to ensure the success of the war against economic odds by increasing productivity and supporting the implementation of government's fiscal and marketing policies. For instance, in the oil and gas sector of Nigeria, Chevron and Texaco makes difference by rooting their business in a solid partnership with host communities and government. This has over the years led to substantial investments in community development projects. Since 1999, Chevron, Texaco and its partners invested more than 56 million USD in community development projects and this has manifested in substantial improvement in healthcare, schools, scholarships, roads as well as employment and income generating schemes particularly in the company's areas of operation (Ndebbio, 2002).

Furthermore, between 1996 and 2004, some Multinationals in the Niger Delta did relatively well in the sponsorship of education and training programmes (Agba & Ushie, 2005). According to Ekanem (2003), Shell Petroleum Development Company (SPDC) in 1996 awarded a total of 3,237 scholarships to Nigerians of which 427 University Scholarships was given to operational areas. In 1997, SPDC also awarded 3,469 scholarships out of which 430 University Scholarships were given to undergraduates from the Niger Delta region. In 1998, more than 3,620 scholarships were awarded. In the area of skill acquisition, SPDC trained 3,447 youths between 1995 and 2000 in welding and fabrication, auto – mechanics, computer, bakery, catering, carpentry, fashion design, electronic, building, candle making and palm oil processing.

Other programmes and projects by oil Multinationals geared towards rural transformations and developments of the Niger Delta region include micro credit schemes for small scale entrepreneurs; crop improvement for better yields, better fishing and fish farming; women empowerment, marine transportation scheme; effective agro food processing and preservation and adult literacy. They also include immunization, support for primary healthcare, family planning, sex education, HIV/AIDS enlightenment programme for youths, rural and urban renewal. According to Aminize (2001) MNs have also contributed in waste management and disposals in the region. Although some Multinationals have benchmark records in the socio economic development of the Niger Delta their contributions as compared to their peculiar problem of the region is negligible and far too restricted.

7.2.5 Cooperative Societies

Cooperatives are usually formed by groups of people with a common purpose to address specific need or problems. Most cooperatives exist to capture various opportunities in the economy, to address the needs and aspirations of their members and communities. They aim to empower the people by enabling even the unprivileged segments of the population to participate in economic activities. They can create job opportunities for those who have skills but little or no capital and provide the necessary support to promote self help in communities. Agricultural co-operatives have been the most popular traditional mode of cooperative development and we have a number of them in Nigeria especially various Farmers Co–operative Societies as agriculture remains the backbone and over 80% of the population depends on it for their livelihoods. There are many such cooperatives in the country and there have been reports of many successes as well as many failures. Cooperative societies are founded on good intentions and they are seen to be critical to rural development in general through creation of employment, improve access to markets and social services. Where cooperatives are seen to be achieving their objectives, we see no reason why the government or other development partners should not support them. Their roles are important and they should be seen as agents of change in rural areas where hardly any government services are seen.

In Nigeria, cooperatives can provide locally needed services, employment, circulate money locally and contribute to a sense of community or social cohesion. They can provide their employees with the opportunities to upgrade their skills through workshops and courses and offer youths in their base communities short and long-term employment positions. Students could also be employed on casual-appointment basis during long vacations. Through these, cooperatives will contribute to economic development. The onus is on the cooperatives to demonstrate to their members, their communities, the government, and to the people that they have a purpose to exist and that they are equal partners in development. They should ensure that their roles are clearly defined for us to know exactly why they exist and what is expected of them. While cooperatives are independent organizations, we should consider that they are important partners in development. Cooperatives are therefore, required for nation building in terms of; food production, employment, income, raw materials for industries and foreign exchange. Women, through cooperatives are now displaying their economic empowerment. They are now involved in various economic activities for the overall benefit of the country. Cooperative enjoys economies of scale as resources are pooled for investment, expansion and also starting new investments. Given that Nigeria is to a large extent, an agricultural country, with predominantly small scale farmers thrives mainly on again small-scale industrial production. Cooperatives, therefore, will continue to play major roles in the Nigerian economy. Both the government and the private sector are aware of this and should, therefore, support the operations of cooperatives in Nigeria. Through these activities, rural development objectives are achieved.

7.2.6 Non Governmental Organizations (NGOs)
Using the words of Willetts (2002), the term "Non-Governmental Organizations" or NGOs, came into circulation in 1945 because of the need for the UN to differentiate in its Charter between participation rights

for intergovernmental specialized agencies and those for international private organizations. According to him, at the UN, virtually all types of private bodies can be recognized as NGOs. They only have to be independent from government control, not seeking to challenge governments either as a political party or by a narrow focus on human rights, non-profit-making and non-criminal. To affirm the above, Edwards and Hulme (1996), say that NGOs were the brainchild of Inter-Governmental Organizations (IGOs) such as World Bank and United Nations (UN) which have identified them as magic wand for fostering development strategies. Also, The World Bank according to Shah (2003) defines NGOs as "private organizations that pursue activities to relieve suffering, promote the interests of the poor, protect the environment, provide basic social services, or undertake community development". The World Bank further says that "In wider usage, the term NGO can be applied to any non-profit organization which is independent of government. Wikipedia (2009) sees NGO as a legally constituted organization created by private organizations or people with no participation or representation of any government. In cases in which NGOs are funded totally or partially by governments, the NGO maintains its non-governmental status insofar as it excludes government representatives from membership in the organization. Types of NGOs vary according to the goals and objectives. However, some of the common types include: Business-Oriented NGOs, Technical NGOs, Environmental NGOs, Government-Operated NGOs, International NGOs, and Donor organized NGOs. Although the NGO sector has become increasingly professionalized over the last two decades, basic characteristics within and outside Nigeria some of which have been highlighted above include: Philanthropy, Volunteerism, National or International in form of global hierarchies (having central authority) or single-country based with transnational operation and Non-profit making Independent of government control.

Non-Governmental Organizations (NGOs) are viewed as non profit organizations that are involved at the grass roots to empower the disadvantaged segments of the population (Clark, 1999). NGOs are agencies set up by private citizens' foundations, churches, volunteer workers, etc. to tackle specific problems and particularly the alleviation of poverty and administration of relief to the needy and deprived, war victims and refugees (Ekong, 2000). NGO may be based either in State, Region or Nationally. At times an NGO may have branches all over the country e.g Country Women Association of Nigeria which is presently found in more than 12 States in Nigeria. NGOs in Nigeria are concerned with agricultural production, poverty eradication, capacity building as well as empowerment. Activities of NGOS include: Formation of groups of Small Scale Farmers, Evaluation and upgrading farmers conditions, Meeting with farmers on regular basis which may be monthly, bi-monthly, or quarterly. Visitation to farmers field, linkage of farmers with other institutions, monitoring of activities through staff meetings, farmers forum and meetings.

Non Governmental Organizations NGOs exists in Anambra State with diverse thematic focal areas, Service type and missions. The NGOs have been very useful in development programmes both at the community, Local Government and State levels. They have complemented government efforts in various Social and economic development programmes. The thematic focus of most Non Governmental Organizations in the State revolve around Health, Education, Environment, Gender Equality, Women Empowerment, Child's Rights, Women Rights, Youth Organizations etc. Similarly, the activities of the NGOs have centred on Advocacy, Sensitizations, Mobilizations, Awareness Creation, Capacity Building, Thrift and Credit Micro Credit Administration, and Monitoring of Government Commitments and projects. Apart from the registration with the Corporate Affairs Commission which is the ultimate, the Social Welfare Department of the State Ministry of Women Affairs and Social Development register Non Governmental and Civil Society Organizations in Anambra State. There are more than 100 registered Non Governmental Organizations in the State.

Donor Programme Agencies
In the Community Development efforts of Nigeria, intervention is one unique area that must not be overlooked. This intervention is that which goes beyond what the people or local communities undertake as self-help efforts. Also, Government's realization of the facts and with all indices it has not achieved meaningfully in terms of development. Despite the wealth of Nigeria's resources, including some of the world's largest reserves of oil, the quality of life for Nigeria's population has been steadily deteriorating. According to USAID, the percentage of the population living below the poverty line has increased significantly over the last two decades: from 27% in 1980 to approximately 70% today (Partners for Development, 2009). The 2009 UNDP Human Development Report ranked Nigeria at only 158 out of 175 countries, one of the lowest levels of human development in the world. Healthcare and other government services are highly centralized with doctors and other resources found

primarily in state capitals and other large towns. Lack of access to health and other services has had serious impacts on the population, with 15% of children not living to see their fifth birthday and a maternal mortality rate that is 100 times that found in industrialized societies.

With practical involvement to alleviate and eradicate the plethora of hydra-headed physical and social problems of Nigeria, interventions came as a way of getting the menace addressed. In this regard, support interventions have been witnessed and experienced by the Nigerian communities through an extension of hands of fellowship (gestures or reciprocations) from several International Multilateral Organizations (IMOs), agencies, foundations, as well as other local and foreign Non-Governmental Organizations; responding to the issues of development in the areas of health, constructions/structural development, provision of social amenities, education and several others. In the list of these organizations are the UNDP, UNICEF, UNESCO, USAID, DFID, WHO, IBRD, UNEP, FAO, British Council, Commonwealth, Ford Foundation, Techno-Serve, MacArthur Foundation, Rotary Club International, Carnegie Foundation, etc. Also in the development arena of the Nigerian communities, particularly the oil-producing communities of Niger Delta who are the hosts to foreign oil prospecting or servicing companies receive support and assistance from the Community Development Foundations, Pro-Natura International (Nigeria) which include Total, Statoil Hydro, Chevron, Shell Petroleum Development Company, Agip, Centrica Energy of the Centrica Resources Nigeria Ltd., ADDAX Petroleum, UC Rusal/Atscon, Bellona, Emis, Nexen, European Union, BG Nigeria Ltd., RSSDA, British Foreign and Commonwealth Office (BFCO), Revenue Watch Institute, NNPC, Frontier Oil, World Bank and a host of others. Some of the Donor Agencies and their programmes are:

UNICEF
From UNICEF (n.d), it is gathered that Nigeria was one of the very first African countries where the United Nations Children's Fund (UNICEF) established a programme of cooperation. UNICEF's work for the survival, protection and development of Nigerian children has continued ever since. Today, UNICEF is still working in partnership with many stakeholders including children and families to achieve national and international Documentation goals instrumental in the fulfillment of children's rights. UNICEF's interventions in Nigeria span different facets of human life not excluding health, education, nutrition and others. The following UNICEF's documentation highlights her areas of intervention in Nigeria:

➢ Mass Disease Control

UNICEF's first interventions in Nigeria were related to endemic disease control through mass campaigns. The emphasis then was on the control of leprosy and yaws. The first African campaign was in Nigeria in 1952-1953. Efforts continued throughout the fifties into the early sixties. By the mid-sixties, yaws was no longer considered a significant public health issue. UNICEF and WHO carried out their first leprosy project in Nigeria. Thanks to a new drug, the treatment of the disease had greatly improved and thousands of children were spared its disfiguring effects. Malaria was another priority and one of the pilot projects in Africa was in Sokoto Province of Nigeria.

➢ Development of Maternal and Child Welfare Services

UNICEF also supported the development of basic rural health services for mothers and children. In 1954, the UNICEF Executive Director recommended an apportionment of US $6,600 to Nigeria for the provision of 500 midwifery kits and training of personnel to encourage the expansion of domiciliary delivery within the expanding maternal welfare services. This constituted the first UNICEF assistance of this type to Nigeria. This very first project is a good example of the strategies used by UNICEF to develop 'maternal and child welfare' services: training, pilot projects and supplies.

➢ Nutrition

As reports revealed widespread malnutrition among African children, UNICEF started providing skimmed milk to underfed children. Research was carried out to better understand the prevalence, causes and prevention of malnutrition. A Department of Food, Science and Nutrition was established in the University of Ibadan in collaboration with the London University, FAO and WHO. Following successful promotion of milk conservation in European countries, UNICEF began assisting with milk conservation in Sub-Saharan Africa. The first milk-drying plant supported by UNICEF in Africa was approved for Nigeria in 1954. The objective was to produce and distribute dry milk for infants and young children. UNICEF also focused on the education of mothers as another strategy to combat malnutrition.

United States Agency for International Development (USAID)

In its development partnership with Nigeria, the United States (US) seeks to strengthen social stability through improved social services, support transparent and accountable governance, promote a more market-led economy, and enhance Nigeria's capacity as a responsible regional and trade partner. These goals support the Government of Nigeria's National Economic and Empowerment Strategy, the Seven-Point Agenda, and Vision 20:2020. Given Nigeria's size and limited resources, USAID focuses on the impoverished Muslim north and the oil-rich Niger Delta.

World Bank
During the training of Local Government Chairmen, Heads of Local Government Committees and Desk Officers of CSDP in Minna, Niger State, the National Co-coordinator of the Community and Social Development Project (CSDP), Mr Foluso Okunmadewa disclosed that: The World Bank has expended $200million on community and social developmental projects in the country in the last three years. According to him, a financial agreement between the Federal Government and the International Development Association was reached to increase the access of poor people to improved social and natural resource infrastructure services.

Partners for Development (PFD)
Partners for Development first established operations in 2000 in the central belt of Nigeria, an area composed mainly of ethnic minorities, where poverty and malnutrition are widespread. PFD's programmes began with a poverty alleviation focus in the four central and northern states of Bauchi, Benue, Kaduna and Nassarawa. Since then PFD has built capacity of over 20 local partners to offer integrated micro-finance, reproductive health and agricultural enterprise programmes, including improved marketing access in those four states. In 2008, PFD expanded its scope of activities by adding a comprehensive package of care and support for People Living with HIV/AIDS in Delta and Akwa Ibom States. PFD programmes in Nigeria reach approximately 850,000 people in rural communities with essential health and income-generation services. Their programmes provide capacity-building training and on-going technical assistance to local partner NGOs and CBOs including financial and administrative management, programme design, and project implementation and monitoring.

British Council–DFID Nigerian Community Education Project: Community Education among Nomads of the North: The British Council managed the Nigeria Community Education Project on behalf of the Department for International Development. The development of the nomadic communities of the north in terms of literacy has changed the status and conditions of the nomads. Here are just a few of the responses from those involved with the project.

- "Before attending, writing was just scribbles and meaningless so now writing has become meaningful. I can pick out words and numbers". (Adult learner, nomadic community).
- "They know how to live with people now. The main thing is co-operation between people" (Royal Head, nomadic community at Tashan Uda).
- "As recently as a few years back, not one single person in the community could read a letter, and they had to take it to Kunini to be read. Now there are many people around who can read, so we don't have to do that" (Ardo Umaru, nomad leader).

"Every year the nomadic groups are taxed by the number of cattle in their herds. Tax inspectors count the cattle and submit their figures. This year, a child watched them count the herd and then looked over their shoulder at the number entered on the form. The inspector had entered twelve instead of the nine he had counted. When challenged by the child, the form was corrected" (Ardo Garga, Education Project Committee Chairperson).

Achievements of NGOs in Nigeria

i. NGOs in Agriculture have helped in reaching the poor especially in inaccessible areas of rural Nigeria and providing their needs in the areas of infrastructures such as schools, electricity, sanitation as well as adequate good quality drinking water.

ii. NGOs use advocacy and political influence to hold local officials accountable for activities which are damaging to the poor

iii. They help communities mobilize and form societies to express their concerns.

iv. They provide atmosphere in which officials can consult people about development plans and listen to alternatives presented by the people.

v. NGOs have recorded a huge success in the areas which the governments have failed, for instance the maintenance of public utilities. NGOs adopt the participatory approach thus making the people to be part of the programmes from the initiation stage to

planning, implementation, execution and maintenance. These make most of their projects sustainable rather than abandoned.
vi. NGOs play a major role in transferring of innovations to rural communities.
vii. Their capability to work with local groups has made them to be more successful than government projects. Examples of NGOs in agricultural areas; Nigeria International Rural Development Organization (NIRADO), Nigeria Participatory Rural Development Network (NIPRDNET), Country Women Association of Nigeria (COWAN), Farmers Development Union (FDU), Christian Rural Urban Development Association of Nigeria (CRUDAN), Oyo-Osogbo Catholic Diocesan Agricultural Development Project (OODAP) and Rural Development Programme of Ibadan Archdiocese.

7.2.7 Religious Organizations

Certain religious organizations engaged in agricultural projects with the aim of alleviating poverty and hunger as well as providing employment to the unemployed members of their congregation. At times, they intervene in some rural development programmes. They engaged in the production of food crops such as cassava, rice, and establishment of plantations e.g. oil palm plantation. Some of the religious organizations in Nigeria include; Christian Rural Urban Development Association of Nigeria, Oyo- Osogbo Catholic Diocesan Agricultural Development Project and Rural Development Programme of Ibadan Archdiocese. The people of Anambra State are predominantly Christians. The Church brought Civilization, Western Education and some social and economic infrastructure like Schools, Hospitals etc. Institutions like Dennis Memorial Grammar School, Onitsha (DMGS), Christ The King College Onitsha (CKC), Iyi-Enu Hospital Ogidi and St. Charles Borromeo Hospital Onitsha, are all monumental evidence of the developmental efforts of the early churches in Anambra State.

7.2.8 Community Based Organizations

Community-Based Organizations (CBOs), are not for profit rather, organizations on a local and national level, facilitating community efforts for community development. The purpose of CBOs is to plan, implement, and monitor social and economic development programmes and provide technical and financial help to the communities. CBOs positively affects the process of rural change i.e. increase in income, improvement in health, nutrition and literacy status of the populations. Jegede (2000), CBOs are private, voluntary,, organizations independent of any government and funded through individual and corporate donations, levies imposed on members and grants from international agencies and governments. They are community groups which are found in both rural and urban areas. Though locally based, they can spread upwards and outwards to community groups or professional groups or trade unions (Ogbuozobe, 2000). CBOs may come together to pool their labour, to obtain credit to buy goods in bulk, or to promote and develop more sustainable forms of agriculture. Though CBOs are voluntary organizations, it is believed in certain quarters that they are somewhat compulsory as it is in the case of age-grades, community or clan associations and professional associations (Bratton, 1990). In Nigeria, some of the expressions of CBOs listed below were identified by African Development Foundation questionnaire in one of its studies (Callahan, 2004).

- Residents Associations
- Cooperative Societies
- User Associations of Basic Services
- Producer Associations
- Professional/Occupational Organizations
- Workers Unions
- Community Development Associations
- Youth Associations
- Local Security Outfits
- Faith-Based Community Organizations

The forms of CBOs listed above exist in Nigeria as well as in many other countries across the globe. The nature or characteristics of such organizations include the following:

- ➢ Engaging in not-for-profit activities,
- ➢ Pursuance of community development,
- ➢ Education and enlightenment on multifarious issues,
- ➢ Pursuance of membership welfare,
- ➢ Provision of partnership with government and international organizations,
- ➢ Non-political affiliation
- ➢ Serving as pressure groups towards attaining communal goals,
- ➢ Joint collateral bodies for obtaining financial aid.

Some of their activities are revealed by the characteristics which they exhibit. Some of the ways in which CBOs are relevant in the area of community development include:

1) **Contribution to the local industrial base:** - The provision of equipment and facilities which aid production of goods and services comes in part from CBOs. Partly, this could be in form of donations to the community or members of the community. At times, such facilities could be leased out or sold out at cheap rates and on installment payment basis. Farm lands have been leased out to members of communities in this wise while small factories have come to settlements in this form.

2) **Front for projecting goals and intentions of various businesses or professional groups:** - Groups are better recognized by governments and international organizations as means of intervention in community development. Such groups are put in charge of development projects to monitor or supervise. Also, needs and aspirations of communities are projected through CBOs.

3) **Provision of infrastructure:** – with levies on members and communities, donations from different sources and small business activities, CBOs generate fund to prosecute various projects in communities. The construction of markets, drainage channels, community halls and provision of facilities in some schools, and elsewhere are recognized to have come from Community Development Associations (CDAs).

4) **Provision of loans**: - cooperative societies of different groups in communities make loans available to their members at low interest rate within comfortable payback period.

5) **Opportunity for training and development:** – some of the CBOs create opportunities for training of members in specific skills towards business development. They involve professional organizations that are relevant in the needed skill area. At times, members within the community who are trained in such skills are invited to donate their knowledge in the process.

6) **Access to necessary equipment and facilities:** – necessary equipment for business development is procured either through loans obtained from CBOs especially cooperative societies. At

times they are directly purchased in large numbers by the society and sold to members to take advantage of the low cost. Also combined with this is the opportunity for warranty on purchased equipment for businesses.

7) **Opportunities for bulk purchasing and joint collaterals:** – in order to obtain loans from Banks, the CBOs act as organizations which can obtain huge amount and distribute such among members who are in need of small loans for various projects. Also, the CBOs assist in purchasing perishable and non-perishable goods especially at festive periods and other times for their members and people of the community in order to take advantage of cheap rates.

8) **Security Outfits:** – in cities or urban centres where security is an issue needing attention, CDAs have come to form "Vigilante" groups which help in keeping watch over communities and community projects or infrastructure. Members of the community are at times organized by the CDAs to take turns in night watches over their communal properties and households.

9) **Entertainment and Tourism:** – In modern times especially in cities, carnivals have been organized by youth organizations especially towards the end of the year to bring entertainment and fun to city dwellers. This has become a way of developing the tourism industry in cities of Nigeria. The very popular ones are the Calabar carnival and the Lagos carnival.

The Need for the Improvement of the Performance of CBOs
Due to various limitations that CBOs have encountered until now, there is the need to assist their efforts towards community development. Some of the constraints in the way of CBOs include:

a) **Overdependence on Government for Financial and Material Support** – according to the findings of Emmanuel (2010), 42% of investigated CBOs in rural coastland of Ilaje were expecting assistance from government alone compared with just 11% expecting assistance from government alone in the urban hinterland. The need to diversify expectation and seek for further assistance in the rural areas was emphasized in this book.

b) **Lack of Access or Affordability Problem in the Area of Good Equipments in the Rural Areas** – also the problem of non-affordability of good equipment in the rural areas to assist or support existing businesses to aid economic development has been perennial. The cost of high quality and highly productive equipment is high and so members of such communities have had to make-do with what they could afford at any point in time. This generates the need for support in this area both for small businesses and for the general welfare of the rural communities.

c) **Lack of General and Business Education in the Rural Areas** – about 57% of the populace in Ilaje had at least secondary school education. This seems to be an enlightened society but this seemed insufficient to increase the skills to reduce poverty and increase development level of the rural areas. This consequently affects the operation of the CBOs in the rural areas (Emmanuel, 2010).

d) **Overload on Infrastructural Backbone of Urban Communities** – Most CBOs in urban community are formed for the purpose of infrastructural development. In most cities, the inward population surge has often led to overload on the existing facilities. Consequently, associations focus more on alleviating this problem but they are often limited in the area of road construction and electricity provision, hence, the need for further support for CBOs in the process of community development.

e) **Insufficient Membership Contribution** – In certain areas, the fact that members' contributions have not been regular or sufficient has hindered the effectiveness of the CBOs in executing their objectives. Since most CBOs depend on residents or members' contribution, there is limit to what could be achieved within reasonable length of time.

Chapter Eight

DEVELOPMENT PLANNING

8.1 MEANING OF DEVELOPMENT PLANNING

Planning is the French word `prevoyance', which means to look ahead. According to Pfiffner and Presthus (1960), planning is "a rational process characterized of all human behaviour." Dimock and Dimock (1970) gave this definition: "Planning is an organized attempt to anticipate and to make rational arrangement for dealing with future problems by projecting trends." According to Simon, Smithburg and Victor A. Thomson; "Planning is that activity that concern itself with proposal for future, evaluation of alternative proposals and with methods by which these proposals may be achieved." A plan is a series of thoughts, processes, and actions, written and agreed in the present, in order to be implemented or carried out in the future. The plan consists of a written statement of objectives and a map or series of maps. Planning is a mental predisposition to do things in an orderly way, to think before acting and to act in the light of facts rather than guesses. Planning is deciding the best alternative among others to perform different managerial functions in order to achieve predetermined goals. Planning is deciding in advance what to do, how to do and who is to do it. Planning bridges the gap between where we are to, where we want to go. It makes possible things to occur which would not otherwise occur. The plan also helps development to take place quickly by describing how any new or improved facilities, such as roads, schools and parks will be provided.

The development plan is a document that sets out how places should change and what they could be like in the future. It says what type of development should take place where, and which areas should not be developed. Development planning is essentially a way of organizing and utilizing resources to the maximum advantages in terms of defined social ends. A development plan is a written text and a map which guides the future use and development of an area. It is prepared in consultation with the public and interested groups and organizations. Planning decisions are made in accordance with your area's development plan. A development plan sets out agreed planning policies for your area and is the background against which planning decisions are made. The development plan is the main public statement of planning policies for the local community. The development plan is a blueprint for the planning and development of your area i.e. for the next six years, for example, it sets out where roads, water supplies, sewerage are to be provided and it zones land for particular purposes (housing, shopping, schools, factories etc.). This will affect what type of buildings can be constructed and the use to which land can be put. It affects many facets of daily, economic and social life - where you can live, what services are available and where developments with job opportunities are to be sited. Planning is a process which involves the determination of future course of action, i.e. why an action, how to take an action, and when to take action are main subjects of planning. Planning involves the creation and maintenance of a plan. As such, planning is a fundamental property of intelligent behaviour. This thought process is essential to the creation and refinement of a plan, or integration of it with other plans; that is, it combines forecasting of developments with the preparation of scenarios of how to react to them.

Good planning gives direction to civic leaders, businesses and citizens to make meaningful decisions for the long term and how best their communities can grow into that future, while allowing for essential services to be provided in the near term. Planning is done not only by trained professionals working in the public sector for planning departments or in the private sector for developers; planning is also done by lay persons who volunteer on local committees or commissions, including a planning commission, zoning board of appeals or historic district commission. A plan is like a map. When following a plan, you can always see how much you have progressed towards your project goal and how far you are from your destination. Knowing where you are is essential for making good decisions on where to go or what to do next. Planning is also crucial for meeting your needs. During each action, step with your time, money, or other resources. With careful planning you often can see if at some point you are likely to face a problem. It is much easier to adjust your plan to avoid or smoothen a coming crisis, rather than to deal with the crisis when it comes unexpected. Good planning helps create communities that offer better choices for where and how people live. Planning helps communities to envision their future. It helps them find the right balance of new development and essential services, environmental protection, and innovative change.

8.2   CHARACTERISTICS OF PLANNING
1. Planning is goal-oriented.
    a.   Planning is made to achieve desired objective of development.

      b. The goals established should be generally accepted otherwise community efforts and energies will be misguided and misdirected.

      c. Planning identifies the action that would lead to desired goals quickly & economically.

      d. It provides a sense of direction to various development activities in the community.

2. Planning is looking ahead.
   a. Planning is done for future.
   b. It requires peeping into the future, analyzing it and predicting it.
   c. Thus planning is based on forecasting.
   d. A plan is a synthesis of forecast.

It is a mental predisposition for things to happen in future.

3. Planning is an intellectual process.
   a. Planning is a mental exercise involving creative thinking, sound judgement and imagination.
   b. It is not a mere guesswork but a rational thinking.
   c. A manager can prepare sound plans only if he has sound judgement, foresight and imagination.
   d. Planning is always based on goals, facts and considered estimates.

4. Planning involves choices and decision making.
   a. Planning essentially involves choice among various alternatives.
   b. Therefore, if there is only one possible course of action, there is no need planning because there is no choice.
   c. Thus, decision making is an integral part of planning.
   d. A devloper is surrounded by a number of alternatives. He has to pick the best depending upon requirements and resources of the community.

5. Planning is the primary function of development in a community the most important or first function.
   a. Planning lays the foundation for other activities of community development.
   b. It serves as a guide for organizing, staffing, directing and controlling.

    c. All the development activities are performed within the framework of plans laid out.

    d. Therefore planning is the basic or fundamental function of leaders.

6. Planning is a continuous process.
   a. Planning is a never ending function due to the dynamic business environment.
   b. Plans are also prepared for specific periods of time and at the end of that period, plans are subjected to revaluation and review in the light of new requirements and changing conditions.
   c. Planning never comes into end till the community exits issues, problems may keep cropping up and they have to be tackled by planning effectively.

7. Planning is all pervasive.
   a. It is required at all levels of community development.
   b. Of course, the scope of planning may differ from one level to another.

8. Planning is designed for efficiency.
   a. Planning leads to accomplishment of objectives at the minimum possible cost.
   b. It avoids wastage of resources and ensures adequate and optimum utilization of resources.
   c. A plan is worthless or useless if it does not value the cost incurred on it.
   d. Therefore, planning must lead to saving of time, effort and money.
   e. Planning leads to proper utilization of men, money, materials, methods and machines.

9. Planning is flexible.
   a. Planning is done for the future.
   b. Since future is unpredictable, planning must provide enough room to cope with the changes in community's demand, government policies etc.
   c. Under the circumstances, the original plan of action must be revised and updated to make it more practical.

8.3   IMPORTANCE OF PLANNING

I.   **Planning increases the community's ability to adapt to future eventualities:** The future is generally uncertain and things are likely to change with the passage of time. The uncertainty is augmented with an increase in the time dimension. With such a rise in uncertainty there is generally a corresponding increase in the alternative courses of action from which a selection must be made. The planning activity provides a systematic approach to the consideration of such future uncertainties and eventualities and the planning of activities in terms of what is likely to happen.

II.   **Planning helps crystallize objectives:** The first step in planning is to fix objectives which will give direction to the activities to be performed. This step focuses attention on the results desired. A proper definition and integration of overall developmental objectives would result in more co-ordinated development activities and a greater chance of attaining the overall objectives.

III. **Planning ensures relatedness among decisions:** A crystallization of objectives as mentioned above would lead to relatedness among the decisions which would otherwise have been random. Decisions of the members are related to each other and ultimately towards the goals or objectives of the community. Creativity and innovation of individuals is thus harnessed towards a more effective development of the community.

IV.   **Planning helps the community to remain more focused in its development:** Planning may suggest the addition of a new line of actions, changes in the methods of operation, a better identification of development needs and segmentation and timely expansion of carrying capacity all of which make the community better fitted or more focused.

V.   **Adequate planning reduces unnecessary pressures of immediacy:** If activities are not properly planned in anticipation of what is likely to happen, pressures will be exerted to achieve certain results immediately or in a hurry. Thus adequate planning brings orderliness and avoids unnecessary pressures.

VI.   **Planning reduces mistakes and oversights:** Although mistakes cannot be entirely obviated, they can certainly be reduced through proper planning.

VII.   **Planning ensures a more productive use of the community's resources:** By avoiding wasted effort in terms of labour, money and machinery, adequate planning results in greater productivity through a better utilization of the resources available to the community.

VIII. **Planning makes control easier:** The crystallization of objectives and goals simplify and highlight the controls required.

IX.   Planning enables the identification of future problems and makes it possible to provide for such contingencies.

X.   **Planning can help the community secure a better position or standing:** Adequate planning would stimulate improvements in terms of the opportunities available.

XI.   **Planning enables the community to progress in the manner considered most suitable by its members:** members, for example, may be interested in stability and moderate project rather than huge projects and risk of discontinuity. In terms of its objectives, the plan would ensure that actions are taken to achieve such objectives.

XII.   **Planning increases the effectiveness of a leader:** As the goals of community people are made clearer, adequate planning would help the leaders in deciding upon the most appropriate act.

8.4   PRINCIPLES OF PLANNING

Planning is a dynamic process, it is very essential for every community to achieve their ultimate goals, but, there are certain principles which are essential to be followed so as to formulate a sound plan. They are only guidelines in the formulation and implementation of plans. These principles are as follows:

1. **Principle of Contribution:** The purpose of planning is to ensure the effective and efficient achievement of development objectives, in-fact the basic criteria for the formulation of plans are to achieve the ultimate objectives of the community. The accomplishment of the objectives always depends on the soundness of plans and the adequate amount of contribution of community towards the same.

2. **Principle of Sound and Consistent Premising:** Premises are the assumptions regarding the environmental forces like raining season, economic and market conditions, social, political, legal and cultural aspects etc. These are prevalent during the period of the implementation of plans. Hence, plans are made on the basis of premises accordingly, and the future of the community depends on the soundness of plans they make so as to face the state of premises.

3. **Principle of Limiting Factors:** The limiting factors are paucity of material resources, shortage of capital funds, government policy of price regulation, etc. The community requires monitoring of all on factors and need to tackle the same in an efficient way so as to make a smooth way for the achievement of its ultimate objectives.

4. **Principle of Commitment:** A commitment is required to carry-on the development plan that is established.

5. **Principle of Coordinated Planning:** Long and short-range plans should be coordinated with one another to form an integrated plan, this is possible only when the latter are derived from the former. Implementation of the long-range plan is regarded as contributory to the implementation of the short-range plan. Functional plans of the community too should contribute to all other plans i.e. implementation of one plan should contribute to all the other plans, this is possible only when all plans are consistent with one another and are viewed as parts of an integrated development plan.

6. **Principle of Timing:** A number of major and minor plans of the community should be arranged in a systematic manner. The plans should be arranged in a time hierarchy, initiation and completion of those plans should be clearly determined.

7. **Principle of Efficiency:** Cost of planning constitutes human, physical and financial resources for their formulation and implementation as well. Minimizing the cost and achieving the efficient utilization of resources shall have to be the aim of the plans. Cost of plan formulation and implementation, in any case, should not exceed the community output's monetary value. Members satisfaction and development, and social standing of the community

are supposed to be considered while calculating the cost and benefits of plan.

8. **Principle of Flexibility:** Plans are supposed to be flexible to favour the community cope with the unexpected environments. It is always required to keep in mind that the future will be different in actuality. Hence companies, therefore, are required to prepare contingency plans which may be put into operation in response to the situations.

9. **Principle of Navigational Change:** Since the environment is not always the same as predicted, plans should be reviewed periodically. This may require changes in strategies, objectives, policies and programmes of the community. The leader should take all the necessary steps while reviewing the plans so that they efficiently achieve the ultimate goals of the community.

10. **Principle of Acceptance:** Plans should be understood and accepted by the members, since the successful implementation of plans requires the willingness and cooperative efforts from them. Communication also plays a crucial role in gaining the members understanding and acceptance of the plans by removing their doubts and misunderstanding about the plans and also their apprehensions and anxieties about consequences of plans for achievement of their communal goals.

8.5   PLANNING PROCESS
What are the steps involved in the Planning Process?
Planning means one looking ahead and chalking out future courses of action to be followed. It is a preparatory step. It is a systematic activity which determines when, how and who is going to perform a specific job. Planning is a detailed programme regarding future courses of action. It is rightly said: "Well planning is action half done". Therefore planning takes into consideration available and prospective human and physical resources of the community so as to get effective co-ordination, contribution and perfect adjustment. It is the basic development function which includes formulation of one or more detailed plans to achieve optimum balance of needs or demands with the available resources. The various stages in the process of planning are as follows:

1. **Establishment of Objectives**
   a.   Planning requires a systematic approach.
   b.   Planning starts with the setting of goals and objectives to be achieved.
   c.   Objectives provide a rationale for undertaking various activities as well as indicate direction of efforts.
   d.   Moreover, objectives focus the attention of developers/leaders on the end results to be achieved.
   e.   As a matter of fact, objectives provide nucleus to the planning process. Therefore, objectives should be stated in a clear, precise and unambiguous language. Otherwise the activities undertaken are bound to be ineffective.
   f.   As far as possible, objectives should be stated in quantitative terms. For example, number of men worked, wages given, units produced, etc. Such goals should be specified in qualitative terms.
   g.   Hence objectives should be practical, acceptable, workable and achievable.

2. **Establishment of Planning Premises**
   a.   Planning premises are the assumptions about the lively shape of events in future.
   b.   They serve as a basis of planning.
   c.   Establishment of planning premises is concerned with determining where one tends to deviate from the actual plans and causes of such deviations.
   d.   It is to find out what obstacles are there in the way of community during the course of development.
   e.   Establishment of planning premises is a step taken to avoid these obstacles to a great extent.
   f.   Planning premises may be internal or external. Internal includes capital investment policy, labour relations, philosophy etc. Whereas external includes socio- economic, political and economical changes.
   g.   Internal premises are controllable whereas external are non-controllable.

3. **Choice of Alternative Course of Action**
   a.   When forecast are available and premises are established, a number of alternative course of actions have to be considered.

    b.   For this purpose, each and every alternative will be evaluated by weighing its pros and cons in the light of resources available and requirements of the community.

    c.   The merits, demerits as well as the consequences of each alternative must be examined before the choice is being made.

    d.   After objective and scientific evaluation, the best alternative is chosen.

    e.   The planners should take help of various quantitative techniques to judge the stability of an alternative.

4. Formulation of Derivative Plans

    a.   Derivative plans are the sub plans or secondary plans which help in the achievement of the main plan.

    b.   Secondary plans will flow from the basic plan. These are meant to support and expediate the achievement of basic plans.

    c.   These detailed plans include policies, procedures, rules, programmes, budgets, schedules, etc.

    d.   Derivative plans indicate time schedule and sequence of accomplishing various tasks.

5. Securing Co-operation

    a.   After the plans have been determined, it is necessary and rather advisable to take members into confidence.

    b.   The purposes behind taking them into confidence are :-

        i.   Members may feel motivated since they are involved in decision making process.

        ii.   The community may be able to get valuable suggestions and improvement in formulation as well as implementation of plans.

        iii.   Also the members will be more interested in the execution of these plans.

6. Follow up/Appraisal of plans

    a.   After choosing a particular course of action, it is put into action.

    b.   After the selected plan is implemented, it is important to appraise its effectiveness.

    c.   This is done on the basis of feedback or information received from community members or persons concerned.

    d.   This enables the community to correct deviations or modify the plan.

e. This step establishes a link between planning and controlling function.

f. The follow up must go side by side with the implementation of plans so that in the light of observations made, future plans can be made more realistic.

8.6 TYPES OF PLANNING

i. **Physical Planning:** It is a planning technique in which the size of the plan is determined by the potential physical resources (men and materials) of the country rather than by the financial resources. Objectives and targets are also determined in physical quantities.

ii. **Farm/Home Planning:** This type of planning is also known as balanced farming which came into existence as a result of the conflicts and confusions often created by segmented or specialized approach to farming and home-making. This type of planning is aimed at bringing the farm and home as an integrated unit into controlled focus.

iii. **Organization/Agency Planning:** Since organizations and agencies are usually a major part of the community functioning process, this type of planning is a very important part of the total community planning process. Hence, it is important therefore, that organizations and/or agency planning be in support of and not contradicting to the community process.

iv. **Project Planning:** This is concerned with the planning and execution of one special unit of the overall programme of the community. Therefore, the project planning is part of the community or organizational planning.

v. **Community Planning:** This type of plan cuts across special interest lines and attempts to interrelate these special phases of planning in terms of an integrated whole but depends on the area to be served. That is, if the term community is used instead of town-country community sense. The planning is considered as community planning.

vi. **Country Planning:** Sociologically, it may be seen as community planning used for different functional units. Its primary center of focus is usually governmental because its limit stops at country-lines, which are also arbitrary in a mutual sense. This broadness distinguishes it from community planning.

vii. **Financial Planning:** It refers to a technique of development planning in which there is allocation of resources, fixation of targets of objectives and their achievement in terms of money. Financial planning is an important technique to remove maladjustments between demand and supply and for calculating cost-benefits of various projects. It ensures the exploitation of physical potentialities and aims at securing a balance between demand and supply, checking inflation and maintaining economic stability. However, the technique has its own limitations.

viii. **Perspective Planning:** It is also called long term planning or terminal year planning in which the long term targets and objectives are fixed in advance for a wider time horizon of 15 or 20 or 25 years. It is only an outline or blue print of development prgrammes to be undertaken over a longer period. In such a planning technique, the broad objectives and targets are fixed for different important sectors of the economy, which are achieved over a long period. For this, the perspective planning is divided into several short periods plans of four or five years or six years as the case may be. These short period plans are further divided into annual (yearly) plans, which are classified into regional and sectoral plans. All these plans and sub-plans are fitted into the perspective plan in such a way that the broad objectives and targets are achieved over a long period. Thus, perspective planning is nothing but the projection of short term planning in terms of long period objectives.

ix. **Rolling Plan:** It is also called short term or inter-temporal planning. This planning technique has been advocated for the developing countries of the world. Rolling plan is a continuous planning process in which there is a periodical revision of the plan in the light of new information, improved data and analysis. Under such a planning technique, every year, new plans are formulated and implemented on the basis of the experience of previous plans. However, there is a plan for a number of years, say 3, 4 or 5 years, which is changed every year according to the requirements of the economy.

8.7 WHY PLAN FOR RURAL - COMMUNITY DEVELOPMENT

Just as each community has unique set of strengths, weaknesses, opportunities, and challenges, each community needs a unique solution or plan. Building and sustaining an economically, environmentally, and culturally, healthy community may require innovative thinking and new attitudes. Solutions need to be developed through collaborative, community-based approaches that involve an expanding leadership base and actively seek input from all works of life. The community planning process needs to honour the past, assess the present, and describe the desired future. A community plan and an economic development strategy can empower communities to maintain a sense of place, become more resilient given economic challenges and opportunities, and can increase their well being. A plan helps individuals and communities see where they want to go and make decisions on how to get there. Increase the likelihood of success while each community has a unique set of economic development challenges, several common factors have been found that increase the likelihood of a community's successful economic development. Local leadership that brings together the human knowledge and financial resources of three sectors of society: government (tribal and city), business, and the third sector (non-governmental organizations). Social planning and policy change is oriented towards policy solutions -- changing or passing laws or regulations to address problems or conditions -- particularly those initiated by officials or other leaders from inside or outside the community. These policies should be determined through a participatory process that involves everyone they benefit or otherwise affect. This model often involves people with expertise from outside the community working with community members on strategy and planning. Policies and programmes planned around local needs and use of local resources is paramount. A planning facilitator with the right attitudes, skills, and knowledge willing to assist your community, strengthens existing economic activity, institutions and promotes workforce development and training as well as develops infrastructure (public services and facilities) by stimulating economic diversification through locally based small business development.

8.8 CONDITIONS FOR SUCCESSFUL PLANNING

The successful implementation of a plan for economic growth and development depends largely on the conditions and circumstances prevailing in the country. They are as follows:

i. Strong and Efficient Government: The first condition for successful planning is the existence of a strong and efficient government. Since planning requires efficient centralized direction, it is obvious that a weak and unstable central government cannot formulate or carry out efficiently any comprehensive national programme of economic development.

ii. Competent Planning Agency (Commission): A competent planning agency or commission is needed for formulating, implementing and reformulating the plan. The commission should consist of persons who should be authorities or experts in their own lines- say in education, technology, finance, etc. besides being experts in their respective spheres, these people must also have sufficient administrative skill and experience.

iii. Sound Administration: Sound administrative machinery is a sine qua non for effective planning. Public administration is strategic in the sense that it influences and determines the success of the entire development plan and that it is susceptible to deliberate social control and charge. A good system is required not only in the initial stage of planning but also to tackle many problems that may crop up in the course of carrying out the plan.

iv. Financial stability: An underdeveloped country should have sufficient financial stability for steady development progress. Deficit financing and inflationary rise in price should be avoided as far as possible.

v. Existence of certain well-defined objectives: Another requirement for successful planning is the existence of certain well-defined objectives. It shall make planning purposive, help in the greater concentration of national efforts towards the attainment of the objectives and give direction and meaning to the various steps taken in that direction.

vi. Accurate data: To a large degree, success of planning depends on whether the formulation of the plan is based on accurate data. Adequate statistical data are of prime importance not only in the drafting of a realistic plan, but also needed in the course of its implementation. Periodic check-up of progress of the plan and revisions that may be called for in view of current developments would not be possible unless the data available for the planning authority are exhaustive and correct.

vii.   Maintaining proper balance: Successful functioning of the plan requires the presence between investment goods sector and consumption goods sector, public sector and private sector, home and external trade, internal finance and foreign exchange and also between labour intensive techniques and capital intensive techniques. To maintain these balances, the government must undertake necessary steps e.g the state should reorganize agriculture, introduce reforms, organize cooperatives and encourage domestic industries.

viii.   Pre-requisites of good planning: The standard modern development plan is an investment plan and its primary goal is to bring about adequate rate of economic growth and development. In such a plan, great care should be taken to match the various segments of the plan and also provide for the requisite investment resources – from where internally generated and externally generated capital will come. A good plan should have these three points:

    a.   It must provide a strategy for economic advancement;

    b.   A good plan should emphasis both the visible and invisible dimension of communal achievements; and

    c.   Modern development planning must have a theory of consumption.

8.9   ADVANTAGES OF PLANNING

The military saying, "If you fail to plan, you plan to fail," is very true. Without a plan, leaders are set up to encounter errors, waste, and delays. A plan, on the other hand, helps a leader organize resources and activities efficiently and effectively to achieve goals.

The advantages of planning are numerous. Planning fulfills the following objectives:

- **Gives a community a sense of direction.** Without plans and goals, communities merely react to daily occurrences without considering what will happen in the long run. For example, the solution that makes sense in the short term doesn't always make sense in the long term. Plans avoid this drift situation and ensure that short-range efforts will support and harmonize with future goals.
- **Focuses attention on objectives and results.** Plans keep the people who carry them out focused on the anticipated results. In addition, keeping sight of the goal also motivates members.

- **Establishes a basis for cooperation.** Diverse groups cannot effectively cooperate in joint projects without an integrated plan. Examples are numerous: Plumbers, carpenters, and electricians cannot build a house without blueprints. In addition, military activities require the coordination of Army, Navy, and Air Force units.
- **Helps anticipate problems and cope with change.** When communities plans it can help forecast future problems and make any necessary changes up front to avoid them. Planning for such potential problems helps to minimize mistakes and reduce the "surprises" that inevitably occur.
- **Provides guidelines for decision making.** Decisions are future-oriented. If leaders don't have any plans for the future, they will have few guidelines for making current decisions. If a community knows that it wants to embark on a new project three years into the future, its leaders must be mindful of the decisions they make now. Plans help both leaders and members keep their eyes on the big picture.
- **Serves as a prerequisite to employing all other development measures.** Planning is primary, because without knowing what a community wants to accomplish, members can't intelligently undertake any of the other basic development measures: organizing, coordinating, leading, and/or controlling.

8.10   DISADVANTAGES OF PLANNING

Various barriers can inhibit successful planning. In order for plans to be effective and to yield the desired results, leaders must identify any potential barriers and work to overcome them. The common barriers that inhibit successful planning are as follows:

Internal Limitations

There are several limitations of planning. Some of them are inherent in the process of planning like rigidity and others which arise due to the shortcoming of the techniques of planning and in the planners themselves.

1.   **Rigidity**
    a. Planning has the tendency to make an administration inflexible.
    b. Planning implies prior determination of policies, procedures and programmes and a strict adherence to them in all circumstances.
    c. There is no scope for individual freedom.

     d. Planning therefore introduces inelasticity and discourages individual initiative and experimentation.

2. **Misdirected Planning**
     a. Planning may be used to serve individual interests rather than the interest of the community.
     b. Attempts can be made to influence setting of objectives, formulation of plans and programmes to suit ones own requirement rather than that of a whole community.
     c. Machinery of planning can never be freed of bias. Every planner has his own likes, dislikes, preferences, attitudes and interests which are reflected in planning.

3. **Time consuming**
     a. Planning is a time consuming process because it involves collection of information, its analysis and interpretation thereof. This entire process takes a lot of time especially where there are a number of alternatives available.
     b. Therefore planning is not suitable during emergency or crisis when quick decisions are required.

4. **Probability in planning**
     a. Planning is based on forecasts which are mere estimates about future.
     b. These estimates may prove to be inexact due to the uncertainty of future.
     c. Any change in the anticipated situation may render plans ineffective.
     d. Plans do not always reflect real situations in spite of the sophisticated techniques of forecasting because the future is unpredictable.
     e. Thus, excessive reliance on plans may prove to be fatal.

5. **False sense of security**
     a. Elaborate planning may create a false sense of security to the effect that everything is taken for granted.
     b. Leaders assume that as long as they work according to plans, it is satisfactory.
     c. Therefore they fail to take up timely actions and an opportunity is lost.

    d. Community leaders are more concerned about fulfillment of laid out plans and performance rather than any kind of change.

6. **Expensive**
    a. Collection, analysis and evaluation of different information, facts and alternatives involve a lot of expense in terms of time, effort and money.
    b. According to Koontz and O'Donell (1980),' Expenses on planning should never exceed the estimated benefits from planning.'

External Limitations of Planning

1. Political Climate- Change of government from Congress to some other political party, etc.
2. Labour Union- Strikes, lockouts, agitations.
3. Technological changes- Modern techniques and equipments, computerization.
4. Policies of competitors- e.g. Policies of Coca Cola and Pepsi.
5. Natural Calamities- Earthquakes and floods.
6. Changes in demand and prices- Change in fashion, change in tastes, change in income level, demand falls, price falls, etc.

The good news about these barriers is that they can all be overcome. To plan successfully, leaders need to use effective communication, acquire quality information, and solicit the involvement of others.

Classification of Development Plans

Development plans are classified according to their time, horizon, activity, coverage, geographical scope, institutional character and level of detail. Let us discuss some of the various types of plans:

1. Development plans according to time horizon – short, medium and long-term plans:
    (a) **Short –term plans:** The typical short-term plan that people are used to are the annual "set-aside" which we describe as the budget. Most people however do not know that there is a daily plan. The work people do in the office every day is based on a daily plan. From daily plans we move to weekly plans, monthly plans and annual plans.
    (b) **Medium-term plans:** these cover a time horizon of between two to six years. However, the typical medium term plans are

the four or five year's plans. Development plans in Nigeria between 1962 and1985 belong to this category.

(c) **Long-term plans:** Any development plan of over 10 years is described as a long time plan. There are certain things which cannot be planned within a short time, e.g. population growth, transportation system, etc. these are better handled within the strategy of long term plans.

2. Plans according to activity coverage;

(a) **Overall plans:** These cover all the major sectors of the economy such as production, consumption, capital formation and distribution of income.

(b) **Sectoral plans:** These relate to the planning of specified sectors of the economy. The often cited example is the famous GoeLRO plan of electrification in Russia in the 1920s. Sectoral plan can be made.

(c) **Functional plans:** this can be made for any major functional areas of the state. Typical examples are the 6-3-3-4 educational plan, the EPI/ORT health plan in Nigeria.

3. **Plan of key projects:** Special plans are usually made for key projects. For example, the Kainji Dam project in Niger state and the Balanga Dam project in Gombe State.

4. Plans according to geographical coverage:

(a) **Local plans:** These are usually restricted to a local government.

(b) **Regional/State plans:** This is a plan made for any geographical area of a country which is more than a local government area but at the same time smaller than the area of the country.

(c) **National Plans:** This usually covers the entire area of the country. It is similar to the overall plans except that the former covers the entire geographical area of the country and the latter focuses on the economic variables.

5. Plans for groups of countries: Groups of countries usually introduce and initiate plans. This usually happens under the framework of international organizations e.g. ECOWAS, EEC, and OPEC.

8.11 OVERVIEW OF THE NIGERIAN NATIONAL DEVELOPMENT PLANS OVER THE YEARS

Pre–Independence Period

Government's involvement in infrastructural provision began as far back as 1917 when the colonial government promulgated the Township Ordinance. This ordinance classified settlements in the country into three classes: namely, the first, second and third class townships. The first class townships harboured the whites and their workers. There was heavy concentration of infrastructure in these settlements (an example being Lagos). They differ from the second and the third class townships, which received little or no facilities. The situation continued until 1952 when the Local Government Councils were established in the then Western Nigeria. The Local Government Councils were seen as avenues through which infrastructural facilities could be extended to the rural areas. But then, the fund allocations to the local governments were hardly enough to maintain facilities in the council headquarters. In fact, little or no fund was available to initiate new schemes for rural development. Yet ironically, in spite of the limited benefits of the colonial policies, the investment pattern established during the colonial period was further consolidated by subsequent governments after independence. This is evident in all the development plans initiated since 1960.

Post Independence Plan Period (1960 - Date)

We shall attempt to summarize the post independence plan period under five major groupings: -

- The First National Development Plan Period (1962-68);
- The Second National Development Plan Period (1975-80);
- The Third National Development Plan (1975-80);
- The Fourth National Development Plan Period (1980-85); and
- The Post Fourth Plan Period (1985 to 1990).

Table 8:1 **Summary of the Post-Independence National Development Plans Total Capital Expenditure (N Million)**

Plans	Period	Total expenditure	% of Total
First National Development	1962-68	1,353,00	3.7
Second National Development	1970-74	2,050,738	5.7
Third National Development	1975-80	32,854.616	90.6
Fourth National Development	1981-85	-	-
Post Fourth National Development	1985-1990	-	-

Source: Olayiwola and Adeleye (2005: 93).

The First National Development Plan (1962-68)
The First National Plan of Nigeria (1962-68) had a total budget allocation of N1, 353 million (see Table 8:1). The plan made no clear statement on rural infrastructural development. As agriculture was still an important exchange earner, the plan's objectives were to encourage the assemblage of agricultural produce for export purposes.

The Second National Development Plan (1970-74)
The Second plan was launched shortly after the end of the civil war. The plan attempted to rehabilitate economic activities in the war-affected areas. The plan spelt out five principal national objectives meant to achieve a united, just, strong and self-reliant nation. Some N 2,050.738 million was allocated as expenditure. But just as in the first plan, government did not make any clear statement on rural infrastructural development. However, it was stated in the plan that government was committed to spending N500,000 for village regrouping. This was perhaps to reduce the cost of providing economic and social infrastructure such as health, electricity, water and educational facilities for the rural areas. The sum allocated to rural development looks too paltry, and, generally like the previous ones, the plan failed to introduce any radical package towards rural infrastructural development.

The Third National Development Plan (1975-80)
Serious concern for rural development at the national level was first highlighted in the third national development plan. The objectives of the plan were similar to those of the second national development plan. The plan emphasized the need to reduce regional disparities in order to foster national unity through the adoption of integrated rural development. The total budget allocation in the third national development plan was N32 billion (see Table 8:1 above). The plan provided for: - the allocation of N90 million towards nation wide rural electrification scheme: - the establishment of nine River Basin Development Authorities (RBDAs) in addition to the two existing ones (Sokoto and Rima (RBDAs); - the construction of small dams and boreholes for rural water supply and the clearing of feeder roads for the evacuation of agricultural produce and - the supply of electricity to rural areas from large irrigation dams. At the State level, some governments, like Oyo State, showed their intention to transform the rural areas through the provision of basic infrastructural facilities. The Oyo State Government spent N15.98 million for the execution of rural electrification for some rural settlements. In addition, the state government planned for the construction of 150 Rural Health Centres

and 725 Health Clinics all over the state. The health facilities were to be provided at a cost of N31.719 million.

The Fourth National Development Plan (1981-85)
The Fourth National Development Plan exhibits several distinguishing features. First, it was formulated by a civilian government under a new constitution based on the Presidential system of government. Second, it was the first plan in which the local government tier was allowed to participate fully in its own right. Fourth National Development Plan, 1981: the plan emphasized among other things the need for balanced development of the different sectors of the economy and of the various geographic areas of the country. It emphasized the importance of rural infrastructural development as a vehicle for enhancing the quality of rural life. Consequently, about N924 million was allocated to the eleven River Basin Development Authorities whose functions include among other things, the construction of boreholes, dams, feeder roads and jetties. About 12, 064 kilometers of feeder roads, 2,650 boreholes, 2,280 wells, 29 farm service centres and 249 earth dams, were expected to be constructed by the River Basin Development Authorities.

The Federal Government allocated N645 million for a country- wide electrification, in addition, all the States of the Federation allocated N700.4 million for the electrification of about 1,600 towns and villages. In terms of rural transportation development, the local government in the country planned for the provision of inter city/village bus services, for the construction of motor parks, and for petrol filling stations during the fourth plan period (1981-85). In order to increase the access of rural dwellers to safe drinking water, rural water supply schemes were planned apart from the huge boreholes drilling programme. The total allocation for this sector was N2, 805 million. Local Governments in some States such as Anambra, Plateau, Cross-River States, former Bendel state and Borno also made fund allocations totaling N311,824 million for water projects. At the State level, the various State governments spelt out different policy issues in the fourth development plan. For instance, in Oyo State, the government identified four cardinal programmes for itself. These include: -
- Free education at all levels
- Free medical services
- Integrated rural development and
- Gainful employment

In line with the above programmes, the sum of N1, 642,401 million were allocated to the various sectors of the economy. The rural sector received much attention in the attempt to

- Upgrade some local government roads.
- Establish 27 Primary Health Centres, 105 health clinics and 6 comprehensive health centres. All these were to be located mostly in the rural areas. - Provide wells in rural areas where piped water is not available.
- Extend rural electrification scheme to phase five in addition to the existing phases one to four.

The Post Fourth Plan Period (1985 to Date)

The post fourth plan period witnessed the establishment of the Directorate for Food, Roads and Rural Infrastructure (DFRRI) in 1985 for the purpose of providing rural infrastructure in the country side. The laws establishing the Directorate was promulgated under Decree No. 4 of 1987. The core of the Directorate's programme is the promotion of productive activities. Besides, the directorate recognized the provision of rural infrastructure such as feeder roads, water, electricity and housing as essential for the enhancement of the quality of life in the rural areas. The programme of the directorate includes:

- ❖ The organization and mobilization of the local people to enhance or facilitate closer interaction between the government and the people. In addition the local communities were asked to form unions or associations for the purpose of providing common facilities for themselves;
- ❖ The provision of rural infrastructures such as rural feeder roads, rural water and sanitation, rural housing and electrification;
- ❖ The promotion of productive activities such as food and agriculture, rural industrialization and technology;
- ❖ The promotion of other extra curricular activities such as socio-cultural and recreational programmes, intra and inter community cohesion activities.

The plan for the implementation of DFRRI programmes was organized into two phases. In phase one; the target was to provide water for 250 communities in each of the states of the Federation, to construct 90,000km of feeder roads, and to promote rural housing, health and agriculture. To facilitate industrial growth, and improve the attractiveness of the rural environment, the Directorate planned to commence its rural electrification programme in the second phase starting in June 1987. In pursuit of its objectives, DFRRI also planned to co-operate with organizations like Nigerian Building and Road Research Institute (NBRRI) as well as rural water supply and sanitation programme (RWATSAN). The Directorate of food, roads and rural infrastructures (DFRRI), does not get involved in direct implementation of the programmes. Rather, for the purpose of the programme implementation, the directorate uses as its main agents, the states and the local governments, to execute its programme. The funds for the programme of the Directorate are made available directly to each state government who then sees to the disbursement of such funds to the local governments. The local governments in the Federation are constituted into rural development committees. These committees embrace the local government officials and the rural communities. Overall, about N433 million was allocated to the Directorate in 1986 for the purpose of implementing its programme. But only N300 million was actually disbursed. In 1987 and 1988, N500 million and N1 billion respectively were allocated to the Directorate.

8.12 IMPEDIMENTS TO EFFECTIVE PLAN IMPLEMENTATION IN NIGERIA

➢ First, until recently, the planning exercise in Nigeria has failed to satisfy the most important requirement of good and effective planning process-wide consultation. As professor Adedeji, a former Federal Commissioner for Economic Development and Reconstruction notes our development plans have tended to be prepared rather hastily, kept secret from the public until they are published, and their publications have invariably taken place several months after the commencement of the plan period. This was particularly the case with the first and second National Development Plans. Consequently, very little attempt was made by their authors to enlist the interest of the average citizen in planning process or to evolve suitable media for communicating the plans. i.e their aims and priorities to the masses. Even the participation of the intellectuals, professionals and other non-governmental groups, whose activities and experience can assist in enriching the national planning effort, was greatly restricted.

➢ Secondly, the absence of a well-defined and inclusive national ideology on which to base overall development policies, another deficiency in Nigeria's planning process. Although the five cardinal principles of national objectives, as enunciated in the Second National Development Plan can be regarded as the underlying philosophy, these objectives have neither been set in sufficiently operational terms nor taken seriously by the public policy makers. They represent more of statements of policy objectives than a plan for action. The fact that none of these objectives have been achieved to any significant extent lends weight to this proposition.

➢ Thirdly, planning process in Nigeria suffers from serious distortions the implementation of plans. Indeed, a review of economic activities both during the 1962-1968 and the 1970-1974 plan periods reveals that the various governments of the Federation do not adhere strictly to the spirit of their plans. Aside from the general tendency to channel the bulk of the available resources to low priority sectors (i.e. social and administrative), the planned allocations and expenditures often differed significantly from actual allocations and expenditures. In majority of cases, new prestige projects were inserted on an ad hoc basis without any plan review exercise having been undertaken.

➢ Successive reliance on foreign aid is also another shortcoming of the planning process in Nigeria. During the 1962-1968 plan period, for instance, it was assumed that 50% of the capital investment would be financed from abroad. Yet only N171 million (out of the accepted six-year total of N678m) came from external sources during the first four years of the plan.

➢ Political interference also constitutes another short-coming of the planning process in Nigeria. The political problem did not consist only of the hospitable climate to foreign investors caused by the prevailing political crisis. It had an additional dimension in the strong disregard of politicians for planning priorities. This resulted either from regional ethnic rivalries over the location of planning projects or from the introduction of new (unplanned) projects for partisan considerations on the part of the ruling parties.

➢ There is also the problem of inadequate infrastructure. A successful plan implementation largely depends on the effectiveness of the services rendered by the country's public physical infrastructures such as roads, railways, ports and shipping line and airways. Unfortunately, the Nigerian transport system is characterized by poor co-ordination, disinvestments, operational deficits, lack of maintenance, inadequate utilization of human and natural resources and poor management and operational control.

➢ Perhaps, the most intractable constraint achieving the objectives of Nigerian third national development plan is the one posed by inadequate organizational resources. Lack of adequate organizational resources is affected in shortages of certain cadre of manpower, poor organizational co-ordination and the inability of organization structures to adapt to the change needs of the economy. These constitute constraints to plan implementation because without the necessary manpower, the execution of the plan becomes difficult if not impossible.

➢ There is also the problem of outmoded technology particularly with regards to agriculture. Although Nigeria is an agricultural economy, the bulk of agricultural production is done by peasant farmers whose average land holdings are between 3-7 acres. The machinery used for production consists mainly of hoes, cutlasses and other primitive hand tools. Given the outmoded farming technology the area under cultivation represents only 11 to 16 percent of the land potentially suitable for agriculture. Thus, outmoded technology results in under-utilization of land and labour resources.

Chapter Nine

COMMUNITY DEVELOPMENT RESOURCES

9.1 DEFINITION OF RESOURCES

The term resources are used in many contexts. It is often understood to mean money; however, in the context of community development it may mean far more than that. They include money, skills, time contributions and services of humans, equipment and materials. Thus, resources are materials, finance, men and women, means, and time that are used and mobilized to meet the objectives of groups and communities. Resources are crucial to effective community development. While the involvement of community activists and volunteers are unpaid. The process of community development has to be supported by funding, staffing, information and a range of other resources. It is important that these resources are accessible and allocated on a basis that is secure, equitable and transparent.

9.1.1 Community Development Resources

Resources are the financial and non-financial supplies that help to fulfill the needs of the community. Here, Community development resources includes; natural, human, financial and infrastructure resources.

Natural Resources: Natural resources are all the things that nature provides. Oftentimes, community development focuses on the natural resource industry that extracts the natural resources, creating jobs and wealth but, if not managed properly, may not be sustainable over time. Part of effective community development is to be good stewards of the land and maintain a healthy balance between the environmental, economic and social undertakings in the community. Natural resources comprises of features such as:

- Land, air and water;
- Minerals and surface/subsurface metals and ores;
- Oil, gas and petroleum;
- Trees and other plants;
- Wildlife; and
- The standards, legislation and policies relating to the above.

Human Resources: Human resources in this sense means the skilled, semi-skilled and unskilled labour force required to implement a plan. Human resources are all about people. People who are at the heart of all community matters and, as such, they are critical to success. But just having people involved is not enough. In community development, it is important to have the right people for the right jobs with the right skills, knowledge and abilities. This is not an easy matter. As often we are not sure who should be doing what or what the required skills are, or where to get the necessary skills if they are missing. Placing people in the right roles and building skills or developing human capacity is called human resource development. Occasionally, it is referred to as building or increasing social capital. Either way, it acknowledges the value of people and their talents and recognizes that this type of development is as important as natural resource development. Unlike many of the natural resources on the planet, people are renewable and should be treated as the most valuable resource in a community. Human resources comprises of features such as:

- Healthy families and lifestyles;
- Skills building, education and training;
- Career planning and employment;
- Effective and legal hiring practices;
- Workers compensation and pensions; and
- Human rights and labour laws.

Financial Resources: The term financial resource is well understood. We know that it means money and it often implies having the ability to acquire it. What gets complicated is how to locate and successfully attract the type and amount of financial resources to community development initiatives. Just like having the right people doing the right jobs, it is important to have the right money at the right time. Traditionally, community development is funded (in part or in total) through economic development channels, taxes or government grants. This leaves little power or control in the hands of the people who want or need to do things that are not on the government or private sector agenda. Fundraising and the seeking of grants have become full-time jobs for many organizations and groups involved in community service and development. Financial resources comprises of features such as:

- Fundraising and grant-seeking;
- Banks and other financial institutions;
- Community loan funds and lending circles;

- Access to capital and investment funding;
- Government loans and programme funds;
- Cooperatives and other forms of investment; and
- Policies and guidelines related to finance lending and reporting.

Infrastructural Resources: Infrastructure is part of the resources needed to be effective in community development and it includes obvious features such as:

- Physical building and structures;
- Transportation and access;
- Communication systems; and
- Electrical, hydro, sewage, garbage and heating.

However, infrastructure also refers to the political systems and leadership needed to support a community, as well as the policies, standards and laws established in the community. Without infrastructure there would be no physical community. When considering resourcing a community development initiative it is important to consider what infrastructure is required, what the relationship is to what currently exists and whether or not there are policies or existing support systems to which contact or adherence are required. A community development undertaking often has its own infrastructure, such as leadership or a physical building, but it should exist within a healthy relationship to that which exists.

9.1.2 Classification of Resources
Table 9.1: Resources Categorized by their Physical Traits and Characteristics

Types of Resources	Examples of Resources Available in the Local Area	Examples of Resources that are not Available or that are Difficult to Acquire in the Local Area
a) Human Resource (Women and Men)	Educated (literate) women and men, carpenter, mason, semi-skilled labours.	Engineer, Overseer, Doctor, Trained men and women.
b) Natural Resource	Forests, rivers, land, stone, etc., (depends on the area).	Water, arable land, etc. (depends on the area).
c) Physical Resource	Plough, spade, table, pick.	Polythene pipes, GI pipes, corrugated sheet, and cement.
d) Financial Resource	Local funds.	External funds.

2. Resources Categorized by Geographic Location

a) Local (community level) resource	Community itself, CBOs, local forests, rivers, land, stone, locally made equipment, etc.	Time contribution, money, and technical services.
b) Resources outside the community	National and international organizations working in the community, or with programmes in that area available to the local community.	National and international organizations and resources located outside local area.

Source: Author's Field Survey Data (2012).

Every community, however rural, isolated, or poor, has resources within it. When those resources, or assets, are invested to create new resources, they become capital (Flora, Flora & Fey, 2004). According to the Community Capitals Framework, capitals can be divided into two main groups the 'human or intangible' and the 'material or tangible' factors. The seven capitals in Community Capitals Framework (CCF) are examined in the table 9.2 below:

The seven capitals in community capitals framework (CCF)
Table 9:2

Human/Intangible Factors	Definition
Social Capital	Social capital is made up of the interactions among groups and individuals such as networks and the norms and trust that facilitate cooperation for mutual support. It includes the subset of spiritual capital, which is the aspect of social capital linked with religion or spirituality (Carnegie Commission, 2007).
Political Capital	Political capital is the ability of a community to influence the distribution and use of resources (Carnegie Commission, 2007). It is also the capacity to change the structures of power, the ability to inspire policy, and the collective organization to hold political representatives to account.
Cultural Capital	Cultural capital is the multi-layered world-views and cultural norms/ innovations, which inform how we see and interpret the world, our sense of place and belonging, and the future potential we imagine for ourselves.
Human Capital	Human capital refers to the characteristics of 'individuals who contribute towards their ability to earn a living, strengthen community, and contribute

	to community organizations, to their families and to self-improvement' (Flora, Flora & Fey, 2004). The components of human capital includes the emotional, spiritual, aesthetic, and musical intelligences and skills present in people; the interpersonal skills, values and leadership capacity of individuals; the skills, education, experience, and knowledge of the community; and the self-esteem and confidence and capacity to contribute to the wider community.

Material/Tangible Factors:	Definition
Natural Capital	Natural capital can be landscape and any stock or flow of energy and materials that produces goods and services. Natural capital includes both renewable and nonrenewable material resources (Carnegie Commission, 2007).
Financial Capital	The incomes, savings, credit and loans, which facilitate investment into other assets—adding value (in formal and complementary currencies). However, when money is spent on consumption, it is not capital but becomes capital when oriented to create other capitals.
Built Capital	Built capital refers to the permanent physical installations and facilities supporting activities in a community. It includes transportation networks, communication systems, utilities, protective services, education and health facilities, and public and commercial buildings. Built capital also includes any fixed assets which facilitate the livelihood or well-being of a community (Carnegie Commission, 2007).

Source: *Carnegie UK Trust (2009) What Are Asset-Based Approaches to Community Development? International Association for Community Development (IACD) November 2009* www.carnegieuktrust.org.uk

9.1.3 Importance of Resource Mobilization

Resource mobilization is the process of identifying and obtaining resources for the community. Communities need both financial and non-financial resources. Resource mobilization is essential for the existence of a healthy, strong and sustainable community. A community cannot exist without resources. They are needed to provide continuity and stability to the community and its work. A community needs resources in order to: carry out its ongoing work, aimed at achieving its mission and goals; undertake new work or initiatives; maintain and increase linkages with government, donor agencies, individuals, private organizations, and other communities. They also needs resources for funding community and develop various aspects of the community. For instance, it helps to;

- develop into a learning community;
- maximize community knowledge and skills;
- develop leadership capacity;
- increase gender awareness and skills within the community; improve leadership capabilities, including the ability to manage resources (e.g., strategic management of excess resources, ability to carry out cost-benefit analyses, ability to develop resource generation schemes, diversification of resource sources, decrease in dependence on foreign donors, etc.).

9.2   MANPOWER DEVELOPMENT
9.2.1   Definition of Manpower Development
There are a number of factors that contribute to the success of any community development, these factors include: capital, equipment, manpower, etc. All these factors are important but the most significant factor is the human factor. Since it is the people who will put the other resources to work, it should be viewed as such by community by giving it due attention in order to achieve its developmental goals and objectives. Manpower development is a process of intellectual and emotional achievement through providing the means by which people can grow on their tasks in the community. It relates to series of activities, which a community would embark upon to improve its development project. Manpower development is important in any discussion of strategic human resources management. These emphasis on manpower and development is influenced by the belief that it is now desirable to focus more attention on areas which in the past has been relatively neglected because every community regardless of its size must provide for the needs, interest and desire of its individual within the work environment if it is to earn loyalty, dedication, involvement and commitment necessary to thrive effectively.

Specifically, Caroline and Charles (1997) argued that manpower development involves activities that enable people to comfortably and conveniently perform community tasks. The human resource is the single most important resource any community has. This means that without manpower no community development or establishment can function. In essence, human effort is greatly desirable and crucial in achieving the goals and objectives of the community. They are planned activities which focus on increasing and enlarging the capabilities, improving the technical and conceptual skills of individuals so that they can posses the necessary abilities to handle complex situations and better perform their task. The central idea underlying manpower development in any community, is how best to keep members current, vibrant and versatile so that they can continuously perform their roles effectively in this age of rapid socio-economic, political, scientific and technological changes and globalization.

Manpower development is critical to any community that wants to continue to grow and remain effective in its development. Manpower development is a process that seeks to optimize the community's usage of its human resources. It requires an integrated approach that addresses multidimensional aspects of community development, ranging from enhancing technical and interpersonal skills to creative thinking and leadership. Communities with high productivity levels have made manpower development an integral part of their development culture. The development of manpower could be viewed as a concept which is generic because of its focus on turning out human resource that is needed for the development of the community (Drucker 1999). Of all the factors of production, human resources are regarded as the most difficult to manage. This difficulty has been traced to the fact that human beings are "thinking beings" with emotions, sentiments and attitudes which are rather complex. As a result, development of manpower views man as the most important asset in the society (Chalofsky and Reinhart 1988; Ekpo 1989; Drucker 1999; Muchinsky 2000). A typical example of the manifestation of this concept could be viewed from the perspective of the Nigerian educational system which is anchored on the 6-3-3-4 system which sought to address the manpower need of the country through mechanisms geared towards developing manpower that would boast the nation's socio-economic and technological advancement (FGN, 1998).

Thus, manpower planning is the development of strategies that match the supply of labourers to the number of jobs available at a community, state, regional or national level. Most writers have concerned themselves essentially with putting forward arguments for and/or against the very idea of manpower planning and development in community. Some other writers have emphasized the need for manpower planning and how to ensure increased efficiency and productivity through the use of manpower plans and development programmes. Manpower Planning which is also called Human Resource Planning consists of putting right number of people, right kind of people at the right place, right time, doing the right jobs for which they are suited for the achievement of goals of the community development. Olusola (1992:68) defined manpower planning or human resource planning as a possible tool for determining and assuring that a community will have, adequate number of skilled and experienced persons available at the right time and place performing tasks which meet the needs of the community and which provides satisfaction for the individuals involved. This approach goes beyond mere consideration of supply but is not specific on what other aspects of objectives manpower hinges on. It also comes with the impression that the only concrete matter it deals with is future supply of manpower. Ibekwe (1984:19) asserted that human resources of a community are collectively known as manpower which could be unskilled, skilled, supervisory functions and it is aimed at ensuring that the right person is available for the job at the right time. Manpower planning is an ongoing process (integrated approach), not a once and for all phenomenon. Its process involves interrelated activities and the plan must continue to be modified to meet prevailing circumstances. While, manpower management is the practice of controlling the quality and levels of manpower within a community or economy so that available manpower is used efficiently and economically.

Since the early 1960, the human factor of production or manpower as it is alternatively called, has been recognized as the most critical resource of the factors without which an effective utilization of all other factors remain a dream. Although, it might be tempting to attach more importance to the availability of physical resource such as capital and equipment undermining that they are mere passive factors of production, which depend on human intellectual which is the active agent to exploit them in order to achieve the objective of development. Thus, the human factor (manpower) is the main stay of the community or an organization. In other words, the success of any community development project or programme depends on the ability and expertise of those who handles it both at the managerial and lower levels of operation, such abilities and expertise usually stems from the knowledge they possess and training received. The main objective of embarking on community project is to improve the standard of living of the people and to achieve this development goal; adequate manpower planning and development programmes should be put in place to enhance performance.

9.2.2 The Need for Manpower Planning and Development

Drucker (1980:130) is of the opinion that the most important factor underlying manpower planning and development is the understanding of human behaviour and the resulting social process. This goes to buttress how environmental influence affects the behaviour of workers which in turn affects the productivity. This is even more important when talking about adequate manpower and the right type of individual especially in a community where technical and managerial skills are few. According to him, the days of unsystematic and intuitive improvement in the use of manpower has come to a close. He sees manpower planning as part of development, which should not be seen in isolation but in the context of the growth of the community. It covers more than simple planning of the manpower requirement of community since it hinges on all aspects of the development and concerned with the future. Manpower planning and development has maintained its imperatives for several reasons:

➢ A growing awareness of the need to look into the future.
➢ A desire to exercise control over as many variables as possible which influence development success or failure.
➢ The development of techniques which make such planning possible.
➢ To achieve more effective and efficient use of community members / human resources.
➢ It helps the community to realize the importance of manpower management which ultimately helps in the stability of a concern.
➢ It also helps to identify the available talents in a community and accordingly, training programmes can be chalked out to develop those talents.
➢ Reduction in labour cost—Manpower development ensures recruitment and maintenance of better developed manpower resource which results in reduced manpower costs. Forecasting of long-term manpower needs to help the community to forecast the compensation costs involved.
➢ To achieve a higher rate of satisfied and better developed community.
➢ Ensure community is responsive to changes in environment.

9.2.3 The Relevance of Manpower Development in Nigeria

a) **Economic Development:** The relevance of manpower development in Nigeria could be situated vis-à-vis economic development. This is because manpower development captures the actual meaning of development in that it is people centred (World Bank 1991;

Grawboski and Shields 1996). In addition, it involves the building of capacity and harnessing the State's human resources which constitute a sine-qua-non for development. The above advantage was vividly conceptualized by Harbison (1973) when he stated that: Human resources constitute the ultimate basis for wealth of nations, capital and natural resources are passive factors of production; human beings are the active agents who accumulate capital, exploit natural resources, build social, economic and political organizations, and carry forward national development. Clearly, a country which is unable to develop the skills and knowledge of its people and to utilize them effectively in the national economy will be unable to develop anything else.

b) **Political Stability:** There is no doubt that a country which fails to adequately develop her manpower would be doing so at the expense of her socio-economic and political stability. In the aspect of political stability, Omodia (2004) stressed the dysfunctional use of the nation's human resources among the youths in propelling political instability when he stated that: ...there has been a situation in which the Nigerian youths especially, those of poor family background were used as tools for disrupting the political democratic system through rigging, thuggery and ethnic conflicts. These factors of rigging, thuggery in addition to economic mismanagement, personal ambition or selfishness among others, were the factors that terminated the First and Second Republic. Thus, manpower development could help the youths in the development of self and in improving the quality of their political participation.

c) **Poverty Alleviation:** It has been argued that effective poverty alleviation scheme must involve the development and utilization of local resource including human for solving local problems (Robb 2000; Omodia 2005). Thus, manpower development is central to solving the present problem of poverty in Nigeria.

9.2.4   Problems of Manpower Development in Nigeria
1) **Colonial Experience:** There have been several arguments regarding the distortions in manpower development of national growth in Nigeria as a result of colonialism which was fashioned towards economic exploitation (Ekpo 1989; Ake 2001; Dauda 2003). It could be recalled Rural Manpower Development and Utilization in Nigeria that the advent of colonialism led to the integration of the

Nigerian economy into the World Capitalist System thereby placing minimum premium on labour when compared to other factors of production. This poor performance of indigenous labour by the colonial government no doubt has persisted in the post-colonial Nigerian State. As a result, this problem account for the lack of adequate attention given to labour as a critical part of the production process in Nigeria.

2) **Poor Political Leadership:** Closely related to the problem of colonial experience as a problem of manpower development in Nigeria is poor political leadership which is further deepening the problem of manpower development in Nigeria. This factor has manifested itself in poor funding of education over the years (Baikie 2002), disparity or class in manpower development between children of the rich and the poor (Omodia 2006).

3) **Poor Manpower Planning:** This problem is associated with the poor data base that is needed for manpower planning in Nigeria both in the rural and urban centres. This problem no doubt constitutes a major hindrance on effective manpower development in Nigeria (Baikie 2002; Oku 2003).

9.2.5   Options for Effective Manpower Development in Nigeria

The options for effective manpower development in Nigeria could be viewed from two basic perspectives:

1. The option of an enhanced regulatory capability on the part of government for effective enforcement of manpower policies. This is quite indispensable based on the need to ensure quality manpower development irrespective of sex, class, and ethnic affiliation to mention but a few. This point could best be appreciated considering the liberal nature of most government policies which tend to snowball into elitist benefit in terms of policy outcome.

2. The need for government to be persuasive in making organizations embraces well designed policies at improving the development of manpower in Nigeria. This could be done both internally and externally. Internally, organizations should be made to see reasons why a careful manpower development plan should form part of their plans and objectives for the financial year. As a matter of fact, the success of organizations should not only be measured in terms of the magnitude of profit through the adoption of outdated personnel administration technique, but, basically on the contribution of the

organization in enlarging the confidence of its workers through manpower development. The external factor involves the contribution of organizations to the development of manpower through financial support meant to boost adult education, vocational education, and specialized research institutes to mention but a few.

Chapter Ten

FUNDING OF RURAL AND COMMUNITY DEVELOPMENT

10.1 FUNDING OF RURAL AND COMMUNITY DEVELOPMENT

Obtaining financial resources can be a major challenge for a community development initiative. This is particularly true when you are beginning the process. As you move to concrete action it usually becomes easier to find and secure funding from local financial institutions, investors, government programmes, foundations and private sector sponsors, or from community members themselves. The key to finding financial support is to be able to clearly identify what you want to do, why you want to do it, and the benefits that will result from your action.

There is no doubt that starting a grass-roots community development activity can be a challenge. Remember that the first steps of the community development process do not need to be cost-intensive. What they do require is a committed and creative group of community members, or organizations, to get things started. If your community development group is informal, it will be important to find an organization within the community that will agree to act as your sponsor for funding requests. Many funders, due to their regulations or tax laws, are unable to give funds to a group of individuals who are not formally organized.

Finding financial support is only the beginning of the resource issue. Good financial management is also essential for maintaining the credibility of your community development effort. You not only want to manage the money wisely, but you also want to get the maximum value or benefit from the resources that are available. Take care to:
- make sound financial decisions,
- meet funding agencies' requirements for record-keeping,
- undertake a monthly assessment of your financial situation, and
- be open about the resources you have and how you are using them.

Financing a community development initiative occasionally involves a variety of financial vehicles or sources of funds. Some groups require less money and can cover the costs through traditional fundraising. Others are of a larger scale and may require bank loans, government grants or some sort of external funding assistance. Community development often reaches a point where generating ongoing revenue or creating a sustainable resource fund becomes important or even a necessity. It can also happen that, as a result of a community development initiative, revenue or resources are generated and this, in and of itself, is the community development activity.

10.2   SOURCES OF FUNDING IN RURAL AND COMMUNITY DEVELOPMENT IN NIGERIA

It is one thing to prepare a plan for community development projects, and it is quite another to execute the projects. Four most important determinants of success or failure of a plan are availability of human and financial, natural and physical resources and prudent management and utilization of these resources. The funding of community development are available from the following sources if properly explored and tapped.

Contribution

The people of a community embarking on community development programme of all types owe it a duty to contribute their quota financially to the execution of the programmes. Financial contribution of the people can take one of many forms such as development levy on flat rate basis for all male and female adults; development levy in accordance with level of income of individuals or voluntary contribution according to individual wish or capability. The community may launch an Appeal Fund. Some members of the community both home and abroad may contribute materials and equipment in place of cash.

Donations

A donation is a gift given by physical or legal persons, typically for charitable purposes and/or to benefit a course. A donation may take various forms, including cash offering, services, new or used goods including, clothing, toys, foods and vehicles. It also may consist of emergency, relief or humanitarian aid items, development aid support, and can also relate to medical care or needs i.e. blood or organs for transplant. Donations are given without return consideration. In some cases, rather than compulsory levies and contributions, wealthy benevolent individuals in the community may decide to offer free-will gift as donations to engender development activities of the community. Some donations are made open while some others are made anonymous. In some communities, individuals, groups and NGOs both national and international have donated money, built schools, churches, health centre, post office, recreational centres, town halls, scholarships and other projects in their various communities.

Loans
These are incomes generated by borrowing from private individuals or from foreign countries to finance projects. The local government in Nigeria was established for the purpose of rendering services and supplying amenities to the people in both rural and urban areas according to the document establishing the local government reforms 1976. Federal government cannot perform all the activities of the rural areas by themselves, but this can only be done by the people elected for that, it does not prevent or stop the Federal government from implementing their roles by providing all the social amenities such as construction of roads, provision of pipe–borne waters, hospitals, good education for the youths, stadium, electricity and museum etc. All these are not really independent because they require government authorization before they can be collected. A typical example of NGOs that get involved in assisting rural dwellers particularly, the women group, is known as Country Women Association of Nigeria (COWAN) and Nigerian Agricultural, Rural Development and Cooperative Bank (NARDCB). The bank was established for the purpose of giving loans to farmers to enable them accomplishe their farming activities. However, lack of record keeping by the farmers often makes it difficult for them to be aided with such loans. Example here, IFAD provides loans to its developing Member States on highly concessional, intermediate and ordinary terms for approved projects and programmes. Lending terms and conditions vary according to the borrower's per capita GNI.

Grants
These are income received in form of aid from other countries or from international organizations like the World Bank, IMF etc. Within a country, government may also receive grant from another government e.g. Local government council receives grants from Federal and State government. However, in the past, substantial (foreign) grants were received from organizations like the United Nations Educational Scientific and Cultural Organization (UNESCO), the United Nations Development Programme (UNDP), the Ford Foundation, the Rockefeller Foundation, the Carnegie Foundation, Organizations such as MacArthur Foundation, the Commonwealth of Learning (COL), British Council, and the United States

Agency for International Development (USAID), etc., are quite notable. It is important to note too that most of the established Non-Governmental Organizations (NGOs) in Nigeria and around the globe equally contribute substantially to community development in Nigeria. Another example in Nigeria is IFAD. IFAD provides grants to institutions and organizations in support of activities to strengthen the technical and institutional capacities linked to agricultural and rural development. Grants are limited to 10% of the combined loan and grant programme. IFAD has financed eight programmes and projects in Nigeria since 1985, with a total loan commitment of US$144.3 million. All programmes and projects have addressed the livelihood needs of rural poor people, including smallholders, rural small businesses, poor fishing communities, young people, landless people and women.

Commercial Ventures
Commercial ventures which are different kinds are being explored by the local communities to generate additional funds. These ventures include amongst others: Built up shops for rent, Market, Motor Park dues and Toll gate fees, Cybercafés, Launderettes, Transportation services, Renting of halls in idle time, Bookshops, Catering services etc. All these and more could generate financial resources needed for community development. However, one problem with this kind of commercial ventures is their management. According to Obikeze (2002), some people see them as places where they could enrich themselves to the detriment of the community. Such levity and disregard lead to the demise of such ventures and this does not augur well for the community.

Local, State and Federal Government
One effective way of encouraging communities to take part in their own development is through financial contributions to execute projects. Sometimes, Local, State and Federal governments place emphasis on the development of certain services, infrastructure or amenities like road, agriculture, hospitals, schools, security among others. In that case, communities too are requested to pay more attention to those areas in their development plans or annual budget. The higher a community lays emphasis on those priority areas, the greater financial contribution it receives from the Local, State and Federal governments. Farmers, in some States of the Federation, are assisted by their various governments, sometimes in form of subsidy, direct cash or inputs. Some Local and State governments have performed well in this respect. Others have failed to meet up with their promises. They either fail to contribute at all or waste

too much time before their widow's mite goes to the various communities. Worse still, some Local and State governments deny some communities such financial contribution for political reasons.

Cooperative Savings Group (Thrift Society)

Cooperative savings group or thrift society has become a veritable instrument of fostering development in our communities. When people come together to form a group and in the process pool their resources together from where loans are granted to members, it is referred to as cooperative savings group. In some parts of Nigeria, it is known as "Ajo" or "Esusu". Cooperative savings group is a non-institutional source of credit and it thrives more in rural areas than institutional sources (Adegeye, et. al. 1985). This is attributed to the inability of rural dwellers to satisfy the collateral security required by the institutional sources. It has also, been reported that out of the 83 percent of those who fund their farming activities through personal savings, 33 percent subscribe to cooperative savings group.

Donor Agencies and Non-Governmental Organization (NGOs)

This is another essential tool of promoting development in our communities. Big firms, companies and investors such as Julius Berger, Chevron, etc. do contribute to community development ventures in Nigeria. The organizations such as Rotary Club and Lion Club also donate money, buildings, farming tools etc. to the Nigerian communities. For instance, some donor agencies and NGOs give loans and credit to farmers at low interest or interest free rates. Under early aid efforts, donors funded projects that extended the influence of the donor; considered poverty as a destabilizing force for globalization; international aid to reduce poverty funding was seen as a stabilizing force; made funding available for market expansion; sought to foster political reform and democracy; sought to reduce migration pressure in developed countries. Much of the funding/aid provided using the above approaches was ineffective, and the level of sustainability was low. In response, donors are: moving to policy based funding – donors are interested in supporting policies that correspond to the perceived needs of the recipient country; moving to unified funding frameworks and local government ownership; large donor agencies and consortiums of donors are moving to harmonize aid/funding packages that stress the importance of local government ownership of projects and initiatives funded with donor support; asking governments in receipt of international funding to be responsible and accountable; promoting multi-actor partnerships between government, business and civil society; recognizing gender and poverty as determinants of health, stability and good governance.

Chapter Eleven

LEADERSHIP IN RURAL AND COMMUNITY DEVELOPMENT

11.1 MEANING OF LEADERS AND LEADERSHIP
11.1.1 What is leadership?

Leadership is and has been described as the "process of social influence in which one person can enlist the aid and support of others in the accomplishment of a common task. According to Alan Keith of Genentech as quoted by (Wikipedia 2009) "Leadership is ultimately about creating a way for people to contribute to making something extraordinary happen." Leadership is a process by which a person influences others to accomplish an objective and directs the community in a way that makes it more cohesive and coherent. Leaders carry out this process by applying their leadership attributes, such as beliefs, values, ethics, character, knowledge, and skills. Although your position as a manager, supervisor, leader, etc. gives you the authority to accomplish certain tasks and objectives in the organization or community, this power does not make you a leader, it simply makes you the boss. Leadership differs in that because it makes the followers want to achieve high goals, rather than simply bossing people around. Leadership is defined as the ability to lead; i.e. the ability to guide, to direct or influence people. It also refers to the position or office of leader (Encarta, 2009). Leadership is defined as the process whereby an individual directs, guides, influences or controls the thoughts, feelings or behaviour of other human beings. It is essentially a group phenomenon and occurs in a situation calling for interaction between a group of people, the leader or leaders, the problem or task and its possible solution. It is a function of personality and there can be no leadership without follower-ship. From the foregoing, some key elements of leadership could be highlighted:

- Leading takes place in a social setting among people
- No leader without follower[s]
- Leadership is a group attribute
- Leader's ideas and action influence the thoughts and behaviours of others
- Implies role-playing for some time
- Leading roles must be performed repeatedly under varying conditions.

Furthermore, Leadership is the process by which an individual directs, guides, influences or controls the thoughts, feelings or behaviour of others. Leadership is the process of leading, but a leader is one who leads. Leadership is a group phenomenon arising by interaction among members of the group. It is the process by which one member of the group assumes responsibility for identifying a group problem that requires solution, a group task that needs to be performed and the ways to solve the problem or achieve the task. Leadership is a personality attribute which is exhibited and reciprocated in a group. There is no leadership without followership. The followers must move, by a perceptible degree in the direction indicated by the leader. Leadership requires some higher levels of knowledge on the subject-matter, the alternative means of addressing the issues at hand and a better picture of the final outcome of the chosen course of action. It is a process of mutual stimulation that allows an effective interplay of individual differences, vested interests, communication and social control in the pursuit of a common course.

11.1.2 Definition of a Leader
A leader can be a person who initiates interaction with other members of the group; a person who initiates interaction with others more frequently than anybody else in the group; a person who moves the group towards attaining its goals. A leader is adopted as: a vital, integral individual who operates within the group to promote, stimulate, guide, or otherwise influence members to action (Chitambar, 1973). The Encarta Dictionary (2009) describes a leader as:
1. Somebody whom people follow; somebody who directs and guides others;
2. Somebody in the lead: someone in front of others as in a procession.
3. Somebody in charge of others as in the head of a nation, political party, legislative body or military unit.

In simple terms, a leader is one who leads or goes first. In other words, a leader is the person who sees the goal ahead of others in the group, then plans and enlists the support of others to achieve the goal. In any given situation, the leader is the one who influences the thoughts and actions of others in his group or community. The concept of a leader is therefore one of role-playing. That is, performing certain roles that would be perceived by others as a leading role. It is also important that one cannot be a leader in isolation. A leader can only emerge in a group. There must be followers to identify with and be influenced by a leader.

11.1.3 Basic Elements of Leadership Relationships

If leadership is the act of leading others towards achieving a common goal, then, four basic elements could be identified: the leader, the followers, the situation, and the task.

- **The Leader:** This implies a role relationship with others in the group and interaction over a period of time within which the leader repeatedly performs functions and acts of leadership in the group. Such acts may be shared with other group members; however, the buck stops at the leader's table.

- **The Followers:** Followers also have a role to play under the direction of the leader. Followers are not mere aggregation, but people in constant active interaction in direction toward desired goals.

- **The Situation:** It refers to a set of values and attitudes that have to be faced by the group members, wherein activity for achievement of those goals has to be planned and implemented (Chitambar, 1973). The situation includes:
  - ✓ Interpersonal relationships within the group
  - ✓ Characteristics of the group as a unit
  - ✓ Characteristics of the culture within which the group exists and from which members are drawn
  - ✓ Physical conditions within which the group is to act and
  - ✓ The perceptual representation of these elements and the attitudes and values held by the members, within the group and among themselves.

- **The Task:** The task defines the activities which are to be performed in common movement and achievement of desired goals by the group. The task sets varying demands and requirements for leadership and hence their nature is of importance and significance to the motivation of leaders.

11.2 QUALITIES OF EFFECTIVE LEADERSHIP

Honesty: The sign of a good leader is the honesty towards his/her work and followers. A leader should be very honest to himself as well as to the members of the association. A leader should not loose his integrity, whatever be the circumstances, because a leader will not be considered reliable and worth following, if he/she looses honesty.

Confidence: Confidence should exude in every word said and in everything done by a leader. He should have the confidence to manage people and show them the right path, whenever they seek guidance. People who see panic or uncertainty in the eyes of their leader won't consider him/her worth depending upon, in the time of crisis. A good leader always keeps a cool head in times of crises and finds solutions to get everybody out of any difficult situation.

Patience: If you want to be known as a good leader, it is very important to be patient. Be cool, calm and collected. Do not panic or loose your temper when the situation is nerve-wracking. A good leader considers crisis, emotions and tricky situations a part of his journey and never looses his composure.

Focus: To become a good leader, one should always remain steadfast to the goal, without wasting time in checking for the possibility of hindrances that might creep in. If you find any obstacles in this process, consider it as your moral responsibility to solve them and find better ways to make progress towards the target.

Dedication: People will respond more openly to a leader who is dedicated towards his/her work and constantly works for the betterment of the people as well as the community at large. He/she should be zealous about the community development and prove his/herself as a source of inspiration for the people around him/her.

Consistency: Consistency is an important leadership quality. Displaying inconsistency will confound others. A leader should remember that he is part of the team, therefore, should be stable before expecting consistency from others.

Motivate Others: A good leader should always encourage his/her members and congratulate them for all their achievements, whether small or big. This will create a healthy environment in workplace, which will in turn motivate members to give their best performance every time they are assigned a task.

Effective Communication: A good leader should be able to reach the people around him/her effectively. Good communication skills are, in fact, key to become a good leader.
Tolerance: A leader should be tolerant of uncertainty and should always remain tranquil, composed and persistent to his/her goals.

Enthusiasm: A good leader is always enthusiastic about the cause of the problem. He/she must have the capability to see what is good or bad for the people in the long run. He/she approaches a problem in a holistic manner and never believes he is different from his people and subject.

Discipline: A leader believes in discipline. He/she follows an orderly manner and routine but still he/she is tolerant. He/she takes decision keeping emotions and personal matters aside. Skillfully, he/she looks each and every aspects of the situation before arriving to any decision and never loses his/her temper in difficult situations. He/she should think positively in each and every situation. A great leader is proactive and committed to excellence. He always maintains high standard and acts as an idol for his/her followers. His/her personal and public life both are remarkable and stain free. A good leader is the one who can give people voice and direction.

11.3   PRINCIPLES OF LEADERSHIP

i.   Know yourself and seek self-improvement - In order to know yourself, you have to understand your endowed attributes. Seeking self-improvement means continually strengthening your leadership attributes. This can be accomplished through self-study, formal classes, reflection, and interacting with others.

ii.   Be technically proficient - As a leader, you must know your job and have a solid familiarity with your community's tasks.

iii. Seek responsibility and take responsibility for your actions - Search for ways to guide your community to new heights. And when things go wrong, they always do sooner or later -- do not blame others. Analyze the situation, take corrective action, and move on to the next challenge.

iv.   Make sound and timely decisions - Use good problem solving, decision making, and planning tools.

v.   Set the example - Be a good role model for your followers. They must not only hear what they are expected to do, but also see. We must become the change we want to see - Mahatma Gandhi.

vi.   Know your people and look out for their well-being - Know human nature and the importance of sincerely caring for your community members.

vii. Keep your members informed - Know how to communicate with not only them, but also patron, advisers and other key people.

viii. Develop a sense of responsibility in your followers - Help to develop good character traits that will help them develop professional responsibilities.

ix.   Ensure that tasks are understood, supervised, and accomplished – Communication is the key to this responsibility.
x.   Train as a team - You should see your members as one and also work as a team.

11.4   CHARACTERISTICS OF LEADERS

Regardless of whether an individual is born with the ability to lead or the skills are developed, there are certain traits leaders will be expected to reflect. These characteristics are as follows:

1.   **Trustworthiness:** A leader cannot exist if he or she does not enjoy the trust of the people being led. The leader must be considered of being of high integrity and honesty which makes him/her remarkable such that the people trust they would be represented well even in their absence. Community members believe what he/she says to the extent that even when they are yet to perceive the motive, they believe the leader to be doing whatever in their interest. A good leader practices what he/she preaches, thus earning the right to lead others and responsibility to them. To the contrary erodes trust. Trustworthiness is the source of the real authority, based on the trust of other people.

2.   **Enthusiasm:** Enthusiasm is an important element of leadership which energizes group members. The true leader is passionate and dedicated about what is to be done and encourages others to move to accomplish the task. Also, a real leader should not be scared to perform hard work, offering a good example to his or her followers. A leader exhibits the 'we can do it spirit' and so 'let's go and take the land'. The biblical examples of Joshua and Caleb reflect this attribute that launched them into leadership position.

3.   **Confidence:** A true leader must be confident in his role and position towards others. The result will be a trustful team that looks up to the leader, following his or her orders and performing the tasks well. The team members will be highly motivated to do a good job when there are no traces of doubt in the steps the leader is recommending. Confidence however, is based on pre-knowledge, fore-sight or pre-conceived vision of the on-going effort.

4.   **Orderliness:** A good leader must be orderly in his/her approach to things. Fluctuation in decisions and work should be avoided. As

much as possible, the leader should try to maintain good order towards work and purpose. This gives the team more confidence and positive thinking. In times of uncertainty and stress, the leader must prove to be orderly and able to work towards the final purpose.

5. **Calmness:** Many challenges may rise along the way and the leader must treat them equally, inspiring others not to let bad influences overcome them. Any crises, any emotions must find the leader calm, composed and steadfast to the main purpose. Others may lose their temper but the leader must keep his/hers. The one that succeeds to keep a cool head in times of pressure is a great leader.

6. **Analytic mind:** A true leader must possess ability to think analytically. He/she should be able to consider the many facets of the problem that needs to be dealt with. While keeping the goal in focus, the leader is able to analyze the matter, by breaking it into parts meant to be inspected and concluded in logical manner. An analytic mind is needed when progress must be made by dealing with every step in particular.

7. **Ambition:** Any good leader should not settle for second best. The focus should be on being the best. Success is a matter of who wins the top. If you settle for less, it implies that you may even attain lesser. A true leader will always have high standards and he or she will strive for excellence in every aspect. The seven qualities described above are essential for a good leader. They can be personal traits, but they can also be developed and strengthened. But, whether these characteristics are natural or developed, a great leader will always work to make the best of these traits and to achieve excellence. Other leadership traits that help a leader to be more effective include competence, honesty, forward looking, inspiring and enjoying good health. Leaders that are open, intelligent, broad-minded, fair-minded and straightforward will impact more on the group members and move them better towards achieving a common goal. It should be noted that developing good leadership skills requires practice and it takes time.

There are certain qualities that are exhibited by an individual that make him or her leader among peers or in a community. The peers or other members of the community need to identify these qualities before conferring the status of a leader on such a person.

- A leader must have the ability to influence others. This may be influenced by a person's personal characteristics such as height, handsomeness or a special appeal that radiates around the individual. It may be an ability for fluent speech that moves a crowd or being wealthy or generous; having known connections with external bodies or occupying a known official position. In many rural areas, age, being married, honesty, humility and industry are highly valued qualities that leaders are expected to have. For instance, late Chief M. K. O. Abiola has been characterized as a leader because of his generosity. He is acclaimed to donate part of his wealth to both Muslim and Christian organizations despite his being a strong Muslim.
- A leader must have the ability to identify with the group. This quality requires some level of empathy or placing oneself in the other's position; having consideration for the feeling of others; being emotionally stable, ready to work with others, love and constantly identify with the group, selflessness, loyalty to the group ideals and goals. These are qualities often demonstrated by many successful union leaders. Members of their union can readily feel a mutual identity. Mr. Adams Oshiomole, former President of the Nigerian Labour Congress (NLC) and present Governor of Edo State is seen as a leader by many people because of his ability to feel the pulse of Nigerians and use it as the basis of labour struggles.

There may also be some innate or psychological characteristics that propel a person to leadership. But such a person needs to have other qualities readily perceived by others to become a leader, thus, lacking in these qualities such a person will become a self-imposed leader. For instance, a person who happens to be a general in the Army when a coup takes place may be readily acceptable as a leader. From the foregoing, leaders can be categorized in many different ways. A leader can therefore posses several qualities that may even appear conflicting sometimes.

11.5   TYPES OF LEADERS
➤   Situational Leader

A situational leader foresees a crisis or need of the group and takes the initiative to address it usually by mobilizing others to tackle it. A situational leader usually holds the position as long as the situation persists. An illustration of situational leader may be taken from the biblical story of David confronting Goliath; who defied the army of Israel but no soldier in the Israel's army was bold enough to confront Goliath. The defeat of Goliath by David brought the latter to limelight. However, other factors would have to come into play to sustain him. In other words, situational leaders persist as long as the condition which brought them into the forefront remains. They can continue if such situation that brought them out becomes institutionalized or by self-imposition on the group. In the case of David he won several battles for Israel after Goliath's defeat. In Nigeria, Odumegwu Ojukwu emerged as a situational leader to lead the Biafran Civil War. Think of other situational leaders you know and indicate whether (and how) they were able to sustain their leadership position or not? Another example is the manner Professor Charles Soludo mobilized Nigerians for the Banking Consolidation exercise in 2006-2007.

➤   Dictatorial Leader

A dictatorial leader is one who feels the people owe him continuous allegiance after having being entrusted to the leadership position by a particular situation. When situational leaders refuse to quit the position after the situation ceases, they often become dictatorial imposing their views rather than seeking to influence others to follow them. A dictatorial leader may claim to have moral obligation to remain at the helm of affairs to watch over peoples' interests or sees his clinging to power as the reward for his effort. A dictator would want to control all phases of life in the community and takes no suggestion from his subordinates except where such suggestions are in his own favour (Ekong, 2003). A ready example is found in most coup d'etat by military rulers. They claim to come up to correct some abuses by a ruling class only to wish to perpetuate themselves in power.

➤   Hereditary Leader

A hereditary leader emerges by birth-right. The custom or tradition of the group recognizes the right of the individual to lead them even before he or she is born. This way, tradition confers on the leader the right to loyalty and unquestioning followership even if other circumstances do not make him or her suitable to hold the office. In Agbor, Delta State of Nigeria, the 18th Obi was crowned when he was 2½ years old.

Here the leader is born into a hereditary leadership position as recognized by custom and tradition. It implies that the leadership status is ascribed rather than achieved. Ascribed status is attained through competition and individual efforts while achieved status is designed culturally and due to no effort of the incumbent. Traditional leaders are very important to the work of the change agent because of the natural power and influence they wield, especially in the rural setting. Their authority might have waned and replaced with constituted political authority; they still have remarkable influence on their subjects and often the respective politicians who align their support on intended programmes. The traditional leader has authority by virtue of the community's tradition; as such he enjoys unlimited loyalty and undisputed obedience as a mark of respect for the stool or office, irrespective of the qualities of the incumbent. Ekong (2003) cites the case of a child king – Ben Keagboekuzi, the 18th Obi of Agbor, Delta State of Nigeria, who took reigns at 2½ years old. When you have a weak infant as the monarch, other people overtly or covertly are vested with the role of leading the community on his behalf.

> ➤ **Professional Leader**

Persons who become leaders by virtue of some expertise or technical competence are professional leaders. Even though professional leaders do not emerge by virtue of personal qualities, possession of a good character can boast the acceptability of a professional leader. So an agricultural extension officer who is also perceived as a good person by his farmers will be more readily acceptable to one who is perceived as a bad person. Other categories of professional leaders are the village teacher, the veterinary officer among a group Fulani herdsmen, the village medicine man etc.

This describes someone who attains the leadership position through hard work and technical competence. The position is achieved and not ascribed. His status is not based on personal charm, although, such characteristics can enhance his acceptability to his group or community (Ekong, 2003). At the local community level, skilled professional leader may include, the pastor, diviner or traditional healer. A village headmaster might be a member or consultant to the village council by the virtue of his expertise, exposure or professional competence. In rural communities they are influential because people look unto them for their knowledge and skills for direction and assistance on various matters both within and outside the scope of their expertise. They are sometimes asked to represent their communities/groups in outside engagements.

> ➢ **Visible Leader**

A leader is called visible when followers and other leaders in a community assign to him similar levels of power and recognition. They play roles that are readily perceived by all members of the community, they are therefore 'visible'. These are leaders accorded the same amount of power and recognition by both leaders and non-leaders. They perform 'visible' roles which are recognized by all in the community.

> ➢ **Concealed Leader**

These are persons within a community recognized by other leaders for their influence but not by non-leaders or other members of the community. They are called 'concealed' because their influence is more evident in the circle of leaders. These are leaders who are not publicly acknowledged as leaders but have so much influence within the leadership cadre for reasons not so obvious to the larger community. On important matters, they are consulted by those in position of authority for quality advice before actions are taken.

> ➢ **Cosmopolitan Leaders**

The interest of cosmopolitan leaders goes beyond the local community. They often represent the community outside its boundary. They tend to be knowledgeable about affairs outside the local community and can facilitate influx of external resources into the community. Their influence is often dependent on what they know than who they know. Cosmopolitan leaders are those whose scope of interests transcends their local environment. They represent their community on outside engagements and they attract beneficial projects to their community. They read widely to be abreast of news that could be of benefit to their community and for personal development. Their power in this case lies on what they know rather than on whom they know.

> ➢ **Action Leaders**

Action leaders are lay people who are actively involved in every aspect of community programmes from planning to evaluation. They use their knowledge and experience to key into programmes to serve as volunteers in whatever capacity community workers would deem them fit. An action leader is a non-professional leader who is actively involved in the planning, execution and/or evaluation of community programmes. Such a person may serve as a volunteer subject-matter specialist or as a programme planner, councilor or committee member. They are usually sought after by change agents for training and active involvement in community programmes.

➢ Opinion Leaders

Opinion leaders are lay people who influence opinion of others on programmes initiated in the community. Over time people have learnt to respect their views which might be as a result of several factors such as social status, age, family background, education, wealth, prestige or political contacts. Change agents should identify them to give legitimation to innovations and programmes in the community. These are non-professional leaders, who by virtue of some qualities they posses (age, education, ancestry, wealth, prestige or political contacts) influence opinions in most activities in the community. It is usually for people to wait until such a person has formed an opinion on a subject before they make up their minds on where to sway (for or against) on the issue.

➢ Traditional Leaders

Traditional leaders' leadership positions are either based on or identified by past traditions of the people. Traditional leaders are usually indigenes of the community and their first loyalty is expected to be to their community. Traditional leadership is associated with kinship, titles, authority over land and resources, and their allocation. They are given special places and recognition in formal occasions and they perform special functions. Traditional leadership is a system where the leaders are expected to serve the people by active engagement in community building. This service attracts a reciprocal relationship between traditional leaders and the people. Traditional leaders are needed by the people as much as the people needed them. In modern time, this restraint is frequently absent because of deterioration in the traditional check and balance system. There were instances, when traditional leaders had extended their authority beyond what was proper to enrich themselves and not the people as a whole.

➢ Modern Leaders

Modern leaders' leadership positions are based on present, cosmopolitan or non-traditional values. Their powers derive from a combination of sources. They may act in concert on major community issues or as linked cliques of individuals specializing in specific issues except the generalist position of a community or village head. Most of them belong to modern governmental bureaucracies while others belong to external voluntary formal organizations. They are often trained professionals whose first loyalty is to the community they represent. The fact that most modern leaders represent external social systems implies that, very often, decisions concerning a village community are taken outside of the community. Modern leaders constitute a main channel through which new ideas, customs and values flow into the local community. At its extreme, the development of modern leaders often results in an erosion of the powers of traditional leaders and therefore a conflict in the maintenance of leadership for the different types of leaders. Despite this fact, a majority of local people look up to traditional leaders for legitimization on issues concerning the community. This is one reason for incorporating traditional leaders into community development programmes. The requirement for legitimization of the intention of modern leaders is informed by the fact that the use of coercive powers is often unsustainable and costly.

11.6   LEADERSHIP STYLES

Leadership is the process of influencing others. The different types of leaders described in the foregoing discussion can adopt different styles for performing their leadership roles, depending on their abilities and the circumstances surrounding the exercise. Leadership can be categorized in two broad ways; that is, by function or by method.

Leadership Style by Function
❖   **Directing**

This occurs when the leader gives instructions on how to address the community goal. The leader assumes a position of superior knowledge of the situation and how best to address it. This approach does not focus on succession as a necessary or possible outcome of leadership.

❖   **Coaching**

This leadership style emphasizes on the teaching component of leadership. The leader is concerned with the followers being able to address similar situation in future using the approved means.

❖   **Supporting**

Supporting is leadership style by mentoring. The leader provides the necessary conditions for the followers to solve a community problem or tackle a community task using approaches that work best for them. This style recognizes the inevitability of succession and the need to create a pool of potential leaders in the community who could use their initiatives under any condition to address similar or different problems or issues in future.

❖ Delegation
This style recognizes that nobody is an island of knowledge. The leader seeks to provide opportunity for qualified member of the community to display their leadership qualities under different circumstances. The more the level of delegation by the leader, the less the leader needs to worry about routine matters in the community.

Leadership Style by Method
❖ Autocratic
An autocratic leadership style is one which thrives on the whim of the leader. The leader is always right and allows no second opinion. The will of the leader is law. Every other opinion that does not tally with that of the leader is not tolerated.

❖ Democratic
This is a leadership style that allows inputs into decision making by followers. It encourages debates on all alternative courses of action proffered and the leader guides the community toward the position favoured by the majority of the followers.

❖ Laissez–faire
The laissez faire leadership style adopts an 'I don't care' attitude to leadership. The leader does not appear to influence the group one way or another. The laissez-faire leadership style is also known as the "hands-off" style. It is one in which the leader provides little or no influence on the path or course of action that the community takes. Most often, laissez-faire leadership works for teams in which the individuals are very experienced and skilled self-starters. Unfortunately, it can also lead to a situation where the leader becomes complacent and therefore provides no leadership at all.

11.7   SELECTION OF LEADERS
Good leaders are instruments to the success of any development programme in the rural communities. Williams et al. (1984) observed that different types of leaders are needed to execute all the stages of development programme in the community. The variation in group situations often determines the types of leaders to be used. This is why the issue of leader selection is most important. Without leaders of the proper

kind and interest in the work at hand, the development programmes may suffer greatly. Williams et al. (1984) discussed five methods of leader selection.

(a) **External selection -** This is the selection of the leader by someone outside the community. The outsider may likely be a professional leader, who asks or appoints someone to serve. The method is commonly used in the military, churches, government and business organizations, where it is usually accompanied with reasonable success. It is not likely to be successful when employed in a community commonly used for the development purpose

(b) **Self-aggrandizement -** This method is based on clever manipulation of the community by the leader by making sure that he is at the right place and at the right time in order to get elected or appointed. The method is usually used by a person who has a strong desire to lead. Usually, the leadership does not last very long in a democracy as the people soon become fed up with him. The community he leads soon disintegrates or gets a new leader due to his inability to harmonize the community toward its tasks.

(c) **Selection on basis of tradition -** This method relies on tradition and culture of the people who makie up the community. Older people or those who had been in top positions for long are most highly respected in the traditional society. When community action is desired on new ideas and practices, then this method of leader selection will probably prove unsatisfactory. This is because when traditional leaders are consulted on any innovation, and are opposed to it younger people who want the innovation may be debarred. For any development programme to be successful in this situation, the social worker must have the approval of the traditional leader.

(d) **Selection by group -** This is achieved through either appointment or election by the community, and is the best method of getting leaders who will have the respect and confidence of the community. Members of the group, who participated in selecting the leader, are ready to give full cooperation and support. The social worker needs the skill to facilitate the method of leader selection. Members could be asked to vote for the people the community wants as leaders.

11.8   THEORIES OF LEADERSHIP

Knowledge of concepts of leader and leadership may be superficial without providing some ground theories of leadership. It is in this recognition that these theories are examined.

The 'Great- Man' Leadership Theory

The 'great-man' leadership theory sees leadership as a quality of the individual who endeared the community members to him as an enigma. In its boldest form the theory states that certain individuals possess just the right blend of looks, personality traits, and intelligence to be almost automatically thrust into leadership position anyhow. These individuals – who are said to have charisma – will always become leaders in any situation or in any community. Charisma is a kind of personal magnetism and hypnotic appeal too imposing not to be recognized. Several examples of history's charismatic leaders include; Mahatma Ghandi, Winston Churchhill, John F. Kennedy, Martin Luther King, Jesse Jackson and Pope John Paul II. In Nigeria a shop-list of charismatic leaders in history may include; Herbert Macauley, Chief Obafemi Awolowo, Sir Nnamdi Azikiwe and Sir Ahmadu Bello. Leaders that used their charisma to negative end could be listed to include; Adolf Hitler and Jim Jones of the Guyana Tragedy.

Functional theory

Functional leadership theory (Hackman & Walton, 1986; McGrath, 1962; Adair, 1988; Kouzes & Posner, 1995) is a particularly useful theory for addressing specific leader behaviours expected to contribute to organizational, community or unit effectiveness. This theory argues that the leader's main job is to see that whatever is necessary or the needs of the group is taken care of; thus, a leader can be said to have done their job well when they have contributed to group effectiveness and cohesion (Fleishman et al., 1991; Hackman & Wageman, 2005; Hackman & Walton, 1986). While functional leadership theory has most often been applied to team leadership (Zaccaro, Rittman & Marks; 2001), it has also been effectively applied to broader community leadership as well. It is imperative to highlight functional leadership; five broad functions a leader performs when promoting community development activities. These functions include environmental monitoring, organizing community activities, teaching and coaching members, motivating others, and intervening actively in the community's work. A variety of leadership behaviours are expected to facilitate these functions. In initial work identifying leader behaviour, Fleishman (1953) observed that subordinates perceived their supervisors' behaviour in terms of two broad categories referred to as consideration and initiating structure. Consideration includes behaviour involved in fostering effective relationships. Examples of such behaviour would include showing concern for a subordinate or acting in a supportive manner towards others. Initiating structure involves the actions of the leader focused specifically on task accomplishment. This could include role clarification, setting performance standards, and holding subordinates accountable to those standards.

The Path-Goal Theory

The path-goal theory of leadership was developed by Robert House (1971) and was based on the expectancy theory of Victor Vroom. According to House, the essence of the theory is "the meta proposition that leaders, to be effective, engage in behaviours that complement subordinates' environments and abilities in a manner that compensates for deficiencies and is instrumental to subordinate satisfaction and individual and work unit performance" (House, 1996). The theory identifies four leader behaviours, achievement-oriented, directive, participative, and supportive those are contingent to the environment factors and follower characteristics. In contrast to the Fiedler contingency model, the path-goal model states that the four leadership behaviours are fluid, and that leaders can adopt any of the four depending on what the situation demands. The path-goal model can be classified both as a contingency theory, as it depends on the circumstances, and as a transactional theory, as the theory emphasizes on the reciprocity behaviour between the leader and the followers. The path-goal theory holds that a leader can affect the performance, satisfaction and motivation of a group by: Offering rewards for achieving performance goals; Clarifying paths towards these goals; Removing obstacles to performance. However, whether leadership behaviour can do so effectively also depends on situational factors. Situational Factors of the path-goal theory have two major dimensions: Subordinate personalities:

- ❖ Focus of control: A participative leader is suitable for subordinates with internal focus of control; a directive leader is suitable for subordinates with external focus of control.
- ❖ Self-perceived ability: Subordinates that believe they have high abilities themselves do not like directive leadership.

Characteristics of the environment:

- When a group is working on a task that has a high structure; directive leadership is redundant and less effective,

- When a highly formal authority system is in place, a directive leadership can again reduce workers satisfaction,
- When subordinates are in a team environment offering great social support, supportive style leadership becomes less necessary.

Situational Theory
The situational leadership model proposed by Hersey and Blanchard (2008) suggests four leadership-styles and four levels of follower-development. For effectiveness, the model posits that the leadership-style must match the appropriate level of follower-development. In this model, leadership behaviour becomes a function not only of the characteristics of the leader, but of the characteristics of the followers as well. Situational theory also appeared as a reaction to the trait theory of leadership. Social Scientists argued that history was more than the result of intervention of great men as Carlyle suggested. Herbert Spencer (1884) (and Karl Marx) said that the times produce the person and not the other way around. This theory assumes that different situations call for different characteristics; according to this group of theories, no single optimal psychographic profile of a leader exists. According to the theory, "what an individual actually does when acting as a leader is in large part dependent upon characteristics of the situation in which he functions (Hemphill, 1949)."
Situational theories propose that leaders choose the best course of action based upon situational variables. Different styles of leadership may be more appropriate for certain types of decision-making. This could be exemplified in a situation where the leader is the most knowledgeable and experienced member of a group, an authoritarian style might be most appropriate. In other instances where group members are skilled experts, a democratic style would be more effective.

Contingency Theory
The Fiedler contingency model bases the leader's effectiveness on what Fred Fiedler (1967) called situational contingency. This results from the interaction of leadership style and situational favourability (later called situational control). The theory defined two types of leader: those who tend to accomplish the task by developing good relationships with the group (relationship-oriented), and those who have as their prime concern carrying out the task itself (task-oriented). According to Fiedler (1967), there is no ideal leader. Both task-oriented and relationship-oriented leaders can be effective if their leadership orientation fits the situation. When there is a good leader-member relation, a highly structured task, and high leader position power, the situation is considered a "favorable

situation". Fiedler found that task-oriented leaders are more effective in extremely favourable or unfavourable situations, whereas relationship-oriented leaders perform best in situations with intermediate favourability. Contingency theories of leadership focus on particular variables related to the environment that might determine which particular style of leadership is best suited for the situation. According to this theory, no leadership style is best in all situations. Success depends upon a number of variables, including the leadership style, qualities of the followers and aspects of the situation.

Integrated Psychological Theory
The Integrated Psychological theory of leadership is an attempt to integrate the strengths of the older theories (i.e. traits, behavioural/styles, situational and functional) while addressing their limitations, largely by introducing a new element – the need for leaders to develop their leadership presence, attitude toward others and behavioural flexibility by practicing psychological mastery. It also offers a foundation for leaders wanting to apply the philosophies of servant leadership and authentic leadership. Integrated Psychological theory began to attract attention after the publication of James Scouller's "Three Levels of Leadership Model" (2011). Scouller argued that the older theories offer only limited assistance in developing a person's ability to lead effectively. He pointed out, for example, that: Traits theories, which tend to reinforce the idea that leaders are born not made, might help us select leaders, but they are less useful for developing leaders. An ideal style (e.g. Blake & Mouton's team style) would not suit all circumstances. Most of the situational/contingency and functional theories assume that leaders can change their behaviour to meet differing circumstances or widen their behavioural range at will, when in practice many find it hard to do so because of unconscious beliefs, fears or ingrained habits. Thus, he argued, leaders need to work on their inner psychology. None of the old theories successfully address the challenge of developing "leadership presence"; that certain "something" in leaders that commands attention, inspires people, wins their trust and makes followers want to work with them.

Scouller in 2011 therefore proposed the Three Levels of Leadership Model, which was later categorized as an "Integrated Psychological" theory on the Business-balls education website. In essence, his model summarizes what leaders have to do, not only to bring leadership to their group or organization, but also to develop themselves technically and psychologically as leaders. The three levels in his model are Public, Private and Personal leadership

The first two– public and private leadership– are "outer" or behavioural levels. These are the behaviours that address what Scouller called "the four dimensions of leadership". These dimensions are: (1) a shared, motivating group purpose; (2) action, progress and results; (3) collective unity or team spirit; (4) individual selection and motivation. Public leadership focuses on the 34 behaviours involved in influencing two or more people simultaneously. Private leadership covers the 14 behaviours needed to influence individuals one on one.

The third – personal leadership – is an "inner" level and concerns a person's growth toward greater leadership presence, knowhow and skill. Working on ones personal leadership has three aspects: (1) Technical knowhow and skill (2) Developing the right attitude toward other people – which is the basis of servant leadership (3) Psychological self-mastery – the foundation for authentic leadership.

Scouller argued that self-mastery is the key to growing ones leadership presence, building trusting relationships with followers and dissolving ones limiting beliefs and habits, thereby enabling behavioural flexibility as circumstances change, while staying connected to ones core values (that is, while remaining authentic). To support leaders' development, has introduced a new model of the human psyche and outlined the principles and techniques of self-mastery.

11.9   DISTINCTION BETWEEN A LEADER AND A BOSS

The dictionary meaning of these terms attempt to establish their differences. Oxford Advanced Learner's Dictionary defines a boss as a person who is in charge of other people at work and tells them what to do. Encarta drives home the point further by describing a boss as somebody that is dominant. He is the dominant partner in a relationship or the dominant member of a group, who tends to make decisions and give instructions. On the contrary, a leader is described as somebody who others follow. In more practical terms, the distinguishing features between a boss and a leader are presented as follows: While a boss operates in authoritarian capacity, a leader operates in democratic dispensation. Though, the 'boss approach' to getting things done is prevalent in formal institutional setting, where the boss gets things done by riding on the power of authority, democratic approach is likely to be more effective in informal work relations. Managers in formal setting, however, have realized that work is more effective when leadership principles are applied to their tasks

LEADER	BOSS
1. Depends on people's good will	Depends upon authority
2. Coaches the men	Commands or drives his/her men
3. Makes work a privilege, challenging and worth the while	Makes work a drudgery and an awful experience
4. Leads by inspiring enthusiasm	Gets things done by instilling fear
5. Focus on team work, says, 'We'	Arrogates effect to self, says 'I'
6. Fixes any breakdown	Fixes blame for breakdown
7. Knows but believes others know something, too	Knows it all disposition
8. Says "get there ahead of time"	Says "get there on time"
9. Sets the pace	Assigns tasks

Table 11.1: Source: *Author's field survey data (2012).*

11.10 DUTIES AND RESPONSIBILITIES OF A COMMUNITY LEADER

For any community or group to survive, there must be in existence an effective leadership to give direction to the efforts of all members in accomplishing the goals of the community. The absence of leadership will make the link between individual and goal difficult. Thus, achievement of individual goals rather than group goals becomes prominent and important. This often leads to a situation in which individuals work to achieve their own goals while the overall community or people become inefficient in achieving its objectives. The essence of leadership is reflected in the statement that: "Without leadership, a community is but a muddle of men and machines. Leadership is the ability to persuade others to seek defined objectives enthusiastically, it is the human factor which binds a group together and motivates it towards goals. Management activities such as planning, organizing, and decision-making will be dormant and ineffective until the leader triggers the power of motivation in people and guides them towards achieving goals. Leadership transforms potential into reality. It is the ultimate act which brings to success all of the potential that is in a community and its people. The role of a leader is to help people solve problems, to offer respect and to empower individuals to do the best that they can.

(a) As a leader, he should be able to study his community and be able to identify its felt needs: it is imperative for community leaders to assess the communities they serve. Furthermore, his role in his community entails familiarity with the problems and aspirations of the people. He/she needs to know the problems of the community, such as poverty, health, substance abuse and crime. Once they identify the problems bothering the community, they can work to solve them. You must provide a mission (what needs to be done) and a strategy (a path for how to accomplish the mission and a way for the group to get there). But developing a clear vision and a careful strategy is not enough; you must also clearly communicate them to your community. Community leaders must also know the strengths of the community. Communities may have some strong institutions, such as churches, schools, law enforcement or labour unions. There may be common facilities such as community centers and public parks to serve as locations for meetings and gatherings. Community leaders should develop personal relationships with community members to better integrate themselves into the community. When leaders have wider focus and dedicated to the growth of their communities socially, politically and economically, they usually perform such functions below:

- ✓ Identification of felt – needs
- ✓ Planning to meet the needs
- ✓ Organizing human, material and financial resources to meet the needs
- ✓ Contribution of material and financial resources
- ✓ Physical participation in project execution
- ✓ Evaluation of progress made in plan execution
- ✓ Utilization and maintenance of facilities provided
- ✓ Development of team spirit to work together always
- ✓ Dependence or reliance on self or the community to improve their living standard.

(b) As a leader, he serves as a link between the community, government and other external bodies. Governmental and other external bodies are in constant touch with the community either for delivery of services or for extraction of human, material and financial resources. Some of these activities are beneficial to the community while others are detrimental to the well-being of people. The community leader in this sense serves as the feedback loop between his community and structures of government within the political system.

(c)   Create Programmes to Address Community Needs: When community members can agree with pursuit of common goals, the community leader's role is to develop programmes to utilize the strengths of the community to reach those goals. For instance, a health screening campaign can use a common space like a community center or church as a location. Local health officials can supply medical staff and equipment and churches, local media and organizations can reach out to members or the public at large to increase participation.

(d)   The Community Leader Assists in Keeping Peace and Maintenance of Law and Order: Keeping of peace and maintenance of law and order is therefore one of the social services a community must enjoy before it can pursue other goals. Thus, no physical or human development is possible in a state of insecurity, disorder and lawlessness. The community leader has an important role to play in this sense. This he can do through his familiarity with the problems of his people. He tries to settle inter personal and intra community conflicts over land, streams, economic trees, over business transactions and inherited property, this he does in accordance with customary rules of the area.

(e)   Connecting with Other Communities for Shared Goals: Community leaders may also work with other communities as part of larger scale projects. Large scale projects like public transportation, economic development and zoning laws can affect multiple communities. The community leader needs to work with other communities to share common interest in large projects as well as advocate for the special circumstance of their community.

Virtual Contact Leadership
One of the benefits of modern technology is the ability to communicate with anyone, anywhere in the world. While this is a benefit for businesses working to expand, it presents unique challenges for leaders. Many leaders have a leadership skill set that relies heavily on their personality and "presence". Many of these skills do not translate well into electronic communication. Leaders need to be aware of this and work to improve their skills in communicating and leading using modern tools. They can no longer rely on the power of their personality to give them an edge. One of the biggest areas leaders must develop is the ability to communicate well through the written word. In the past,

leaders were often able to rely on assistants for written communication. However, with the ubiquitous use of email, this is no longer an option. Leaders who cannot communicate well in writing will find themselves at a disadvantage. Leaders preparing for the future should make a conscious effort in the following areas:

(a) Developing strong writing skills
(b) Understanding different forms of electronic communication
(c) Understanding the culture of different forms of electronic communication.

11.11 EVALUATION OF LEADERS

Leadership evaluation guidelines indicate the behaviour that can be used to evaluate a leader (Human Resources, 2006).

i.   **Vision:** He clearly and simply communicates the Strategic Plan and inspires and energizes others to commit to the Strategic Plan. He leads by example.

ii.   **Ownership:** He reinforces the Strategic Plan in all operational activities. He communicates development challenges in a positive manner. He uses expertise to effectively influence the behaviour/decisions of rural leadership. Accept responsibility for failures and successes.

iii. **Accountability/Integrity:** He adheres to highest standards of ethics. Follows and promotes development policies and procedures ("does the right thing"). Actions consistent with words ("walk the talk"). He is absolutely trusted by others. He delivers on commitments to constituents, leaders and followers. He demonstrates courage/self-confidence to stand for beliefs, ideas, and people.

iv.   **Inspires excellence:** He continuously seeks new ways to improve the work environment both practices and processes. He strives to improve his/her own areas of relative weaknesses and assumes responsibilities for own mistakes. He sets challenging standards and expectations for excellent performance. He recognizes and rewards achievement. Fully utilizes team members of all cultures, races and genders.

v.   **He positively stimulates change:** He creates real and positive change. Sees change as an opportunity. He questions the status quo and implements new and better ways of doing things. He promotes alternative points of view as being essential to positive change.

vi.   **Teamwork:** He functions effectively both as a leader and team member and respects the talent and contributions of all team members. He creates an environment where everyone feels able to participate. He links goals of own organization, team members with Strategic Plan. He respects diversity of opinion in constituency, peers, and subordinates. He enthusiastically supports the team, even during bad times. He assumes responsibility for the team's mistakes and settles problems without alienating others.

vii. **Self-Confidence:** He acknowledges strengths and limitations, seeks candid feedback from peers. He maintains an even disposition when things are not going well and treats all others with respect, fairness and dignity. He shares problems and concerns openly and honestly. Shares information across traditional boundaries and is open to new ideas.

viii. **Communications:** He explains Strategic Plan and other rural initiatives and messages to members of the community. He communicates in an open, candid, clear, complete, consistent, interactive manner that initiates response/discussion. Listens effectively, demonstrates genuine interest in others.

ix.   **Development Skills:** He structures jobs/assignments for people's development and growth. He shares knowledge, information and expertise with team members. Positively sets challenging goals that stretch current performance levels and drives new skill development. Gives frequent, candid coaching/feedback on performance and career development. He documents results and treats everyone with dignity, trust and respect.

x.   **Motivation:** He motivates others to behave and perform at their highest level. He inspires through words and actions.

xi.   **Empowerment:** He delegates important tasks, not just what he/she does not want to do. Gives authority commensurate with responsibility, and resources necessary to get the job done. Promotes visibility of staff/team members and peers, gives credit where due.

xii. Fully utilizes diversity of team members to achieve success.

Chapter Twelve

AGENTS AND AGENCIES IN RURAL AND COMMUNITY DEVELOPMENT I

12.1 THE ROLE OF COOPERATIVE SOCIETIES IN RURAL AND COMMUNITY DEVELOPMENT

12.1.1 Meaning of Cooperative Societies

Cooperative Societies are legal, institutionalized and voluntary organizations characterized by the values of self-help, self-responsibility, democracy equality, equity and solidarity. The International Cooperative Alliance (ICA) in its statement on the Cooperate Identity, in 1995, defines a cooperative as, "an autonomous association of persons united voluntarily to meet their common, economic, social, and cultural needs and aspirations through a jointly-owned and democratically - controlled enterprise" (ILO, 2002). It is a business voluntarily owned and controlled by its member patrons and operated for them and by them on a nonprofit or cost basis (UWCC, 2002). It is a business enterprise that aims at complete identity of the component factors of ownership, control and use of service, three distinct features that differentiate cooperatives from other businesses (Laidlaw, 1974). A cooperative is an enterprise with broader objectives than other corporate forms. Thus, a co-operative society is an association of individuals who voluntarily pool their resources and carry on the business for their own welfare and not for a profit seeking business.

A co-operative society has been formed behind the following broad objectives:
- To render service to its members instead of making profits.
- It encourages a state of mutual help in the place of competition.
- It assures a state of self-help in the place of dependence.
- It develops a state of moral solidarity in the place of unfair business activities.

Figure 12:1.

Cooperative businesses are unique from other types of commercial enterprises in that they exist to meet the needs of people, not to maximize profit. All over the world, people due form cooperatives to better their lives and build more successful communities. A commitment to community is one of the seven cooperative principles and building stronger communities—for the good of all—is at the heart of why people form cooperatives. One of the most important things about cooperatives is that they can meet peoples' needs when for-profit enterprises are unwilling or unable to do so. The success of cooperatives around the world in providing for these needs takes many forms. Cooperatives are enterprises that put people at the centre of their business and not capital. They follow a broader set of values than those associated purely with making a profit. Because cooperatives are owned and democratically-controlled by their members (individuals or groups and even capital enterprises) the decisions taken by co-operatives balance the need for profitability with the needs of their members and the wider interests of the community. Members make equitable contributions to the capital required and accept a fair share of the risks and benefits of the undertaking. Co-operative societies work on the principles of self-help and mutual assistance to provide services for their members in a prudent and effective manner. Every co-operative society must be registered under the Co-operatives Law. It is a form of business where individuals belonging to the same class join their hands for the promotion of their common goals see Figure 1. It reflects the desire of the poor people to stand on their own legs or own merit.

Cooperative Societies are found in every Village, Town, State, Region and National Level in Nigeria. Examples of cooperatives in Nigeria include-Pan Foundation Multi-Purpose Cooperative Society Limited, Nigeria Labour Cooperative Society, National Cooperative Insurance Society of Nigeria and Capital Investment Cooperative Society Limited, to mention but a few. Cooperative societies according to Juhász (2001) are traditional organizations of mainly the poorer segments of society which have the potential to play an important role in developing a strong "social capital" in rural areas. Rural contexts can host a variety of cooperatives, in agriculture (production, processing, marketing, purchasing and sales), but also financial services (banking, credit and loan, insurance), in health, electricity, telecommunications, water, consumer goods and services, housing, tourism, and handicrafts. Members may belong to several kinds of cooperative societies namely: Marketing Cooperatives; Processing Mills Cooperatives;   Producers   Cooperatives-   Groundnut   Producers

Cooperative; Cocoa Producers Cooperative; Oil Palm Producers Cooperative; Garri Producers Cooperative; Rice Producers Cooperative; Sugar Cane Producers Cooperative; Yam Producers Cooperative; Goat Producers Co-operative; Beef Producers Cooperative and Fish Producers Cooperative etc.

12.1.2 **History of Cooperative**

In early human societies people learned to cooperate and work together to increase their success in hunting, fishing, gathering foods, building shelter, and meeting other individual and group needs. Historians have found evidence of cooperation among peoples in early Greece, Egypt, Rome and Babylon, among Native American and African tribes, and between many other groups. Early agriculture would have been impossible without mutual aid among farmers. They relied on one another to defend land, harvest crops, build barns and storage buildings, and to share equipment. These examples of informal cooperation – of working together – were the precursors to the cooperative form of business.

The cooperative movement began in Europe in the 19th Century, primarily in Britain and France, although The Shore Porters Society (2007) claims to be one of the world's first cooperatives, being established in Aberdeen in 1498 (although it has since demutualized to become a private partnership). The industrial revolution and the increasing mechanization of the economy transformed society and threatened the livelihoods of many workers. The concurrent labour and social movements and the issues they attempted to address describe the climate at the time. In the first half of the nineteenth century, living conditions were extremely harsh for working class people in the textile milling towns of northern England. Mill workers laboured long hours under dangerous working conditions for low pay. Plagued by unending poverty, they were forced to buy food on credit from merchants who charged high prices for goods that were poor quality and often adulterated. Owning no property, workers were unable to vote. These conditions gave rise to labour movements which drew great numbers of followers.

During this period, cooperative initiatives were common, offering their working class members the promise of economic opportunity and democratic control. But until the founding of the Rochdale Equitable Pioneers Society in 1844, none were successful. When the self-described "Rochdale Pioneers" opened their first cooperative food shop, they sold only five products – butter, flour, oatmeal, sugar, and candles – but promised to provide members with "purest provisions, giving full weight and measure." They went on to establish many other member-owned businesses. Learning from earlier failures, the founders of the Rochdale society developed a series of operating principles which ensured their success and the success of hundreds of cooperatives in England and beyond which soon imitated them. Today, these basic principles still guide cooperatives around the world.

Growth of Cooperatives in England: The Rochdale Equitable Pioneers Society

In 1843, workers in the textile mills of Rochdale, England went on strike. When the strike failed, the millworkers began to look for other ways to improve their lives. Instead of calling for another strike or asking charitable groups for help, some of these people decided to take control of one of the most immediate and pressing areas of their lives. They believed they needed their own food store as an alternative to the company store. Twenty-eight people founded the Rochdale Equitable Pioneers Society. After saving money for over a year, these pioneers opened their co-op store at 31 Toad Lane on a cold December evening in 1844. Although the founders agreed to sell just butter, sugar, flour, and oatmeal, they also offered tallow candles for sale that night. They were forced to buy candles because the gas company refused to supply gas for the new group's lights. They bought candles in bulk and sold what they didn't use to their members. The Rochdale Pioneers weren't the first group to try forming a co-op but they were the first to make their co-op succeed and endure. To avoid the mistakes made by earlier co-op societies and to help others, they developed a list of operating principles governing their organization. These formed the basis for what are now known as the cooperative principles. Rochdale is still considered the birthplace of the modern cooperative movement.

The Growth of Cooperatives in the United States

In the United States, cooperatives of one sort or another have roots going back to colonial times. Like their counterparts in England, these early groups experimented with ways to band together and gain economic clout. One of the earliest co-ops was established in 1752 by Benjamin Franklin and is in operation to this day – the Philadelphia Contributorship for the Insurance of Homes from Loss by Fire. It is the oldest continuing co-op in the United States and predates the historical Rochdale group but its place in co-op history is less well known. From colonial times on, most early American co-ops were formed primarily for the benefit of farmers. Some co-ops helped farmers keep their costs low through joint purchases of supplies, such as feed, equipment, tools, or seed. Some marketing co-ops helped farmers obtain the best prices for their goods by combining their crops and selling in large quantities. Others provided storage or processing services, such as grain elevators or cheese making. Consumer groups in the United States began taking note of the early British consumer co-ops and the success of American farmers who worked together. They began forming consumer protection associations in 1845, one group started a store in Boston, founded on the same principles the Rochdale Pioneers had applied a year earlier. These "protective unions' eventually became divided over political and social issues of the time and were all out of business by the end of the Civil War. Most early American co-ops failed due to insufficient capital (money invested by the owners), poor management, and a lack of understanding of the cooperative principles by their members. It wasn't until the early 1900s that co-ops began to have true, long-lasting success in the United States.

Consumer Co-ops Make Waves

The first documented consumer cooperatives was founded in 1769, in a barely furnished cottage in Fenwick, East Ayrshire, when local weavers manhandled a sack of oatmeal into John Walker's whitewashed front room and began selling the contents at a discount, forming the Fenwick Weavers' Society. In the decades that followed, several cooperatives or cooperative societies formed including Lennoxtown Friendly Victualling Society, founded in 1812. By 1830, there were several hundred co-operatives (Doug, 2008). Some were initially successful, but most cooperatives founded in the early 19th Century had failed by 1840 (Doug, 2008). However, Lockhurst Lane Industrial Co-operative Society (founded in 1832 and now Heart of England Cooperative Society), and Galashiels and Hawick Co-operative Societies (1839 or earlier, merged with The Co-operative Group) still trade today. It was not until 1844 when the Rochdale Society of Equitable Pioneers established the 'Rochdale Principles' on which they ran their cooperative that the basis for development and growth of the modern cooperative movement was established (David, 1994; Ihimodu, 1988).

In rural and urban areas alike, consumer co-ops were first organized to provide consumers with control and to fight the unfair practices of private and company stores. Over the years, consumer co-ops have experienced "waves" of growth and development, followed by periods of decline. The first of these waves began in the early 1900s with what was called, The Rochdale plan." Under this plan consumers organized into buying groups to purchase from a cooperatively owned wholesaler. The wholesaler would then gradually help these buying clubs convert their operations into retail outlets by supplying management, inventory, and capital. In 1920, there were 2,600 consumer co-ops in the United States – all but 11 were general stores – and 80% were in towns with populations of less than 2,500. Combined sales volume for these stores was about $260 million. Unfortunately, when the wholesalers began having problems due to rapid growth, the whole system crumbled, and most co-ops were closed within the decade (Karen, 2011).

The Great Depression the 1930s triggered another great wave of co-op organizing in cities and in rural areas. In California, the "End Poverty in California" (EPIC) campaign established and promoted "self-help" cooperatives and worked unsuccessfully to elect the reformer Upton Sinclair Governor. Several national "consumers' unions" were formed to promote consumer education and protection. In 1936, Toyohiko Kagawa, a Japanese Clergyman with a social gospel, inspired the development of many co-ops in the United States by preaching"brotherhood economics," his term for cooperation. "Cooperatives," he said, "are the foundation of world peace. They are the love principle in action. Whether we like it or not there is no other way but cooperatives." These efforts, bolstered by Franklin Roosevelt's New Deal, supported urban co-ops with technical assistance. Some leading consumer co-ops were launched in this period – in Berkeley, Palo Alto, Eau Claire (Wisconsin), Hanover (New Hampshire), and Hyde Park (a Chicago, Illinois neighborhood), and Greenbelt (Maryland – a Washington, D.C. suburb). All of these stores survived to their 50th anniversaries but in the 1980s, the co-ops in Berkeley and Greenbelt closed, and those in Eau Claire and Palo Alto greatly scaled back their activities. The co-ops in Hanover and Hyde Park were thriving and growing– both with dynamic membership programmes (Karen, 2011).

In the late 1960s and 1970s the "new wave" of consumer co-ops began. Born out of the ideas and philosophies of the 1960s counterculture, these stores were opened by young and idealistic members. They set up co-ops to fit their belief in equality, not to follow their co-op predecessors. Most of the new co-ops sold only whole, unrefined, and bulk foods. Their operating practices were diverse and experimental. Some stores had limited store hours; others were open seven days a week. Some were run by volunteers, others by fully paid staff. Some had various forms of worker self-management; others had more traditional management structures. Some paid year-end patronage refunds; others gave members a discount at the cash register. These co-ops were pioneers in what came to be known as the "natural foods" industry. But not all were successful. Some failed because of their experimental structures and operating systems. Most were unable to escape the same problems that had troubled older, earlier co-ops – insufficient capital, inadequate membership support, and inability to improve operations as the natural foods industry developed a stronger commitment to idealism than to economic success, the lack of adequate support from their wholesalers, and resistance to consolidation. But the "new wave" co-ops which survived are strong and well-established. The consumer co-op movement in the United States has had mixed success – especially in contrast to consumer co-ops in Europe and Asia. But each wave of cooperative growth produces renewed enthusiasm for a time-tested idea and innovations that prove successful in the consumer marketplace – at least for a time.

Pre-Independence Development of cooperatives in Nigeria
Government involvement in a purposeful agricultural and cooperative extension development started with the colonization of the country by the British. The main purpose then was to increase the agricultural production of the export crops. This was aimed at getting a ready source of raw materials for their industries in Britain. As a result of this, all extension works at that time were directed towards the development of export crops. The period between 1890 and 1905 can be described as a period of trial and error. Many projects were tried but all failed.

The present day cooperatives in Nigeria derived their origin from the traditional financial organization variously referred to as "adashi" or "esusu" in the local language. The "adashi" or "esusu" is a widespread indigenous system of thrift and credit which seems to be well managed and successful (Seibel, 2004). In 1934 however, C. F. Strickland, a British cooperative expert, examined the "adashi" or "esusu" systems as a possible basis for introducing modern day cooperative societies in Nigeria (Strickland, 1934). Following the recommendations of Strickland, the cooperative society's ordinance was introduced in 1935 and modeled after the British-Indian Cooperatives as the blueprint for the British Colonies in Africa (Siebel, 2004). Later the government saw the need to promote savings habit among the low-income people. With another report which Mr Strickland submitted in 1936, (C.T.C.S) Co-operative Thrift and Credit Societies were formed and it spread all over Eastern and Western Nigeria (Ihimodu, 1988).

The initial achievement of the government on co-operatives was the promulgation of Cooperative Laws and the Co-operative Regulations which followed on the 6th February, 1936. In 1937, Gbedun Co-operative Produce Marketing Society became the first Co-operative Society to be the first Registrar of Co-operative Societies in Nigeria. After these developments, several Co-operative Societies and Union were formed and registered by the government through the Western Ministry of Trade, Industry and Cooperative. In 1953, The Co-operative Bank Plc was established by the Co-op Movement to provide for financial needs of members of Co-operative Societies in Nigeria. A sum of One Million Pounds (part of the proceeds realized on cocoa export) was approved for the take off of the bank by the late Chief Obafemi Awolowo, then Premier of the Western Region. For instance, in 1952, as a result of constitutional changes three regions were created Northern, Western and Eastern Regions. Separate regional Ministries of Agriculture were also created. This is also led to the creation of a separate extension units under the ministries. Due to this major reorganization, extension service was given a prominent role to play in the education of the farmers and the supply of essential farming materials. Departments for co-operative development were created in the appropriate ministries and this helped in the promotion of co-operatives in all parts of Nigeria. The Co-operative Federation of Nigeria was formed in 1945 and formally registered in 1967. It is the National Apex Organization which represents the entire cooperative movement in Nigeria.

Post-Independence Development of cooperatives in Nigeria
Nigeria got her independence in October, 1960. Three years after the independence. Midwest region was created in 1963 and this brought the number of Ministries of Agriculture to four and Department of Cooperative. As a result of the regional creation of the Ministries of Agriculture and Cooperative, development of Agriculture and Cooperative became a regional concern. Each region made several attempts to make use of all the Agricultural and Cooperative potentials in their areas. Such attempts included the establishment in their rural projects, farm settlements, Agricultural Financing agencies, Marketing Boards Cooperative Societies etc. Most of these projects could not succeed due to political and financial problems. However, they were able to make significant impacts on Agricultural and Cooperative development especially in the area of extension. More purposeful agricultural programmes were initiated during the 1970s, all aiming at increasing agricultural productivity. Notable among them were the National Accelerated Food Production Project (NAFPP),

Agricultural Extension and Research Liaison Services (AERLS), River Basin and Rural Development Authorities, Operation Feed the Nation (OFN) etc. 1980s witnessed further development of Agriculture and extension. During the change to civilian rule between 1979 and 1983, the Green Revolution Programme was launched. This programme could not succeed for political reasons. Despite all the transformation, the country has witnessed in the agricultural sector and cooperative, the Country continues to experience food shortage and the extension unit of the sector is still at the mercy of our policy makers.

12.1.3 Values of Cooperative Society
Cooperatives are based on the values of self-help, self-responsibility, democracy, equality, equity, and solidarity. In the tradition of their founders, cooperative members believe in the ethical values of honesty, openness, social responsibility, and caring for others.

12.1.4 Principles of Cooperative Society
Cooperatives around the world generally operate according to the same core principles and values, adopted by the International Co-operative Alliance in 1995. Cooperatives trace the roots of these principles to the first modern cooperative founded in Rochdale, England in 1844.

The cooperative principles are guidelines by which cooperatives put their values into practice.

1) **Voluntary and Open Membership:** Co-operative societies are voluntary organizations, open to all persons who are able to use their services and willing to accept the responsibilities of membership, without gender, social, racial, political or religious discrimination. However, the eligibility of an individual's admission into a co-op's membership is however still confined within the criteria as set out in the individual co-op's constitution and the laws of the jurisdiction.

2) **Democratic Member Control:** Co-operative societies are democratic organizations controlled by members, who actively participate in setting policies and making decisions.
Men and women serving as elected representatives are accountable to the membership. In primary co-operatives, members have equal voting rights (one member, one vote) and co-operatives at other levels are organized in a democratic manner.

3) **Members' Economic Participation:** Members contribute equitably to, and democratically control, the capital of their co-operative. At

least part of that capital is usually the common property of the co-operative. They usually receive limited compensation, if any, for capital subscribed as a condition of membership. Members allocate surpluses for any, or all, of the following purposes:

- developing the co-operative,
- setting up reserves,
- benefiting members in proportion to their transactions with the co-operative,
- supporting other activities approved by the membership.

4) **Autonomy and Independence:** Co-operative societies are autonomous self-help organizations controlled by their members. If they enter into agreements with other organizations, including governments, or raise capital from external sources, they do so on terms that ensure democratic control by their members and maintain their co-operative autonomy.

5) **Education, Training and Information:** Co-operative societies provide education and training for their members, elected representatives, managers and employees, so they can contribute effectively to the development of their co-operatives.

6) **Co-operation among Co-operatives:** Co-operative societies service their members most effectively and strengthen the co-operative movement by working through local, national, regional and international structures.

7) **Concern for Community:** While focusing on members' needs, co-operative societies work for the sustainable development of their communities through policies they agree on.

12.1.5 Importance of Cooperative Societies

Cooperative societies are important in order to help organize mutual benefits. Within a cooperative structured society in its original tribal form, jobs are allocated and resources are exchanged among each other and trading is only done with external communities. Now cooperative societies are extremely important in the savings market and for mortgage and professional credit within banks. Cooperative societies are businesses that are set up by a number of individuals with the intention of gaining mutual benefits from them. These societies are important to ensure that everyone who has put an investment into them gets a fair and equal return.

i.   Co-operative societies according to Gertler (2001) are practical vehicles for cooperation and collective action, both of which are crucial to sustainable development; build and reinforce community.

ii.   They are therefore media for measuring and sustaining development.

iii.   When they work effectively, co-operatives reproduce and expand social capital, which then contributes to the success of other projects.

iv.   Co-operatives play an integrating and stabilizing role, foster alliances and coalitions, and can help to reduce social inequality.

v.   Co-operatives are not tightly constrained by the discipline of capital markets—at least in the short run.

vi.   Co-operative managers do not need to demonstrate growth and profits (surplus) every quarter, nor do they risk their jobs if they fail to generate competitive rates of return on shareholder investments.

vii.   Co-operatives can raise capital via retained earnings and various forms of member equity contributions and loans.

viii.   Co-operatives do not need to make a profit in the conventional sense. They can persevere in the long term without more than break-even performance; co-op capital is "patient" capital. Co-operatives can thus make longer term investments that promise important returns in the future, even if that future is more than one business cycle away. Members derive other kinds of benefits besides those enjoyed by owners of a firm. They are likely to be positively affected by investments in environmental sustainability, for example, because they live and work in the region directly affected by the co-operative. Co-operatives help to stabilize regional economies and provide a favorable climate for further investment.

ix.   Cooperative societies tend to outlive many private firms (Direction des Coopératives1999), and their presence in rural areas helps to stabilize economies that are typically the most vulnerable. This allows others to plan and invest with greater confidence, and to reap the benefits of long-term projects designed to enhance productivity or to protect the resource base.

x.   Co-operatives reduce inequality and promote equitable sharing of the costs and benefits of sustainable development.

xi.   Co-operatives promote economic democracy and the empowerment of marginalized groups—a hallmark of sustainable development and a pre-condition for shared responsibility.

Cooperatives promote greater economic democracy through shared ownership and shared control. More people gain direct roles in the allocation and management of resources, and their skills and creativity are more fully engaged (Sen, 1999).

xii. Co-operatives serve as facilitating partners in alliances involving local and national, and public- and private-sector organizations.

xiii. Cooperatives are often key partners, trusted and respected by Non-Governmental Organizations (NGOs), State agencies, and private-sector firms. As brokering partners, they frequently provide leadership resources and may serve as facilitators for projects involving complex alliances (Ortíz, 1994; Ketilson et al. 1998). Sustainable development is knowledge-and management-intensive;

xiv. Co-operatives have organizational capacity for communication, training and education. Educating members, employees, and the public is a co-operative principle, and many co-operatives have been successful in upgrading the technical, managerial, and organizational skills of their membership and staff. Short courses, advanced education, peer instruction, and learning by experimentation all become more feasible in a co-operative context.

xv. Co-operatives are also conduit channels by which Government or Non-Government Organizations (NGOs), can effectively deliver training, technical support, and adapted technologies.

xvi. Given the prospect of long-term relationships, co-operatives can valorize investments in members, employees, and customer education. As locally controlled organizations, co-operatives are in an advantageous position when it comes to effective communication (Ortíz, 1994). There is less reason to conceal product or business information, and members can be confident that they are not being misled.

xvii. Co-operatives are part of a world movement that has strong links to other contemporary social movements focused on the environment.

xviii. Some co-operatives have pioneered in providing sustainable livelihoods to marginalized peoples.

xix. Co-operatives have provided needed links between socially conscious consumers and innovative producers who wish to implement more sustainable forms of production and consumption.

xx. Co-operatives in agriculture have a number of obvious advantages among which are economies of scale, reduced transaction costs, increased business safety and new services. According to Earnshaw (2000), "[food] co-operatives must pay out at least 20 percent of the surplus in cash, but may reinvest 80 percent in the business for the good of members." The benefits to members of this reinvestment may include reduced prices, a larger store, or extra services. Some members may desire a discount when purchasing their goods.

12.1.6 **Characteristics of Cooperative Society**
Based on the above definitions some of the main features of Co-operative enterprises are:

1. **Voluntary Association:** A co-operative enterprise is essentially a voluntary association of individuals seeking to improve their economic status through joint efforts. Individuals having common interests can join a cooperative enterprise as members of their own accord. They are also free to leave the enterprise after giving due notice. While leaving, a member can withdraw his capital from the society but he cannot transfer his share to another person. There is no binding either to become a member or to continue as a member similarly, a member of co-operative society may or may not avail the services provided by the co operative society. This is the specialty of any cooperative society.

2. **Open Membership:** Membership of co-operative enterprise is open to all irrespective of their caste, creed, religion, sex, colour, political affiliations and beliefs. Besides, normally, the membership list is not closed. New members are always welcome to a co-operative society. The membership fee or the value of the share in the capital of the society is kept low so as to enable the persons of low income to join as members. But a member cannot own more than 10% of the total share capital of the society and sometimes it can even be less if it's by laws so provide.

3. **Variable Nature of Member's Liability:** A co-operative may be organized on the basis of either limited liability or unlimited liability. The credit societies in rural areas, where the majority of the members are farmers, are generally formed with unlimited liability. In the case of limited liability societies, the word, "limited" is being used as a part of their name.

4. **Democratic Control:** Equality is the essence of co-operative enterprises; each member is entitled to a single vote regardless of his contribution to the capital of the society. The basic principle of co-operatives, "one man one vote" ensures that nobody can dictate terms to other members just because of his greater command over excessive wealth. Administration of co-operative society is entrusted to a Board of Directors elected on the principle of equality of vote. Thus, co-operative society is an emblem of true democracy.

5. **Limited Reward to Capital Invested:** The capital invested in a co-operative is not given an under preference. It is rewarded in the form of a limited rate of interest. All members contribute capital at the time of joining as members in the society. In return to the capital contributed, the members are assured of a fixed rate of return maximum to the extent of 9 per cent per annum on the sum deployed by them. This is an incentive extended by the society to its members met from the surplus of that year.

6. **Distributive Justice:** The profits earned by a co-operative society are distributed equitably among its members according to the extent of the business transacted with it by the respective members. A specified portion (one fourth of its total profit) of the profits is transferred to Statutory Reserve and then a fair rate of interest is paid on the capital subscribed by the members. As per the cooperative society act up to 10 per cent of the surplus generated by the society must have to be spent for the welfare of the members. The remaining profits are disbursed on the basis of the dealings of the individual members within the society.

7. **Service Motive:** The primary motive of co-operative societies is to provide service to their members. The aim is not to earn profits as is the case in all other forms of enterprises. The spirit of co-operation operates under the noble motto, "Each for all and all for each". Service to others is expected to be given primary importance, while self-interest should be given only a secondary priority. Even though profit is not at all an aim of the cooperative society, still members like it so because, they can take up any activities of their choice to generate surplus in order to meet their day to day expenses.

8. **Perfect Unity:** The basis of co-operation is united and joint action. Co-operatives thrive on the principle of mutual help. They are the

enterprises of financially weaker sections of the society. A poor man cannot individually fight against the evils of capitalism. But when many poor persons unite they get real strength. Co-operatives convert the weakness of members into strength by adopting the principles of "Self-Help Through Mutual Help" and "Maximum Strength Through Perfect Unity".

9. **Moral Emphasis:** A co-operative lays more emphasis on the development of the moral character of its members by capitalizing on the honesty, integrity and loyalty of its members. Honesty is regarded as the best security. A co-operative is expected to prepare a band of selfless workers for the good of humanity.

10. **Cash Trading:** "Cash and Carry" system has become a universal feature of the co-operative enterprises. Generally cooperative society operates with limited capital at their disposal collected from its members. It is not a position to afford the liability of credit sales which is a common phenomenon with all other forms of business. It is because a cash sale, as a rule, has always helped in avoiding the risk of bad debts and in conserving the limited resources of co-operatives. But members can only purchase on the basis of credit, which is an exception to the present rule.

11. **Principle of Thrift:** One of the fundamental principles is to inculcate a habit of thrift among its members. This, in turn, implies economical management and avoidance of wasteful expenditure.

12. **State Control:** The co-operative societies are to follow certain rules and regulations framed by the government. In India, all cooperative societies are registered under the Co-operative Societies Act. The Central and State Government provides a number of incentives for the promotion of co-operatives.

13. **Co-operative education and training:** The success of a co-operative will depend upon the awareness of its members towards the principles of co-operation. The members should be properly educated about the aims and objectives of the society. The members should be trained to perform various activities of the society. Thus, proper education and training of its members are the basis ingredients of its success.

14. **Legal Entity:** A cooperative society after registration is recognized as a separate legal entity in the eyes of law. It acquires an identity quite distinct and independent of its members. It can purchase, dispose its own assets, can sue and can be sued. The income of the cooperative society is legally taxable as per the Income Tax Act.

15. **Equal voting Rights:** The organization of cooperative society is a democratic body. Every member has got equal right over the function and management of that society. As such, each member is empowered to one vote irrespective of the number of shares held or capital contributed.

12.1.7 Types of Co-operatives

Cooperative societies may be classified into different categories based on the objectives, and purpose for which they are formed and nature of activities they are performing.

(a) **Consumer Cooperatives:** Consumer's cooperatives are formed with the objective of fulfilling the needs and requirement of its members. They do this by supplying goods and services at cheaper rates and by eliminating the middlemen. They build relationship directly with the manufacturers, purchase the goods at wholesale price and sell them to members at comparatively less than market price. The profit margins which the wholesalers and retailers are supposed to enjoy are passed on to the members by the society, hence charges less price from the members without compromising the quality. In Nnewi, we have Consumer Cooperative Society.

(b) **Producers Cooperatives:** These types of cooperatives are formed to assist the manufacturers/industrial units in setting up, production and marketing their products. It procures plants and machineries, raw materials and other necessary items to facilitate the members in the production of goods and services. It also, at times, takes the responsibility of marketing the products produced by the manufacturers. Small producers mainly benefit out of this process. They are concentrating more and more on production and others are duly taken care of by the cooperatives.

(c) **Marketing Cooperatives:** It is an established fact that many small producers are not successful in their projects because they lack marketing skill and network. Quality production and cheap rate do not come to their rescue in marketing. It is the marketing cooperative whose business is to purchase all the goods produced by the small manufacturer and market them when the market is favourable or at different places where there is demand for the same. The producer benefited by selling and society by earning commission from such sales.

(d) **Housing Cooperatives:** Affording the basic need of a house or to have a land to construct a house is a stupendous task on the part of a common man due to want of requisite fund, proper facility, managerial ability and others. Housing cooperative societies are those voluntary associations of members which engage in acquiring land from the general public, develop the same, and construct houses as per the requirement of members and transfer the ownership in their favour. In consideration, the members pay the price on easy installment basis, or simple term loan basis. Some societies also sell plots to their members.

(e) **Credit Cooperatives:** The very objective behind formation of a cooperative society is to make free, down trodden people in our society from the clutches of village money lender. In the name of financial support, they have exploited the poor and needy people in many ways, thus the poor were not given any opportunity to improve their socio-economic stand. Credit cooperative come in their way. They have been assisting the poor farmers and needy people of the society with the provision of soft loans, easy loans at comparatively lower rate of interest and easy terms and conditions. In this process atheist, exploitation of money lenders has been checked to a great extent.

Credit cooperatives are of two types namely:

i) Agricultural credit cooperatives, and

ii) Non-Agricultural credit cooperatives.

An agricultural credit cooperative extends credit to the rural people for both productive and non-productive purposes, mainly related to agricultural financing. A non-agricultural society is meant for urban as well as rural masses and to meet their financial requirement for any other purposes.

(f) **Agricultural cooperatives:** An agricultural co-operative, also known as a farmers' co-operative, is a co-operative where farmers pool their resources in certain areas of activity. Agricultural co-operatives are forms of co-operatives formed by farmers or agriculturalists who have combined their resources together for the production and marketing of their produce and also getting some equipments and items to enhance the effectiveness of their production and marketing of the items with the hope of benefiting members financially and economically. As societies usually formed by farmers, who on their own, each member has his own farmland, agricultural societies contribute to agricultural development. By coming together to form a co-operative, the reason is for them to benefit from the special services, which include; receiving loans, farm inputs such as fertilizer, professional advice in financial education, mobilization of savings, provision of extension services, management of credit and attraction of government's support, land/soil conservation and irrigation. A practical motivation for the creation of agricultural co-operatives is sometimes described as "overcoming the curse of smallness". A co-operative, being an association of a large number of small farmers, acts as a large business entity in the market, reaping the significant advantages of economics of scale that are not available to its members individually. Agricultural co-operatives are widespread in rural areas. In the United States, for instance, there are both marketing and supply co-operatives (some of which are government-sponsored) which promote and may actually distribute specific commodities. There are also agricultural supply co-operatives which provide inputs into the agricultural process. We should note that in Europe, there are strong agricultural/business co-operatives, and agricultural co-operatives banks. In contrast, while there are notable exceptions, co-operatives have generally struggled to succeed in developing countries, particularly Africa, despite heavy injection of funds and technical assistance by donors.

Functions of Agricultural Cooperatives

We should remember that farmers formed co-operatives for many purposes, including marketing of produce, purchasing of production and house supplies, and provision of credit. Farm marketing associations are the most important type of agricultural co-operative. Farm purchasing co-operatives rank second in importance. The modern farmer – member, who depends increasingly on off – farm products, can realize maximum savings by ordering goods through co-operatives. Regional co-operatives order some items from manufacturers and produce others in their own plants. The most important manufactures of these co-operatives are feed, fertilizer and petroleum products; other co-operatively produced items include paint, lumber, and farm equipment. Trends in agriculture since World War

II have vastly increased the size of farmer investments in land, buildings, and equipment and, therefore, the need for farm credit. A co-operative farm – credit system satisfies this need. In Nigeria, the Central Bank of Nigeria (CBN) guarantees agricultural credit loans given to farmers by commercial banks. The Nigerian Agriculture, Co-operative and Rural Development Bank Ltd. (NACRDB) also give loans to farmers and other forms of co-operative societies. The functions of agricultural co-operatives are summarized as follows:

> Farm production: Agricultural co-operatives encourage members to engage in joint cultivation of food and cash crops among others.
> Co-operatives joint supply of farm machinery. The membership of an agricultural co-operative can afford a farmer the opportunity to use modern farm and agricultural tools and implement which he could not afford on his own.
> Produce Marketing: The Produce Marketing Co-Operative Society help to stabilize prices of farm produce.
> Irrigation: An individual farmer may not be able to practice irrigation due to costs involved. But by joining a co-operative, he and the members may be engaged in irrigation programme to the benefits of the members (farmers).
> Land and soil conservation: Land and soil conservation can be better achieved through co-operative effort.
> Access to credit facilities: Government and her agencies easily grants credit facilities to co-operatives rather than an individual, who may lack collateral securities to obtain loans. Even this is also applicable to commercial banks.
> Training and Education: Agricultural co-operatives provide to their members, training and education.
> Extension service: The introduction of new ideas, new methods, new techniques (innovation) is also a function of an agricultural co-operative.
> Attraction of Government Support Agricultural Co-operatives attracts government support to their activities.
> Mobilization of savings: Agricultural co-operatives encourage the culture of savings among farmers.

Types of Agricultural Cooperatives
There is no uniform classification of agricultural co-operatives among scholars. However, the major types of agricultural co-operatives are:
1) Indigenous/Traditional Farmer's Society
2) Agricultural Production Co-Operatives; and

3) Service Co-operatives. Enikanselu, Akanji, and Faseyiku, (2005) gave the following classification of agricultural co-operatives:
   a) Farmers' Multipurpose Co-Operatives
   b) Produce Marketing Co-Operatives
   c) Food Crop Production and Marketing Co-Operatives
   d) Livestock Co-operatives
   e) Fishery Co-operatives
   f) Piggery Co-operatives
   g) Agro – Industrial Co-Operatives etc.

i. **Indigenous/Traditional Farmers' Society:** We should note that, co-operative action takes place when individuals pool their resources together (which are often meager) in an effort to obtain what is needed by all but cannot be obtained by the use of an individual's resources, talents, time, effort or information. This mutual assistance habit has existed since the origin of humanity that is, since the time, human beings started living together on the basis of family unit and/or in a community. Co-operative is, therefore, customary and instinctive solidarity. The first co-operative act of man was when the first human family started gathering food even before agriculture was invented. Long before the advent of modern co-operative societies, Africans by nature have been their brother's keepers. Prior to the introduction of money, Africans lived a communal life, where they collectively assisted one another to build their houses or till their farmlands. In Nigeria, for instance, the various tribes had their own ways of helping each other through co-operative activities.... The method and manner of such assistance differ from each ethnic group to another. In traditional societies we have examples of mutual aid and assistance. You would have noticed instances where helps were rendered to others on such events as birth celebrations, death and funeral ceremonies and assistance to the injured or the sick or those involved in legal tussles. We should note that within these traditional societies existed customary arrangements for securing assistance from neighbours on these occasions. The more advanced forms of traditional co-operative is demonstrated in saving and lending, joint action, joint possession of land, etc. our elders did not leave life's risks and emergencies to chances. They developed various patterns of mutual assistance, reduced them to custom, and handed them down as tradition and as a legacy from the past through formal and informal education. These customs or practices were enforced with the authority of the elders. They are common in various communities in Nigeria. These societies are usually called self – help organizations.

a) **Isuzu/Contribution Club:** The pattern of traditional co-operation was dictated by the economic activities predominant in each area of the country. In the western part of the country where the Yorubas live, the mainstay of their economy was trade and commerce. AJO/ESUSU was what they used in helping each other where every member of the group contributes to a fund and each member takes his own turn in receving the totally contributed fund. The more advanced forms of traditional co-operative demonstrated in savings societies are common in Nigeria. For instance, while it is called Esusu in Yorubaland, it is known as Adaghe in Hausa land. The other AJO in the Yoruba land is not a co-operative effort in the strict sense but a programme to encourage savings which is very prevalent among traders.

b) **Labour Clubs:** There are also labour exchange activities in farming. These are common in Nigeria. In this kind of co-operative, all members will on a rotation plan assigned to work in each other's farm according to designated days. In the same vein, in those communities where homes are still being built in the traditional way, labour exchange activities do exist. Members of the group will decide on agreed days to work on each other's house for the purpose of erecting shelters for themselves. On a large scale, self – help organizations do exist in various communities where common projects are carried out not for individual benefit but for the common use of the entire community. Such projects include: constructing access roads to the healthcare delivery system by building clinics and/or hospitals among other numerous projects. The Hausas, for instance, used a collaborative arrangement called gayya where every member of the society would come together to partake in either the construction of roads, bridges, market squares for the community by combining their efforts and resources. We should note that this form of co-operative that we have been describing (mutual construction of projects) end at the time when the object of the co-operative is accomplished. This is more or less ad hoc co-operative.

ii.   **Agricultural Production Cooperative Society:** This is formed by farmers who produce similar agricultural product. They organize co-operative production and undertake joint marketing of the product on wholesale or retail basis. The farmers could still retain their individual farmlands or they may jointly own farms. Agricultural production co-operative, encourage members to engage in joint cultivation of food and cash crops among others. The importance of agricultural production co-operatives to the attainment of food security for Nigeria can not be over emphasized. This is because of our level of underdevelopment in which an individual farmer cannot achieve his desires for mass production for the needs of the country. It is in the interest of farmers that resources are combined so as to gain a tremendous advantage individually and severally, which would widen the industrial base of any economy and the management techniques of these farmers. Types of agricultural production cooperative society include:

a.   **Group/Joint Farming Cooperative:** This society is formed by the farmers of a particular locality. Instead of going for individual farming, they go for mass farming to get higher rate of return from economies of scale. Combined they contribute land, labour, and capital in the field of agriculture and share of benefits in a desired proportion among the members. This process is more beneficial because of (i) Mass production (ii) Maximum output, (iii) Application of advanced technologies, fertilizers, seeds and others, (iv) pooled resources fund, land and labour etc. (v) no financial crunch. Groups of farmers can decide to team together to form agricultural production co-operatives. They can practice joint ownership of farmlands, machinery and equipments. The money they contribute can, for instance, be used to procure a principal machine (tractor) that members of the society will be using. This will enable members to have access to modern machineries and equipment. As a Farmers' Co-operative Society, it performs the functions of extension of credit to their members, collective purchase of fertilizers and seeds, collective storage of agricultural produce, collective processing of agricultural outputs, collective marketing of farm produce and establishment of day care centers. Some agricultural production co-operatives even have consumer shops, and other conveniences for the joint use of the entire members.

b. **Tenant Farming Co-operatives:** As the name implies, tenancy here is used in the sense of hiring someone's farmland for the purpose of cultivation. The land owner gives his land to a tenant farmer on agreed terms. Repayment is usually in the form of certain percentage of the farm produce although monetary repayment for the hire of the land is not uncommon. Such tenant farmers may realize the benefits of co-operative and decide to pool their resources together for the betterment of the members. It has been established in the previous chapters the benefits that co-operatives generate to its members and societies. We recall that agricultural production co-operatives encourage members to engage in joint cultivation of food and cash crops among others.

c. **Farm Settlement Scheme:** Farm settlements were very common in the old Western Region. In this set up, the farm settlement had, in addition to farming, and other related activities such as provision of amenities (water, electricity power, schools, clinics, etc). A new generation of enlightened farmers were trained in modern farming techniques and placed in a particular area to engage in large scale farming. Farm settlements were established and funded by governments as part of its agricultural development programmes.

iii. **Service Cooperatives**: Farmers form service co-operatives for the purposes of economically purchasing supplies and of profitably marketing their produce as well as savings and obtaining loans (credit). Farm marketing associations are the most important type of agricultural co-operative. Farm purchasing co-operatives rank second in important. The modern farmer – member, who depends increasingly on off-farm products, can realize maximum savings by ordering goods through co-operatives. Regional co-operatives order some items from produce and produce others in their own plants. The most important manufactures of these co-operatives as earlier pointed out are feed, fertilizer, and petroleum products. Other co-operatively produced items include paint, lumber, and farm equipment.

Functions of Service Cooperatives

Members of these co-operatives remain independent, whether they are grouped together as enterprises or households, and make their living as self employed farmers. Each member earns according to the extent of his participation in the production of agricultural product or the provision of a service. The co-operative supplies its members with production services and facilities at cost price, or at the lowest possible price. Among the various functions of a service co-operative societies are:

> ➤ Trading in cash crops such as cocoa, palm kernel, coffee etc.
> ➤ Assemblage of agricultural cash crops, that is, the society buys in small bits from farmers.
> ➤ They conduct market research in order to establish which product has better market potentials.
> ➤ They store agricultural produce until they are sent to the marketing board and co-operatives. We should remember that the marketing boards were responsible for the selling of the cash crops to the international markets but after their dissolution, private exporters have taken up the responsibility of selling agricultural products to the international markets.
> ➤ They are responsible for the packaging or bagging of the cash crops.
> ➤ They participate in the transportation of the cash crops either from the farm to their warehouses or from their warehouses to the exporters' warehouses (Enikanselu, Akanji, Faseyiku, 2005).
> ➤ They provide extension of credit to their members, collective purchase of fertilizers and seeds, establishment of day care centres and consumer shops.

a) **Thrift and Credit Cooperative Societies:** Agricultural co-operative society extends credit to their members as well as mobilizes savings among their members. The co-operative thrift and credit society is a credit society that can be formed by all classes of people, especially farmers. Okonkwo (1980} stated that the main objective of the co-operative thrift and credit society is to mobilize capital among their members and give loans to the members at a minimal interest rate. We should note that in many parts of Nigeria, Thrift and Credit Co-operative has been found to be the most successful kind of society because of its simplicity in terms of organization and financial service it renders to its members. Credit and thrift society is, therefore an association of low income earners who jointly pool large resources or fund together by contributing on a weekly or monthly basis. This type of society encourages saving habits among their members and grant loans to the members out of the accumulated fund. The loan attracts a low rate of interest. At the end of the year, surplus will be distributed to members as dividend. The members can also be afforded the opportunity of purchasing household items like television, fridge, etc. The benefits of credit and thrift co-operative society can be summarized as:

- It promotes the social and economic conditions of the members.
- It enhances the saving spirit of the members.
- It encourages and promotes banking habit among the members.
- It grants loans and credit facility to its members at a reasonable rate of interest.
- Usually, the interest rate is far below the banking rate of interest on loadable fund (Enikanselu, Akanji and Faseyiku, 2005).

b) **Supply Cooperatives Societies:** It is a common practice among farmers to take the advantage of membership of co-operative society to meet their supply needs. Many farmers, apart from farm inputs, need other things like clothes, household items, provisions etc. These supplies are better purchased collectively through a supply co-operative. The co-operative can buy in bulk direct from the manufacturers, thus cutting off the middlemen. This will lead to lower unit prices of such supplies to the members.

c) **Marketing Cooperative Societies:** We should note that farmers do form marketing co-operative society. This is important because while the farmers will be concentrating their efforts in the activities of farming, the society will be looking for markets to sell the farmers' products after harvest. With good market arrangement, the co-operative can secure better bargain and good prices for the products. The society can buy in bulk, farming inputs such as fertilizers, herbicides, fungicides, and pesticides among others, which it distributes to farmers on credit. The money for these inputs will be paid when the produce of the farming members would have been sold. Similarly, money can be given to the members by the society particularly at the period of planting and preparing the land. The money so received will be used to meet other expenses. This removes worries and anxieties from the farmers. Many cocoa farmers, for instance, do group themselves together to form this type of co-operatives, and derive the benefits of membership through large scale marketing of their products. We should note that the Marketing Co-Operative Societies represent a unique method of organizing business in agricultural product marketing.

12.1.8 Formation of a Cooperative Society

Like other businesses, cooperatives start with the recognition of a need or an opportunity. In fact, the economic motivation for starting a cooperative is very much the same as for starting other businesses. Starting a new cooperative takes energy and resources. By following a planned step by-step procedure, the process can be completed in an efficient and timely manner. Because cooperatives are people-driven organizations, the first key to their success is to identify individuals with like needs who want to explore the feasibility of forming a cooperative business. Without this important first step, the chance for a successful cooperative business is slight. The original group of individuals is usually potential users of the cooperative. They often have leadership and organizational skills. They organize informational meetings for other potential users and discuss topics such as: how the proposed cooperative could meet identified needs, cooperative operational practices, advantages and disadvantages of the cooperative business structure, member investment and financial requirements, and member commitment needed. Use of outside advisors experienced in cooperative development work, legal, tax, and finance issues, and product experts may save the group from making expensive mistakes and losing valuable time. Criteria used for selecting advisors should include: level of cooperative experience, ability to work as a team, understanding of issues related to start-up organizations, and objectivity. There seem to be absence of consensus as to the steps involved in starting a cooperative society. Various authors, cooperators and cooperative consultants view the steps differently. In this book, we borrow leave from RBCDS (1995) and UWCC (2002). In an attempt to ensure conciseness, precision and comprehensiveness, we synthesize the various steps developed by these sources. Thus, starting a cooperative involves the following steps:
1.   **Hold an organizing meeting; establish steering committee**

A core group of interested individuals should hold an informational meeting of potential cooperative members and others in the community. The primary purpose of the meeting is to explain the identified need and how a cooperative would address it. It is important that the group come to general agreement on the nature and importance of the problem and the potential for a cooperative to address it. Such an agreement will become the group's shared vision, so it is worth spending as much time as necessary to achieve it. If sufficient interest is generated, a steering committee is selected from the group. Although these six to eight individuals have no legal authority, they will be responsible for bringing the interests and concerns of the group to outside parties and meeting with resource people. The steering committee meets regularly and reports its activities and findings to the larger group. Leadership skills, sound business judgement, and a desire to reach decisions are valuable qualities for committee members. Critical questions this step poses include: is there general agreement on the nature of the problem? Does the cooperative form of business meet the group's needs? Is there sufficient interest among potential cooperative members to proceed with a feasibility study? Are there individuals willing to serve in a leadership capacity? Sub-committees on business plan, by-laws and policies, purchasing and construction, and personnel could be formed.

2. Survey on potential members

Under the guidance of the steering committee and resource persons, potential cooperative members are surveyed. Topics include: need for services, volumes to be purchased or marketed, willingness to join, finance, and use of and familiarity with cooperatives.

3. Feasibility study of the business; then report on the results

The steering committee can either conduct a feasibility study (using the guidelines provided), or hire a consultant to carry out the study. The purpose of a feasibility study is to examine critical opportunities and obstacles that might make or break the proposed cooperative business. The feasibility study should give the group a good idea of whether the cooperative is likely to be successful as a business. The critical issues that a feasibility study analyzes include the number and interest level of potential members; market issues (can the cooperative get better prices, better quality or better services than potential members currently get through other means?); operating costs; start-up costs; and availability of financing. The quality of the feasibility study is critical because it will influence all future decisions on the development of the cooperative.

Contributions by potential cooperative members are often used to help cover the cost of a feasibility study.

These members will be the primary beneficiaries of the cooperative, so naturally they should assume some responsibility for the financial costs of assessing its feasibility. The steering committee should hold a follow up meeting with potential cooperative members to report on the results of the feasibility study. A summary of the feasibility report should be distributed to participants, and the full report made available to anyone who wishes to see it. The preliminary financial projections should tell the group how much equity will be required from each member of the cooperative, and whether or not the cooperative is projected to return any patronage refunds (shares of the profits) to members during the first few years of operation. These are key pieces of information that will influence each person's decision about whether to join the cooperative. This should be a major decision point. If the feasibility study indicates that the cooperative is not a viable business, or if sufficient commitment does not exist among the group, the steering committee should not proceed with forming the cooperative.

4.   **Develop a business plan**
If the feasibility study results are favourable, the steering committee carries out or hires a consultant firm to develop a detailed business plan. The business plan serves two primary purposes: to provide a blueprint for the development and initial operation of the cooperative and to provide supporting documentation for potential members, financial institutions and other investors. A typical outline of a business plan includes a description of the company, a market analysis, research and development related to the cooperative's product or service, a marketing and sales plan, capitalization supplied by members and loans, description of facilities and equipment, and financial business projections such as fixed and variable operating costs, sources of income, and pro forma statements.

5.   **Develop legal documents**
Under the guidance of professional advisors, the steering committee should draft legal documents for approval by prospective members. These documents are: articles of incorporation; bylaws and other legal documents. The articles of incorporation declare the cooperative's purpose, kind and scope. The bylaws provide instructions on how the cooperative will conduct its declared purpose and must be approved by the membership. Other legal documents, such as membership applications and marketing agreements, are necessary to meet a

cooperative's special needs. The next thing would be to incorporate the association. In Nigeria, incorporation takes place when a cooperative files its articles with the Corporate Affairs Commission. As soon as the cooperative is incorporated and thus exists as a legal entity, two or three members of the steering committee should open a bank account in the cooperative's name. This account will be used to deposit equity contributions from new members.

6.   Secure financing for the cooperative

Cooperative businesses vary greatly in the amount of capital they need to get up and run. The business plan should include the amount and type of financing needed by the cooperative and a strategy for obtaining it. The steering committee and its advisors are responsible for implementing this strategy. Virtually all cooperatives require some level of member financing, usually in the form of stock purchases or membership fees. Member financing not only provides equity for the cooperative, it also provides a financial base that helps other investors, particularly banks, feel more secure in investing in the cooperative. The steering committee should prepare a membership application for new members to fill out and sign. It should identify the member's name, address, and phone number; the number of shares of stock being purchased (or the amount of the membership fee if it is a nonstick cooperative); and a stated agreement that the new member agrees to belong to and abide by the bylaws and contracts of the cooperative. Each member's initial financial contribution should be collected at the time the membership application is submitted.

7.   Recruit members for the cooperative

During their organizational phase, many cooperatives hold meetings for potential members, conduct surveys and mail organizing updates to them, and collect initial down payments on membership fees. All of these activities provide a good indication of the level of interest in, and commitment to, the cooperative. Thus, when the time comes to actually "ante-up" and join, potential members are more primed to act. Even so, the steering committee may need to recruit new members in addition to those who have attended one or more of the organizational meetings. This should be a major decision point. If the cooperative is unable to obtain the necessary debt financing, or if sufficient commitment does not exist among potential members to provide sufficient equity capital, the steering committee should not proceed with developing the cooperative at this time.

8. Hold Cooperative's First Membership Meeting, Hire Management and Staff

After financing has been secured and sufficient members have signed up, the first general membership meeting is convened. There are two major pieces of business that must be conducted at this meeting: the members adopt the cooperative's bylaws; and the members elect a board of directors for the cooperative. This meeting marks the transition from a steering committee and interim leadership group to a formally elected board and legally approved bylaws. In their capacity as owners, members elect the board of directors to function as their representatives in overseeing the administration of the cooperative. It is this mechanism through which a cooperative is member-controlled. As the members' representatives, the board's primary responsibilities are to develop policies, conduct long-range planning, hire and supervise the cooperative manager, and guide the cooperative in pursuing its mission and goals. Some new cooperatives identify management personnel early in their organizing process, especially if members of the steering committee already know one or more key individuals. However, recruiting staff personnel is listed as a latter step in the cooperative formation process because the cooperative is not a definite "go" until the necessary financing has been secured. One or more of the key individuals can be hired as consultants at an early stage with the mutual intent that they will work for the cooperative once it is formally established. This approach also has the effect of making investors feel more comfortable about financing the cooperative because proposed management staff have been identified. For some lenders, competent management is the most important thing they look for in making a loan decision.

9. Start Cooperatives

The directors must acquire the necessary facilities for business operations. Actual operations may begin after all facility transactions are completed and the manager has hired the needed complement of employees. It is important to note, however, that forming a cooperative is not a guarantee for success. Cooperatives are subject to the same marketplace demands and planning requirements as any business, including careful market analysis; sound business planning; competent management; and adequate capital to start-up and grow. A good cooperative is the one, which is viable, efficient, self-reliant and project-oriented. A cooperative must not only meet its members' needs, but also survive in the marketplace while doing so.

12.1.9 Cooperatives as Agents of Rural and Community Development in Nigeria

A cooperative society is an autonomous association of persons united voluntarily to meet their common economic, social and cultural needs and aspirations through a jointly owned and democratically controlled enterprise (ICA, 1995). Cooperatives seek to enable individuals and groups to tackle their own needs on the basis of participation, collective action, empowerment, sharing, enabling and equality (Maghsoudi, 2010). Cooperatives are major players in the development process. Cooperative societies all over the globe have been seen as one of the ways of reaching out to the un-banked and the neglected in the society, and not a few have come to see it as an alternative to the regular banking, since it, in most cases, provides members of the group with the financial incentives, without the rigours usually experienced in banking halls. Cooperative enterprises provide the organizational means whereby a significant proportion of humanity is able to take into its hands the task of creating productive employment, overcoming poverty and achieving social integration (UN Secretary General, 2003). Available statistics (Chavez, 2003), indicate that one-half of the world's population is supported by cooperatives and that 100 million jobs are provided yearly by cooperatives; more than even the multinational corporations. Cooperatives contribute significantly to rural development by empowering women and other marginalized groups and bringing them fully into the development process.

In Africa, cooperatives have contributed immensely to the development process (Agbo, 2010). For instance in Benin, cooperatives provided over USD 18 million in rural credits in 2002. In Cote d'Ivoire USD 26 million was invested by cooperatives for community development in schools, rural roads, maternity clinics, etc. in 2002. Rural savings and credit cooperatives in Burkina Faso have introduced health insurance schemes and HIV/AIDS education. The same feat has been replicated by cooperatives in other parts of the world. For instance, in Costa Rica cooperatives dominate businesses in eco-tourism and environmental conservation. Agro-tourism cooperatives make significant contributions in Brazil, Italy and Thailand. Cooperatives in Sweden have begun to provide substantial social services in rural areas of the country.

An informational document released by the Federal Department of Cooperatives traced the history of the establishment of the earliest cooperative societies in the country to the 1930s in the Lagos Colony. From then onward, they grew and spread across Nigeria. There are an estimated 800, 000 cooperative societies, mostly agricultural, in all the 774 Local Governments of the 36 States of the Federation and the Federal Capital Territory. They are usually named to reflect their purpose: Consumer Cooperative Society; Thrift and Credit Cooperative Society; Retail Cooperative Society; and Wholesale Cooperative Society. "A 2007 survey (in Nigeria) inventorised about 125, 000 registered cooperative groups servicing about 1.4 million farm families," the document indicates. "The range of services offered by these cooperatives and groups vary depending on the type of commodity, ecological location and value chain activity," the document further explained.

Cooperatives have been used by government to drive several agricultural and rural development projects in Nigeria with mixed results. Successes have been recorded here and there. Patrick (1995) indeed, the services offered by cooperatives to their members are varied and many. The document listed these examples: they facilitate the provision of agricultural inputs to farmers; they provide tractor and farm mechanization services; engage in the provision of storage and warehouse facility services; they facilitate marketing and market information; cooperatives facilitate the provision of processing services and access to credits for their members. Regular and optimal performance of these roles will accelerate the transformation of agriculture and rural economic development. Ijere (1981) further explains that, it is the cooperative that embraces all types of farmers and a well organized and supportive cooperative is a pillar of strength for agriculture in Nigeria.

However, Co-operative societies have the following impact on rural development.

❖ Opportunities for co-operators to building capital to finance their business through gradual but regular savings of money. Co-operative societies have helped individual members especially those in ten rural areas to build up capital to finance their business by either savings or assistance. This has helped in the increased dependency of rural people on government.

❖ Employment opportunities. The co-operatives are the second largest employer of labour after the government. This has helped in the reduction of unemployment as well as crime rate in the rural areas.

❖ The co-operative society contributed substantially to the commercial growth and development of the country by undertaking business ventures, economic productions and small-scale enterprises financing. The rural areas are not left behind in this significant contribution.

❖ It has also helped by the promotion of physical and social development of the rural areas through transportation business (Nnewi Mass Transit), low-cost housing units and community development efforts.

❖ Significant contribution to the rural output as well as the national output by way of massive production of goods and services. This contribution of the co-operative can not be over emphasized, it brings about exchange as well as wealth creation in the rural are.

❖ It promotes workers to ownership of houses, cars and other properties by virtue of being members of one co-operative society or the other.

❖ Apart from assisting members to participate in international trade, co-operatives make it possible for the rural people, through members representing the co-operative at international apex, to sit among the community of nations.

❖ Co-operative leaders are being trained as good community leaders through the training and skill acquired from the democratic principles and co-operative practices.

❖ Co-operative provides ready market for members produce in the rural area. Members are encouraged to engage in economic production and services that enhance gross domestic product and national income.

❖ It has made provision for retail goods to be available for the consumption of the co-operatives in the rural areas as well as the public at affordable prices.

❖ It makes provision for bonuses to be given to members in the rural areas on patronage, which enhance their personal income as well as savings, and investment.

❖ Co-operative members readily benefited from government and non-government organization of expert advisory services in various ways.

❖ Functional co-operatives education and training imparted on the members enable them to do well in their business.

❖ Standard of living of the rural dwellers and co-operators is raised/improved on thus, guaranteeing quality of members' lives.

❖ Co-operative societies in Nigeria have for decades, resolved some of the financial challenges faced by workers or low income business owners by using the power of numbers to provide individual needs from resources pooled by the collective efforts.

Co-operative societies provide opportunities for millions of people in all economic sectors, particularly in the rural low-income groups, to escape poverty in a sustainable way. One important common characteristic of the services provided by cooperatives to millions of their members in the country is that they are all relevant to the current drive and determination of the Federal Government to transform the agricultural sector. They are, therefore, a veritable tool that could be useful in the successful implementation of the Agricultural Transformation Agenda (ATA) of the government. "The cooperative medium has been successfully used to provide the small-holder farmers with credit, agro-inputs and market access," Mr. Jonathan Dangwaran, the Director of Federal Cooperatives said in a presentation on using cooperatives as effective vehicle for delivering rural finance at a workshop. Rural finance, which will make it possible for smallholder farmers to access credit facilities, is one of the key performance indicators of the successful implementation of ATA.

It is surely in recognition of the important roles and services provided by cooperatives worldwide that the General Assembly of the United Nations Organisation (UNO) declared 2012 as the International Year of Cooperatives by resolution No. A/RES/64/136 of February 11, 2010. The resolution itself is the outcome of a series of studies by the organisation, capped with a report recommending it by the Secretary General. The resolution explains the rationale for the declaration: "cooperatives, in their various forms, promote the fullest possible participation in the economic and social development of all peoples, including women, youth, older persons, persons with disabilities and indigenous peoples, are becoming a major factor of economic and social development and contribute to the eradication of poverty." Given the roles of cooperatives in promoting social and economic inclusion as testified by the UN as quoted in the preceding paragraph, paragraph three of the UN resolution explicitly said it encourages "All Member States, as well as the United Nations and all other relevant stakeholders, to take advantage of the International Year of Cooperatives as a way of promoting cooperatives and raising awareness of their contribution to social and economic development."

Finally, one will say here that Nigeria is surely paying serious attention to the development of cooperatives for the benefit of its citizens- to promote the growth of cooperatives as business and social enterprises that can contribute to sustainable development, eradication of poverty, and livelihoods in various economic sectors in urban and rural areas and provide support for the creation of cooperatives in new and emerging areas. As with its important contribution to world peace through peace keeping operations in various conflict areas of the world, it is encouraging sister African countries to develop and benefit from the activities of cooperatives in their jurisdictions by hosting the Regional Cooperative Development Centre for West and Central Africa at Sheda, Federal Capital Territory, Abuja.

12.1.10 Advantages of Cooperative Society

1) Easy to Form: The formation of a cooperative society is very simple as compared to the formation of any other form of business organizations. Any ten adults can join together and form a cooperative society. The procedure involve in the registration of a cooperative society is very simple and easy. No legal formalities are required for the formation of cooperative society.

2) No Obstruction for Membership: Unless and otherwise specifically debarred, the membership of cooperative society is open to everybody. Nobody is obstructed to join on the basis of religion, caste, creed, sex and colour etc. A person can become a member of a society at any time he likes and can leave the society when he does not like to continue as; member.

3) Limited Liability: In most cases, the liabilities of the members of the society are limited to the extent of the capital contributed by them. Hence, they are relieved from the fear of attachment of their private property, in case the society suffers financial losses.

4) Service Motive: In Cooperative Society members are provided with better goods and services at reasonable prices. The society also provides financial help to its members at concessional rates. It assists in setting up production units and marketing of produces for small business houses so also small farmers for their agricultural products.

5) Democratic Management: The cooperative society is managed by the elected members from and among themselves. Every member has equal rights through its single vote but can take active part in' the formulation of the policies of the society. Thus, all members are equally important for the society.

6) Stability and Continuity: A cooperative society cannot be dissolved by the death insolvency, lunacy, and permanent incapability of the members. Therefore, it has stable life and continues to exist for a longer period. It has got separate legal existence. New members may join and old members may quit the society but society

continues to function unless all members unanimously decided to close the same.

7) Economic Operations: The operation carried on by the cooperative society economical due to the eliminations of middlemen. The services of middlemen are provided by the members of the society with the minimum cost. In the case of cooperative society, the recurring and non-recurring expenses are very less. Further, the economies of scale-per production or purchase, automatically reduces the procurement price of the goods, thereby minimizes the selling price.

8) Surplus Shared by the Members: The society sells goods to its members on a nominal profit. In some cases, the society sells goods to outsiders. This profit is utilized for meeting the day-to-day administration cost of the society. The procedure for distribution of profit that some portion of the surplus is spent for the welfare of the members, some portion kept reserve whereas the balance shared among the members as dividend on the basis of this purchase.

9) State Patronage: Government provides special assistance to the societies to enable them to achieve their objectives successfully. Therefore, the societies are given financial loan at lower rates. Government also extends many types of subsidies to cooperative societies strengthening their financial stability and sustainable growth in future.

12.1.11 Disadvantages of Cooperative Society

Cooperatives the world over are in a state of flux. In almost all parts of the world, cooperatives face one or more of the following crises: crisis of ideology, crisis of capital, crisis of credibility and crisis of management (Taimni, 1997). Cheney (1995) identified five challenges facing cooperatives. These are cultural transformation, competition and expansion, wage solidarity, centralization and reorganization, and programme to increase productivity and participation. Groves (1985) on the other hand, posits that one of the major problems of cooperatives is how to keep balance in the two parts of cooperative business, efficiency and democracy since those who are charged with the operation of a cooperative chiefly the board and manager must serve two masters: the imperatives of good business practice and the social purpose of a community of people. Hence, to maintain their special character, cooperatives must be two things in one: a business organization and a social movement. This is what makes a cooperative a business enterprise with a human face and so, very difficult to manage. In striving for efficiency, cooperatives often tend to imitate other businesses, but in pursuing a social purpose they bring out the features, which make them different (Laidlaw, 1974). Educating, training and retraining of members in general and officers in particular are always a challenge to cooperatives especially in developing countries. A cooperative without a strong component of education is in danger of losing its essential character, that is, the human and personal characteristics which distinguish it as a cooperative. Be that as it may, the general limitations or drawbacks cooperatives suffer are as follows:

(A)   Limited Resources: Cooperative society's financial strength depends on the cap contributed by its members and loan raising capacity from state cooperative banks. The membership fee is limited for which they are unable to raise large amount of resources as their members belong to the lower and middle class. Thus, cooperative are not suitable for the large scale business which require huge capital.

(B)   Inefficient Management: A cooperative society is managed by the members only. They do not possess any managerial and special skills. This is considered as major drawback of this sector. Inefficiency of management may not bring success to the societies.

(C)   Lack of Secrecy: The cooperative society does not maintain any secrecy in business because the affairs of the society are openly discussed in the meetings. But secrecy is very important for the success of a business organization. This paved the way for competitors to compete in a better manner.

(D)   Cash Trading: The cooperative societies sell their products to outsiders only in cash. But, they are usually from the poor sections. These persons require an availing credit facility which is not possible in the case of cooperatives. Hence, marketing is a shortcoming for the cooperatives.

(E)   Excessive Government Interference: Government put their nominee in the Board of management of Cooperative Society. They influence the decision of the Board which may or may not be favourable to the interest of the society. Excessive state regulation, interference with the flexibility of its operation affects adversely the efficiency of the management of the society.

(F)   Absence of Motivation: The members may not feel enthusiastic because the law governing the cooperatives put some restriction on the rate of return. Absence of relationship between work and reward discourage the members to put their maximum effort in the society.

(G)   Disputes and Differences: The management of the society constitutes the various types of personnel from different social, economical and academic background. Often they strongly differ from each other on many important issues. This becomes detrimental to the interest of the society. The different opinions and disputes may paralyze the effectiveness of the management.

12.1.12 The Road Ahead

Strengthen the cooperative business model using ILO's Promotion of Cooperatives Recommendation, 2002 (No. 193)

- Develop policies, legal frameworks and administrative practices (e.g. registration procedures, taxation policies, accounting standards, capital standards for financial institutions as well as ability to access funding) that support the establishment and growth of cooperatives, in consultation with cooperative organizations.
- Develop and implement an adequate regulatory framework for cooperatives, including for instance, labour law, taxation law, accounting standards and competition law.
- Establish equal treatment between cooperatives and other enterprises, taking into consideration the distinctive structure of cooperatives and their member-driven approach.
- Strengthen the autonomy of cooperatives: Necessary regulation needs to focus, first of all, on the self-control mechanisms of cooperatives.
- Provide special support for cooperatives that address specific social and public policy needs and activities benefiting disadvantaged groups or regions.
- Provide for an efficient and effective implementation of the regulatory framework, such as provisions on registration of cooperatives and auditing.
- Promote the establishment of secondary and tertiary cooperative structures (that is, associations of cooperatives) as well as horizontal linkages between primary cooperatives, so that the

value-added in the processing and commercialization of products remains with cooperative members.

- Raise awareness among policymakers, for instance, to promote entrepreneurial diversity in the banking industry, including cooperative banks.
- Promote education and training on the cooperative business model and its advantages, at all appropriate levels of the national education and training systems, and in the wider society. Strengthen the productivity of existing cooperatives and their competitiveness, among others by providing for training and other forms of assistance to members, office-bearers and staff of cooperatives in order to develop technical, entrepreneurial and managerial skills.
- Establish links and collaboration between employers' and workers' organizations, and cooperatives.
- Encourage employers' organizations to extend membership to cooperatives wishing to join them.
- Encourage workers' organizations to advise and assist cooperative members to join them, and to assist their own members to establish cooperatives.

Chapter Thirteen

AGENTS AND AGENCIES IN RURAL AND COMMUNITY DEVELOPMENT II: THE YOUTHS AND WOMEN IN COMMUNITY AND RURAL DEVELOPMENT

13.1 THE ROLE OF YOUTHS IN RURAL AND COMMUNITY DEVELOPMENT

The development of community is a dynamic process involving all segments of the locality, including the often-overlooked youth population. The key component to this process is found in the creation and maintenance of channels of interaction and communication among diverse local groups that are otherwise directed toward their more individual interests. By facilitating interaction and developing relationships, these diverse individuals interact and begin to mutually understand common needs. When relationships, consistent interaction, and channels of communication can be established and maintained, increases in local adaptive capacities materialize and community can emerge. While much of the attention given to building local capacities are often focused toward adults, youths are an increasingly visible and active component in community development efforts. Such involvement contributes to both the development of community and the social and psychological development of the youths involved. To encourage youth involvement in the community, it is vital to understand the influences, motivations, obstacles, and feedback that they receive from the community.

The merging of community building and youth development has been at the core of recent youth engagement literature (Nitzberg, 2005; Kubisch, 2005; Cahn & Gray, 2005; Lynn, 2005). It has identified that youths must be fully engaged and involved in change efforts at the community level if they are to learn to function as effective members of society (Nitzberg, 2005). Community building, for individuals, focuses on building the capacity and empowerment to identify opportunities for change within or outside the community. Community development is facilitated by the ability of local people to mobilize resources to address local needs. Historically, youth input in decision making, problem solving, action, and evaluation in communities have received limited attention. However, recent trends suggest that youths are playing an increasingly important role in the development of their communities (Brennan, Barnett, & Lesmeister, 2006). Youth represent a vast and often untapped resource for immediate and long-term community development efforts. They also provide an invaluable resource for programme planning and effective evaluation. As youths engage in more sustained positive relationships with adults, other youths, and community organizations, they will learn that they are valued citizens of their communities. Such collaborations will lead to skill enhancement. Experiences of different countries reflect the fact that broad participation of different age groups, especially youth, has played an effective role in the development of rural community.

There is a need for community workers, programme developers, and policy planners to better understand the role of youth in the community development process. Equally important, a need exists to better recognize the benefits and opportunities presented through youth involvement in community development activities. Through active engagement, youths can take on ownership and become lifelong contributors to local well-being. If youths are included in programmes to meet needs and empower communities, they can become lifelong participants and take on a sense of ownership towards developmental efforts.

13.1.1 Definition of youth

Youth is a concept with a variety of definitions. Youth is generally the time of life between childhood and adulthood (maturity) (Macmillan Dictionary, 1981: 1151). Definitions of the specific age range that constitutes youth vary. An individual's actual maturity may not correspond to their chronological age, as immature individuals can exist at all ages. Youth is also defined as "the appearance, freshness, vigour, spirit, etc., characteristics of one who is young". Youth is a term used for people of both sexes, male and female, of a young age. The report of The Political Bureau (1997) classified youth as those between 16–30 years. This range conforms with the formal education years – from primary to post-secondary education. But not all youths have been opportuned to either go to or finish school. According to Last and Sa'id "youth include young adults in their twenties (20–29 years old). (1991: iv)". Vision 2010 Report defined youth as persons aged from 12–30 years. In an earlier work Abdullahi (1982) defined youth as any person in the period between early childhood and old age. This permits further differentiation of youth stratum on the basis of seniority for example youth of 19–24 years, 25–30 years and 31–

36 years. Odekunle (2002) provided socio-economic variegation and typologies of youth: "male/female, educated/uneducated, employed/unemployed, rich/poor parental background stable/unstable family environment, able/disable etc".

The United Nations, for statistical purposes, defines 'youth', as those persons between the ages of 15 and 24 years, without prejudice to other definitions by Member States. This definition was made during preparations for the International Youth Year (1985), and endorsed by the General Assembly (see A/36/215 and resolution 36/28, 1981). All United Nations statistics on youth are based on this definition, as illustrated by the Annual Year Books of Statistics published by the United Nations System on Demography, Education, Employment and Health. Many countries also draw a line on youth as the age at which a person is given equal treatment under the law – often referred to as the "age of maturity". This age is often 18 in many countries, and once a person passes this age, they are considered to be an 'adult'. However, the operational definition and nuances of the term 'youth' often vary from country to country, depending on the specific socio-cultural, institutional, economic and political factors. Within the category of "youth", it is also important to distinguish between teenagers (13-19) and young adults (20-24), since the sociological, psychological and health problems they face may differ.

Around the world, the terms youth, adolescent, teenager, kid, and young person are interchanged, often meaning the same thing, occasionally differentiated. Youth generally refer to a time of life that is neither childhood nor adulthood, but rather somewhere in-between (Webster's New World College Dictionary, 2004 Fourth Edition). Youth also identifies a particular mindset of attitude, as in "He is very youthful". The term youth is also related to being young (Konopka, 1973). The term also refers to individuals between the ages of 15-24 (Altschuler, Strangler, Berkley & Burton: 2009). Youth is an alternative word to the scientifically-oriented adolescent and the common terms of teen and teenager. Another common title for youth is young person or young people (Konopka, 1973). Youth is the stage of constructing the self concept. The self-concept of youth is influenced by several variables such as peers, lifestyle, gender and culture. It is this time of a person's life when they make choices which will affect their future.
Youth has been defined severally by scholars from various regions. For instance the way Nigerians view youth is quite different from other nations. According to Nigeria's National Youth Development Policy (2001), the

youth comprises all young persons of ages 18 to 35, who are citizens of the Federal Republic of Nigeria. Some writers focus on youths from the point of view of behaviour, arguing that young people themselves, through antisocial attitudes and activities, are a threat to society. Globally, youth is described as the period in an individual's life this runs between the end of childhood and entry into the world of work (Onuekwusi and Effiong, 2002). Youth is seen as a universal stage of development. According to Carrino (2005), youths are the largest generation ever to enter the transition to adulthood. Comprising 30 percent of the population in the developing world, young people present a set of urgent economic, social, and political challenges that are crucial to long term progress and stability. People in this age bracket definitely constitute a sizeable chunk of a nations' population on which the burden of nation building falls. In Nigeria, for example, youths are seen as "vital sources of manpower for development" (Odusanya, 1972; Olujide, 2008). Youths are rightly seen as leaders of tomorrow. The youth also constitute the major resource base for any country that want to embark on any meaningful rural development projects. Hence, the kind of education (formal or informal) that youths are exposed to or have access to will determine the nation's overall development.

According to the National Youth Policy, youths are all the young persons of ages 18–30 years. They have for long been making important contributions to the development of their individual societies in the areas of agriculture, defense, hunting, transmission of cultural values. Youth is seen as a relational concept. This refers to the social processes whereby age is socially constructed, institutionalized and controlled in historically and culturally specific ways. In relation to adulthood, the notion of youth is perceived by comparing the characteristics of youths and adults as shown below:

Table 13.1: Notions of youth and adult

Youth	Adult
1. Not adult/adolescent	Adult/grown up
2. Becoming	Arrived
3. Pre-social self that will emerge under the right conditions	Identity is fixed
4. Powerless & vulnerable	Powerful & strong
5. Less responsible	Responsible
6. Dependent	Independent
7. Ignorant	Knowledgeable

8. Risky behaviours	considered behaviour
9. Rebellious	Conformist
10. Reliant	Autonomous

Source: Rethinking Youth, 2009.

13.1.2 Characteristics of Youth

Youths according to Adedoyin (2003) and Torimiro (2008) are said to posses the following characteristics:

❖ Greater physical strength
❖ Greater knowledge acquisition propensity
❖ Faster rate of learning
❖ Faster reaction time
❖ Innovative proneness
❖ Love for adventure and preference for boldness
❖ Minimal risk aversion
❖ Often unclear of needs and values
❖ Less fear of failure - Sensitive to criticism—do not accept failure well
❖ Less conservation
❖ Experimental—like to explore
❖ Social needs and desires are high
❖ Developing community consciousness

13.1.3 The Role of National Youth Service Corps in Rural and Community Development in Nigeria

A measure of regaining the lost confidence of Nigerians especially the youths and to demystify the strong resentments ebbs and surging away the efforts of nation building i.e. the fallouts of thirty-six months of Civil War (1967-1970). The Gowon Military Administration drew up the famous or infamous 3r's policy: Reconciliation, Rehabilitation and Reconstruction. One can therefore simply state that the NYSC Scheme was designed to make Nigeria one. The NYSC Degree 24 of 1973, was promulgated on May 22, 1973, and the National Directorate was inaugurated on June 4, 1973 Prof. Adebayo Adedeji was appointed its first Chairman (National) and (colonial), (Dr) Ahmadu Au its first Director National. The Degree stated that NYSC is being established:

> With a view to the proper encouragement and development of common ties among the youths of Nigeria and the promotion of National unity

Objectives of NYSC

The objectives of the service corps were spelt out in some detail in Section 1(3) of the Decree. While the scheme has itself undergone several changes and amendments, its objectives have remained constant.

a. To inculcate discipline in Nigerian youths by installing in them a tradition of industry at work and of patriotic and loyal service to the nation in any situation they may find themselves.

b. To raise the moral tone of our youths by giving them the opportunity to learn about higher ideals of national achievement and social and cultural improvement.

c. To develop in our youths the attitude of mind acquired through shared experience and suitable training which will make them more amenable to mobilization in the National interest.

d. To develop communities among our youths and promote National unity by ensuring that:

   - As far as possible youths are assigned to jobs in States other than their state of origin.
   - Each group, assigned to work together is as representative of the country as possible,
   - The youths are exposed to the modes of living of the people in different parts of the country, with a view to removing prejudices, eliminating ignorance and confirming at first hand the mains similarities among Nigerians of all ethnic groups;

e. To encourage members of the service corps to seek at the end of their corps service, carrier employment all over the country, thus promoting the free movement of labour.

f. To induce employers, partly through their experience with service corps members, to employ more readily quantified Nigerians irrespective of their states of origin, and

g. To enable Nigerian youths to acquire the spirit of self reliance

In essence, the main aim of this programme, without any doubt, is exposure to the variegated socio-cultural, multi- religious, multi-ethnic condition of this giant of the black world. An Igbo graduate of Nsukka origin posted to Benin- Kebbi, in the far North-East, a Yoruba graduate of Yawa extraction deployed to Abakaliki, east of the Niger River, an Urhobo graduate posted to the North West Nigeria; all ethnic nationalist be they majority or minorities interacting at both physical and intellectual level, for national cohesion and development

THE RELEVANCE OF NYSC

The relevance of this scheme can be seen on what past leaders of Nigeria have said about it for instance, General Yakubu Gowon's message to the first batch of corps members, July 2, 1973:

> *The Nigerian Youth Service Corps provides for the youths a much needed platform for self-realization and for contributing their essential quota in the realization of our national objectives of building a strong, united self reliant nation.*

Rtd. General Gowon, as already mentioned was the Head of State who created this programme. Not done yet, Gowon made another statement regarding the NYSC, Rtd. General Yakubu Gowon, during the informal inauguration of NYSC Directorate on June 4, 1973 thus; "The purpose.... is primarily to inculcate in the Nigerian youths, the spirit of selfless service to the community and to emphasis the spirit of oneness and brotherhoods of all Nigerians irrespective of cultural background. The history of our country since independence has clearly indicated the need for unity amongst all peoples."

Rtd. General Olusegun Obasanjo at the swearing in ceremony of corps members on Saturday 6 August, 1977, in his first time as military leader also elegized the scheme he said:

> *I believe it is an opportunity to remind you that the nation expects you to make appreciable contributions towards implementing various social and economic programmes now in the process of execution. It is expected for instance, that in the field of education, youth corps teachers will reinforce the thinned ranks of secondary school teachers, and assist in training of teachers for the universal primary education scheme.*

The amiable Sokoto teacher turned politician and president; Shehu Shagari (1979-1983) made the following statement about NYSC:

> *Through the NYSC, the nation has started a gradual process of total mobilization. Participants of the NYSC have continually made us proud and have justified the optimism of the foundation fathers of the corps scheme.*

After a military putsch, which swept the NPN administration out of power, Rtd. General Mohammed Buhari took over with his non-smiling Deputy-General Tunde Idiagbor. Rtd. Major General M. Buhari at the passing out parade of 11th batch of Corps1 members July 12, 1984 had this to say about NYSC:

> *The nations' hope and pride lie in her youth members of the NYSC who constitute a reservoir of highly skilled, talented and vigorous manpower whose energies and visions, if tapped and properly harnessed would lead us to the desired social economic upliftment and threshold of greatness.*

Another coup d' etat that took Buhari out and the deceptively smiling, self-styled military dictator came in. IBB at the swearing in ceremony of corps members November 1992 thus sees NYSC as:

> *In spite of initial misconception about the scheme, it must be pointed out that NYSC has, to a large extent, achieved the objectives for which it was established. It is incontrovertible that corps members graduate from the scheme better equipped to appreciate and proffer solutions to various socio-economic problems that face this country. They have since the inception of the scheme, influenced and accelerated local community development efforts.*

At this time, late General Sani Abacha took over power and he awesomely applauded NYSC. General Sani Abacha, at the swearing in ceremony of the 21st batch of corps members, November 22, 1993 had this to say:

> *As we reflect on the 20 years of the scheme, we must put in increased resources that will substantially permit more dynamic and innovative activities in the coming decade. The need to encourage you to actively participate in community and national development is dedicated by the commitment you have as active partners, rather than passive beneficiaries of the process of change in society (Adopted from Obodoechi, 2006).*

One of the most significant attributes of pre-colonial African societies was their regular resort to collective community efforts as a means of meeting common challenges. For many centuries, it was through this indigenous arrangement that communities built fortifications for their collective security, built roads and bridges to facilitate transportation and cleared forest to make way for farms. Long before the colonial administrators came with their "development plans" many Nigerian societies had perfected mechanisms by which their people could identify common needs, mobilize the human and material resources for meeting such need and execute collectively adopted programmes of action for achieving their goals. These arrangements, among other things, helped to install in young members of the community, the spirit of self-help and reliance, frequently reinforce the idea that the members of each community were the primary architects of their own destiny.

It is true that over the last few decades, this concept of communal service has been eroded by the growth of urbanization and other modern influences, particularly the increasing individualism and anonymity of urban life. Furthermore, as governments have tended to shoulder increasing responsibility for infrastructural development since, 1960, urban dwellers have tended to rely more on the promises of the State than on the power of their own communal efforts. But, in vast areas in rural Nigeria, where majority of the nation's population continually reside, both the spirit and the practice of traditional community are still alive and well. And annually it is particularly to these rural communities that thousands of National Youth Service Corps members have been deployed, to work hand-in- hand with the rural people, in the service of their fatherland.

Under the National Youth Service Corps Scheme, the objectives of community development can be summarized as six-fold (Obodoechi, 2006).

1) Community development service is supposed to install in corps members, the traditions of dignity of labour. As the entire national service scheme instills in the youths the spirit of selfless service to the fatherland, the community development programme imbues them with a sense of pride at having contributed, in a practical visible manner, towards the completion of a development project. In having a work hand-in-hand with local people, the youths learn that there is nothing disdainful, say in molding blocks, weeding grass off a farm or clearing a refuse dump which had been identified as a threat to public health. They also learn that all Nigerians, the educated and the unlettered alike, should work together, indeed must strive together, towards the achievement of our common aspirations.

2) The NYSC community development programme is designed to enlist the corps member's commitment to his or her host community by deploying them to serve in various communities. By so doing, the expectation is that corps members would not conduct

their lives in the manner of tourists or visitors, but as full members of their host communities. The community development programme, therefore, by compulsorily involving corps members in local project, to take active interest in the airs of the community. This involvement with local project and people makes it impossible for them to remain aloof to, or isolated from, day-to-day development around them. !n this way, the community development programme ensures that for the one-year ration of their service, the corps members are part and parcel of the communities to which they are deployed, sharing in the pains and joys of the local people.

3) The NYSC community development programme affords the corps members, through their interaction with members of the rural communities, greater insight into peoples customs, traditions, and overall culture, In course of executing projects jointly with the local communities, corps members are exposed, at first hand, to the peoples' work habits, their communal values developmental aspirations. In this intimate working partnership with the local people, corps members are afforded the opportunity of asking questions regarding any aspect of the people's history, customs, traditions, folklore and philosophy. This close interaction is supposed to enable the corps members to attain a clearer d better appreciation of the culture of the host community, so that long-held prejudices can be dispelled. The positive impression made on corps members during this close interaction with the local people and their culture, is expected to sustain a much healthier attitude towards Nigerians of other ethnic religious and cultural groups, long after the service year has come to an end.

4) The community development programme designed to rekindle the self-help spirit among local communities and motivate their people towards greater emphasis on self-reliance. In some parts of the country, we pointed out earlier, particularly the urban and semi-urban communities, the spirit of self-help have been progressively eroded and the people have tended to look up to government as the sole agent of development. The trend was particularly fuelled by the illusion of an oil boom, which availed government of enormous resources. But even before the recession started in the earlier 1980s the NYSC scheme had been emphasizing self-help as the most important ingredient of development. Now that it is becoming increasingly clear that their is severe limits to what government can do, the NYSC Community Development

Programme has emerged in the forefront as an instrument for re educating the people and re-orientating their attitude in the direction of communal self-help.

5) Also, the purpose of NYSC Community Development Programme has been to enlighten, and educate the people on the operation of the NYSC and on life in other parts of the country. The presence of the corps member in rural areas, and their involvement in projects within the local community, serves to stimulate greater interest in the NYSC among curious villagers. The presence of the corps members in their midst affords the villagers the opportunity to meet, some times for the first time ever, a Nigerian from some other part of the country. By making enquiries from such a novel visitor, some of the villagers and learn a great deal about life in the corps member's area of origin. The information and ideas impacted by such a corps member to his or her host may for instance enable the local people to realize that the problems of development are similar in various parts of the country and that in no single state or community has the scourge of poverty being vanquished. Such a realization should bring the local people to a better appreciation of government's efforts towards a more balanced development of the entire country. The corps members are also expected to serve as positive models for the rural youths.

6) Another objective of the NYSC Community Development Scheme is to provide a forum for training youths in the leadership of development initiative. The process of conceiving and implementing a project involves a long sequence of activities, demanding various levels of decision-making. At each stage, such as the identification of a public need, design of the project, motivation of local people for work, mobilization of material recourse and evaluation of executed jobs; corps members informally acquire practical training in leadership and management. Participation in community development activities thus assists the corps members in developing their individual leadership talent and encourages them not to shy away from social responsibilities. As it is expected that that country's future leadership will evolve from her contemporary youths, the community development service is suppose to develop the leadership capabilities of these youths and give them some basic preparation for the challenges of the future.

ORGANIZATION OF THE NYSC DEVELOPMENT PROGRAMME
Since the NYSC scheme was inaugurated in 1973, it has been obligatory for all corps members to participate in the community programme. At its inception, the programme was designed as a vacation assignment and carried out during the short Easter school vacation. Over the years, however, and the light of changing circumstances, the programme has undergone various modifications, all geared towards ensuring greater effectiveness and achieving better result. Today, the NYSC follows a two-way approach in implementing the programme.

First, there is the Traditional Community Development (TCD) exercise, in which corps members participate working alongside rural communities, in concrete identifiable projects such as constructing roads and bridges or building the local school, health center, post office, etc. Secondly, there is year-round community development programme under which corps members are expected to undertake, in their spare time, projects in any of the following areas:

a. Education
i. Campaign against illiteracy
ii. Extra-mural and adult literacy classes
b. Health
i. Public health campaigns
c. Conduct of feasibility study (designed and costing);
d. Final selection of project;
e. Procurement tools and materials;
f. Mobilization of local communities to work alongside corps members;
g. Launching and publicity arrangement;
h. Transportation and accommodation arrangement;
i. Record keeping;
j. Evaluation of projects and the entire exercise; and
k. Arrangement for community maintenance of the completed project.

Some corps members also serve as liaison officers between the various communities, other corps members and the state secretariats. This liaison officer, among other things has the following responsibilities in relation to community development service:
   a. Ensure that every corps members take active parts in community development project within his or her host community;

b. Assist the zonal inspectors in keeping proper records corps members' participation in the community development service exercises;
c. Assist zonal officers in ensuring that corps members are properly mobilized (with due regarded to their talent, skills and professional training) to implement such programmes as would be of benefit to the host community;
d. Ensure that any corps members' projects which are of commercial value are properly verified and documented, and subsequently brought to the knowledge of the state director, for possible commercialization and mass production; and
e. Liaison with the local government community schedule officers, local government chairmen. traditional rulers and community leaders in monitoring and assessing corps members' performance in the year-round community development with a view to recommending outstanding projects for national recognition.

Funding of CDS Projects

Funds for NYSC community development service projects come from various sources. For construction projects, the host community normally provides the necessary funds and materials, while corps member contribute their labour and skill. The NYSC directorate annually provides substantial grants for the purchase of non-expendable tools for the CDS exercise in all state secretariats in the Federation. In addition to these, where necessary, corps member may solicit for funds through:

a. Donations from wealthy members of the community;
b. Launching of the project;
c. Donations from the Local Government
d. Donations from the State Government
e. Donations from the commercial enterprises, industrialists, philanthropists, social clubs   and other voluntary agencies, etc.

Whatever the source of funding, however, great emphasis is laid on prudence and accountability in the application of funds.

ACHIEVEMENT OF NYSC COMMUNITY DEVELOPMENT SERVICE

Over the two decades since the NYSC was inaugurated, the community development programme has continuously earned acclaim as one of the most effective aspects of the entire scheme. In states, local government areas and rural communities across the country, corps members have left their marks both as selfless patriots and as catalysts of socio-economic development, through their execution of numerous CDS projects. The success of the CDS has been particularly note worthy in the following areas:

(a) Development of Basic Rural Infrastructure
Corps member have contributed actively to the execution of numerous communal works all over the country, notably roads, culverts, bridges, post offices, medical centers, bus stop shelters, markets, town halls and public toilet systems. They have also carried out plot numbering exercises in many cities and have contributed immensely to environmental protection programmes (including landscaping and beautification, erosion control and afforestation efforts etc.

(b) Implementations of Literacy Programmes
Corps members have always been engaged in adult literacy programmes and extra-mural classes as part 1 the CDS programme. Reports from various parts of the continually testify that corps members are playing leading roles in mass literacy campaigns and in extramural classes for school drop outs.

(c) Provisions of Health Service
Through their community development activities, corps members have greatly assisted in propagating preventive healthcare delivery systems. They have been doing this through immunization campaigns against AIDS and drug abuse and pilot project to improve waste disposal methods and enhance water purification.

(d) Promotion of Cultural and Sporting Activities
Over the years, many corps members have been actively involved in promoting sporting and cultural activities in the communities to which they are deployed. The NYSC itself has been involved in organizing competitive sports in 1986 when the National Director Cup Competition was inaugurated. This competition featuring soccer and volley ball for male and female corps members respectively, is designed to enhance the mental and physical alertness of corps members, create an avenue for greater interaction among them and help in stimulating sporting interest among the local community. Corps members, during their CDS, have also contributed to the development of community theatre, specifically by organizing performances of the local peoples drama, music and dance. This has help in keeping the artistic heritage of many host communities alive.

(e) Contributions of Food Production and Small-Scale Industrial Development

Since 1984 when the CDS was expanded to include agricultural activities, corps members have established farms in all States of the Federation, including Abuja. The CDS farming programme has evolved to embrace both arable and livestock farming. The scheme now cultivates a minimum of 100 hectares of land in each of the State, producing a large tonnage of food annually.

The NYSC, under its CDS has also established a great number of agro-based industries at selected locations across the country. There is now:

i.   An NYSC Feed Milk industries in Ikeja, Lagos State;
ii.   A Garri Processing Factory in Afon, Kwara state;
iii.   Two Rice Mills at Ezillo- Ebonyi state, Taraba, Zamfara and Sokoto States.
iv.   A Garment Factory in Minna, Niger State: and
v.   A Shoe Factory in Benin City, Edo State.

(f) Invention or Fabrication of Simple Machinery

Since the inception of the NYSC in 1973, corps members have, as part of their contributions to community development, designed, fabricated or even invented simple machinery made purely from local materials. These fabrications and inventions have been applied in the improvement of agriculture and food production, health service delivery, educational instruction and small-scale industrial processes.

In November 1992, the NYSC management mounted a three-day national exhibition at the national theatre, Iganmu, Lagos, and tagged it: "The NYSC Inventors Forum". The exhibition brought to national focus, the scientific ingenuity and the technological creativity of the corps members. Among the inventions on display were phototherapy sets, combined incubator, Dz sterilizer, and sang taken tube and Breathalyzer tube. Also exhibited were light machinery such as water pumps, hand corking crown machine, simple slice, trisect local oven, vegetable cutter and local food warmer. There were also electrical and electronic inventions including a digital ignition lock, a digital electronic safe, a radio broadcasting transmitter, steam pressing iron and an uninterrupted power supply system. Particularly noteworthy at the exhibition was the fact that most of the inventions and fabrication on display were produced from locally-sourced materials. The obvious implication is that if tools and appliances could be mass-produced within Nigeria, the country will thereby conserve a huge amount of its foreign exchange.

However, assessed from whatever perspective, it is clear that the National Youth Service Corps Community Development Programme has been a resounding success. In the light of the accomplishment listed above, the activities of corps members under the scheme continued to impact positively on the lives of the local people and on the welfare of numerous communities all over the country even if only on account of its contributions thus far, the CDS has already earned itself a place of pride in the history of the nation's rural development acclaimed as a quiet but effective mechanism for rekindling and sustaining the spirit of self-help and self-reliance particularly among our rural communities.

In the decades ahead, both the NYSC management and corps members themselves will need to work even harder in other to uphold the impressive record of the past 20 years. This will demand greater imagination and planning on the part of management, and a higher degree of patriotism and commitment on the part of encouraging or acceding proposals aimed at brooding the scope of the CDS so as to include the following:

a. Family Life Education
i. Home management
ii. Child upbringing; and
iii. Family planning

b. Work Among Women
i.   Nutrition requirement cookery principles and food preservation
ii.   Textile designs, clothing laundry services and interior decoration
iii.   House hold management, home improvement practice, consumer education, economy of time, effort and money.
iv.   Importance of family and relations.

c. Public Enlightenment and Extension Services
This is expected to cover such themes as:
i.   Food production and food self sufficiency;
ii.   Fertilizer application;
iii.   Land use;
iv.   Pest control;
v.   Village layout and housing;
vi.   Oral hygiene (common diseases and preventive measures).

In spite of several difficulties and constraints attendant of the planning and execution of these proposed programmes, it is to be expected that they will come on stream before long, continuing the saga of community service which the NYSC has thus far written in glorious colours.

Table 13.2: CDS Projects in the States (1999-2005)

State Construction Projects	Educational Projects	Health Programmes	Charity/Social Work	Environmental Improvement
Constructions of Bridges, Culverts, It-latrine, Markets Stalls, Classroom blocks, Feeder Roads etc.	Adult Literacy, Extra-moral, Drama etc.	Health Campaign, Immunization, Community Health services etc.	Legal/aid, Donations to destitutes and handicapped homes, presentations for health services etc.	Clean-up, flower planting etc.

Source: Obodoechi (2006).

State	Construction Projects	Educational Projects	Health Programmes	Charity/Social Work	Environmental Improvement
Abuja(FCT)	22	64	26	15	18
Abia/Imo	36	87	30	25	19
Adamawa/Taraba	21	63	28	12	17
Akwa-Ibom	28	58	24	8	21
Anambra/Enugu	23	64	38	16	19
Bauchi	18	47	18	12	4
Delta/Edo	32	84	28	10	12
Benue/kogi	21	85	24	12	14
Cross River/ Akwa ibom	29	83	17	10	11
Borno/Yobe	28	61	21	8	12
Kogi/Kwara	48	98	32	16	14
Lagos	34	216	28	17	16
Niger	21	90	14	6	13
Ogwi	34	11	2	28	11
Ondo	36	133	22	10	8
Osun/Oyo	44	140	26	11	14
Plateau	33	111	13	12	8
Rivers	28	89	21	13	9
Kebbi/Sokoto	22	91	19	12	10
Total	735	2,074	501	243	266

Source: Obodoechi (2006).

Table 13.3: A Few Examples of the CDS Projects Executed by Corps Members

Project	Location
1. Maternity Center	Igbo-OyoState
2. Bridge	Nono-Ime (Now in Abua)
3. Building of an Incinerator	Igbajo-Oyo State
4. Construction of Classroom Blocks	Mani-Kaduna State
5. Construction of culvert	Anpka town-Benue (Now in Kaduna)
6. Car park	NTA-Sokoto State
7. Constructions of Dispensary	Bwari-FCT
8. Construction of Science laboratory	Vandeikya-Benue State
9. Construction Roundabout	Ekiti-Ondo State
10. Construction of a Mosque	Lugbe Village FCT
11. Amusement Park	Tundun Wada-Kano
12. Building of School Dinning	Azere-Bauchi State
13. Construction of Library block	C.C.A, Ado-Ekiti, Ondo State
14. Construction of Park & Round-about	Ogoja Urban-Cross River
15. Poultry House	Bwukie-BenueState
16. Construction of Market Stall	Maiduguri- Borno State
17. Rehabilitation Road	Odeda-Ogun State
18. Modern Motor Park	Oka-Akoko, Ondo State Mowe—
19. Fencing of Stadium	Abak, Akwa-Ibom State
20. VIP Toilet	Duduguru- Plateau State
21. Bus Stop Shed	Irepodun-Kwara State

Source: Obodoechi (2006).

Table 13.4: CORPS Members Fabrication/Innovations Project

S/No	Project	Service Year	Location	Remarks
1.	Automatic power sien	87/88	FCT	project was completed and put in practical use
2.	Millet shelling machine	88/89	Katsina	Machine can shell 0.14kg approximately one bundle per operation. It can run for seven hours continuously on a one horse prime mover.
3.	Fabrication of an all purpose cutting and scaling machine	88/89	FCT	Used in sealing & cutting polythene materials (useful in packaging)
4.	Grain plant and applicator	88/89	Edo	Found very useful in farms fertilizer
5.	Construction of a	89/90	Ogun	It is a broadcast

	Radio			transmitter that reaches up to 200 metres it could be useful at NYSC orientation camp.
6.	Combined wheat/rice	89/90	Oyo	Has the singular Mechanism of harvesting, threshing and harvester and collecting. Minimizes loss of produce. Manually operated
7.	Solar Dryer	89/90	Kwara	The device uses sun rays to dry fresh fish and seeds preservation. All components can be sourced locally. Efficiency depends on suns ray.
8.	Construction of photographic	90/91	Ogun	A *form* of x-ray device used in photography for colour separation
9.	Corn shelling machine	90/91	Katsina	Works on the principle of rotation and can be electric motor, internal combustion engine or Mechanically. Has capacity of shell 2.5 metric tones of maize per day
10.	Digital electronic safe	90/91	FCT	Provide security system for safe and car keys.

Source: Obodoechi (2006).

Problems of N.Y.S.C

The activities of NYSC have spanned every field of human endeavour, and its contributions to national development are no longer a matter of debate. But the relevance and achievements of the NYSC have become a matter of historical records, its future remains some what surrounded in uncertainty and doubt. Brigadier- General Edet Akan who was NYSC Chief Executive 84-1988 gave insight into the problems of the scheme. These problems include:

(i.) Inadequate Funding: For the scheme to effectively mobilize eligible participants, it is unlikely the scheme will get anything near what it actually needs. One must appreciate the societal constraints as all sectors are competing for a share out of the limited resources. Because of this, the NYSC has to live with a number of problems:
- Lack of adequate number of problems: orientation camps.
- Lack of accommodation and social services for corps members
- Lack of resources and incentives for corps members and staff. The allowance for a corps member is grossly too small.

(ii.) Effect of National Un-employment on Productivity of the Service Corps: When the scheme started in 1973 it was possible to arrange selection interviews for serving corps members so that they were virtually guaranteed permanent after- service employment. This gesture went a long way to motivate corps members and keep them busy on their service assignments instead of roaming all over the country.

(iii.) Societal Factors: The implementations of the goals of the NYSC rely very much on a number of inputs, support and cooperation from the Federal Government, State Governments down to the Local Government, including the in-puts from the general citizenry. One major problem area is the unrelenting lobbying by Nigerians (particularly the well placed in society) for their children and wards to serve in selected States, urban areas and places where the corps members have contacts to secure after service employment. This militates against the goal of the scheme and erodes discipline in the service corps badly.

(iv.) Perennial Under Utilization of and Non- utilization of Corps Members in their Places of Primary Assignment: In many places corps members are reduced to glorified clerks and office assistants, and entrusted with the real duties for which, they have been posted and unable to contribute meaningfully to national development. Worse still, in other cases, corps members are out-rightly rejected even in areas they do not have business working in.

(v.) There is the Problem of Monitoring and Evaluation of Corps Member's Performances: The state secretariats are charged not only with posting the corps members to their respective primary assignment places, but also with monitoring their performance and ensuring that the objectives of the scheme are attained. The employees of the secretariat are therefore expected k make sure that the corps participants are given tasks related to their academic training, that they report conscientiously for work everyday and that they carry out their duties in a manner satisfactory to both their employers and the NYSC secretariat. This responsibility has been unevenly carried out, due to the unsatisfactory employee/corps participant ratio and the inadequate number of vehicle and other logistic aid.

13.2 THE ROLE OF WOMEN IN RURAL AND COMMUNITY DEVELOPMENT

13.2.1 Women: Who Are They?

A woman is a female human being. According to Wikipedia (2012) the term woman is used to identify a female human regardless of age. We usually use different words for a woman like, girl, lady, mother, wife, daughter, widow, maid etc. All these terms seemed to be different, but in fact represent the one soul, which is called "woman" universally. They are of the sex in animals or plants that produce or are capable of producing fruits or bearing young ones, pertaining to any reproductive structure that contains elements to be fertilized by male elements (Umobi, 2008). Therefore, for the purpose of this book, the word women also incorporates girls, and babies as they all have the same attributes of feminine gender.

13.2.2 Understanding the Issues: Why Women's Participation in Community and Rural Development Matters

Nearly one in every four women in sub-Saharan Africa is a Nigerian. Because of its sheer size, the country significantly influences the achievement of the Millennium Development Goals (MDGs) in sub-Saharan Africa. The situation of women in Nigeria has a key role to play in determining the progress of the whole region. According to Afolabi et al. (2003), women constitute over half of the world's population and contribute in vital ways to societal development generally. In most societies, women assume five key roles: mother, producer, home-manager, community organizer and socio-cultural and political activists. Essentially, the 1985 United Nations Report avers that seventy-five percent of the world's population lives in the Third World, and seventy-five percent of the Third World population is in rural areas. The majority of the population in LDCs lives in rural areas, approximately seventy percent being women (Cartledge, 1995). The socio-economic problems in developing countries have encouraged different communities to engage in strategies which enable them to uplift their standards of living and promote their social function. In an attempt to address their community problems, women, in particular, engage in activities that lead to the process of community development project. Traditionally, there has been a perception that community development was a male activity. Development activities have always existed in most countries with women leading the way. However, since women were never given any recognition for their contribution, it thus appeared as if men were the only ones influential to the process of development.

Rural women's participation in the development process has been the focus of intensive debates by most international forums in the past years. Among the forums that have recognized the plight of Third World's women's participation in the development process are the 1995 Nairobi Forward Looking Strategies for the Advancement of Women held in Kenya, the 1995, The Beijing Declaration, and the United Nations Development Fund for Women (2000). According to the philosophy of these forums, each member state should promote women's economic independence, which includes the creation of employment, access to resources and credit, the eradication of the persistent and increasing burden of poverty, malnutrition, poor health and illiteracy on women. Although, such declarations have been able to increase an awareness and understanding of the problems facing women and their needs, as such they have not yet resulted in significant development priorities for rural women (UNIFEM, 2000).

The impact of development on women in Nigeria is quite different for both urban and rural women. In fact, there is substantial evidence that rural women are mostly neglected, and consistently have lost in this process (Meer, 1998). There is also overwhelming evidence of development policies and projects formulated bypassing the involvement of rural women in most African countries (Hunger Project, 2000). Development, according to Olopoenia (1983) and Pradip (1984), is not an isolated activity, for it implies a progress from a lower state to a higher and preferred one. Development is a process by which people are awakened to opportunities within their reach. Development, therefore, starts with people and progresses through them (Seer, 1981; Gwanya, 1989). According to these authors this is the reason why rural women should be involved in on going development initiatives. They are the most marginalized group in terms of their needs, while being the people who produce almost 80% of the food consumed in most of Nigeria's rural areas (Hunger Project, 1999).

The focus on rural women in this book is a concern; it implies that these people have a certain consciousness about their position as rural women, although there are no strategies developed to affect change on them (McIntosh & Friedman, 1989). Following the Lagos Plan of Action for Economic Development of Africa, it is advocated that the needs, rights and concerns of all women be fully integrated into individual country's development planning to benefit all sections of the population (Hunger Project, 2000). The critical levels of poverty and unemployment currently experienced in Nigeria mean that considerable pressure must be exerted on the economy to increase growth rates and to provide all people with access to economic opportunities (Lightelm and Wilsenach, 1993). Dlamini and Julia (1993:3) maintain that as women have historically been a major force in the social and economic development of the country. They deserve recognition and participation as a significant element in such development.

There are good reasons to focus on, and to emphasize rural women's participation in development. The most fundamental reason is that they play crucial roles in both subsistence and commercial food production in Nigeria. Not only because they are working harder than the average man, but also because they are reliable and committed to their tasks (Burkey, 1993; Hunger Project, 2000). Not only are women the majority in rural areas in Nigeria, but they are responsible for more than 50% of all productive activities, even in those households where men are present (Burkey, 1993). Many rural areas of less developed countries are commonly characterized by deforestation, loss of soil fertility, low productivity and poor living standards. All these have detrimental effects to the well-being of rural women. Therefore, overlooking the plight of rural women will have negative impacts on the development of rural areas and that of the nation. The contributions women make have to be taken into consideration, because history shows that families have survived because women were always there and the duties they perform indicate that they are indispensable to their communities. Dlamini and Julia (1993:346) explain that prior to colonization (up co the nineteenth century) women were once a dynamic force of economically independent people who assumed responsibility for food production for the family. In spite of these constraints, rural Nigerian women have gone a long way in community development. To this end, there is a need to reverse this negative approach to development by retrieving and revising the potential for participation by rural women (Buvinic et al, 1978). Equally important, those who are not in crisis are often the beneficiaries of development efforts, while those entrapped in poverty remain exactly where they are with no hope of relief (Van Rooyen et al, 1993).

Nigerian women in agriculture

At a time, when smallholder agriculture is changing rapidly as a result of commercialization, globalization, climate change, new technologies and migration patterns, it is important to recognize the key role women play in agriculture. They need support to help them adapt to these changes and to seize emerging opportunities. On the basis of available evidence and statistics, the role of women in agricultural production in Nigeria cannot be trivialized. They perform crucial roles in the domestic and economic life of the society. Rural and national development can hardly be achieved with the neglect of this important and substantial segment of the society. Women comprise an average 43% of the agricultural labour force of developing countries. One feature of modern agricultural value chains is the growth of contract farming or out grower schemes for high-value produce. Evidence shows that women supply much of the labour under contract farming arrangements, but female farmers are largely excluded from signing contracts themselves, because they lack a secured control over land, family labour and other resources required to guarantee delivery of a reliable flow of produce. Women are heavily engaged in the livestock sector. In particular, women often have a prominent role in managing poultry and dairy animals. In some countries, small-scale pig production is also dominated by women. Available data shows that about 12% of fishers and fish farmers in the primary sector are women. In most developing countries, women who are employed are just as likely as, or even more likely than men to be in agriculture.

Individual-based projects

For many rural communities, farming period starts in March or April depending on when the rains start. Because of this, crops that are produced are limited to traditional crops like cassava, yam, corn, cocoa yam, etc. However if new farming methods are introduced, so that nontraditional crops are cultivated, the income of the rural women can be increased. One of the methods that can be adopted to increase income of the rural women is off-season or dry season farming. In Nigeria, temperature supports plant growth throughout the year, but at certain times of the year, particularly in the rainforest zone, water limits plant growth. Also, there are many popular crops that are produced in the Northern Nigeria which do not produce good yield in the south, because of too much rain during the growing season. These crops can be produced in the south if they are grown during the dry season. There are other crops such as corn, and melon, which can be grown twice within a year. Dry season farming has great advantages, e.g., the menace of weed is greatly reduced and incidence of plant diseases is also low.

Dry Season Farming

i) Green vegetables: Green vegetables are usually very expensive during the dry season, so those people who can grow a few stands of Ugu (Triferia occidentals) or greens (Amaranthus sp) can increase their income. To grow these vegetable in the rural communities where there is no pipe-borne water, the crops should be planted from middle September to early October. This gives the plant enough time to get properly started before the rains ceases. For Ugu, which has long growing duration, all that is needed is for the crop to be watered everyday. However, ensure that the plant has enough organic manure and that it is also properly mulched. Greens may require to be watered more regularly. After the first crop of greens are harvested in January, it is more expensive to start a new crop, except if you live in areas, where the rains comes early in the year.

2) Tomatoes and melons: Tomatoes do not grow well during the rainy season. A good harvest of tomatoes can be obtained in the south if they are planted in mid-August. Make the nurse of the crop in container pots or basins in late June to middle July. Transplant the seedlings to well-prepared beds when they are seven to eight weeks old. The crops can be fertilized with organic (poultry, refuse) or mineral fertilizers. These crops usually ripe before every dry weather sets in. Tomatoes may be difficult to grow between December and March, because the crops does not do well during the wet weather, they require water to produce good yield. So, if you want to grow tomatoes in January, you must invest in water. Melons (Egusi) are one of the crops that produce abundant harvest during second planting. The crops are sown in September and by December the fruits are matured and no watering is required.

3) Orchards: Setting up of fruit orchards can also provide a reasonable income to the rural women. Pineapples are very popular and are sold at good prices. These can be grown very easily at the backyard or small plots. The farm requires regular weeding and mulching too. The crops should be spaced at least, four feets apart to make weeding easier.

4) Citrus fruits: Orchard, oranges, grape fruits, lemon and lime are in higher demand throughout the year. So, a rural woman can make investment in these fruits very early in her life. These orchards are not very difficult to maintain, but the returns are worth the efforts. Other fruit trees worth planting that can provide reasonable income include coconuts, avocado pears and bananas. Rural women can plant these near their homes or in farms.

5) Small poultry farms: Rural women can increase their income by setting up poultry farms. This should be at very small scale, not more than 15 to 20 chickens at a time. Usually, broilers are preferred as they mature faster and are in high demand.

Gender specific labour constraints due to household and community responsibilities and gender-specific labour requirements mean that women farmers cannot farm as productively as men, and make it more difficult for them to respond when crop prices rise. In most rural parts of Nigeria, men and some women work in farms for wages, but in their households, women are the ones who make sure that fields are cultivated for the production of food for immediate consumption by the family. Female-headed households, face more severe labour constraints than male-headed households because they typically have fewer members but more dependents. In some areas, male out-migration adds to the constraint already imposed by gender specific farming tasks.

Extension services provide good and timely information on new technologies and techniques; help farmers when deciding whether to adopt an innovation, and can lead to significant yield increase. Yet, the provision of extension services in developing economies remains low for both women and men, and women tend to make less use than men of extension services. Even when women have access to extension services, the benefits may not be obvious. Also, the way in which extension services are delivered can constrain the way women farmers receive information on innovations. Women tend to have lower levels of education than men, which may limit their active participation in training that requires a lot of written materials. Time constraints and cultural reservations may hinder women from participating in extension activities, like field days, outside their village or within mixed groups.

Financial services such as savings, credit and insurance provide opportunities for improving agricultural output, food security and economic vitality at household, community and national levels. There is a substantial amount of evidence showing that there is a significant gender gap in the access to credit in many developing countries. Women also often get smaller loans and may not retain control over the use and/or income generated by the loan. Many studies have shown that improvement in women's direct access to financial resources leads to higher investments in human capital in the form of children's health, nutrition and education. Access to new technology is crucial in maintaining and improving agricultural productivity. The use of purchased inputs depends on the availability of complementary assets such as land, credit, education and labour, all of which tend to be more constrained for female-headed households than for male-headed households. The evidence points to significant gender differences in the adoption of improved technologies and the use of purchased inputs, such as fertilizer, across regions.

In recognition of the importance of women in national building, the Nigerian Government, more than ever before, is keen on rural poverty alleviation as a way of improving the economy. Focus is on planned and desirable change in the rural societies in the form of agricultural development. The success of these planned change programmes is hinged largely on the rational decision-making process of the women.

13.2.3 The "August Meeting" Concept and Rural/Community Development in the South East of Nigeria

The "August Meeting" concept is an example of grassroot mobilization of women towards community development through self-help. Everywhere worldwide, women are known for their acceptable and responsible leadership role which stands as the reason for the respect usually accorded to them. In Nigeria, there are three major ethnic groups- Hausa, Yoruba and Igbos. The Igbos lives predominantly in South East of Nigeria. They speak common language-Igbo. Anambra, Enugu, Ebonyi, Abia and Imo are the core Igbo states. Their unity arose out of common traditions of origin, worldview, cultural features and ties, and as a result of practical and integrated coexistence over centuries.

Historically, one thing that cannot be taken from the Igbo people in Eastern Nigeria is their love for community associations. In Igbo communities, women have long had meetings of their own, and such congregations have been rightly emphasized as the base of women's political power in traditional Igboland (Allen, 1972). These womens' associations, with pre-colonial and ancient roots have given Igbo women strong and powerful political voices and symbolism (Dine, 1983). Irrespective of where they are, they hardly miss the monthly association meetings, where they deliberate on matters of common interest. But, if the Igbo generally hold the monthly meetings sacrosanct, their women do not joke with the month of August. It has remained so since the 1940s, when the Church Missionary Societies (CMS) thought it wise to devise a way to get women involved in the affairs of their communities. Its prominent was heightened immediately after the Nigeria-Biafra Civil War, when the displaced Igbo people of the South East – the area then known as "Biafra," returned to homes, communities and towns that had been devastated and ravaged by war. Schools were destroyed and hospitals were razed to the ground. Expected government help was not forthcoming, and the people known for their resilience, determination and enterprise adopted the self-help method to rebuild their communities. Today, the "August Meeting" is a regular occurrence in the South East of Nigeria. Every Igbo woman, particularly married women, is expected to attend the women's meeting on a date agreed upon by all the branches of the organization.

The formal leadership roles by which women became politically significant in Igbo traditional communities are at two inter-related levels: the "Umuada" and the "Otu Alutaradi". The "Umuadas" are daughters of the community who have married into other villages but retain their ties with their community of birth. "Otu Alutaradi" are wives of the men of the village whose common bond is their place of marriage. Both groups maintain order, promote life and create consolidation, joy and solidarity for themselves and for the entire village community. This meeting, usually organized during the month of August, is the exclusive preserve of married women.

The reasons why such meetings are held in the month of August may not be far-fetched. In the month of August, there is a short period of dry whether popularly known as "August break". This makes August suitable for gatherings. It is the month when most people are relatively free in the area. Being the month of the New Yam festival, people are free from farm work; teachers and students are also on holidays. So, rather than while away the time, the women gather from all walks of life, with those abroad sending delegates home to felicitate with their kith and kin, and brainstorm on what to do to uplift their communities. Being the eight month of the year, it is well spaced out from the festivity periods like January of New Year, Easter and Christmas seasons. These festive periods attract so many persons to their towns and villages and in order not to travel too frequently, August seems most appropriate. These Igbo-speaking women gather in their home towns in a grand meeting that lasts for days to discuss and deliberate on issues that affect them in common.

The modus operandi of the usually week-long event is structured so that the women first meet in their villages and wards to articulate ideas based on community development. From the second day, they converge at the central venue usually church, where all the women of the town will commence the five-day meetings to brainstorm on the respective outcomes of their village and quarters' meetings, before capping it with a final decision on the project/s that they consider to likely benefit the majority of people in the area. They then put machinery in motion on what is required to get the project/s for the year start. It is soul-lifting that despite the individualistic nature of the Igbo people, this idea of coming together to execute communal projects has somewhat enhanced unity and cooperation, as well as keep the spirit of oneness among the race alive over the years, irrespective of religious beliefs or faith. This has helped in different ways as a veritable tool for community and rural development.

There are many reasons why women come together from their different places of abode to hold August meeting. It is a period of re-union for home and 'abroad' women. It is a forum for women, who were married from outside the community to interact with and know more about his people, their customs and traditions. Through this forum, with its seminars and workshops, women have the opportunity to know everything they need to know about womanhood and how to chart new courses of action where these are needed. The gathering gives women the opportunity to be integrated into their community development projects, and having women as stakeholders and not mere observers helps guarantee a speedy and steady community development progress. It is an avenue for women to rub minds together on various issues affecting womenfolk. Such issues include health matters, children's welfare, marriages and family life. Spiritual matters are not left out as church leaders are invited to give talks on issues bothering on spiritual matters, church's teaching on family planning, divorce, abortion, temporary separation and so on. During August meetings, women discuss and make inputs on sustainable development of the local church in particular and the community in general. Through it, women have fought against cultural malpractices against women, attracting government intervention resulting in legislation in some instances.

The women conceived the idea of August meeting as a platform to make their contributions to the development of their communities. Before long, the concept had spread and it has become a rallying point for women in service of their communities. Actually, some communities have made progress in both projects developments, building of civil centers or town halls, markets, while some engaged in settling of disputes where there are problems usually between town union executives and the traditional stool. Further more apart from all these, other activities like recognition of men and women who have contributed to the growth of the local church are carried out. Improvement of the lots of women is another major aim of August meeting, and of course, fund raising for the achievement of goals and objectives. In many places, they try other women for stealing, committing adultery or even for speaking lightly to men about matters of childbirth or listening to the conversation of a husband with a co-wife at night. These women had the right to convict or to acquit and to levy fines on other women (Meek, 1937). They would insist on their decisions and could go to any length to carry them out. They are the watchdogs of the constitution and their leaders promptly call a general meeting when anything appeared to be going wrong in the town. They would bring the matter to the attention of the elders, whose refusal to act could make the women leave the village en masse in protest. The women use their organizational skills to raise money, which is used effectively for the reconstruction of schools, hospitals, markets and civic centres. Community development projects are financed through: annual dues, levies, donations, fines, sales, and income from money-yielding ventures, endowment, and investiture.

The Adazi-ani Community is our case study in self help community development; it is a town in Aniocha Local Government of Anambra State. During the August Meeting, different fund raising events are held; some of the popular ones include the cake cutting, kola breaking and award of titles to wives, mothers or daughters of distinguished and wealthy members of the community, who have played cardinal roles in bring about their community's development. Previous officials of the association who performed well during their tenure are honoured and rewarded with titles. Children and relatives of the awardees make generous donations towards ongoing infrastructures and projects. With the huge sums of money accruing from these activities, the Adazi-ani Women Group has the following completed projects to its credit: The "Eke" Market, which is the first ever project completed by the community, continues to function as the nerve centre for buying and selling of goods and services. Through a scholarship scheme, the AWG provides assistance to needy students.

Of course, such good initiatives come with their challenges which oftentimes threaten their essence. The August meeting has not been without its own challenges, chief of which is the unnecessary display of affluence and all kinds of indecency. It is also usually riddled by incessant power tussle. But the church, which is behind the idea, has somewhat been able to curtail these influences, as the women are now compelled to wear identical dresses specially called for the usually annual event, and even dictated the type of style in which they must be sown. This has somewhat reduced the tendency to show off, as well as checked the temptations for women who lack the means to want to take to unorthodox means so that they can fit into what their mates and colleagues are doing. We can only hope that the women would continue to use the occasion for the propagation of the noble ideas for which it was conceived. Its imperfections or vainglories notwithstanding, the August meeting remains an avenue through which the women can fight some of the societal ills, as it was in many places this year, where indecent dressing was the focus.

"August Meeting" is a force to reckon with in Igboland: several communities now plan their communal activities to fall within the meeting period. Many state governments now partner with these women groups. The Igbo women have carefully designed this forum to ensure that peace and love reign in their communities and that they keep their dignity intact so as to give womanhood the pride of place it deserves in national integration and development.

13.2.4 Inhibitions to Women's Role in Development
It is a statement of fact that there are a lot of discriminations against womenfolk for reasons of beliefs, attitudes, norms, or lack of respect for right of women. This has resulted to the wide gap between men and women in all spheres of life. The militating factors are as follows:

i. **Mass illiteracy (women's low education):** Education constitutes the basic constraint to women development in Nigeria as in many third world countries. For example, most customs often prefer sending the male child to school to the female, who is expected to nurture siblings and to be married off. This manifests in the preference to male education and anti-women education, traces of which are still visible in some parts of the country, particularly the far north. The consequent mental under- development of women population presses itself in a double negative outcomes, namely: a few number of educated women and low educational quality or contents of women education as most women shun courses in the sciences, accounting and other fields that would equip them for work in modern sector (Warren & Stokes,1985).

Available statistics on male-female educational imbalance in developing countries is discouraging. Women accounted for at least 480 million (60%) of the third world's 795 million illiterates in 1980. The proportion of illiterate adult females outweighed the male by 73% to 48% in Africa, 47% to 30% in Asia, and 23% to 18% in Latin America (Harrison, 1981). Besides, the female illiterate's position rose more than 5 million annually in the seventies as against only 2 million yearly for men which indicates perhaps, unconsciously sustained gap in acknowledging the existence of this problem. In the same boat is the African Development Bank which described resource constraint, especially credit, as a major stumbling block to the effective participation of women in development process. Following the awareness, the bank organized a seminar to deal more specifically with African women's access to credit in 1986. The seminar *was* preceded by the bank's sponsored surveys on credit availability to women in six African Countries - Cameroun, Cote d' ivoire, Kenya, Mali, Tunisia and Zimbabwe. There are instances, where women are denied of access to extension services. Rather, extension workers relate mostly with men and expect them to transmit whatever they have learnt to their wives with the disadvantage of being unable to correctly impart all they have learnt in the process. There are even instances of misplaced extension services as in the case of a project in Bolivian Altiplano "Where women have responsibility for livestock, but training in livestock care was nevertheless given to the men, who passed the information to their wives with inevitable and costly omissions", (Warren & Stokes, 1985).

ii.   **Home challenges:** It must be emphasized that no matter the career of a woman, her penury, the care of her home and children should be done with pride and joy. Women in politics are wives and mothers and in fulfilling these various roles, they are likely to be faced with the problems of balancing the interest in the home front with that of their political life. In doing this, the consent of the spouse is a condition for the woman politician's success. Naturally, a pregnant women or a nursing mother may not be too effective in politics so also the aged it must be emphasized too that sleeping away from home occasionally on political trips or passing the night or a nights in place other than with ones husband or children could be very challenging, especially for young mothers. The truth of the matters is that men cherish the food and companionship of their wives. Therefore, a negative suspicion or disagreement of the husband at any stage of women in politics could spell doom of that career or ambition however determined.

The multiple work programmes of women, rural women in particular, which are recreated daily, make it very difficult for them to participate in modern activities. Such multiple work tasks include numerous agricultural activities and unending household chores cleaning, preparing food, collecting water, caring for children, etc. The double day activities of the urban women are also excruciating and energy-sapping. They work in the office; cope with urban life pressures and return home to wrestle with numerous domestic chores including the tantrums of some overly commanding husbands.

iii. **Discriminatory customs and laws:** The customary practices of many contemporary societies are biased by subjugating women to men and undermining their self-esteem. The overall impact of gender bias, cultural norms and practices has entrenched a feeling of inferiority in women and placed them at a disadvantage vis-à-vis their male counterpart in the socio-political scene even in urban centers. These socially constructed norms and stereotype roles make women overplay their 'feminity' by accepting that they are 'weaker sexes', overemphasizing the dainty nature of their sex and regarding exceptional achievement as masculine.

Influence of traditional practices which places women at great disadvantage is also still pervasive. Where a husband dies, even when testate, attempts are made (very often successful) by the extended family of the late husbands to disallow the bereaved wife and children from inheriting the property of the deceased. Worst still, the mourning period for the bereaved wife is often turned into a period of extreme torture and extortion of confessions from the wife as she is generally assumed to be responsible for the death of the husband, particularly in a situation of premature death of an affluent young man. The situation is worse when the man dies intestate. In many of the cultures, male children are given preference in inheritance compared with female children. In some other cultures, the women/female is not allowed to inherit property at all. All these traditional practices retard progress of women in terms of opportunity for capital formation, power, status and influence.

Other aspects of the cultural milieu of some parts of the country, Nigeria also constitutes, problem to women development. In Nigeria, and other countries with similar cultures, women in purdah do not attend public gathering and also do not interact with people outside their households. In such circumstances, they remain unexposed to modern development ideas and creative innovations. Similarly, penetrating women with modern development activities amounts to cultural taboo in some cultures. Above all, traces of the culturally rooted negative feeling that women education is irrelevant are yet to be completely erased from some traditional and conservative parts of Nigeria. It is worthy of note, however, that the Better Life for Rural Women Programme of Babangida's military regime, FEAP and FSP Programmes of Abacha military regime succeeded in pulling out many of the women in purdah for necessary exposure.

iv. **Women poor economic base (poverty):** Women cannot own or inherit properties such as land, even though 80% of Nigerians subsistent farming is done by the women; it is no exaggeration to claim that Nigeria has more women farmers than men. It is true that over 90% of women live below the poverty line in Nigeria. The educated ones are not rich and the rich ones are uneducated or are not politically inclined. This disadvantage cannot allow the women to match Naira for Naira in Nigeria's monetized politics; it is a fact that most rural communities are affected by the problems, which are politically related. Oppression has for decades caused great damage to many people of developing countries. Women have suffered due to marginalization and exclusion in all levels of decision-making. As the effects of the past unequal distribution of resources are still with Nigerians, it adds to the plight of women, who in most instances are the ones who have to fend for their families. If there are no means to do that, they become trapped in poverty and this phenomenon is generally associated with women.

The development programmes stipulate that the role women play and their standard of living is so low that they form part of the syndrome, which has internationally been labeled "the feminisation of poverty". The crucial issue faced by most developing countries is that of high population rate, which has become so difficult to be addressed. It is envisaged that it can be tackled if the status of women is improved and their right to be involved in decision making is honoured by the leaders of the countries concerned. All these are issues, which left women powerless. Nigeria being so highly populated, like many African countries, which are also in the process of developing, faces this great problem, because the population contained does not correlate with the resources the country has. These results in problems like diseases, malnutrition, unemployment and many others. Although, there are programmes being implemented to address these problems, the process will be hindered by the imbalances, which previously existed amongst different racial groups, vast differences between urban and rural life and the fast growing trend of squatting.

There is also the problem of technological bias resulting in the displacement of women from certain economic activities. In this regard, nothing is done to retrain women traditional labour in the art of using tractors and other sophisticated and complex machines, which are the ingredients of farm mechanization. Rather, such training are given to men and in the final analysis, women are displaced from some of the activities for which they have been responsible. Women in India were victims of this problem when tractors were first introduced in that country. This is also true of Nigeria.

v. **Gender roles – patriarchy:** The family is the main institution of patriarchy (Kate Millet, 1970), which is an important concept in explaining gender inequality. Literarily, it means "the rule of the father"; more broadly, it refers to a society ruled and dominated by men over women. This is inherent in most African families. Giving men a higher social status over females has crept into public life, which reflects in state activities. The family plays an important role in maintaining this patriarchal order across generations. The socialization of children to expect and accept different roles in life has created a social mechanism for the development of values that engender the several forms of discrimination against the female sex. The greatest psychological weapon available to man is the length of time they have enjoyed dominance over women, who have taken it for granted especially in the area of politics and development that often continue to stereotype women and justify their subordination. A woman does not take a separate or opposing decision apart from her spouse's. Traditionally, a male child (even the least born) is assured to be superior to his mother who is a female.

vi.   **Lack of affirmative action quota:** Affirmative action is usually a measure intended to supplement non-discrimination; it is a broad term encompassing a host of policies that seek a support to the weak groups in society. They include policies, where deliberate action is used to stop discrimination. A policy process of this kind allows for rules that have the objective of enhancing equal opportunity for individuals and the improvement in the situation of marginalized groups. In 1979, the United Nations General Assembly adopted the convention on the Elimination of All Forms of Discrimination against Women (CEDAW). This convention has variously been described as the "Bible of women empowerment" and "Women's International Bill of Rights." Since its adoption, it has become a reference point for the women's movement in the demand for gender equality. The convention "reflects the depth of the exclusion and restriction practiced against women solely on the basis of their sex by calling for equal rights for women, regardless of their marital status in all fields – political, economic, social, cultural and civil. It calls for national legislations to ban discrimination against women and recommended temporary special measures to speedy equality between men and women" (UNESCO). The constitution of the Federal Republic of Nigeria takes no cognizance of the disadvantaged position of women and has no provision for gender equality. Apart from the general reference to non-discrimination on the basis of sex there is nothing in the constitution that is aimed at redressing the disparities that exist along gender lines in Nigeria.

Chapter Fourteen

AGENTS AND AGENCIES IN RURAL AND COMMUNITY DEVELOPMENT III: TRADITIONAL RULERS IN RURAL AND COMMUNITY DEVELOPMENT

14.1 THE ROLE OF TRADITIONAL RULERS IN RURAL AND COMMUNITY DEVELOPMENT

14.1.1 Definition of Tradition

Tradition is commonly regarded to be the basis of any traditional ruler's authority; it is this characteristic which differentiates traditional rulers from all other leaders in any society. Any attempt to define traditional ruler and, hence, identify such individuals, must start with a discussion of the notion of tradition. Tradition commonly refers to that which is "old". According to Encarta Dictionary of English, the word 'tradition' can be defined in five senses, three of which are relevant to its usage in this book. First, it refers to custom or belief which is a long established action or pattern of behaviour in a community or a group of people, often one that has been handed down from one generation to other. Second, it presupposes body of customs, i.e., a body of long-established customs and beliefs viewed as a set of precedents. Third, tradition refers to handing down of customs i.e., the handing down of patterns of behaviour, practices and beliefs that are valued by a culture.

However, Hobsbawm & Ranger (1994) have drawn our attention to the existence of what they have termed; "Invented Traditions". These are traditions that are claimed to have been around since time immemorial; yet historical evidence proves the opposite. According to Hobsbawm and Ranger (1994:1):

> An invented tradition constitutes ... [A] set of practices, normally governed by overtly or tacitly accepted rules of a ritual or symbolic nature, which seek to inculcate certain values and norms of behaviour by repetition, which automatically implies continuity with the past. In fact, where possible, they normally attempt to establish continuity with a suitable historical past.

According to Hobsbawm and Ranger (1994: 4-5), traditions are likely to be "invented" when and if ... [A] rapid transformation of society weakens or destroys the social patterns for which "old" traditions have been designed, producing new ones to which they are not applicable, or when such old traditions and their institutional carriers and promulgators no longer prove sufficiently adaptable and flexible, or are otherwise eliminated: In short, when there are sufficiently large and rapid changes on the demand or supply side. The notion of invented tradition suggests, therefore, that tradition can be used as a strategic resource. In this sense, tradition is considered to be flexible and fluid and can be changed to suit a current purpose. The carriers of tradition are also its creators and, hence, are agents who use this resource to shape or influence current outcomes. Treating tradition in this manner freed it from the rigid mould introduced by Max Weber (Gerth & Mills 1946:78); but it also introduced some degree of cynicism amongst students of tradition and traditional leaders. The cynicism is at least partly based on the understanding of the purpose of the inventions: to give "rapid and recognizable symbolic form to developing types of authority and submission" and "to allow Europeans and certain Africans to combine for 'modernizing' ends" (Hobsbawm & Ranger 1994:237). Thus, on the African continent at least, invented traditions have their roots in colonial rule. Both the colonizer and the colonized invented traditions, and in more than one way these inventions were employed in the strategies of decentralized despotism and tribalism. Perhaps the most commonly used definition of tradition as a basis of authority is Max Weber's (Gerth & Mills 1946:78):

> *[It is] ... the authority of the "eternal yesterday", i.e. of the mores sanctified through the unimaginably ancient recognition and habitual orientation to conform. This is "traditional" domination exercised by the patriarch and the primordial prince of yore. Many contemporary scholars have remained in this mould. Adewumi and Egwurube's (1985:20) definition of traditional leaders serves as an example: ...The group referred to as traditional leaders/rulers or tribal leaders/rulers are individuals occupying communal political leadership positions sanctified by cultural mores and values, and enjoying the legitimacy of particular communities to direct their affairs. ... Their basis of legitimacy is therefore tradition, which includes the whole range of inherited culture and way of life; a people's history; moral and social values and the traditional institutions which survive to serve those values.*

14.1.2 **Traditional Ruler Defined**

But what tradition are they referring to? More often than not this question is not answered. Where answers are given, a clear preference for the pre-colonial traditions is expressed. The definition offered by His Royal Highness Erediauwa, the Oba of Benin in Nigeria (cited in Aborisade 1985: vii), is a case in point:

> *Traditional ruler means the traditional head of an ethnic community whose stool conferred the highest traditional authority on the incumbent since before the beginning of British rule.*

In many respects, definition of traditional ruler has become a political exercise. The quest of His Royal Highness, the Oba of Benin is for more powers to traditional rulers in Nigeria. His project is to "purify and protect" the institution of traditional leadership from the "contamination" of the colonial period, hence his reference to the pre-colonial as a source of authority. The romantic portrayal of such leadership as a "consensus-driven institution that involves all affected parties", as the "unifying factor" in their communities, and "as a mere catalyst for decision-making" has to be placed in the current (postcolonial) political context. The fact is that, like all other social groupings, traditional rulers compete for political space in the postcolonial dispensation. Given their tarnished image, this was never going to be easy; hence the attempts at present to "reinvent" the institution and its basis of authority.

The truth of the matter is that traditional rulers derive their authority from custom and not so much from tradition; and custom, not tradition, is the basis of appointment. Customs, although closely intertwined with tradition, are generally more flexible than tradition and thus, more useful in facilitating change. Hobsbawm (1994:2) argues as follows in this regard: It does not preclude innovation and change up to a point, though evidently the requirement that it must appear compatible or even identical with precedent imposes substantial limitations on it. What it does is to give any desired change (or resistance to innovation) the sanctions of precedent, social continuity and natural law as expressed in history.

Custom, therefore, is a source of legitimacy. There is no actual distinction between "real" or "invented" customs; nor is there any limitation on the time during which they supposedly developed. In many respects the only "real" or "legitimate" customs are the ones in use today. These customs may or may not be the same as those that were obtained in earlier times, and they may or may not be recent in origin. In all cases, however, these customs will reflect some of the changes that took root in the various communities. Most of these Traditional Rulers are not 'traditional' in that their position because they have no direct pre-colonial pendant; if any, their office is based on a tradition created rather recently. Nor do they 'rule' in a formal sense. Nonetheless, as Nwaubani (1994) in one of the very few long-range historical analyses of the institution, has put it, in contemporary Igbo society, Traditional Rulers have become permanent and influential 'guest[s] on the center-stage'.

Traditional rulers are, therefore, not traditional rulers in the true sense of the word, but rather customary leaders. In fact, there is little traditional about traditional rulers/leaders. Many are educated, belong to Christian denominations, speak and understand the official language and are by no means uninformed about what happens in areas outside their own. They are mobile and some are regular participants in affairs that are often regarded as "modern". The only real issue that distinguishes traditional rulers from other types of leaders is that they are appointed by members of a relatively closed community, usually defined in terms of some form of ethnic criteria, and that they are appointed by means of the legitimate customs of that community. Hence, traditional ruler/leader can instead be defined as "individuals who are appointed by members of a specific, ethnically-defined community by means of the accepted customs of the day, to preside over that community". The traditional rulers discussed in this book in the context are the kings and similar personalities by whatever name they are called in their respective vernaculars. These are the persons who by custom occupied the highest social and political positions in their respective communities over a given politically recognized area.

14.1.3 Traditional Institutions

By traditional institutions, we refer to the indigenous political arrangements whereby leaders with proven track records are appointed and installed in line with the provisions of their native laws and customs (Orji, & Olali, 2010:402). The essence of the institutions is to preserve the customs and traditions of the people and to manage conflicts arising among or between members of the community by the instrumentality of laws and customs of the people. Traditional institutions are the custodian of their people's norms, cultures and practices. In most African setting, just as it is obtainable in Nigeria, selection of persons into the offices of traditional institutions is hereditary or by selection or election by the instrument of relevant traditional methods. The mode of selection of the occupant of traditional institutions varies in Africa in general and in Nigeria in particular from ethnic groups to ethnic groups or communities to communities. Ethnic nationalities in Nigeria have a rich heritage which predates colonization. Prior to the advent of British colonialism in Nigeria, the various ethnic nationalities within that entity had well established political institutions which met the social, economic and political needs and aspirations of their peoples. These institutions are today commonly referred to as traditional institutions, which are part of the deep-rooted and rich cultural heritage of those ethnic groups. Traditional institutions are symbols of indigenous peoples' rights, privileges, laws, customs and traditions which include but not limited to paramount rulers and their councils. The traditional institutions in the Nigerian context is inclusive of the chiefs-in-council, elders-in-council, title holders who may be appointed based on their contributions to the growth and development of their communities with or little no executive, legislative or judicial powers.

There exist two main types of traditional institutions in the pre-colonial Nigeria. These include; centralized authority structure and decentralized authority structure. The Hausa/Fulani pre-colonial society falls within the centralized structure whereas; the Igbo society/South-East is a decentralized system. However, the Yoruba pre-colonial society had a combination of both. Corroborating the above position, Imaogene (1990) cited in Roberts (2004:26) observes that in Nigerian traditional societies, there were a plethora of structures and values in place, for example, there existed centralized political systems with strong monarchies co- existing with decentralized political structures with the kind of lineage politics characterized as 'excess of democracy'. He asserted that traditional institutions were central features of pre-colonial governance in Nigeria. We can define an institution within the context of this book as an organization whose purpose is to further public welfare and learning, while tradition is a cultural continuity transmitted in the form of social attitudes, beliefs, principles and conventions of behaviour, derived from past experience and used to shape the present and the future. Thus by definition, "Traditional Institutions" are agencies and custodians of traditional practices, which include the customary regulatory bodies that moderate the ordinary business of life in a particular community. They include the following, amongst others:
- ❖ Traditional rulers/chiefs
- ❖ The lineage
- ❖ The extended family
- ❖ The nuclear family

- ❖ The age grade
- ❖ Professional guilds
- ❖ Administration of justice
- ❖ Court historians, Court jesters, and praise singers.

However, our emphasis here is on Traditional rulers. It is generally acknowledged that kingship was the earliest form of government known to man. In contemporary African society, kings are referred to as traditional rulers in two ways. Firstly, they are rulers who evolved by the laws and customs of the people and, are therefore, part of the people's cultural heritage. Secondly, it is used in contra-distinction to the modern system of government or rulership introduced in Africa by European colonialists. The king (Obi; Oba; Sultan; Emir; etc.) was before British rule, the personification of state and sovereignty, although there were usually a collection of other institutions that exercises this function in conjunction with him.

14.1.4 Traditional Rulers in Pre-Colonial Era
A traditional ruler is a person who by virtue of his ancestry occupies the throne of an area and who has been appointed to it in accordance with the customs and traditions of the area, and whose throne has been in existence before the advent of colonialism in Nigeria. Traditional rulers were part of the natural environment of their societies. They assumed leadership position being the founders of the political communities.

In the Eastern part of Nigeria, the Igbos' were organized in a non-centralized system whereby the heads of the different clans formed the highest political authorities in Igbo villages (Afigbo, 1980). The Edo and Igala kingdoms had enormous influences on the move towards centralization among the Western and Northern Igbo groups before the advent of colonialism. In the Northern part of Nigeria before the coming of the Europeans, the category of traditional rulers include the Mai of Borno, the Habe rulers in Hausaland, the Attah in Igalaland, the Etsu of Nupeland and a host of others. Consequent upon the Islamic Jihad led by Sheikh Usman Dan Fodio in the 19th century in Northern Nigeria, the Habe rulers (Sarki) in Hausaland and other parts of Northern Nigeria were replaced by Fulani Emirs while the Mai rulers in Borno became Shehu rulers (Abubakar, 1980). In the Southern part of Nigeria, the Yoruba and Edo peoples of the Southwest were led by Obas as traditional rulers in their various towns and villages (Atanda, 1970). In the different parts of pre-colonial Nigeria, the peoples had different systems of traditional political system which were either centralized or decentralized and under the leadership of recognized heads as traditional rulers.

Most societies in Nigeria were governed through the monarchical system. The Yorubas, Edos (Benin), Hausas, Kanuris, Junkuns, were among the societies governed through this method. These monarchs were referred to in various names and appellations such as Oba, Emir, Obi, Aku and Saki resepectively. They were seen as divine and they also have political and religious powers to back them up. They were seen as representatives of God, the Supreme being on earth, and they possessed great power and were assisted by priests in spiritual matters. Absolute political power was centralized in the traditional rulers in pre-colonial era.

The Yorubas, for example had a well organized political system of government right from the pre-colonial era. The political system was monarchical and process of succession was hereditary. The Oba (king) was the head of state and government. He was also seen as a divine ruler who had control over all the people and groups in his domain. All established towns are ruled by Oba who is the political as well as the corporate personification of the town. He is regarded as 'sacred' because it is believed that Olodumare gives the scepter to Orisanla who in turn gives it to every ruler. The Oba therefore ruled their subjects on behalf of Olodumare whom they represent. According to Idowu, a paramount Yoruba clan-head who is virtually a priest-king because he is regarded as divine in consequence of his scepter which he derived from the divinity to whom he is vice-regent. The administration of the town belongs to him, therefore, he is called Oba.

It is on record that the Benin Empire stands out as one of the finest examples of purely African States-craft unaided by foreign influence. The government of Benin Empire revolved around the Oba, who was regarded as the incarnation of the people's soul. He was an absolute monarch, and by his divine attributes, he had the fear and respect of his entire subjects. The royal officials held office at his pleasure. According to Oloko (1976), the traditional ruler under the Benin kingdom was at the head of a well organized system of government. As the sole authority, he was the legislature, executive and the judiciary. Traditional institution during the pre-colonial era was quite clear, since law and order were maintained through a normative system that was part of the general social structure though, the system was not sophisticated, the machinery of government was organized enough to manage affairs, resolve tension and administered justice in the society. Also, the institution was controlled by certain unwritten laws which ensure the security of the institution. This implies that, traditional rulers had positive impact on the evolution of political, economic and social institutions in which they had dominant control.

In the Hausa/Fulani areas of Nigeria, the defeat of the Hausa States by the great Islamic leader and scholar, Sheikh Usman Danfodio from 1804-1809, led to the abolition of Hausa kingdoms and the establishment of Emirates mostly headed by Fulani scholars who received flags from Danfodio. Sokoto and, to a lesser extent, Gwandu served as the headquarters of the Caliphate. The Emir was the political, spiritual and administrative head of the Emirate and he assigned specific security duties to a number of institutional heads like the Waziri, a senior official; Madawaki, a military commander; Galadima, who administered the capital city; while the Alkalis administered justice based on Sharia law. Consequently, it was considered sacrilegious to violate such orders and as such, there was always unflinching obedience to all rules and regulations.

The Igbo structure was, in the first place, not hereditary, not ascribed but achieved. It was by direct democracy that a ruler emerged and the powers were usually limited to his immediate village. Most classical social anthropological and historical accounts of Igbo society have described it as prototypically 'stateless', 'acephalous', or 'segmentary' (Meek 1937, Green 1947, Forde/Jones 1950, Jones (1957), Uchendu 1965 - for a review see Goltzsche: 1976, Isichei: 1976, Ifemesia: (1978), consisting of autonomous villages and village groups (Obodo, 'town') ruled by 'diffused' authority without formalized, permanent, or hereditary leadership positions. Uchendu (1965) described the prototypical Igbo traditional local political organization as 'an exercise in direct democracy' on the village level, with a 'representative assembly' on the level of the village group.

To be sure, there were exceptions to this general picture: Some Igbo communities, especially trading cities along the Niger like Onitsha and Oguta (Nzimiro, 1972) and the 'holy city' of Nri (Afigbo 1981: 31-68) had elaborated chieftaincy institutions in pre-colonial times. Especially the case of Nri has fuelled both academic and popular imagination, because the stirring archaeological findings at Igbo-Ukwu seem to suggest to some authors (Onwuejeogwu: 1980, 1981; Hahn-Waanders: 1985, Grau: 1993) the existence of a one thousand year-old tradition of Nri sacral kingship and 'hegemony' over large parts of Igboland. This theory is welcomed in current popular and political debates about Igbo chieftaincy, as it seems to be able to prove the traditional character of contemporary Igbo Traditional Rulers' titles. Nonetheless, even in current debates in Nigeria, most people continue to view Igbo society as being traditionally based on 'democratic principles' (Aguwa 1993: 20), as expressed in the common proverb; Igbo enwe (ghi) eze, 'the Igbos have no king'.

Traditional rulers occupied important positions among the peoples of pre-colonial Nigeria. Their positions were sanctioned by the traditions, history and culture of their respective peoples who held them in high esteem and reverence (Amusa, 2010). For example, among the Yoruba of the Southwestern Nigeria, traditional rulers are regarded as the representatives of the gods of the land (Alase Ekeji Orisa) and the custodians of the people's history and culture. An Oba of Yoruba personifies the kingdom and represents the reincarnation of the past ancestors of the community (Falola and Akinrinade, 1985). Among the Hausas, Kanuris and other peoples of Northern Nigeria, the traditional rulers, i.e., the Emirs and Shehu wielded strong political power, authority and influence and were well respected by the people. Since the traditional rulers derive their authority from the traditions of the people, they were considered to have divine rights over the people to rule and govern them. Their words were orders and their actions were divine and sacred (Atanda, 1973). They were hardly seen in public except during important traditional festivals and religious celebrations.

To this end, during the pre-colonial period in Nigeria, the position of traditional rulers was not only divine but it was based on ritual leadership and political power was seen as sacred trust between the people and the rulers (Cohen, 1970; Ashiru, 2010). The people submitted themselves and were absolutely submissive to the authority of the rulers who in turn were expected to rule for the general good and welfare of the community as a whole. They were seen as the symbols of the peoples past, custodians of their history and past, upholder and preserver of their culture and customs, epitome of cultural norms and values of the society such as truth, discipline, courage and responsibility and so on (Emordi and Osiki 2008). In theory, traditional rulers in pre-colonial societies had permanent tenures of office and the positions were hereditary. However, in practice, they had a number of advisers, assistants and other courtiers and their final decisions were based on consensus of opinions of all the stakeholders. Although traditional institutions in pre-colonial Nigeria were in most cases absolutely monarchical, they were not in any way autocratic or totalitarian.

In fact, various mechanisms were put in place for checking the abuses of tending autocratic rulers in pre-colonial Nigerian societies (Atanda, 1980). This was the situation of traditional rulership that the British colonial rule met when Nigeria was colonized in 1900 and the various people forced together in the 1914 amalgamation.

14.1.5 Traditional Rulers in Colonial Era

The advent of colonial rule ushered in a transformation in the role of traditional rulers. This change was necessitated by the desire to realize the objectives of colonialism, which where to exploit the natural resources of Nigeria to meet the industrial needs of the capitalist metro poles. Traditional rulers were therefore, used to serve these objectives. According to Aidelokhai (2008), traditional rulers before the advent of colonial rule in Nigeria were the political, cultural, economic and social administrators and lords of their various domains. The status of traditional rulers changed with the advent of colonial rule as the colonialist who imposed their power on traditional rulers usurped their sovereign authority. This development was meant to enable the colonialist perfect their exploitation through the use of traditional rulers. Crowder (1978) asserts that chieftaincy institution were maintained and used by the colonialist for colonial interest. The indirect rule in Northern Nigeria attests to this phenomenon. Arguing further, Crowder believes that whether they had fulfilled the entire traditional pre-requisite for assumption of office, which would have allowed them rule in pre-colonial days, their right to rule depended on the colonial authorities.

More often than not, scholars often misrepresent the role of traditional rulers in the colonization and colonial rule in Nigeria, particularly their participation in the trans-Atlantic slave trade. They have also been accused of complicity in the sustenance and prolongation of colonial rule in Nigeria for their support for the British colonialists. The fact is that people tend to look at the past with the eyes of the present, thereby seeing the negative sides of the activities of past heroes and heroines who had done what they did in the light of the realities and situations of their time. While it is an established fact that traditional rulers were actively involved in the trade in human beings with the Europeans, the truth is that the trade was not considered bad at its time. In fact, it was the global commerce of its time which brought together the major world continent of that era- Europe, Americas, Asia and Africa (Curtin, 1976). Therefore, the involvement of Africans in such a global trade was a benefit then rather than curse. Also, the active involvement of traditional rulers in the 'heinous' trade could be explained from the perspective of the fact that, by traditions, they were supposed to represent their peoples in all manners of dealings with foreigners. Hence, they had the traditional rights to negotiate with the Europeans the sales of their war captives and condemned criminals. It can be categorically stated here that no African traditional ruler offered the sale of his people on subjects, apart from condemned criminals and war captives to the Europeans. In fact, the sale of male slaves was prohibited by most traditional rulers in Nigeria (Ryder, 1980). Unfortunately, scholars have not emphasized the nationalist role of traditional rulers during the period of colonial subjugation of African states by the Europeans.

Indeed, traditional rulers constituted the early opposition to the colonization of Nigeria during the period of the 'legitimate' trade which followed the abolition of the Atlantic slave trade. They saw the desire of the Europeans to take over the control of the commerce in their domains as an affront against traditions and as the custodians of peoples custom, they rose to the occasion by challenging the European domination and control. Examples of traditional rulers abound in this regard. They included; Kosoko of Lagos, Jaja of Opobo and Nana Olomu of Itshekiri in the Oil Rivers and a host of others (Coleman, 1958). Because of the European possession of superior fire-arms, all these rulers were captured and deported to enable the Europeans control the commerce of the areas under them and puppets were appointed in their positions. This deposition and enthronement of traditional rulers by the European official during this period was to have disastrous impact on traditional chieftaincy institutions in Nigeria.

The Europeans were to follow up their economic control of Nigerian territories with active political control following the commercial rivalries which led to the Berlin West African Conference of 1884/1885 and its recommendation of 'effective occupation' of the areas of influence of individual European States (Coleman, 1958). The traditional rulers were also instrumental to the opposition to the formal colonization of Nigeria. Such rulers included; Oba Overami of Benin and other traditional rulers in Southern and Northern Nigeria who engaged the British troops in several battles for the defense of his traditional domains. The defeat of these traditional rulers resulted in the formal colonization of their territories. These were some of the impressive efforts of Nigerian traditional rulers to maintain the integrity of African traditions in the face of alien European domination which has not been appreciated by some scholars calling for the total scrap of traditional institutions in Nigeria. It was not until the

British colonial official began to realize that colonial success depended greatly on the recognition and involvement of the traditional rulers that they began to patronize and incorporate them into the Indirect Rule system. This realization was not unconnected with the fact that the Europeans discovered that Nigerian peoples were so bound with their traditions and traditional rulers to the extent that whatever they ordered was what the people would do or not do as the case may be. This was the origin of the involvement of traditional rulers in colonial government which has received great criticisms from scholars as 'criminality' (Emordi and Osiki, 2008). Again, this category of scholars tends to look at the past with the eyes of the present.

In order to legitimize their control over the territories after the amalgamation of Nigeria in 1914, the colonial masters introduced a system of administration that utilized the already perfected structure put in place by the traditional rulers. This was the development that gave birth to the Indirect Rule system of administration. In the colonial era, the British system of colonial administration employed the system of indirect rule. Indirect rule was a British system of ruling her colonies with the use of local chiefs or other approved intermediaries and traditional laws and customs with British officials merely supervising the administration. Indirect rule used the existing traditional system of administration and it recognized the status of traditional rulers who served as the priest of indirect rule (Abdullahi, 2007). Undoubtedly, the introduction of the Indirect Rule system, first in Northern Nigeria and later in Southern Nigeria gave the traditional rulers the opportunity of active participation in the colonial government through the Native Authority. The Indirect Rule not only strengthened the power and influence of traditional rulers, it also attempted to create it where it did not exist at all (Adesoji, 2010). This was the situation in the Eastern part of the country among the Igbo where the colonial government experimented with the establishment of 'Warrant Chiefs' to act like the Hausa Emirs or Yoruba Obas (Adesoji, 2010). This was a manifestation of the colonial ignorance of the different peculiarities of the traditions of the various peoples of Nigeria.

Although the Indirect Rule served the purpose for which it was created in the places where it was successful such as Northern Nigeria and Yorubaland, it altered the balance of power in traditional political systems in several of these areas. Indeed, it was a total failure in the East as it led to more problems that it met. Yorubaland offered perfect example of the disruption of traditional chieftaincy institutions by the Indirect Rule. It excessively altered the traditional arrangement of balance of powers and made the paramount rulers above board (Atanda, 1970). However, it must be emphasized that they only danced to the tunes of colonial officials, collected taxes and remitted such to them and were therefore, stooges of colonial government rather than being the protectors of the interest of the people which they used to be in the past. Convinced of the enormous powers and recognitions wielded by traditional rulers in Nigerian communities, the colonial government made move to give constitutional backing to their participation in colonial government in Nigeria. This was achieved in 1914 after the amalgamation of both the Northern and Southern Protectorates of Nigeria. In the 1914 Constitution of Nigeria, six Nigerian traditional rulers were made unofficial members. These were Sultan Attahiru of Sokoto, the Alaafin of Oyo, the Emir of Kano, Chief Richard Henshaw of Calabar and the Shehu of Borno (Adesoji, 2010). From this period, traditional rulers began to enjoy constitutional recognitions throughout the colonial period even at the expense of the educated elite who formed the bulk of the nationalist leaders.

The matter came to a head during the period of decolonization when the colonial officials adopted 'divide and rule' tactics to prolong the attainment of Nigerian independence by setting both the educated and traditional elites against each other (Coleman, 1958). Thus, when self-government drew near, traditional rulers were given a say in governmental matters. Significantly, the Richards Constitution of 1946 created a House of Chiefs in Northern Nigeria members of which were all first-class traditional rulers in the Region (Odumosu, 1963). The same arrangement, with some differences, was replicated in the Western Region through the Macpherson Constitution of 1951 and in the Eastern Region through the Lyttleton Constitution of 1954. While this strengthened the political influence of traditional rulers in Nigeria, it increased their partisanship as they began to lend their supports to the ruling political parties which had the rights to select the traditional rulers that would be at the House of Chiefs (Vaughan, 2000). Thus, traditional rulers had begun to flout traditions which required them to work for the interest of their subjects irrespective of their political affiliations.

The climax of the involvement of traditional rulers in colonial politics was in the last years of colonial rule in Nigeria in the late 1950s and in the First Republic between 1960 and 1966. During these periods, ruling political parties in the three regions began to patronize leading traditional rulers and lure them into their folds through political appointments and offices.

For instance, in the Western Region, Oba Adesoji Aderemi, the Ooni of Ife was appointed as the Governor of the Region by the Action Group (AG) government of the West in 1959 (The Guardian, July 16, 2007; Adesoji, 2010). In addition to this, some prominent traditional rulers in Yorubaland such as the Olubadan of Ibadanland, Osemawe of Ondo, Oluwo of Iwo, Olu of Warri and a host of others were given ministerial appointments during this period (Vaughan, 2000). The unfortunate situation during this period was that, while the favoured traditional rulers were given political appointments, those who were not in the good books of the ruling party were dealt with severely. This was the situation in the First Republic in Nigeria during which the traditional institutions became instruments of political rewards or punishments as the case may be in the hands of the politicians. Interestingly, this was the situation regarding the status of traditional ruler's vis-à-vis modern politics when the military struck in January, 1966 bringing the First Republic to an end.

14.1.6 Traditional Rulers in Post-Colonial Era
The post-colonial era undoubtedly, witnessed radical changes in the administration of native authorities, changes that the traditional rulers were not prepared for. The military came into power in January 1966 and suspended the Constitution, took over all spheres of governance hitherto manned by the politicians (Kirk-Greene, 1976; Alao, 1990). With its conviction that, while traditional rulers are very powerful and respected in among the Nigerian peoples, they must not be partisan, the successive military regimes in Nigeria covertly and overtly excluded traditional rulers from government. This was done through the Local Government Reforms of 1976 and the 1979, 1989 and 1999 Constitutions designed by military regimes in Nigeria (Emordi and Osiki, 2010). Through these avenues, traditional rulers were legally and formally insulated from the governmental affairs and administration as they were given very limited advisory roles to play. Even at the local levels which are the levels in which the traditional rulers commanded great respects, the military governments made the local government administrator/chairman superior to the traditional rulers (News watch, April 18, 1988; Emordi and Osiki, 2008). Thus, from the hitherto exalted positions of being the only recognized leaders by the authority, traditional rulers tumbled out of government with limited powers. Some even suffered humiliation in the hands of the politicians when they failed to play along with the government of the day. Thus, for personal security, many of them became involved in subterranean politics for survival. Those who did not comply were deposed. Only those who cooperated were co-opted into governance.

In spite of this formal constitutional relegation, traditional rulers still had modicum of recognitions during the successive military regimes. For instance, the Aguiyi Ironsi military regime appointed traditional rulers as Chancellors of Federal government owned universities in 1966 as a mark of honour and respect for traditional institutions in Nigeria (Nigerian Tribune, July 28, 1966). Also, the 1989 Constitution stipulated the establishment of a State and Local Government Council of chiefs in every State and Local government area in Nigeria. Furthermore, the General Sani Abacha led autocratic regime decreed that 55 of statutory allocations of local governments should be set aside for the upkeep of the traditional institutions in such Local Government Areas (Aiyede, 2003). The military made use of the traditional rulers mainly in the area of legitimizing their regimes and in the area of settling disputes during crises. This is why the military, particularly the Babangida administration saw the traditional rulers as "the most valuable asset the nation had" (Newswatch, April 18, 1988).

It was also under the military regimes of Generals Babangida and Abacha that the actions and utterances of traditional rulers were mostly criticized in Nigeria. For instance, the annulment of the 1993 Presidential elections adjudged the fairest and freest in the history of elections in Nigeria by the Ibrahim Babangida administration which was unanimously condemned by all classes of Nigerians including the traditional rulers. To the utmost surprise of Nigerians, it was not long before prominent traditional rulers in Nigeria began to befriend the dictator that succeeded General Babangida, Late General Sani Abacha and supported his succession (Conscience International, 1998; Onoja, 2007). Some of them started to justify the annulment of June 12, 1993 Presidential election and the incarceration of the presumed winner, Chief M.K.O. Abiola. They became regular visitors at the Aso Villa, the official residence of the Nigerian Head of State, during the dark years of General Sani Abacha. No doubt, they benefited immensely from Abacha's loots in the forms of contracts, gift of cars and cash, oil blocs and oil lifting opportunities among others (Onoja, 2007). By the end of last millennium, the position of traditional rulers in governance in Nigeria has been reduced to that of advisory and placed under the control of Local Government Councils. However, this does not mean that traditional institutions have died a natural death as they were to play prominent role in the democratic dispensation that ushered in Nigeria into the 21st century.

14.1.7 Traditional Rulers and Community Development
The role of traditional rulers in Nigeria has been undergoing changes as the democratic dispensation within the country develops. It has therefore been necessary that they redefine their role as heads of their polities within the framework of developmental efforts by the Federal government and its adjuncts especially the Local government. Traditional rulers stand as a structure within a given system which has functions to perform in the transformation and development process within Local government environment as well as in a large society.

Traditional leaders in Nigeria remain, for a variety of reasons, important to the design and implementation of development projects within their areas of jurisdiction. Indeed, today, traditional rulers perceive their role as being primarily initiators of development or catalysts of development processes. They are keenly aware of the fact that their functions have been transformed from serving in merely political, military and ritual capacity that they derives from their traditional role as moral and social leaders. Their core functions include mobilization of their communities for development purposes in this capacity; they act as linkages between their communities and development agencies including central government departments, Local government organs, NGOs, diplomatic missions, religious bodies and welfare associations. This includes the provision of infrastructure; settlement of disputes through arbitration, revenue collection and resource mobilization; provision of services and infrastructures; The management, protection and allocation of natural resources; social community workforce mobilization; promotion of economic activities such as advocacy and peer control for micro-credit schemes; planning, implementation and monitoring of local development initiatives; broker between the people and the State.

Sometimes, traditional rulers initiate development projects and secure the support of both internal and external development agents for the execution of these projects for the enhancement of standard of life of the members of their communities. Besides, they are expected to ensure that peace and stability which are essential conditions for development through adjudication of cases, distribution and sale of land and the management of communal resources such as land, water bodies and forest resources. For instance, in the early colonial period, traditional rulers collaborated with Christian missions and the Central Government in the construction of school buildings and health centers as well as the provision of potable water and much later electricity in their respective areas. As their contribution, the rulers gave out land grants and also organized communal labour. Traditional rulers work in conjunction with their subjects and therefore carry the whole community along to accomplish development projects that will be of benefit to the entire community. Traditional rulers have been very useful in giving publicity to government policies and programmes at the grass-root level as the case in Anambra State, where the State has engaged all the traditional rulers in the fight against insecurity currently facing various communities and Nigerian State at large.

Communities who have active traditional rulers, who take steps to quickly address the problems of their subjects, are usually peaceful. Igwe Orizu in Nnewi town of Anambra State, the traditional ruler, apart from documenting and developing a data base for the unemployed youths of the community organizes lectures for the youths and keeps in touch with them. Also, he has been making efforts to develop his community which is already attracting a lot of investments. The community is relatively at peace. This Igwe understands the concept of human security, the need to invest heavily in agriculture and seek job placement for the unemployed without resorting to the Federal or State governments. The Sultan of Sokoto, Alhaji Muhammad Sa'ad Abubakar III is yet another traditional ruler to be emulated. He has consistently condemned the security breaches in the country and advised the youths and leaders at different levels to address key issues leading to insecurity. Other leaders in this category should act positively.

14.1.8 Factors Responsible for the Waning Influence of Traditional Rulers in Nigeria

There is no doubt that traditional rulers in Nigeria have gradually witnessed the erosion of their powers, from depending upon British colonial administration to dependence upon elected politicians. As their roles narrowed, that of the political parties increased. Perhaps, it may be necessary at this point to identify the key issues that have contributed to the waning influence of the traditional rulers:

- Self-inflicted (partisanship in politics, defecation of traditional values, lack of integrity by some, money-for-chieftaincy policies, in-fighting and 'Igweship'/'Ezeship'/'Obaship'/'Emirship' tussles).
- Military dictatorship (clipping of wings and enthronement of subservient culture).
- Social malaise (moral decay in the society, lack of respect for elders and constituted authority – including traditional institutions).

- Dwindling sphere of influence (creation of new States and Local government areas have further balkanized the 'kingdom' overseen by the traditional rulers).
- The Young, Bold and Restless and their brash manners (The appointment of the likes of the late Igwe John Nebolisa as the Igwe of Awkuzu further eroded the public's confidence in traditional institutions).
- Conflict of interest between local government authorities and traditional rulers, and a need to clarify who should do what in local community matters.
- Globalisation (waning influence and interest in monarchies, and traditional institutions worldwide).
- Politics (Party politics have been played in a manner to undermine the influence of traditional rulers over local voters).
- The Economy (Dwindling economic fortunes which also affected the traditional rulers have further eroded their influence and authority, a situation where some traditional rulers ride on Okada motorcycles and 'beg for bread' does not say much for the institution they represent).
- Civilisation and development (the era of inquiring minds, professionals etc. This era has witnessed lots of social changes including open same-gender relationships and marriages (in the west), doubts and public questioning on the concepts of, and existence of God, and Allah).
- Abuse of privileges (giving chieftaincy titles and honours to less deserving members of the society has created a society with false values, and negative role models).
- The single status movement and the agitation for republicanism (the desire to let the people decide their affairs rather than having a supreme human lording it over them).

14.1.9 **The Road Ahead**

The following recommendations are hereby offered for better performance of traditional rulers in community development in future.

- ➢ Traditional rulers have to adopt the spirit of yearly dialogue amongst the subjects. The outcome of the yearly dialogue will create necessary relationship towards community development programmes.
- ➢ Wealthy individuals from in the community can support the traditional institution to enable traditional rulers embark on huge projects.

- ➤ The entire population or community should be sensitized to respond to self-help development projects of the community.
- ➤ The resources realized for community development projects both money and materials should be utilized in such a way that the people will gain from them.
- ➤ The spirit of honesty, transparency and accountability should be the watch word of any traditional ruler.

Chapter Fifteen

CONFLICT AND CONFLICT RESOLUTION AT RURAL AND COMMUNITY LEVEL

15.1 DEFINITION OF CONFLICT

There is no single universally accepted definition of conflict. However, one issue of contention is whether the conflict is a situation or a type of behaviour. Disagreement, crises, war, violence, opposition, revolt are words synonymous with conflict. Conflict arises in different shapes, patterns or dimension. The emergence of conflict depends on the issue at stake. Conflict is defined as a clash between individuals arising out of a difference in thought process, attitudes, understanding, interests, requirements and even sometimes perceptions. A conflict results in heated arguments, physical abuses and definitely loss of peace and harmony. A Conflict not only can arise between individuals but also among countries, political parties and states as well. A minor conflict not controlled at the correct time may lead to war and rifts among countries leading to major unrest and disharmony. Wikipedia (2012) averred that conflict refers to some form of friction, disagreement, or discord arising within a group when the beliefs or actions of one of more members of the group are either resisted by or unacceptable to one or more members of another group.

Intra-group conflict is a conflict that can arise between members of the same group, while inter-group conflict is the one that can occur between members of two or more groups, and it involves violence, interpersonal discord, and psychological tension. Conflict in groups often follows a specific course. Routine group interaction is first disrupted by an initial conflict, often caused by differences of opinion, disagreements between members, or scarcity of resources. At this point, the group is no longer united, and may split into coalitions. This period of conflict escalation in some cases gives way to a conflict resolution stage, after which the group can eventually return to routine group interaction once again. Conflicts can occur between individuals, groups and communities; examples include; quarrels between individuals, labour strikes, competitive sports, or armed conflicts. Conflicts can be of many types which are verbal conflict, religious conflict, emotional conflict, social conflict, personal conflict, organizational conflict, community conflict and so on.

Conflict is a form of social interaction in which actors seek to obtain scarce reward by eliminating or weakening other contenders. This may be in the form of fist fights, threats, legislation or total annihilation. In rural communities, conflict may arise where there is a difference of opinion between group leaders or where one community is perceived as exploiting the other unfairly. Conflict between individuals may degenerate to conflict between communities or a division of a village community into contending groups. Perceived challenge to the security of a group can also engender conflict. This often triggers a strong defense reaction resulting in the appearance of old alignments with each group trying to obtain dominant positions over the contender. Retaliation to a single act if followed by a rebuttal may soon grow to group conflict. Even in community work, proposed changes or new ideas may be viewed apprehensively as a challenge to the status quo thereby triggering a conflict. Similarly the perceived use of a pressure group to gain an advantage by a community or a section of a community can trigger a conflict among rivals. For example, if a political officeholder from a certain community was perceived to have influenced the naming of his home town, the host community of a new secondary school which other things considered is thought to be more appropriately located in a neighbouring town, this can be ground for a communal conflict.

There are subtle differences in the way individual and communal conflicts play out. While individual conflicts may be expressed by outward signs such as refusal to greet each other or do anything together, group conflict may not produce such ill-feelings among ordinary members of the conflicting group, but leaders in both groups may be more careful in their dealings with members of the rival community. Generally, conflict may not necessarily be exhibited by overt physical violence, but may result in sabotage, undermining of rivals or use of legislative or judicial machineries. Finally, conflicts do not always have to bear a negative connotation. The negative outcomes of conflict are fairly well known. They include disruption of social unity, generation of bitterness, destruction of properties, bloodshed, inter-group tension, refusal to cooperate and diversion of peoples' attention from group goals. The positive impacts of conflicts are, however, not always obvious. For instance, until there is an overt conflict, it may be difficult to appreciate some deep seated issues within or between conflicting parties. Thus, an open conflict can lead to a clear definition of issues. Once these issues are properly defined, finding an amicable solution becomes easier to attain. For instance, it is a common assumption that government interventions in a rural community would be widely accepted by the people as beneficial and that local communities will be willing to make required sacrifice to get the programmes implemented. But when members of local communities make an open display of dissatisfaction, government often realizes its error and set up committees usually including representatives of the local community to have a rethink and address both short and long-term causes of the conflict.

It is not out of place to observe that communities experience conflicts from time to time and this can retard the pace of rural development. Conflicts occur in different ways and if not properly managed can cause serious problems in the community. If there are conflicts, people will not cooperate and will not show any interest in the rural development programmes. There must be ways and means of managing or resolving the conflicts. In addition, inter-group cohesion is usually at its highest point during periods of conflict. The solidarity among group members is higher and it is easier to attain other group goals during this period that may even be unconnected to the issues in conflict. Group members are more alert to group interests and the "we feeling" is stronger at these times. Despite its positive angles, conflict is generally disintegrative and as such communities seek to avoid them. Where this is not possible, mechanisms have been developed to resolve conflicts as they arise.

15.2   PHASES OF CONFLICT
A conflict has five phases.
1. **Prelude to Conflict -** It involves all the factors which possibly arouse a conflict among individuals. Lack of coordination, differences in interests, dissimilarity in cultural, religion, and educational background are all instrumental in arousing a conflict.
2. **Triggering Event -** No conflict can arise on its own. There has to be an event which triggers the conflict. Jenny and Ali never got along very well with each other. They were from different cultural backgrounds, a very strong factor for possibility of a conflict. Obi was in the mid of a presentation when Amaka stood up and criticized him for the lack of relevant content in his presentation, thus, triggering the conflict between them.
3. **Initiation Phase -** Initiation phase is actually the phase when the conflict has already begun. Heated arguments, abuses, verbal disagreements are all warning alarms which indicate that the fight is already on.

4. **Differentiation Phase -** It is the phase when the individuals voice out their differences against each other. The reasons for the conflict are raised in the differentiation phase.
5. **Resolution Phase -** A conflict leads to nowhere. Individuals must try to compromise to some extent and resolve the conflict soon. The resolution phase explores the various options to resolve the conflict.

15.3   TYPES OF CONFLICT

Political Conflict: This emanates from political institutions and, systems. It is characterized by revolutionary political ambition to disrupt or reform the constitutional order in practice. In political terms, conflict can refer to wars, revolutions or uprisings that involve the use of force. This can also be referred to as armed conflict. In early times, virtually most parts of Nigeria were decentralized states but they transformed to a centralized state before 1900. A critical analysis of this statement would necessitate the question: 'How did decentralized states become centralized before 1900?" An elaborate explanation of these types and modes will enable you to properly define conflict situations in Nigeria. Understanding types of conflict determines the kind of human relations that had existed and the context of time and place that facilitated it, the individuals involved and the roles they played. In attaining the third objective, the concept of conflict cannot be insignificant. This is because, at one time or the other, a group of people moved into inhabited areas by virtue of being migrants, thereby encouraging the fusion of culture, languages and political systems. In this way, people identify with each other and possibly due to the natural law of remoteness after a long time of settlement, there is a change in identity. As explained under human behaviours in conflict, the bid for expansion and subjugation is most applicable in political conflict because the changes were full of reactions, violence and revolts. Anifowose (1982:4) defined violence as a human behaviour in political conflict as "the use or threat or physical act carried out by an individual or group of individuals within a political system against one another and/or property, with the intent to cause injury or death to persons and damage of property." Groups enter into political conflict as a result of feelings of dissatisfaction arising out of compassion between what is currently enjoyed and what ought to or is expected to be enjoyed. In Nigeria, the immediate pre-colonial period that is the 19th century was full of revolutions. These revolutions meant drastic changes in conditions, methods and ideas which formed part of the treaties and agreements which shall be discussed in subsequently units.

Economic Conflict: This is a type of conflict associated with economic issues. In this case, money is the mechanism and decisive factor for the level of opposition or competition. As discussed in the previous unit, competition is behaviour synonymous to this type of conflict, because the principle of capitalism which emphasizes maximization of profit at all cost, makes competition inevitable. There is perpetuity of lack of mutual benefit and less co-operation because the strong group tends to dominate and undermine the weak group. At this juncture, it is pertinent to note that economic conflict has to do with production and distribution processes through the parties/groups involved. For instance, an entrepreneur tends to maximize profit by paying workers less wages than they deserve. Conflicts in form of protests, demonstrations, strikes or boycotts arise to ensure change. The Agbekoya Parapo Revolt of 1968-1969, a peasant revolt in post-colonial Yorubaland was organized by peasant farmers to resist the policy of tax payment. The revolt was dominantly aimed at reduction of taxes to be paid by farmers to the government. Before independence, the colonial government established marketing boards for cash crops, such as: cocoa, cotton, and groundnut and so on. These products were graded, examined and bargained at prices that were not favourable to the peasant farmers. As a result, the Agbekoya Parapo explored the indigenous way to regulatory work standards to protect the interest of peasant farmers as regards to pricing. The crux of the revolt was the activities of the peasant farmers that involved protests which culminated into violence. The defiance on part of the government to consider the resolution of the peasants aggravated the revolt. As explained earlier each party/group to conflicts maintains the position or stands favourable to it. In this case, the peasants resolved to: (i)remove Local government official administering the villages (ii) remove some Baales (iii) reduce the flat tax rate (iv) put an end to the use of force in tax collection (v) increase the prices of cocoa and (vi) improve the roads leading to the villages. Afterwards, the regional government passively agreed to a compromise.

Gender Based Conflict: This cuts across extensively to other types or modes of conflicts. It is usually borne out of oppression and inequality. In Nigeria, the problem of inequality or oppression of women is peculiar to the pre-colonial, colonial and post-colonial periods. Gender conflict implies that women (and girls) are predominantly victims who experience neglect within the dominated organization. Although the status of women varies in pre-colonial Nigerian societies, the level of inequality or marginalization depended more on the group or class which they belonged (Ikpe

2003:130). In spite of this, gender conflict was not so, inherent in the pre-colonial period, rather it could be explained as gender based division of labour, as women had specific roles to play. Some women were able to acquire wealth and rose to positions of authority. For instance, Iyalode Efunsetan of Ibadan, Queen Amina of Zaria wielded strong political authority and influence, as well as Madam Efunoye Tinubu of Egbaland. However, their rise and recognition was not achieved on a platter of gold, it was a product of conflicts with men in the society. Gender conflict was more pronounced in the colonial period. The Aba Revolt of the Igbo women in 1920s was organized and led by rural women of Owerri and Calabar provinces. Basically, the revolt was sparked off by a disagreement between Nwanyeruwa (a woman from Okoko district) and an enumerator Mark Emereuwa who was asked by Okugo (the Warrant chief of the town) to obtain an accurate census of the people as mandated by the District Officer. The census was taken as a plan towards imposition of tax on both men and women. On November 18, 1929, Emereuwa went to Nwanyeruwa to "count her goats, sheep and people," in anger the woman responded that "was your late mother counted?" The verbal encounter triggered off the women's revolt because it is an aberration for women to pay tax in Igbo society. At this juncture, it is worthy of note that the Aba Women's revolt was an aftermath of agreements made with colonial masters at the beginning of the 20th Century.

Religious Conflict: This is a type of conflict that is peculiar to Nigeria. It is mostly prone to violence. It occurs when people of different religions fail to co-exist and relate with each other by respecting what each other stands for. In Nigeria, religious conflict has claimed lives and properties. At any slight provocation, religious conflicts resurge. The violence thereafter contributes to socio-economic and political instability. At times the religious conflict possesses an ethnic undertone or vice versa. In the contemporary period, it is a type of conflict that has permeated the Nigeria polity. To solve the problems, there are Inter-faith mediation centres nationally and globally established to co-ordinate religious teachings to stop conflict situation.

Mode of Conflicts
- **Organizational Conflict:** This is mostly associated with work place. In order to achieve the goals set for progress, conflict occurs in organizations because of clash of interest or clash of necessary priorities.

- **International Conflict:** This occurs among different countries that constitute an international organization. This may occur through varying interests on socio-economic and political policies to be adopted. Each member country would always prefer that the aims and objectives of the organization correspond with its foreign policy objective.
- **Environmental Resource Conflict:** The availability of natural resources in a community serves as source of revenue or livelihood as well as it can cause conflict. In contemporary times, the natural endowment of crude-oil in the Nigerian Niger-Delta has been the bane of the uprisings and crises which continues to resurge by escalating different dimensions of violence.
- **Other modes of conflict:** Are emotional conflict, ideological conflict, diplomatic conflict, military conflict and so on. It is worthy of note that no type or mode of conflict can occur in isolation, they are mostly interwoven.

15.4 MEANING OF CONFLICT RESOLUTION

The term conflict resolution may be used interchangeably with dispute resolution, where arbitration and litigation processes are critically involved. Furthermore, the concept of conflict resolution can be thought to encompass the use of non-violent resistance measures by conflicted parties in an attempt to promote effective resolution. Conflict resolution is conceptualized as the methods and processes involved in facilitating the peaceful ending of conflict. Often, committed group members attempt to resolve group conflicts by actively communicating information about their conflicting motives or ideologies to the rest of the group (e.g., intentions; reasons for holding certain beliefs), and by engaging in collective negotiation. Ultimately, a wide range of methods and procedures for addressing conflict exist, including but not limited to, negotiation, mediation, diplomacy, and creative peace-building.

Conflict Management
This deals on how to control or manage an existing conflict so that it does not escalate, thereby leading to chaos, crisis and war. At this, efforts are made to ensure that constructive conflicts do not degenerate and become destructive, in which case they will be difficult to manage. Conflict management according to Wikipedia's account (2007) referred to the long-term management of intractable conflicts. It is the label for the variety of ways by which people handle grievances—standing up for what they

consider to be right and against what they consider to be wrong. Those ways include such diverse phenomena as gossip, ridicule, lynching, terrorism, warfare, feuding, genocide, law, mediation, and avoidance. Which forms of conflict management will be used in any given situation can be somewhat predicted and explained by the social structure—or social geometry—of the case.

15.5 CONFLICT MANAGEMENT AND RESOLUTION

Conflict management is often considered to be distinct from conflict resolution. In order for actual conflict to occur, there should be an expression of exclusive patterns, and tell why the conflict was expressed the way it was. Conflict is not just about simple inaptness, but is often connected to a previous issue. The latter refers to resolving the dispute to the approval of one or both parties, whereas the former concerns an ongoing process that may never have a resolution. Neither is it considered the same as conflict transformation, which seeks to reframe the positions of the conflict parties. Conflict management differs from Peace Building, which aims to prevent conflicts from even arising in the first place, by engaging individuals, groups, parties and stakeholders in processes that enhance peaceful coexistence outside conflict situations.

A conflict is resolved when some mutual sets of actions are worked out. It involves an orderly and non-violent handling of parties involved. The parties with perceived incompatible goals seek to consider each other. This is peculiar to groups that are mutually dependent on each other. Each group will not wish to spread the conflicts because of cordial inter-group relations that have enhanced growth and development. For instance, scholarly works on the Nigerian Civil War resolved that the crises was a problem that emanated from regionally based elites in their struggle to acquire state power and wealth (Ukiwo 2005:13). Ordinary Nigerians had nothing against each other. Hence to manage and resolve such conflicts require an analysis of the elite and the masses as well as the internal and external socio-political and economic structure in existence.

Figure 15:1.

15.6   METHODS OF CONFLICT RESOLUTION
There are two major classes or methods of resolving conflicts.
- Regular Dispute Resolution
- Alternative Dispute Resolution

(1.) Regular Dispute Resolution
This includes the regular system of reporting a case to the police, getting the offender prosecuted, convicted and sentenced. It also covers civil

litigations. This is basically by litigation in court, that is, through legal process. Under this system, the winner takes it all. There is always a winner/loser ending.

(2.) Alternative Dispute Resolution (ADR)

Generally, alternative dispute resolution (ADR) refers to any process or collection of processes established to resolve disputes without trial or violence. The term "ADR" is often used to refer to a broad category of "ADR processes" such as negotiation, conciliation, mediation, settlement conferences, arbitration, consensus building, and community conferencing. In addition, ADR includes conflict management and prevention systems, such as an ombuds office, which can help people, decide what dispute resolution process they want to use. Often, one or more ADR processes may be appropriate for resolving certain kinds of disputes. Most ADR members practice one or more ADR processes. As its name implies, this includes the methods that are alternative to the regular system. In this type of dispute resolution strategy, people are encouraged to go for a win-win solution (instead of a win-lose or lose-lose situation).

15.7   TYPES OF ALTERNATIVE DISPUTE RESOLUTION (ADR)

There is no specific formula for resolving conflicts. But there are certain procedures and approaches which have been used either singly or in combination to address conflicts. Generally, the first efforts in any conflict are geared towards minimizing the feeling of difference and calm down the conflicting parties, thereby creating an environment where the issues in conflict can get some attention and reflection. The aim of this preliminary stage is to prepare the ground for the conflicting parties to co-exist and work together towards finding a more permanent solution. This temporary working agreement is called accommodation. It is the decision of both parties to overlook minor antagonism with a view to achieving greater aims.

a) **Accommodation: -** The process of accommodation can be found in many day-to-day circumstances. It describes a situation where two strangers live together to form a marriage (as in a family); or where a number of different families co-exist to form a community; or where various communities co-exist to form a nation irrespective of their perceived differences. Accommodation may take different forms depending on the circumstances and the attributes of the group involved. These include: a truce, displacement, institutionalized release of hostility, super- ordination, compromise, involvement of a third party, segregation and toleration.

b) **Mediation: -** This is a process in which one or two neutral mediators help people in a dispute to communicate with one another, understand each other, and if possible, reach agreements that satisfy the participants' needs. Mediators do not provide legal advice or recommend the terms of an agreement. Instead, the mediator helps people reach their own agreements, rebuild their relationships, and, if possible, find lasting solutions to their disputes. In mediation, people speak for themselves and make their own decisions. Participants in mediation may or may not be represented by counsel. In Maryland, mediation is available in the private sector, through community-based mediation services, and in many courts. At the community programmes, two trained volunteer mediators are assigned to each case. In the private market, people select their own mediators based on background and experience. In most court programmes, a mediator will be assigned to a case unless the participants select someone on their own.

c) **Displacement: -** This is a process of ending one conflict by replacing it with another, usually through a process of scape-goating. For instance, sibling's rivalry can be addressed by both siblings fighting a common opposition who can then carry the blame for their earlier conflict. By doing so, they transfer the hostility between them to a third party who is now a scapegoat. The diversion of hostilities to a scapegoat may lead to a more lasting resolution of the original conflict. It is important that the scapegoat need not be a person or another community. It is common to make the devil or evil-doers or unknown enemies the scapegoat in an attempt to resolve a subsisting conflict.

d) **Negotiation: -** Sometimes called "direct" or "unassisted" negotiation, refers to any dialogue involving two or more people in an effort to resolve a dispute or reach an agreement. People negotiate all the time, and negotiation is often the first step in attempting to resolve disputes. However, people also can and do seek relief from the court system or from other dispute resolution processes without first attempting to negotiate with one another. People may also choose to have an attorney or other expert to negotiate on their behalf.

e) **Conciliation: -** This is a process in which a neutral person functions as a "go between" in an attempt to resolve a dispute involving two or more people. The conciliator may have multiple private conversations with the people in dispute in hopes of identifying shared interests and reaching an agreement that meets the needs of the participants and resolves their dispute. The conciliator does not generally bring the people in dispute together or create an opportunity for them to talk directly to each other. The conciliator must remain neutral and has no decision making authority.

f) **Compromise:** - When domination or complete defeat is unlikely, parties in conflict may accept less than their earlier claims to end a conflict. This is known as compromise. Compromises often take place when the contending parties are equally powerful or equally peace-loving. Even when one party is more powerful, but continuous conflict appears disadvantageous, a compromise can still be reached. Compromise is therefore, a bargaining process with neither of the conflicting parties being totally satisfied. The chances of the conflict resurfacing are high when a compromise is reached, especially when one party perceives an imbalance in the outcome of the compromise.

g) **Third-Party Roles:** - The intervention in a conflict by third parties is a common occurrence in many communities. The third party may play the role of a mediator where he or she literally throws him or herself between the warring parties and tries to put them apart. The mediator is not necessarily invited into the dispute and may even get injured in the process. The third party may also play the role of a conciliator trying to calm down or pacify the conflicting parties thereby preparing the way for further resolution of the conflict. Finally, the third party may play the role of an arbitrator or judge. In this case, the third party may have been appointed or invited by the parties to assess the issues in conflict and decide on a binding solution. In most rural communities, the arbitrator is usually a person highly respected by both parties and he or she seeks to resolve a conflict without letting any of the contending parties unduly lose face. Where any of the parties doubts the impartiality of an arbitrator, the disputants may appeal to another.

h) **Segregation:** - In cases where disputants refuse obstinately to yield to any conciliatory moves, segregation is another option at least to allow tempers to cool down. In some cases, a permanent physical distance may be put between contending parties to maintain peace.

In the past, banishment, exile or sale into slavery are instruments used to segregate a quarrelsome party permanently.

i) **Toleration:** - In this case, contending parties agree to disagree knowing that neither of them can or should win. People often accept each other's right to differ because certain values are too cherished to compromise or victory would be too costly even for a more powerful party. Thus, husband and wife may belong to different religions, but they function as a family without discussing religion or accepting each other's right to hold a different belief. Most social systems maintain their identities because of the willingness to tolerate others.

j) **Truce:** - Truce is the temporary cessation of hostilities without the issues being settled to allow the conflicting parties time to regroup, attend to certain religious rites or observances, or for the solution of the conflict to be worked out. A truce can be declared for a few days or for an indefinite period.

k) **Community Conferencing:** - This is a process in which a neutral person brings together everyone in a community who has been affected by an action resulting in serious harm. During the meeting, the participants hear what happened, talk about how they have been personally affected, and work together on a plan to repair the harm. Although most frequently used in response to incidents of crime and delinquency, the process can be used for a wide variety of community conflicts.

l) **Consensus Building:** - This is a process in which a neutral person brings stakeholder groups and individuals together and facilitates their efforts to solve a problem or address a complex issue in a way that best meets the participants' needs. Consensus building is similar to mediation because the process is about people making their own decisions, opening lines of communication, and developing agreements that everyone can support. Consensus building, however, usually involves a much larger group of people than can be accommodated in mediation and is generally used to prevent or resolve disputes about public policy or other complex issues affecting many people.

m) **Institutionalized Release of Hostilities: -** This is a situation where conflicting parties are given the opportunity to release their hostilities on each other or other objects. Among many ethnic groups, a formally arranged wrestling match can provide this opportunity. In other communities, the conflicting parties are allowed to rain abuses on each other. In all instance of institutionalized release of hostilities, the disputants are bound by societal norms and etiquettes. For instance, the use of tools may not be permitted in a wrestling contest or false allegations may not be allowed in an abusive release. The failure to abide by the societal norms guiding institutional release of hostilities may result in the defaulting party being labeled a social outcast by a larger society.

n) **Arbitration: -** This is a quasi-judicial process in which people in a dispute present their views to one or more knowledgeable neutral people who decide how the dispute will be resolved. Arbitrators review evidence, hear arguments, and make a decisions, often in the form of a monetary "arbitration award" paid by one person to the other. Arbitration is generally a binding process, which means that the participants agree up front to abide by the arbitrators' decision. In "high/low" binding arbitration, the participants may negotiate in advance an upper and lower limit for the arbitrators' award.

o) **Super-Ordination: -** Super-ordination involves ending a conflict through the total defeat and submission of one party to the conflict by the other. Institutionalized release of hostilities may result in super-ordination as one party may be declared the outright winner. However, super-ordination may occur without any institutionalized arrangement. In this case, one party can totally subjugate the other. Even though super-ordination is used to imply that the parties in dispute are actively engaged, sometimes a more powerful third party can subjugate both contending parties and force a final end to the conflict between the warring parties. This approach was used to resolve many cases of inter-ethnic conflict by the British Colonialists in their march to acquire Nigeria as a British Colony.

p) **Settlement Conference: -** This refers to a process in which people in a dispute in court present their views to a knowledgeable neutral person who evaluates their case and suggests ways to settle it without trial. The settlement conference facilitator is usually a judge or experienced lawyer who is able to give informed opinions about how the court might decide the case, to indicate how similar cases have been settled, to provide advice, and to suggest the terms of an agreement. In most Nigerian Magistrate courts, complex civil cases are routinely scheduled for a settlement conference prior to trial.

q) **Ombuds Offices: -** They provide a confidential, neutral and informal process for people in conflict. The ombudsperson may provide advice about resolving the conflict and may help arrange for the people in conflict to use any of the above-mentioned ADR services. The ombuds man usually reports to the highest ranking official in an in a community organization, provides statistical data on service delivery, and makes recommendations for systemic changes aimed at preventing and managing conflict.

15.8   CAUSES OF CONFLICTS AT COMMUNITY LEVEL

Conflict is a common feature of all human societies and organizations. It is, therefore, not peculiar at the community level or among those charged with the responsibility of community development. However, there is the need for those managing human affairs, especially at the community level, to endeavour to minimize conflict, to eliminate it completely, so as to ensure the success of their development efforts. The common causes of conflict at the community level include the following points:

i.   **Unhealthy Rivalry among Community Leaders:** This has been identified as one of the major causes of conflict in many communities. In some cases, trouble ensues between the traditional ruler and the executive members of his cabinet, or among the executive members of the town union. Jealousy, power tussle, gang-up and class conflict are common unacceptable behaviour among some community leaders. They are inimical to the progress of a community.

ii.   **Embezzlement of Fund:** The embezzlement of fund targeted for community development brings conflict at the community level. However, there are some cases where unsubstantiated accusations have been made against some community development projects. There is the need for community leaders to exhibit transparent honesty in discharging their duties, especially when handling public or community finance.

iii. **Struggle for Supremacy and Recognition:** The struggle for supremacy and recognition often results in conflict among community leaders. This is common among some traditional rulers and town union leaders. In the 1980s, there were constant clashes either between town unions and traditional rulers or among executive body of town unions. The conflicts among leaders were so common then, especially during Governor Akonobi administration in Anambra State that the government adopted a policy of "prompt dissolution of crisis-between town unions or dethronement of autocratic rulers while replacing them with purposeful leadership or caretaker committees" (Anambra State 1989:35). The struggle for supremacy among community leaders often creates serious problems for community development and may even endanger social stability.

iv. **Maladministration:** Bad leadership at the Local government level is often a source of conflict at both Local government and community levels. Lack of vision and commitment towards people's welfare by those entrusted with power often results in conflict between them and the governed. Moreover, the conflict which, more often than not, exists between the political executive and the senior administrative officers over who controls what, tends to retard efforts towards implementation of community development programme. Degri (1999:18) observed that because of ignorance of bureaucratic process, inexperience or naked display of power, some chairmen of Local government councils tried to bye-pass their secretaries while carrying out certain political or administrative decision and actions. This, according to him, often results in conflict capable of jeopardizing their functions. This is one of the reasons why development in many newly created Local Government Areas is still at snail-like speed.

v. **Class Conflict:** The segregation of members of a community into various socio-economic groups is one of the common causes of conflict. Community leaders should strive to represent a symbol of unity and togetherness of the people. The Local government officials encourage traditional leaders and town union executives to find a lasting solution to disputes in their respective communities, in this way, the objectives of community development can easily be realized. Some Local government officers pay lip service to the welfare of communities under their authority. This often results in strained relationship between them and community leaders.

vi.   **High Handedness:** Some traditional rulers or members of the executive body of town unions exhibit acts of high handedness in the administration of their communities. This often results in conflict of power which is not an acceptable way of governing a people. For, it tends to alienate the leadership from the followership and thus officials, especially the chairman, and vice chairman should ensure that leadership at community levels adopts happiness of all the members of the community.

15.9   PREVENTION OF CONFLICTS AT COMMUNITY LEVEL

As already stated, conflict is a common occurrence in most human societies and organizations. But there is always the need to prevent conflicts and to promote peace and mutual understanding among people for the realization of common goals or for community development. It is necessary that all those concerned with community leadership (including the chairman, vice chairman, supervisors, and community development officers) should evolve strategies for conflict prevention and harmonious inter-personal and inter-group relationship. They can prevent conflict at community level by:

- ➤ Demonstrating sincerity of purpose.
- ➤ Adopting democratic style of leadership whereby they consult with the followers on matters relating to community development.
- ➤ Equitable distribution of social and economic benefits for the welfare of various communities and groups.
- ➤ Demonstrating transparent honesty in the discharge of their duties
- ➤ Avoiding misuse of funds targeted for community development project(s).
- ➤ Seeking expert advice for proper implementation of community development project(s).
- ➤ Liaising with necessary government authorities and agencies for the portion of peace and progress in the community.
- ➤ Seeking the support and assistance of law enforcement agencies in the maintenance of law and order at community level.

15.10   CONFLICT MANAGEMENT AND RESOLUTIONS AS A NECESSITY FOR EFFECTIVE IMPLEMENTATION OF COMMUNITY WELFARE PROGRAMME

There is the need for chairmen and vice chairmen of various Local governments to use their privileged positions to promote peace and harmonious co-existence among people in their council areas. This requires good sense of judgment, impartiality and ability to make mature decisions on the part of the chairman and vice chairman. Besides, the supervisors and community development officers and community leaders should cooperate in the task of improving the welfare of people in their various rural communities. There is need for chairman and vice chairman as well, to evolve a mechanism for conflict management. Such strategies should cover both Local government and community levels. No community can develop in a situation of anarchy, lawlessness and bickering among its people. Lack of cooperation among people often frustrates effort towards community development. The management of conflict is, therefore, a necessity for effective implementation of community welfare programmes for the general well-being of the people.

Conflict resolution is necessary in every human society or organization. This is because the resolution of conflicts helps to ensure peace, orderliness and effective implementation of community welfare programme. The resolution of conflicts resulting from misunderstanding in implementing community welfare programmes is very necessary because of the following reasons:

1) Conflict or disagreement among them results in quarrel and dissipation of energy.
2) Conflict leads to distraction and loss of focus towards the achievement of intended goals.
3) It gives rise to bickering and enemity, which destroy mutual understanding and spirit of team-work.
4) It dampens enthusiasm and spirit of cooperation necessary for successful implementation of community welfare.
5) Conflict may give rise to apathy and nonchalant attitude of some officers towards community welfare programme.
6) Conflict may alienate the intended beneficiaries of community welfare programme.

There is the need for the chairman of Local government council, the vice chairman, supervisors and community development officers to work as a team towards the successful implementation of community welfare programme. They should maintain cordial relationship with the traditional rulers and executive body of town union, to ensure successful implementation of community welfare programme.

Chapter Sixteen

POVERTY AND RURAL DEVELOPMENT

Poverty has many faces, changing from place to place and across time, and has been described in many ways. Most often, poverty is a situation people want to escape. So poverty is a call to action -- for the poor and the wealthy alike -- a call to change the world so that many more may have enough to eat, adequate shelter, access to education and health, protection from violence, and a voice in what happens in their communities (World Bank, 2006).

Poverty is one of the main symptoms or manifestations of under development. The new global call for sustainable development has coincided with an emphasis on poverty alleviation in the decade of the 1990s. This is more pertinent to sub- Saharan Africa, where, on the average, 45 to 50 percent of the people live below the poverty line. This of course is a much higher proportion than in any other region of the world except South Asia (World Bank, 1996; Mbaku, 1994). Most analysts follow the conventional view of poverty as the absence of sufficient income for securing basic goods and services. Many other experts have conceptualized the poor as the portion of the population that is unable to meet basic nutritional needs (Ojha, 1970). Musgrave and Ferber (1976), identify the poor, using the criteria of the level of consumption and expenditure. Poverty is related to entitlements (Sen, 1983), which are taken to be the various bundles of goods and services over which one has command, taking into cognizance the means by which such goods are acquired (e.g. money, coupons etc.) and the availability of the needed goods. Yet, other experts see poverty in very broad terms, such as being unable to meet basic needs–physical (food, health care, education, shelter, etc.) and non-physical (participation, identity etc.) requirements of a meaningful life (Streeten, 1979; Blackwood and Lynch, 1994).

16.1   Meaning of Poverty
The word poverty comes from old French word 'poverté' (Modern French 'pauvreté'), from Latin 'paupertās', from pauper (poor) (Skeat, 2005). Because poverty affects many aspects of the human condition, including physical, moral, and psychological, a concise and universally accepted

definition of poverty is elusive. Different criteria have been used to conceptualize poverty. Poverty is the state of one who lacks a certain amount of material possessions or money. According to United Nations Report (2011), poverty is a denial of choices and opportunities, a violation of human dignity. It means lack of basic capacity to participate effectively in society. It means not having enough to feed and clothe a family, not having a school or clinic to go to; not having the land on which to grow one's food or a job to earn one's living, not having access to credit. It means insecurity, powerlessness and exclusion of individuals, households and communities. It means susceptibility to violence, and it often implies living in marginal or fragile environments, without access to clean water or sanitation. World Bank in 2011 defined Poverty as pronounced deprivation in well-being, and comprises many dimensions. It includes low incomes and the inability to acquire the basic goods and services necessary for survival with dignity. Poverty also encompasses low levels of health and education, poor access to clean water and sanitation, inadequate physical security, lack of voice, and insufficient capacity and opportunity to better one's life.

Poverty is a subjective and comparative term describing a lack of sufficient wealth (usually understood as capital, money, material goods, or resources especially natural resources) to live what is understood in a society as a "normal" life: for instance, to be capable of raising a healthy family, and especially educating children and participating in society. A person living in this condition of poverty is said to be poor. The meaning of "sufficient" varies widely across the different political and economic areas of the world. (www.wikipedia.com accessed January, 17, 2013). Poverty is often strongly correlated with social problems, such as crime and disease (notably sexually transmitted diseases), sometimes in epidemic level. As a result, many societies employ social workers to fight poverty by a variety of methods, which range from moral persuasion, financial subsidy to physical coercion. Poverty is a living condition in which an entity is faced with economic, social, political, cultural and environmental deprivations. Poor people are those who fall below the income poverty line. According to World Bank, any person who is earning less than one dollar a day is poor. Are you poor? Poverty affects many aspects of human condition. These include physical, emotional and psychological aspects.

Figure 16:1.

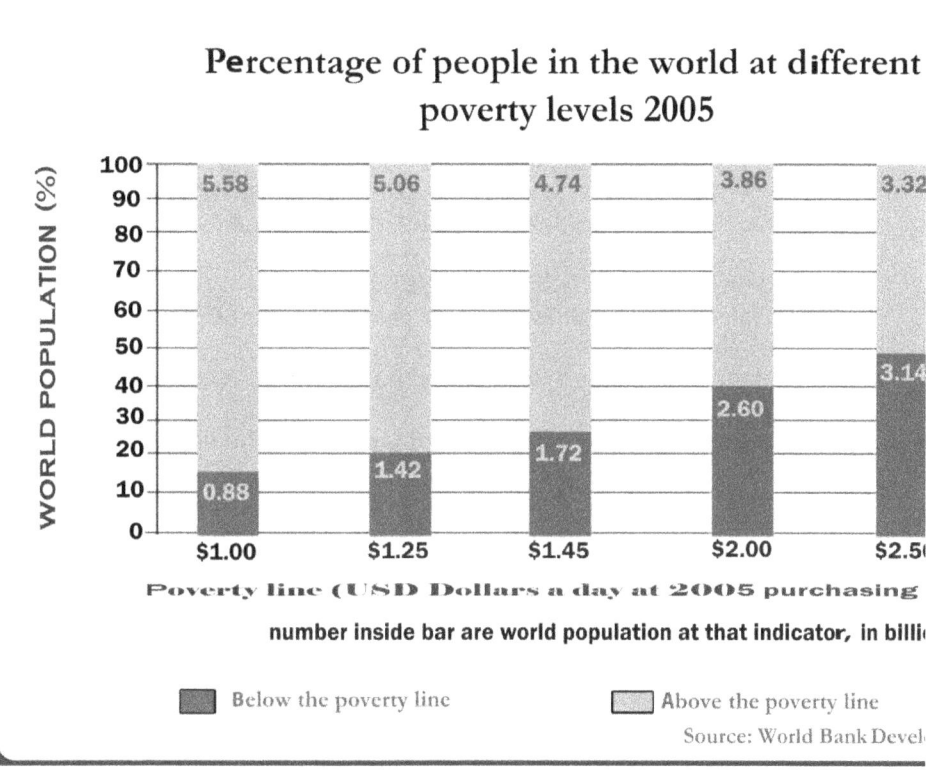

The word poverty provokes strong emotions and many questions. It is a chronic and debilitating condition that results from multiple adverse synergistic risk factors and affects the mind, body, and soul. However, you define it as being is complex; it does not mean the same thing for all people, it is the state of being without, often associated with need, hardship and lack of resources across a wide range of circumstances. However, it is much more than just not having enough money. There is no one cause of poverty, and the results of it are different in every case. Persons with income less than that deemed sufficient to purchase basic needs—food, shelter, clothing, and other essentials are designated as poor. In reality, the cost of living varies dramatically based on geography; for example, people classified as poor in Eastern part of Nigeria might not feel as poor if they live in Northern region of Nigeria. Again, being poor in Nigeria is different from living in poverty in USA or

Zimbabwe. Poverty varies considerably depending on the situation. The differences between rich and poor within the borders of a country can also be great. It is inter-related to other problems of underdevelopment. In rural and urban communities, poverty can be very different. In urban areas, people often have access to health and education but many of the problems caused by poverty are made worse by things like overcrowding, unhygienic conditions, pollution, unsafe houses etc. In rural areas, there is often poor access to education, health and many other services, but people usually live in healthier and safer environments.

16.2 CHARACTERISTICS OF POVERTY

- Subjacent poor: those living on more than US $0.75 but less than US $1 a day
- Medial poor: those living on more than US $0.50 but less than US $0.75 a day
- Ultra poor: those living on less than US $0.50 a day

The poorest are those from socially excluded groups, those living in remote areas with little education and few assets and the landless. To better understand the characteristics of the world lowest poverty level poorest, the summary include:

1. Despite a global trend of poverty shifting toward urban areas, the incidence of poverty is still higher in rural areas. And as poverty deepens, the income disparities between rural and urban areas tend to increase. On average, poverty rates are 2.4 times higher for the subjacent poor and 2.7 times higher for the medial poor in rural areas than for their counterparts in urban areas. But, the poverty rates for the ultra poor are nearly four times higher in rural areas than in urban areas.

2. The poorest and most undernourished households are located farthest from roads, markets, schools, and health services. To some extent, an electricity connection indicates the degree to which a household is "connected" in a broader sense to roads, markets, and infrastructure. It has been found that households living in ultra poverty are on average four times less likely to be connected than households living above the dollar-a-day poverty line.

3. The proportion of poor people who are educated varies from country to country. However, there is one consistent pattern in every part of the developing world: adults in ultra poverty are significantly less likely to be educated, be they male or female. In nearly all studied countries, the proportion of adult males without schooling is almost

double or more among the ultra poor than the non-poor. In Vietnam and Nicaragua, adult males living in ultra poverty are three times more likely to be unschooled than those living on more than $1 per day. In Bangladesh, nearly all women in ultra poor households are unschooled (92 percent), compared to less than half in households living on more than $1 a day (49 percent). The data overwhelmingly show that the poorest are the least educated.

4. In all developing countries, children from poorer families are less likely to go to school. In Nigeria, 48 percent of children living in ultra poverty attend school, compared to 81 percent of children living above the dollar-a-day poverty line, representing a 33 percentage-point gap. In Vietnam, the gap is 30 percentage points, in Ghana, it is 28 percentage points, and in Burundi, it is 24. Without education, the future of children living in ultra poverty will be a distressing echo of their current experience.

5. There does not seem to be a uniform pattern of higher landlessness among the poor, though the relationship varies among Sub-Saharan Africa, Latin America, and Asia. Land is a vital productive asset in rural economies. It would thus be expected the association between poverty and landlessness to be high. In all parts of Asia, those who are landless are the poorest. For example, nearly 80 percent of the ultra poor, in rural Bangladesh do not own cultivable land. In Sub-Saharan Africa, however, little difference was found between the incidence of landlessness among the poorest and less poor households, and in some cases the reverse pattern was found. This corresponds to the findings of other studies that in Sub-Saharan Africa, the poorest often own some land (usually very small plots), but they lack access to markets and other key resources such as credit and agricultural inputs. In Latin America, although the incidence of landlessness is high, it was actually found to be higher among those who live on more than $1 a day than among those living on less than $1 a day.

6. Countries in Asia, Africa and Latin America have minority and other subgroups that have consistently higher prevalence of poverty and hunger, especially in Asia. In Laos and Vietnam, ethnic minorities in upland areas experience a higher probability of being poor. In Sri Lanka, the incidence of poverty is highest among Tamils, and in India, disadvantaged castes and tribes consistently experience deprivation in a number of dimensions. For example, tribal people in India are 2.5 times more likely to live in ultra poverty than others. In Latin America, indigenous people are overrepresented among the

poor, and increasingly so further below the dollar-a-day poverty line. There is some evidence that female-headed households and women are overrepresented among the ultra poor households, but in general, no large differences were found.

16.3 TYPES OF POVERTY

Different people think about poverty in different ways. Because of these differences it is useful to discuss about many types of poverty.

1) **Absolute or extreme poverty:** Absolute poverty is synonymous with destitution and occurs when people cannot obtain adequate resources (measured in terms of calories or nutrition) to support a minimum level of physical health. This arises when the consumption of an individual or household is below a minimum acceptable level which has been fixed over time as a global standard for meaningful human existence known as poverty line (World Bank, 1996). Absolute or extreme poverty is when people lack the basic necessities for survival. For instance, they may be starving, lack clean water, proper housing, sufficient clothing or medicines and be struggling to stay alive. This is most common in developing countries, but some people in the European Union (EU), for instance, homeless people or the Roma in some settlements, still experience this type of extreme poverty. The United Nations tends to focus its efforts on eliminating absolute or extreme poverty. The first goal of the United Nations Millennium Development Goals is to eradicate extreme poverty and hunger. Eradicating extreme poverty is translated into an objective to reduce by half the proportion of people living on less than a dollar a day. However, poverty in most EU countries is more generally understood as relative poverty.

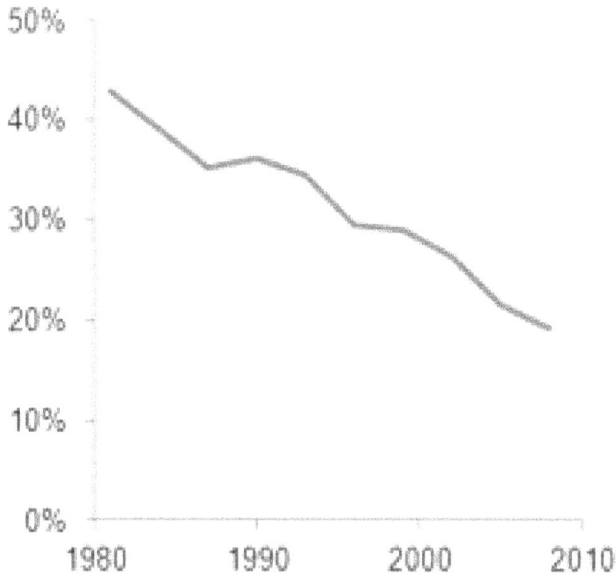

This graph shows the proportion of world population in extreme poverty 1981–2008 according to the World Bank.

Poverty is usually measured as either absolute or relative (the latter being actually an index of income inequality). Absolute poverty refers to a set standard, which is consistent over time and between countries. For a few years starting from 1990, the World Bank anchored absolute poverty line as $1 per day. This was revised in 1993, and though 2005, absolute poverty was $1.08 a day for all countries on a purchasing power parity basis, after adjusting for inflation to the 1993 US dollar. In 2005, after extensive studies of cost of living across the world, the World Bank raised the measure for global poverty line to reflect the observed higher cost of living. Now, the World Bank defines extreme poverty as living on less than US $1.25 (PPP) per day, and moderate poverty as less than $2 or $5 a day (but, note that a person or family with access to subsistence resources, e.g. subsistence farmer, may have a low cash income without a correspondingly low standard of living – they are not living "on" their cash income but using it as a top up). It estimates that "in 2001, 1.1 billion people had consumption levels below $1 a day and 2.7 billion lived on less than $2 a day" (World Bank, 2007). A dollar a day, in nations that do not use the U.S. dollar as currency, does not translate to living a day on the equivalent amount of local currency as determined by the exchange rate (Mukul, 2007). Rather, it is determined by the purchasing power parity rate, which would look at how much local currency is needed to buy the same things that a dollar could buy in the United States, (Mukul, 2007). Usually, this would translate to less local currency than the exchange rate in poorer countries as the United States is a relatively more expensive country, (Mukul, 2007).

The poverty line threshold of $1.25 per day, as set by the World Bank, is controversial. Each nation has its own threshold for absolute poverty line; in the United States, for example, the absolute poverty line was US $15.15 per day in 2010 (US $22,000 per year for a family of four), (US Census Bureau, 2011) while in India, it was US $ 1.0 per day (World Bank, 2010), and in China, the absolute poverty line was US$ 0.55 per day, each on PPP basis in 2010, (The Government of China. 2011). These different poverty lines make data comparison between each nation's official reports qualitatively difficult. Some scholars argue that the World Bank method sets the bar too high, others argue it is low. Still others suggest that poverty line misleads as it measures everyone below the poverty line the same, when in reality someone living on $1.2 per day is in a different state of poverty than someone living on $0.2 per day. In other words, the depth and intensity of poverty varies across the world and in any regional populations, and $1.25 per day poverty line and head counts are inadequate measures (World Bank Report, 2009, 2010).

The proportion of the developing world's population living in extreme economic poverty fell from 28 percent in 1990 to 21 percent in 2001 (World Bank, 2007). Most of this improvement has occurred in East and South Asia (World Bank, 2012). In East Asia, the World Bank reported that "The poverty headcount rate at the $2-a-day level is estimated to have fallen to about 27 percent (in 2007), down from 29.5 percent in 2006 and 69 percent in 1990" (World Bank, 2012). In Sub-Saharan-Africa, extreme poverty went up from 41 percent in 1981 to 46 percent in 2001, combined with growing population increased the number of people living in extreme poverty from 231 million to 318 million. In the early 1990s, some of the transition economies of Central and Eastern Europe and Central Asia experienced a sharp drop in income (World Bank, 2005). The collapse of the Soviet Union resulted in large declines in GDP per capita, of about 30 to 35% between 1990 and the trough year of 1998 (when it was at its minimum). As a result, poverty rates also increased, although in subsequent years as per capita incomes recovered the poverty rate dropped from 31.4% of the population to 19.6% (World Bank, 2010; The New York Times, 2000).

2)   **Relative poverty:** Relative poverty means poverty as socially defined and dependent on social context, hence relative poverty is a measure of income inequality. Usually, it is measured as the percentage of population with income less than some fixed proportion of median income. Relative poverty measures are used as official poverty rates in several developed countries. As such, these poverty statistics measure inequality rather than material deprivation or hardship. The measurements are usually based on a person's yearly income and frequently take no account of total wealth. The main poverty line used in the OCED and the European Union is based on "economic distance", a level of income net at 60% of the median household income (Blastland, 2009). This refers to the position of the individual or household compared with the average income in the country. It is a condition of want in one situation as compared with another, (World Bank, 1996). Relative poverty occurs when people do not enjoy a certain minimum level of living standards as determined by a government (and enjoyed by the bulk of the population) that vary from country to country, sometimes within the same country. It exists everywhere; is said to be increasing, and may never be eradicated. Relative poverty is when some people's way of life and income is so much worse than the general standard of living in the country or region in which they live that they struggle to live a normal life and to participate in ordinary economic, social and cultural activities. What this means will vary from country to country, depending on the standard of living enjoyed by the majority. While not as extreme as absolute poverty, relative poverty is still very serious and harmful. People are said to be living in poverty if their income and resources are so inadequate as to preclude them from having a standard of living considered acceptable in the society in which they live. Because of their poverty they may experience multiple disadvantages through unemployment, low income, poor housing, inadequate health care and barriers to lifelong learning, culture, sport and recreation. They are often excluded and marginalized from participating in activities (economic, social and cultural) that are the norm for other people and their access to fundamental rights may be restricted (European Commission, Joint Report on Social Inclusion, 2004).

3)   **Income poverty:** This happens when a household takes in less than one US dollar per day. It means that people will not have enough food or medicine and they will have poor clothes and houses. Income

poverty is due to people not having access to money or other assets. If people do not have any other assets like land to grow their own food, then income poverty can bring about stunted growth and early death. The best way to reduce income poverty is to encourage and support the development of effective businesses (small, medium and large) which make good use of our natural resources and talents to create wealth and jobs.

Figure
16.2

4) **Non-income poverty:** This is a period when people may have a little bit of money but otherwise the quality of their life is not good. They do not have access to affordable social and physical services (schooling, health care, medicines, safe water, good sanitation, good transport) and they may not feel safe in their homes either because they cannot trust the authorities or because they belong to some particularly vulnerable group. The best way to reduce non-income poverty is to make sure that people have access to affordable and good quality social services and infrastructure that they feel secured in their homes, that they trust the authorities and, if they are vulnerable, that there are safety nets programmes to protect them.

Figure 16.3

5) **Asset poverty:** Asset poverty is an economic and social condition that is more persistent and prevalent than income poverty. It can be defined as a household's inability to access wealth resources that are

sufficient enough to provide for basic needs for a period of three months. Basic needs refer to the minimum standards for consumption and acceptable needs. Wealth resources consist of home ownership, other real estate (second home, rented properties, etc.), net value of farm and business assets, stocks, checking and savings accounts, and other savings (money in savings bonds, life insurance policy cash values, etc.). Wealth is measured in three forms: net worth, net worth minus home equity, and liquid assets. Net worth consists of all the aspects mentioned above. Net worth minus home equity is the same except it does not include home ownership in asset calculations. Liquid assets are resources that are readily available such as cash, checking and savings accounts, stocks, and other sources of savings. There are two types of assets: tangible and intangible assets. Tangible assets are most closely resembled liquid assets in that they include stocks, bonds, property, natural resources, and hard assets not in the form of real estate. Intangible assets are simply the access to credit, social capital, cultural capital, political capital, and human capital.

6) **Rural poverty:** This occurs in nonmetropolitan areas with populations below 50,000. In rural areas, there are more single-guardian households, and families often have less access to services, support for disabilities, and quality education opportunities. Programmes to encourage transition from welfare to work are problematic in remote rural areas, where job opportunities are few (Whitener, Gibbs, & Kusmin, 2003). The rural poverty rate is growing and has exceeded the urban rate every year since data collection began in the 1960s. The difference between the two poverty rates has averaged about 5 percent for the last 30 years, with urban rates near 10–15 percent and rural rates near 15–20 percent (Jolliffe, 2004).

7) **Urban poverty:** This happens in metropolitan areas with population of at least 50,000 people. The urban poverty deals with a complex aggregate of chronic and acute stressors (including crowding, violence, and noise) and are dependent on often-inadequate large-city services.

8) **Transitory Poverty:** This is a situation where individuals find themselves in poverty for a brief period of time.

9) **Situational poverty:** Is generally caused by a sudden crisis or loss and is often temporary. Events causing situational poverty include environmental disasters, divorce, or severe health problems.

10) **Generational poverty:** This occurs in families where at least two generations have been born into poverty. Families living in this type of poverty are not equipped with the tools to move out of their situations.

11) **Poorest-of-the-poor:** These are individuals who are usually disabled, who contribute little and benefit only very slowly from growth process. Poor disabled people live under the double burden of poverty and disability. Without support from the state, it is very difficult for them to access education, special care and jobs. In developing countries, the responsibility of care and support falls on the family.

16.4 MEASUREMENT OF POVERTY

The initial attempts to measure poverty were made more than a century ago by Booth (1889), Rowntree (1901) and Naoroji (1901), (Anyanwu 1997). While Booths and Rowntrees' studies were focused on the urban cities of London and New York, Naoroji's was directed at estimating the extent of poverty. These initial attempts were intended to identify poverty lines, hence it was only later that poverty profiles and indicators were introduced. Also, the initial axiomatically based measure of poverty was not introduced into the debate until 1976, by Sen.

In quantifying poverty and identifying the poor, there are two obvious basic requirements. First, the measure of the standard of living is used (consumption approach) in order to distinguish different individuals, households and countries from each other. Second, a 'cut off point'–the 'poverty line' is chosen which separates those identified as poor from non-poor (Ravallion and Huppi, 1991; Kanbur, 1990). The second requirement is how the degree of poverty relative to a particular poverty line is measured and how this is aggregated across those who are termed as poor. The literature has identified a number of desirable properties for poverty measures. Basic among these properties are the monitoring axiom, the transfer axiom, and addictive decomposability. The measure of poverty should increase when the income of the poor household, for instance, decreases (the monitonicity axiom) or when income is transferred from a poor to a less poor household (the transfer axiom). These properties imply that one desires the measure of poverty to take account of the distribution of living standards among the poor, not simply to indicate how many people are poor (based on the focus axiom, looking at the household's income only). Another desirable property is that the measure of poverty be additively decomposable by population sub-group, so that aggregate poverty can be represented as an appropriately weighted sum of poverty levels in the component sub-group of a population.

As noted earlier, absolute poverty measures refer exclusively to the well-being of those who are defined as poor, hence suggesting that the condition of the poor only, and not of the overall society, is important. There are seven kinds of absolute poverty measures: the Headcount Ratio/ Incidence of Poverty, the Poverty Gap/Income Shortfall, Disparity of Income Distribution, Composite Poverty Measures, the Physical Quality of Life Index (PQLI), the Augmented Physical Quality of Life Index (APQLI), and the Human Development Index (HDI).

Vital Statistics

> ➤ More than 2.8 billion people, close to half of the world's population, live on less than the equivalent of $2 per day. More than 1.2 billion people, or about 20 per cent of the world population, live on less than the equivalent of $1 per day.
> ➤ South Asia has the largest number of poor people (522 million of whom live on less than the equivalent of $1 per day). Sub-Saharan Africa has the highest proportion of people who are poor, with poverty affecting 46.3 per cent or close to half of the regions' population.
> ➤ Nearly 1 billion people are illiterate; more than 1 billion people do not have access to safe water; some 840 million people go hungry or face food insecurity; about one-third of all children under five suffer from malnutrition.
> ➤ The estimated cost of providing universal access to basic social services and transfers to alleviate income poverty is $80 billion, which is less than 0.5 per cent of global income.
> ➤ The top fifth (20 per cent) of the world's people who live in the highest income countries have access to 86 per cent of world Gross Domestic Product (GDP). The bottom fifth, in the poorest countries, has about one per cent.

- ➢ The assets of the world's three richest men exceed the combined Gross Domestic Products of the world's 48 poorest countries.
- ➢ In 1998, for every $1 that the developing world received in grants, it spent $13 on debt repayment.

There are plenty of statistics and data about global poverty these are just a few:

- Each year, more than 8 million people around the world die, because they are too poor to stay alive.
- Over 1 billion people—1 in 6 people around the world—live in extreme poverty, defined as living on less than $1 a day.
- More than 800 million go hungry each day.
- Over 100 million primary school-age children cannot go to school.

Over three million people (see figure above) around the world are considered poor. Lots of men, women and children endure unimaginable obstacles that prevent them from receiving their basic human rights. When the UN created the Universal Declaration of Human Rights in 1948, the signers proclaimed that all people have the right to education, work, health and well-being. Today, however, millions around the world are too crippled by poverty to fulfill these basic rights. Millions continue to go hungry. Scores of children never step inside a classroom. Families watch their loved ones die from largely preventable causes, because they do not have access to adequate medical care. In essence, poverty is a denial of human rights.

While poverty exists everywhere, it is most severe in developing countries, where more than one person in five lives on less than $1 a day – the threshold, which is being used by the World Bank to define extreme poverty. In 2001, over 1 billion people lived in extreme poverty and nearly half the world's population (2.8 billion) lived on less than $2 a day. In developed countries, poverty results in wandering homeless people and poor suburbs and ghettos. In these cases, we talk about relative poverty (in contrast to absolute poverty), which is measured by comparing one group's situation to the situations of those who are more advantaged. Despite the many definitions, one thing is certain; poverty is a complex societal issue. No matter how poverty is defined, it can be agreed that it is an issue that requires everyone's attention. It is important that all members of our society work together to provide the opportunities for all our members to reach their full potential. It makes all of us to help one another.

According to Copenhagen Declaration (2005), absolute poverty is a condition characterized by severe deprivation of basic human needs, including food, safe drinking water, sanitation facilities, health, shelter, education and information. It depends not only on income, but also on access to social services. The term absolute poverty is sometimes synonymously referred to as extreme poverty. There are different types of poverty. It is caused and it has effects on people. Efforts are, however, being made to reduce it as it is difficult to be totally alleviated. The condition in itself is not always considered negatively, even if this is the prevalent interpretation: some cultural or religious groups consider poverty an ideal condition to live in, a condition necessary in order to reach certain spiritual or intellectual states. A notable example is that of the Christian Francisan order. This is called voluntary simplicity, of which voluntary poverty is an extreme form.

Poverty is studied by many social, scientific and cultural disciplines.
- In economics, two kinds of poverty are considered: relative and absolute poverty.
- In politics, the fight against poverty is usually regarded as a social goal and most governments have - secondarily at least - some dedicated institutions or departments for that effect. The work done by these bodies is mostly limited to census studies and identification of some income level below which a citizen is technically considered poor. Active interventions may include housing plans, social pensions, special job opportunities, or requirements. Some ideologies (such as Maxism) argue that the economists and politicians actively work to create poverty. Other theories consider poverty a sign of a failing economic system and one of the main causes of crime.
- In law, poverty is recognized, in most developed countries, as a mitigating factor for the determination of the punishment, being usually considered coincident with a generic and permanent state of need which can affect and alter the correct capability of clearly or freely identifying the legally and socially acceptable behaviour. Poverty is generally argued to cause increased crime rates amongst the poor by increasing their stress.
- In education, poverty affects a student's ability to effectively profit from the learning environments. Especially for younger students

coming from poverty, their primary needs as described in Maslow's Hierarchy of Needs; the need for safe and stable homes, clothes on their backs, and regular meals clouds a student's ability to learn. Furthermore, in education circles, there is a term used to characterize the phenomenon of the rich getting richer and the poor getting poorer (www.wikipedia.com accessed January, 17, 2013).

16.5   WHO ARE WORST AFFECTED BY POVERTY?

a) **Women:** Women form a greater percentage of poor people than men. The main reason for this is that women have historically had less access to education and paid jobs. Many women have always performed unpaid work as mothers, housewives etc. They are employed in poorly paid jobs such as domestic and farm labour. Even within poor household, women usually earn less than men and property and possessions are often in the name of a man. The UN has found that although, women perform nearly two third of the world's work, they receive only one tenth of the world's income and they own only one hundredth of the world's property.

b) **Children:** Poverty has a very severe effect on children. At the moment some of the poorest households in Nigeria are those headed by children where parents are either ill or have died from AIDS or other causes. Even in families where parents are still present, children are very badly affected by malnutrition and it has its most severe effect on children between the ages of six months and two years. Malnutrition also means that the children can more easily get diseases and either die young or have poor physical and mental development as a result. Poverty limits the access children have to educational opportunities, especially early childhood development. Many poor children also are drop out for some years before completing primary basic education. In Nigeria, the geographical region with the largest numbers of poor children is the North, where more than 70% of children live in poverty.

c) **Youth:** Poverty, resulting to lack of education limits employment opportunities for young people. In South Africa, with their high unemployment rate, many young people have no hope of finding work in the formal sector. Urban youths are also very vulnerable to getting involved in crime, gangs and drug or alcohol abuse. These youths are often called "youth at risk" and government targets them for public works and other employment and training programmes.

d) **Disabled:** About 13% of all people in Nigeria suffer from some form of disability. In developed countries, there are usually grants, support, special institutions and special jobs to help people live full lives in spite of their disability. In developing countries, the responsibility of care and support falls on the family. Poor disabled people live under the double burden of poverty and disability. Without support from the state it is very difficult for them to access education, special care and jobs. Public transport is often not accessible to people with certain disabilities and those with hearing or sight impediments are restricted from accessing information and communicating with others.

e) **The elderly:** Older people are usually not working anymore and have to be taken care of by the rest of society. In Nigeria, most poor older people survive on the monthly pensions paid by the state. They also have access to free health care. Because of high unemployment many families share the pensions meant for the elderly and it ends up being insufficient for their needs. Older people also often look after grandchildren and continue to perform unpaid domestic work for their families. This especially applies to older women.

f) **Affected family living with AIDS:** People who carry the heaviest burden as a result of HIV and AIDS are the poor. AIDS increases poverty and families are the first to feel the economic effects of HIV and AIDS. Families lose income if an earner is sick. Often, another one of the family members stays at home to look after the sick person and further income is lost. Families also have increased costs as they have to spend on caring for the sick or paying for funerals. In most cases, orphans are cared for by older female relatives, who are already living in poverty - the additional burden they carry will deepen their poverty. At the moment, Nigeria has an overall HIV prevalence rate of 32% among pregnant women. This means that about 16% of the overall population is HIV positive.

16.6   EVOLUTION OF POVERTY IN NIGERIA

In spite of the abundant human and natural recourses with which the country is endowed, the scope and depth of poverty experienced today has brought with it a plethora of socio-political crises. It is however, necessary to begin with a critical analysis of the Nigerian economy noting that a successful poverty alleviation programme depends on a thorough assessment and understanding of the nature and causes of poverty in the country.

Indeed, the history of the Nigerian Economy shows that people were engaged in traditional economic activities such as farming, hunting, teaching, fishing etc. These activities were not only self-sustaining, but they had a sufficient capacity for the growth and development of the country. Indeed, the causes of poverty in Nigeria could be assessed from two theoretical perspectives viz: the conventional economics and the political perspective. There is some interdependence between the causes and thus some inter-relationship between the remedies as given by both perspectives.

Resource gap, mismanagement of resources, corruption and slow rate of growth in output are two principal contexts within which conventional economics discusses the causes of poverty. This thought explains that poverty is the collective consequences of certain sectoral distortions, shortages or the inevitable results of limited recourses (Edozien, 1975 and Dike, 1997).

While Nigeria always had a large population of poor people, the incidence of poverty has been changing overtime, though not in a consistent pattern. The period from 1980 to 1985 was one of increasing poverty in Nigeria. Total factor productivity in Nigeria declined steadily from 1970s to the mid 1980s. Real average family income in the rural areas and average unskilled labour real wage, in both rural and urban areas, declined throughout the period. Gross Domestic Products at factor cost in 1987 prices declined at an average annual rate of 1.8 percent between 1981 and 1985. Agricultural production stagnated and rate of unemployment increased.

16.7 Nigeria: A Middle-Income Country, Where a Large Number Live in Poverty

Despite impressive growth since democratization, poverty levels remain unacceptably high. The poverty rate is currently estimated to be about 54.4%, at a slight improvement from the peak of 66.9% registered in 1996 (Okojie, 2002). Nevertheless, poverty is at double the rate that it was in

1980, when the poverty level was 28.1%. Table 16.1 shows poverty levels in Nigeria between 1980 and 2010, by region.

Table 16.1: Indicative Poverty Trends by Region, Nigeria

Level	1980	1985	1992	1996	2004	2010
National	28.1	46.3	42.7	65.6	54.4	69
Sector						
Urban	17.2	37.8	37.5	58.2	43.2	61.8
Rural	28.3	51.4	66.0	69.3	63.3	73.2
Geopolitical zone						
South-South	13.2	45.7	40.8	58.2	35.1	63.8
South-East	12.9	30.4	41.0	53.5	26.7	67
South-West	13.4	38.6	43.1	60.9	43.0	59.1
North-Central	32.2	50.8	46.0	64.7	67.0	67.5
North-East	35.6	54.9	54.0	70.1	72.2	76.3
North-West	37.7	52.1	36.5	77.2	71.2	77.7

Sources: Nigerian National Bureau of Statistics (NBS) (2005: 22-24) and NBS (2011).

Although, the data are not directly comparable across the years owing to differences in the way they were collected, they indicate the presence of a consistent North-South divide. Some, like Bello and Roslan (2010), have argued that this pattern can be explained in part by the fact that the North's economy is predominantly agricultural and that particularly low returns from rural enterprises condemn the region to poverty. Table 16.2 shows that people working in the agricultural sector are more likely to live in poverty. This is consistent across all years. The reasons why agriculture in Africa is often associated with poverty are many and varied, but for Nigeria low wages, the poor productivity of land and labour, and depressed commodity prices are often cited, combined with shortages of land, labour and capital (World Bank, 2008). Low productivity in the agricultural sector, where female labour predominates, contributes to the poverty of the rural population, making Nigerians more dependent on food imports and less able to withstand external or other shocks.

Table 16.2: Poverty Head Count by Occupation of Head of Household in Nigeria

Poverty Headcount by Year

Sector	1980	1985	1992	1996	2004
Professional & technical	17.3	35.6	35.7	51.8	34.2
Administration	45	25.3	22.3	33.5	45.3
Clerical & related	10	29.1	34.4	60.1	39.2

Sales workers	15	36.6	33.5	56.7	44.2
Service industry	21.3	38	38.2	71.4	43
Agricultural & forestry	31.5	53.5	47.9	71	67
Production & transport	23.2	46.6	40.8	65.8	42.5
Manufacturing & processing	12.4	31.7	33.2	49.4	44.2
Others	1.5	36.8	42.8	61.2	49.1
Student & apprentices	15.6	40.5	41.8	52.4	41.6
Total	27.2	46.3	42.7	65.6	54.4

Source: Nigerian National Bureau of Statistics (NBS) (2005:24).

16.8   POVERTY ALLEVIATION EFFORTS IN NIGERIA

One of the anti-poverty measures introduced by the government in 1996 budget is the payment of negative income tax by the low income earners, whose total annual income is less than N10, 000. By 1982, the oil boom receded and oil glut surfaced which led to the fall in the government revenue earnings. Before the end of 1982, Nigeria was caught in the throes of depression and found her self among the league of highly indebted nations (HIPC) and hence among the poorest nations. Since 1982, there have been attempts by successive governments to alleviate the high rate of poverty and improve the performance of agricultural sector. See Table 16.3 for the summaries of the various poverty alleviation programmes by successive governments in Nigeria from 1986 to date.

Table 16.3: Anti-Poverty Programmes by Government in Nigeria

S/N	Programme	Year	Target group	Nature of Intervention
1.	Directorate for Food, Roads And Rural Infrastructures(DFRRI)	1986	Rural Areas	Feeder Roads, Rural Water Supply and Electrification.
2.	National Directorate of Employment (NDE)	1986	Unemployed youth	Training finance
3.	Better Life Programme (BLP)	1987	Rural Women	Self help and rural dev. Progr. Skill acquisition.
4.	People's Bank of Nigeria (PBN)	1989	Underprivileged in urban and rural areas	Encouraging savings and Credit facilities
5.	Community Bank (CB)	1990	Rural residence, Micro-enterprise in Urban Areas.	Banking facility
6.	Family Support Programme (FSP)	1994	Families in rural areas.	Health care Delivery child welfare, youth development

7.	Family Economic Advancement Programme (FEAP)	1997	Rural Areas	Credit facilities to support the Establishment of cottage industries.
8.	National Poverty Alleviation and Eradication Programme NPAEP	2001	Unemployed youth and under privileged	Training of youth in different skills and Provision of Social security

Source: Adapted from, Suleiman (2002:7).

16.9   CAUSES OF POVERTY

Poverty is an exceptionally complicated social phenomenon, and trying to discover its causes is equally complicated. The stereotypic (and simplistic) explanation persists—that the poor cause their own poverty—based on the notion that anything is possible in America. Some theorists have accused the poor of having little concern for the future and preferring to "live for the moment"; others have accused them of engaging in self-defeating behaviour. Still other theorists have characterized the poor as fatalists, resigning themselves to a **culture of poverty** in which nothing can be done to change their economic outcomes. In this culture of poverty—which passes from generation to generation—the poor feel negative, inferior, passive, hopeless, and powerless. The "blame the poor" perspective is stereotypic and not applicable to all of the underclass. Not only that most poor people are able and willing to work hard, but have they done so when given the chance. The real trouble has to do with such problems as minimum wages and lack of access to the education necessary for obtaining a better-paying job.

The overall persistent high level of poverty in the world suggest that poverty is primarily the consequence of the way society is organized and resources are allocated, whether these are financial or other resources such as access to housing, health and social services, education and other economic, social and cultural services. Indeed, the fact that there are very different levels of poverty in different member states demonstrates clearly that different approaches to allocating resources and opportunities leads to different outcomes. Poverty does not just happen but is caused.

A. **Overpopulation:** Overpopulation is defined as the situation of having a large number of people with too few resources and too little space. Overpopulation can result from either a high population density (the ratio of people to land area) or from low amounts of resources, or from both. A high population density pressures the available resources in the country, as the resources can only support a certain number of people. Poverty can also depend on the country's mix of population density and agricultural productivity. High birth rates contribute to overpopulation in many developing countries. Children, especially boys, are assets to many poor families, because they provide labour, usually for farming. Cultural norms in traditionally rural societies commonly sanction the value of large families. Also, the governments of developing countries often provide little or no support, financial or political, for family planning (see Birth Control). Families may also not know about family planning due to the lack of education. Hence, most developing countries have high rates of population growth. Moreover, a country's level of poverty can depend greatly on its mix of population density and agricultural productivity. On the other hand, many countries in Sub-Saharan Africa have population densities of less than 30 persons per sq km (80 persons per sq mi). Many people in these countries practice manual subsistence farming. These countries have infertile land and lack the economic resources and technology to boost productivity. As a consequence, these nations are very poor.

B. **Lack of education:** Illiteracy and lack of education are common in poor countries. Governments of developing countries often cannot afford to provide for good public schools, especially in rural areas. Whereas virtually all children in industrialized countries have access to an education, only about 60 percent of children in sub-Saharan Africa even attend elementary school. Poor people also often forego schooling in order to concentrate on making a minimal living. In addition, developing countries tend to have few employment opportunities, especially for women. Poor investment in education also escalates poverty. The 2011 Ibrahim Index of African Governance scored Nigeria 49 per cent in the area of education. This is less than the continental average put at 51 per cent. The 2011 Little Data Book on Africa, compiled by the World Bank, puts gross primary school enrolment vis-a-vis relevant age group at 93.1 per cent, but puts gross secondary school enrolment (percentage of relevant age group) at 30.5 per cent. The implication of this is that while almost all children of primary school age are enrolled in primary school, only 30 per cent of them proceeds to secondary school. The number of children out of school in the country is put at over eight million.

The 2010 Global Monitoring Report of the United Nations Education, Scientific and Cultural Organization (UNESCO) has this to say about the nation's state of education, "Sub-Saharan Africa has registered remarkable progress since 1999 in reducing its out-of-school population by nearly 13 million, down to 32 million in 2007. Yet, the deficit remains large: one-quarter of the region's primary school age children were out of school in 2007, and the region accounted for nearly 45 per cent of the global out-of-school population. Nigeria alone represented over 10 per cent of the global total."

C. **Environmental degradation:** Environmental degradation is the deterioration of the natural environment, including the atmosphere, water bodies, soil, and forests — is an important cause of poverty. Environmental problems have led to shortages of food, clean water, materials for shelter, and other essential resources. As forests, land, air, and water are degraded, people who live directly off these natural resources suffer most from the effects. People in developed countries, on the other hand, have technologies and conveniences such as air and water filters, refined fuel, and industrially produced and stored foods to buffer themselves from the effects of environmental degradation. In developing countries, deforestation has had particularly devastating environmental effects. Many rural people, particularly in tropical regions, depend on forests as a source of food and other resources, and deforestation damages or eliminates these supplies. Forests also absorb many pollutants and water from extended rains; without forests, pollution increases and massive flooding further decreases the usability of the deforested areas.

D. **High rate of unemployment:** Unemployment is rampant now that the global financial crisis has ravaged the world's economy. With a higher number of unemployed people, crime rates in these cities will increase as people grow desperate to survive. It is also believed, however, that some governments of the world intentionally keep a "sufficient" number of people out of work as a replacement batch when the need arises.

E. **Unfair trade laws:** High subsidies and protective tariffs for agriculture in the developed world drains the taxed money and increases prices for consumers in the developed world, decreasing competition and efficiency and preventing exports by more competitive agricultural and other sectors in the developed world due to retaliatory trade barriers and undermining the very type of industry in which developing countries do.

F. **Corruption and poor governance:** (coupled with dictatorial regimes). Poverty can only be fought in the presence of strong institutions, and equitable distribution of resources. This requires a non-corrupt government. However, in Africa, programmes designed to fight poverty are not fully implemented, because the funds end up in the hands of corrupt individuals, who pocket the majority. Corruption is a rampant problem in the world today, especially in third-world countries. It undermines democracy and good governance by flouting formal processes. It often occurs when leaders are not accountable to those they serve. Corruption usually inhibits development when leaders help themselves with money that would otherwise be used for development projects. It increases the cost of business through the price of illicit payments themselves, the management cost of negotiating with officials, and the risk of breached agreements or detection. Also, it generates economic distortions in the public sector by diverting public investments into capital projects where bribes and kickbacks are more plentiful. In Nigeria for example, more than 400 Billion dollars was stolen from the National Treasury by Nigeria's leaders from 1960 to 1999. Forms of such corruption include embezzlement, bribery, cronyism, nepotism, graft etc. Hence, this leads to poverty as leaders should have used the money they usurped to help the poor, which results in a lack of funds. And because of poor governance, those in authority have failed to apprehend the corrupt. This creates an imbalance in society and leads to more poverty because you end up with a few influential and powerful individuals oppressing the poor (who are the majority).

G. **Diseases and poor health facilities:** Another leading cause of poverty in Africa is the prevalence of diseases (such as malaria, HIV/AIDS, TB etc). When a household is affected by any of the diseases, the little resources are spent on treating the sick. In a worst case is as cenario where the bread winner dies, those who are left behind have no resources to support themselves, thus leading to a poor lifestyle. And the situation is worsened by poor health facilities.

H. **The World Bank and IMF Policies:** The loans given out by the World Bank and IMF (the International Monetary Fund) have contributed to the poverty problem in Africa. Such loans come with strict conditions, which usually required governments to adjust some of their economic decisions. For instance, the requirement to reduce total government spending has affected major social sectors such as education, health and infrastructure, which are drivers of economic development.

I. **Unfavourable government policies:** Another cause of poverty is unfavourable government policies. In Nigeria, as in many other countries, the economy is subjected to the whims and caprices of the government. A single government policy can either lift millions out of poverty or sink them deeper into poverty. At the moment, the Federal Government is contemplating withdrawing subsidy from petroleum products. People have viewed this differently. The Organized Private Sector (OPS) has lent its voice to the removal, saying it would not affect the cost of doing business because, according to Alhaji Aliko Dangote, President of Dangote Group, the OPS had been paying market price for diesel for about 10 years. But a number of people think differently, they are of the view that the subsidy removal would have a crippling effect on the well-being of a majority of Nigerians. The Nigeria Labour Congress (NLC) has said that it would result in Nigerians paying more for petroleum products, which would make nonsense of the minimum wage of ₦18, 000 that was recently approved by the government.

So, whether poverty is on the increase or decline in an economy is a function of the economic policies pursued by the government. The policy pursuit of the government cannot be divorced from the perspective of those in government which is shaped by what they have been and where they have been. An economy driven essentially by graduates of Bretton Wood Institutions can only witness depreciation in the citizens' standard of living, which is the rule where they have been.

J. **Poor land utilization:** In most African countries, people own large chunks of land that are underutilized or sometimes not even used at all. This is partly because they are either not educated on what to do with the land, or because some people are just stuck in their rudimentary ways of doing things. Some people just use the land to grow crops, which are just enough for subsistence survival. Nothing goes to the market for sale.

K. **Prejudice and inequality:** Social inequality stems from cultural ideas about the relative worth of different genders, races, ethnic groups, and social classes. Ascribed inequality works by placing individuals in different social categories at birth, often based on religious, ethnic, or 'racial' characteristics. In certain countries in the world, governments tend to favour a specific creed or race or people. This is evident in South Africa. In South African history, apartheid laws defined a binary caste system that assigned different rights and social spaces to different races, using skin colour to automatically determine the opportunities available to individuals in each group. These people enjoy educational, social and welfare benefits. For example, the children of these people are able to enjoy education with subsidized school fees; adults are able to obtain high-paying jobs easily etc. Instead of channeling resources to help those at need, the governments of these countries choose to treat different races and creeds with prejudice and will treat others with less favouritism. Hence, this leads to poverty.

L. **Civil wars and unending political conflicts:** Africa is popular for its civil wars, either between neighbouring countries or within the same country. Such incidences render war zones unproductive, in addition to scaring away investment that would otherwise help foster economic development and create employment, which would help people get out of poverty. Nations experiencing civil war will experience stunted economic growth. For example, from 1990 to 1993, the period encompassing Desert Storm, per capita GDP in Iraq fell from $3500 to $761. This is significant as it shows the drop in the well being of all citizens in the affected country. It however, fails to capture the broader affects of damages to the infrastructure and social services, such as health care and access to clean water, which are not captured. The loss of infrastructure and breakdown of society will inevitably lead to the nation having to spend a hefty sum to rebuild and prepare itself for the economy. Furthermore, civil war diverts scarce resources from fighting poverty to maintaining a military. This is evident in the cases of Ethiopia and Eritrea. The most recent conflict over borders between the two countries erupted into war during 1999 and 2000, a period when both countries faced food shortages due to droughts.

M. **Natural disasters:** Natural disasters such as hurricanes and earthquakes have caused millions of dollars worth of infrastructure and the loss of lives. Developing countries often suffer much more extensive and acute crises at the hands of natural disasters, because limited resources become obstacles for the construction of adequate housing, infrastructure, and mechanisms for responding to crises. Natural disasters, being uncontrollable by man, affect annual agricultural output, as floods destroy the fertility of soils by washing away mineral-rich topsoil, take away natural decomposing agents, and thereby rendering the soil infertile. Droughts cause the land to become barren and unsuitability of such land for cultivation. The states of the U.S.A situated in Tornado Alley face constant fears of poor harvests in the face of frequent tornado occurrences. In the case of the Sichuan Earthquake in 2008 and the 2004 Tsunami catastrophe not only resulted in the loss of agriculture, but the destruction of many infrastructures worth of millions of dollar as well.

N. **Poor infrastructure:** Africa has a very poor infrastructure set up. They have poor roads, railways, water systems, etc, yet these are some of the major drivers of economic development. As a result, only a few areas with better facilities (such as urban areas) have developed over the other (rural) areas, which are occupied by the largest percentage of the population. Take the Sagamu-Benin express road for instance; we all know how many times money has been budgeted for the rehabilitation of that road. For a moment, take your mind away from the money but look at the number of people who have lost their lives on that road. Those are the unlucky ones because for many of them and their families, especially those who are their families' bread winners, it is a plunge into poverty. If a self-employed man is involved in an accident and has to spend six months or one year in the hospital, it means for that period, there is no income for him despite the fact that he has to keep spending money. Let's not forget the cause; it is because some people stole money meant for the repair of that road on which the accident occurred.

O. **Government's anti-poverty efforts:** The Nigerian Government has consistently reiterated its commitment to poverty reduction in the country. The first of the government efforts to scale down poverty in the country was Operation Feed the Nation (OFN), which was introduced by General Olusegun Obasanjo in 1979. The focus of the programme was to encourage Nigerians to embrace agriculture for the purpose of solving two poverty-related problems: malnutrition and unemployment. OFN was replaced with Green Revolution which was introduced by Former President Shehu Shagari in 1980. The focus of this programme was similar to its predecessor's.

The first administration to address access to credit by the poor as a way of alleviating their poverty was that of General Ibrahim Babangida. The administration started the now defunct People's Bank, which had a mandate to provide funding for entrepreneurs that could not access funds in conventional banking institutions. It also introduced community banks, which were meant to assist rural and poor people. Babangida's administration also introduced the Directorate of Food, Roads and Rural Infrastructure (DFRRI). This outfit was meant to open up rural areas while providing them with basic amenities for the purpose of increasing commercial activities in the areas. It was also the administration that started the National Directorate of Employment (NDE) with the mandate to develop programmes that would combat mass unemployment. General Sani Abacha, who became Head of State in 1993, established the Family Economic Advancement Programme (FEAP) as an agency to fight poverty in the country. The modus operandi of the agency was to disburse loans to families through cooperative societies. General Obasanjo, in his second coming as the nation's head, introduced the National Poverty Eradication Programme (NAPEP) to coordinate all anti-poverty programmes in the country from the local government to the federal level.

The Federal Government has also demonstrated its willingness to fight poverty by identifying with the United Nations MDGs. The UN in Year 2000 set 2015 as the target year for developing countries to record some progress in certain developmental areas with a view to scaling down poverty. There is a Senior Special Assistant to the President on MDGs. While there is no doubt that some progress has been recorded by the government in its poverty alleviation activities, the fact that independent international organizations say that 92% of the country's over 150million population live below the poverty line casts a pall on the efforts of the government. What the verdict portrays is that the efforts of the government have not yielded encouraging results despite the billions of naira that has gone into the programmes.

Three reasons are probably responsible for the unimpressive results of the anti-poverty programmes. The first is that the programmes were politicized. The intention behind most of the programmes was not to extricate the suffering masses from their poverty and anguish but to make a political statement. The second reason for the seeming ineffectiveness of the poverty alleviation programmes is corruption. Because of the pervasiveness of corruption in the country, operatives of the poverty eradication agencies often work at cross purposes with the objective of the agencies by converting funds meant for the masses to personal use. So, as a result of corruption, rather than the poverty reduction programmes reducing the number of the poor, it increases the number of the rich. The third factor is the failure of government to institute a system of assessing the success of the programmes. There is no feedback mechanism by which the government can hear directly from the poor on how effective or otherwise the programmes are. By the time it gets to the government that the programme is off target, it will be too late to do anything about it. So, until poverty alleviation programmes are divorced from politics and corruption and a mechanism for assessing their success is instituted, they will be mere motion without movement.

16.10 CONSEQUENCES OF POVERTY
The repercussions of poverty may vary in scale, but all carry a negative effect, regardless of political, economic, and social outcomes.

Homelessness: Extreme poverty carries with it a particularly strong set of risks for families, especially children. Compared to children living in poverty but having homes, homeless children are less likely to receive proper nutrition and immunization. Hence, they experience more health problems. Homeless women experience higher rates of low-birth-weight babies, miscarriages, and infant mortality, probably due to not having access to adequate prenatal care for their babies. Homeless families experience even greater life stress than other families, including increased disruption in work, school, family relationships, and friendships.

Hunger and malnutrition: Rises in the costs of living make poor people less able to afford items. Poor people spend a greater portion of their budgets on food than richer people. As a result, poor households and those near the poverty threshold can be particularly vulnerable to increases in food prices. For example, in late 2007, increases in the price of grains led to food riots in some countries. The World Bank warned that 100 million people were at risk of sinking deeper into poverty. Threats to the supply of food may also be caused by drought and the water crisis. Intensive farming often leads to a vicious cycle of exhaustion of soil fertility and decline of agricultural yields. Approximately 40% of the world's agricultural land is seriously degraded. According to United Nation's Ghana-based Institute for Natural Resources in Africa, if current trends of soil degradation continue, the continent might be able to feed just 25% of its population by 2025. Every year nearly 11 million children living in poverty die before their fifth birthday. 1.02 billion People go to bed hungry every night. According to the Global Hunger Index, Sub-Saharan Africa had the highest child malnutrition rate of the world's regions over the 2001-2006 periods.

Mass emigration of population: In the face of a nation's poor economy and weak rule of the government, the population may seek to migrate to areas with a better-faring economy, where the trade is more profitable; where there is low cost for all. Since the people of such poverty-stricken nations choose to migrate in search of better living/job/social conditions, it may undermine the nation's ability to recuperate from the far-reaching effects of poverty.

Genocide: This is a most extreme case of poverty, where there has only been one example in history - Uganda under the regime of the totalitarian and brutalistic Idi Amin, army colonel turned leader. In this case, Idi Amin spending spree quickly landed the beleaguered nation to total economic collapse. It is known that he systematically organized a pogrom of his fellow countrymen. Relatives of the victims were to pay an exorbitant sum to "recover" the bodies, and this was how he kept Uganda's battered economy afloat.

Violence: According to experts, many women become victims of trafficking, the most common form of which is prostitution, as a means of survival and economic desperation. Deterioration of living conditions can often compel children to abandon school in order to contribute to the family income, putting them at risk of being exploited. For example, in Zimbabwe, a number of girls are turning to prostitution for food to survive because of the increasing poverty. In one survey, 67% of children from disadvantaged inner cities said they had witnessed a serious assault, and 33% reported witnessing a homicide. 51% of fifth graders from New Orleans (median income for a household: $27,133) have been found to be victims of violence, compared to 32% in Washington, DC (mean income for a household: $40,127).

Terrorism: Through recent years, analysts have been able to point out that politically and economically weak nations often fall prey to terrorism. i.e. Nigeria, Afghanistan, Iraq, Yemen etc. Poverty too is a major factor in explaining the spike in terrorism in recent years. Between the years of 1933 to 1973 were times, when Afghanistan experienced political and economic stability. By the end of the Soviet-Afghan War, the country had been ravaged by infighting and devastation caused by the Soviets. Only then did terrorism flourish. Nigeria is not an exception in this instance, where since 2001 when Boko Haram metamorphosed and with its increased activities of bombings and killings since 2009, the state has remained weakened with fear of terror and poverty necessitated by insecurity.

16.11 THE ROAD AHEAD

The dismally slow progress in reducing ultra poverty and the relative lack of success in reaching the very poorest clearly demonstrate that "business as usual" will not be good enough to reach the poorest within an acceptable timeframe. As the world moves toward the deadline for achieving the Millennium Development Goals of cutting hunger and poverty in half, it cannot be content to focus only on the marginally poor and hungry—the desperate, grinding poverty of the world's absolute poorest must also be assuaged. A focus on policies and programmes that are particularly effective at improving the welfare of the world's poorest and hungry is needed.

Thus, in programmes aimed at tackling poverty, specific goals have been created and efforts concentrated or focused on meeting those targeted goals. Through this approach, there have been some progress in poverty reduction since 1970, although it has not been spread equally over the different parts of the world. Most of the decline in poverty took place in East Asia, notably in China. In developing countries, infant mortality was cut by more than 40% and adult illiteracy by 50%. A newborn baby can expect to live 10 years longer, and a combined net primary and secondary school enrolment has increased by nearly 50%. But there have also been reversals over the last few years, and huge problems remain. Based on the experience of the past years, there is now a growing consensus among national and international policy makers on what works and what does not in fighting poverty. Policies that are part of the successful poverty reduction package of different countries include the following:

Inclusive and broad-based economic growth: Economic growth is one of the most important factors in helping to reduce poverty, but it is not sufficient. The effectiveness of economic growth in reducing poverty depends upon the structure of growth, existing levels of inequality and on how the benefits of growth are distributed. Inequality in income is a function of the distribution of economic assets (land, industrial and financial capital), and so-called "human capital" in the form of education and skills. Governments need to work on creating more equity in the distribution of income and assets. The effectiveness of growth in reducing poverty also depends on the extent of growth and employment opportunities created, and whether it takes place in areas and sectors where the poor are located. In most cases, with the exception of the South East Asian countries (South Korea, Taiwan, Malaysia, etc.) in their high growth phase, there has not been sufficient employment generation in the formal sector of the economy. Attention now needs to be paid to the informal sector of the economy.

- According to the Secretary-General's Millennium Report, a 1 per cent increase in a country's gross domestic product can bring about an increase in the incomes of the poorest 20 per cent of the population. But this cannot happen where inequalities in society do not permit growth to benefit the poor.
- China is an example of what could be achieved by rapid economic growth built on investment in people: the gap in average income between China and the rest of the world has decreased by over 50 % compared to 40 years ago.

However, prospects for growth in the world economy currently are rather bleak. The world economy appears to be growing too slowly to create enough jobs or to make a real impact on poverty. Even the industrialized countries appear to be stuck with high unemployment, a major cause of poverty. This suggests that economies cannot rely on growth to pull them out of poverty, but must take specific steps to target poverty reduction directly. Growth, if it is achieved at the cost of environmental degradation, can also undermine the livelihoods of the poor, who are dependent these resources. Hence, development policies need to be sensitive to the social and economic environments of the poor.

- After the 1992 Earth Summit (Rio de Janeiro, Brazil), the Philippine was the first country to establish a council for sustainable development with partners from Government, civil society and private business. Key businesses worked to implement sustainable development initiatives – reusing by-products, controlling pollution levels and including environmental provisions in collective bargaining agreements with labour unions.

Realizing globalization's potential: The phenomenon of large corporations operating in many countries, in the hands of private individuals, who make decisions about opening/closing and reorganizing operations that affect the lives of many people, is a reality of this new millennium. The process called globalization and increased economic integration offer countries many positive market and employment opportunities. But there are also risks and problems associated with it. The poor in poor countries at this time are often victims of this process. Countries need to prepare themselves for globalization by:

- Building up the competitive advantage of their industries.
- Addressing the problems of those who will lose out from global competition; and
- Improving technology and increasing productivity so as to avoid competing on the basis of low wages, poorly regulated working conditions and exploitation of the environment.

Even after they have done all this, nothing is guaranteed. Markets may be saturated and despite globalization, many industrialized countries also still protect their markets with tariffs and quotas and discriminate against the products of developing countries. Better trade policies, fairer rules and terms that allow poor countries to enter developed countries markets need to be put in place. The United Nations Secretary-General has urged all industrialized countries to consider granting duty-free and quota-free access for essentially all exports from the least developed countries. Governments and international agencies also need to work on preparing countries assisting them in developing regulatory policies that will soften the negative impact of volatile financial flows.

Promoting good governance, accountability and participation: Honest and fair government practices, free of corruption; decision making open to the input of the public; and follow-up actions in accordance with decisions made, are measures needed to eradicate poverty. Of prime importance are:

- Good governance - the conduct of a government that is honest and fair (see Briefing on Governance);
- Transparency :- decision making can be open to public input and scrutiny; and
- Accountability - ensuring that follow-up actions are in accordance with decisions openly arrived at, and that they can help ensure that the benefits of growth and poverty reduction policies actually reach the poor.

Key in bringing this about is the role that civil society can play, as is the process of allowing and encouraging the participation of the poor, themselves in the making of policies, especially those that affect them directly. There is a clear link between empowering the poor and overcoming poverty. According to the UNDP Poverty Report 2000:

- In Andhra Pradesh, India, women organized themselves into self-help groups (SHG), which mobilized community savings, created opportunities for income generation for women via the increased access to credit and through a focus on skill formation and improved the status of women. The groups mobilized the community to make recommendations about loan priorities, and also tried to reduce or eliminate child labour and improve the condition of girls.
- Similarly, in Cambodia, local communities developed their own anti-poverty projects. Villagers brainstormed about their problems, they asked questions of officials and expressed their opinions about how best to do things.
- In Bulgaria, self-governing civic organizations increasingly provided vocational training, fostering new businesses, protecting the environment and resolving conflicts.

Provision of basic services and budgetary policies: The way in which public resources are mobilized and spent determines the kind of impact that it has on poverty. A fair and equitable public budgetary policy (relating to expenditure, taxation and government fiscal priorities) can also help to promote economic growth, reduce inequality and make development more pro-poor. Examples of success in pro-poor and participatory budgetary policies can be found in India, Brazil and Uganda. Bringing about improvements in the quality of life, or reducing the level of deprivation, is a function not only of the resources available, but also of the economic and social priorities and policies of government. Reducing the impact of the various dimensions of poverty is possible, even at low levels of income. Government spending on health and education, in combination with other policies that promote equitable growth, is particularly important in addressing poverty. Such social provisioning policies can help:

- Reduce the experience of deprivation and poverty,
- Increase people's productive capacities and possibilities, and
- Reduce the amount that government must spend on dealing with the impacts of health or other crises and deprivation.

Countries such as Costa Rica, Cuba, Sri Lanka and Viet Nam and the state of Kerala in India have secured better health conditions, greater reductions in mortality and improvements in literacy over others with similar or greater economic resources. Viet Nam, with a per capita income of $350, has a lower infant mortality (31 as compared to 60 per 1,000 live births) and higher adult literacy (92.9% as compared to 84.6%) than South Africa, which has a per-capita income of $3,310. Mauritius, a small island nation in the Indian Ocean cut its military budget and invested heavily in health and education. Today, all Mauritians have access to sanitation, 98 per cent to safe water and 97 per cent of births are attended by skilled health staff.

Achieving gender equity: More women than men live in absolute poverty. Economic crises have often hit them harder. Few of them tend to get fewer skilled jobs, and in situations of growing unemployment they are often the first to lose their jobs. This increases their vulnerability and makes them more susceptible to poverty, a phenomenon referred to as the feminization of poverty. It has been observed that investment in girls' and women's education translates directly into better nutrition for the family, better health care and declining fertility. It has also been widely acknowledged that poverty is unlikely to be overcome without specific immediate and sustained attention to girls' education and women's empowerment. According to one estimate, closing the gender gap in education adds 0.5 percentage points to annual growth in GNP per capita.

Chapter Seventeen

POLICIES/PROGRAMMES OF RURAL AND COMMUNITY DEVELOPMENT IN NIGERIA

17.1 WHAT IS A POLICY?

Generally, policy is a plan or principles that guides decision making. Oxford Advanced Learners' dictionary (7th edition) defines policy as a plan of action agreed or chosen by a government, political party, or a business etc. According to Dimock (1970) policy is a consciously acknowledged rules of conduct that guides administrative decisions. Policy is a statement of a principle or group of principles with their supporting rule of action that conditioned and governed the achievement of certain objectives to which a business is directed. A policy can best be described as a framework or strategy, giving a broad outline of the direction and overall strategy for the development of a particular sector. It can also be defined as a high-level overall plan embracing the general goals and acceptable procedures, especially of a government body (Westerinen, 2003). Many factors contribute to the development of policy, such as public debates in various fora, the demands of different political constituencies, reports from commissions and task forces appointed to enquire into perceived problem areas, evaluations of previous policies, and so on. Policies are often enunciated in such documents as government white papers, though not necessarily. A public policy is a deliberate and (usually) careful decision that provides guidance for addressing selected public concerns. In short, any given policy represents the end result of a decision as to how best to achieve a specific objective. Most people actually apply a similar process in the decisions they make in their everyday lives – even around fairly inconsequential choices. Policy is said to be an intervention, a course of action taken by government, or management (in the case of an organization) or, better still, an individual, to influence or arrive at pre-determined outcomes.

17.2 RELATIONSHIP BETWEEN GOVERNMENT POLICY AND PROGRAMMES

A policy can best be described as a framework or strategy, giving a broad outline of the direction and overall strategy for the development of a particular sector. It can also be defined as a high-level overall plan embracing the general goals and acceptable procedures, especially of a government body (Westerinen, 2003). A programme is a planned and organized series of events that seeks to address a particular problem or to promote development. Programmes demand a clear statement of objectives linked to national or higher level policies. They are made up of a number of projects which, when linked together, achieve the programme's objective.

From the definition of policy and programmes; policy can be regarded as the bedrock upon which programmes can come into reality. Without a policy put in place there cannot be a programme. Policy is an action plan on which master plan has been conceived after carefully and painstaking brainstorming on the pros and cons of different steps and then, a conclusion is reached after passing through the various stages. The decision reached is to be implemented through programmes. Example of the rural development policy during the Babangida Administration in Nigeria led to the establishment of the defunct Directorate of Food, Roads, and Rural Infrastructure (DFRRI) in 1986. Different programmes through which the policy was implemented include; rural road construction and rehabilitation, rural water scheme, provision and maintenance, rural housing, rural banking, etc. Policy remains a paper work unless programmes are designed on it to ensure the reality of the policy. Therefore, policy should be backed up with good implementable programmes to make the series of statement in the policy document realizable. They must be well worked out to solve problems.

17.3   AN OVERVIEW OF RURAL AND COMMUNITY DEVELOPMENT PROGRAMMES IN NIGERIA SINCE INDEPENDENCE TO DATE

Since political independence in 1960, various regimes both civilian and military have adopted various strategies and methods at developing the rural areas of the country. However, Ikotun (2002) noted that in spite of colossal amount of money that have gone into implementing rural development programmes and the proliferation of rural development agencies one after the other, much impact has not been made. He went further to state that in spite of pious official pronouncements, and declaration of intentions as contained in the development plans, at the end of each plan period rural life remained unchanged. Each plan came with new promises and raised hopes that were never fulfilled. The First National Development Plan, 1962-1968 for example, had as its priority, agriculture (considered as synonymous with rural development) but capital budget and expenditure on agriculture during the plan period was only 42 percent. The Second Development Plan, 1970-1974, had as its main thrust, the attainment of a just and egalitarian society and claimed to place high premium on reduction of inequality among social groups and between urban and rural areas. These noble objectives not withstanding, this aspect of the plan was partially executed. It is significant to note also that it was only during the Third National Development Plan, 1975-1980 that attempts were made to engage in what has been referred to as "integrated rural development". This refers to the Agricultural Development Programmes (ADPs) that were sponsored by the World Bank. It is to be noted that in spite of the active involvement of the World Bank in the ADPs, for which the country has taken loans worth billions of Naira, the country has continued to be deficient in food production and the standard of living of the people, especially in the rural areas are still very low.

Thus, as far back as early 1970s, rural development has been identified as a strategy for improving the economic and social life of the rural poor in Nigeria since then; successive governments at various levels have embarked on several programmes aimed at rural development. A cursory look at the introduction, establishment, implementation and the objectives of majority of the programmes will reveal that they are mainly targeted at rural development in an attempt to better the lives of rural dwellers, stimulate and enhance economic growth, as well as get the rural sector to contribute meaningfully to the national economic and social development. It is however, sad to observe that from independence to date, there has been a great disparity between successive government pronouncements and the establishment of various development agencies towards attaining rural development and the actual results of implementation efforts. These programmes have direct or indirect impact on rural development. Some of the development programmes established under development agencies since independence to date, apart from the National Development Plan stated above, can be broadly listed as:

- National Accelerated Food Production Programme (NAFPP) 1972;
- River Basin Development Authority (RBDA) 1973;
- Agricultural Development Programme (ADP) 1975;
- Operation Feed the Nation (OFN) 1976;
- The Universal Primary Education Scheme (UPE);
- Mass Mobilization for Social and Economic Reconstruction (MAMSER);
- National Orientation Agency (NOA);
- National Agricultural Land and Development Agency (NALDA);
- Primary Health Care Programmes;
- Green Revolution Programme, (GRP) 1979;

Specifically, however, since early 1980s, rural development agencies that were in place include:

> ➢ Accelerated Development Area Project (ADAP) 1982;
> ➢ Better Life Programme (BLP) 1984;
> ➢ Multi-State Agricultural Development Project (MSADP) 1986;
> ➢ The Directorate of Food, Roads and Rural Infrastructure (DFRRI) 1986;
> ➢ The National Directorate of Employment (NDE) 1986;
> ➢ National Agricultural Insurance Company (NAIC) 1987;
> ➢ Expanded Programme on Immunization;
> ➢ Basic Primary Education Scheme (BPE);
> ➢ The Nomadic Education Programme;
> ➢ The Migrant Fishermen Scheme;
> ➢ Adult Support Basic Education Programme;
> ➢ Federal Assisted Mass Transit Scheme;
> ➢ State Assisted Transport Scheme;
> ➢ Ferry Transport Schemes (in the Riverine areas and Lagos);
> ➢ Low-Cost Housing Estate Scheme;
> ➢ Federal Environmental Protection Agency;
> ➢ Flood and Soil Erosion Control Programme;
> ➢ People's Bank of Nigeria 1990;
> ➢ Community Banks 1991;
> ➢ Nation Insurance Corporation of Nigeria (NICON);
> ➢ Family Economic Advancement Programme (FEAP)1997;
> ➢ National Fadama Development Programme, NFDP (1993);
> ➢ Family Support Programme (FSP) 1994;
> ➢ National Poverty Eradication Programme (NAPEP) 1999;
> ➢ Poverty Alleviation Programme (PAP) 2001;
> ➢ National Special Programme for Food Security (NSPFS) 2003;
> ➢ National Economic Empowerment and Development Strategy (NEEDS) 2004.

At this juncture, a look at the essence and contributions of few of the agencies will be considered.

17.3.1 Farm Settlement Scheme (FSS)

The Farm Settlement Scheme (FSS) was the very first agricultural programme embarked upon by government in Nigeria. This scheme was borrowed from the success story of productive cooperatives in Israel, especially the Kibbutzim option.

The scheme was introduced to perform the following functions:

a. Bring school leavers back to the land
b. Increase agricultural production
c. Teach farmers new techniques in farming
d. Make agriculture more attractive to the youths.

This scheme was very operational in the Western and Eastern regions of Nigeria. The scheme failed due largely to the following:

a. The conditions which made this programme succeed in Israel was absent here.
b. The farms were located far away from the urban areas and employees were finding it difficult sleeping inside the remote farms dotted right inside the villages.
c. Poor remuneration for the farmers.
d. Government bureaucracy and necessary bottlenecks.
e. The scheme was alien to even the practitioners.

17.3.2 National Accelerated Food Production Programme (NAFPP) 1972

This was part of the Second National Development Plan (1970 – 74). The plan itself had no clear statement on rural development, although ₦1, 353 million was voted for it (FGN, 1972). It targeted self sufficiency in the production of rice, maize, sorghum, millet and wheat. It was a joint programme of Federal Government and USAID. Its objectives include accelerating and increasing food production through the adoption of improved packages of production technology, speedy up the transfer of research results to farmers, pursuing intensive and extensive cultivation of crops and linking research to production agencies through extension services. The programme was launched in 1973 as a national network of agro services centres created to facilitate the distribution of tractor and machinery services to farmers to support the promotion of improved packages of technology development by various research institutes under the NAFPP. It was created by Federal Ministry of Agriculture with the primary aim of increasing staple food production through the promotion of improved production technologies among the small-scale farmers, especially in rural areas. The major success of the programme is that it led to an appreciable improvement in food production in the 1970s and above all it laid a good foundation or an effective researcher-farmer linkage. But unfortunately the programme has been kept dormant for a long time since after the regime that introduced it left the stage. These centres are no longer in the mainstream of rural development plans, thus, a gradual collapse of the programme.

17.3.3. **River Basin Development Authority (RBDA) 1973**

The early 1970's can rightly be seen as the period of the conception of the River Basin Development Authorities Decree No. 32 of 1973 thus brought the Chad Basin Development Authority into existence as a result of the Food and Agricultural Organization (FAO) of the United Nations recommendation. The Sokoto-Rima Basin Development Authority was created in April, 1973 under the Decree No. 25 which brought into existence the eight River Basin Development Authorities (RBDAs). The number was increased to eleven in 1978 and to eighteen in 1984, but later reduced again to eleven in 1986. The authorities were created to develop the water resources potential of the country for agricultural and domestic purpose. Their attention was focused mainly on agricultural production including crop, fisheries and livestock even when the name was changed in 1984 to reflect their potential role as rural development agency.

The functions of RBDA as spelt out in section 4 of the Decree No. 78 of 29th September, 1979 were:

a. To undertake comprehensive development of both surface and underground water resources for multi-purposes use.
b. To under-take schemes for the control of floods and soil erosion.
c. To construct and maintain dam, dyes, polders, and well, boreholes; Irrigation and drainage system, other work necessary for the achievement of the Authority's function under this section.
d. To provide a unit for this purpose to farmers and recognized associations as well as for urban water supply schemes for a fee to be determined by the authority concerned, with the approval of the ministry.
e. To control pollution in rivers, lakes, lagoons and creeks in the Authority's area in accordance with nationality laid down standard.
f. To resettle persons affected by the works and schemes specified in this section or under special settlement schemes.
g. To develop fisheries and improve navigation on the rivers, lakes, reservoir, lagoons and creeks in the Authority's area.
h. To undertake the mechanized cleaning and cultivation of land for the production of crops and livestock for forestry in areas both inside and outside irrigation project for a fee to be determined by the Authority concerned, with the approval of the ministry.
i. To undertake large-scale multiplication of improved seeds, livestock and tree seedlings for distribution to farmers and for aforementioned schemes.

j. To process crops, livestock products for the farmers in the Authority's area in partnership with the State agencies and any other person.

k. To assist the State and Local governments in the implementation of the following rural development work in the Authority's area:

- The construction of small dams, well and bore-holes and the development of water ways for the evacuation of farm produce.
- Large-scale mechanized cleaning and cultivation of land;
- The provision of power for rural electrification schemes from suitable irrigation dams and other types of power stations under the control of the Authority concerned;
- The establishment of agro-service centers and tractor hire schemes;
- The establishment of grazing reserves;
- Large-scale multiplication of improved seeds;
- Large-scale production of breeding-stock, cattle and poultry for distribution;
- Large-scale aforestation schemes;
- The training of staff for the running and maintenance of rural development schemes and for the general extension work at the village level.

However, the River Basin Development Authorities Amendment Act No. 7 of 1981 superseded the former decree and widened the scope of the Authorities' activities to include the provision of infrastructure and technical know-how for primary agricultural production. The nomenclature of the RBDAs was also changed to River Basin and Rural Development Authorities (RB & RDAs). The number of RB and RDAs too was also increased to eighteen in each State, except Lagos and Ogun States which had its own RB & RDAs. This new arrangement was, however, short-lived as in 1986, the eighteen RBDAs were organized and merged into the former eleven. This re-organization was completed in 1987. The activities of these authorities were again restricted mainly to the "comprehensive development of both surface and underground water resources for irrigation, urban and rural areas were supplied and electricity generation provided along the main water-sheds in the country rather than on state basis". Accordingly, the nomenclature RD & RDA was changed once more to River Basin Development Authority (RBDA). The Niger Delta Basin Development Authority remained one of these eleven RBDAs. While some believe the authority has some impact, the general consensus is that the output from the authorities does not justify the huge amount of funds channeled into them particularly during the Second Republic. With the long years of existence, the activities of RBDAs and the Ministry of Water Resources have not been felt appreciably by Nigerian farmers.

Despite some visible accomplishments recorded by numerable problems that hindered the effective implementation of River Basin Development Authorities, notable among them include:

i. **Corruption:** There was massive corruption in the operation of some of the basin's authorities. In some instances, not all the money voted for projects were used. Much of the money found their way into private pockets. In some other instances contract were never executed.

ii. **Political interference:** Outside political interference in the operations of the authorities were noticed. At times, this interference comes from the ministry of Agriculture albeit, the Federal military government, at times outside influence from overseas. It was strongly suspected that the U.S.A government worked against the programme because its success will jeopardize importation of wheat from U.S.A.

iii. **Dearth of manpower:** Paucity of high caliber experts in the area of agronomy, drainage and water-shed management, farm management, irrigation engineering, hydrology, soil/water conservation among others. All these were lacking in Nigeria.

iv. **Land tenure system:** The existing land tenure system before creation of the basin authorities hindered the smooth take-off of the projects as land owners disturbed the project over non-payment of compensation for acquired lands and in some instances resisted out rightly the acquisition of their lands. For instance, soldiers have to be called in to stem further riots by land owners over the Bakaliori project in Sokoto State in the early 1980's.

v. **Natural hazards:** Occasionally, rivers overflow their banks thereby washing away dams constructed on them while there are other cases of rivers and dams drying up in the dry season.

17.3.4 Agricultural Development Programme (ADP) 1975

The origin of the ADPs dates back to 1975 when the Federal Government of Nigeria in conjunction with the World Bank and the State Governments of the North-Central, North West embarked on investigations aimed at identifying suitable areas for piloting agricultural development projects. These were to serve as experiments before committing huge amount of money on full scale projects. These investigations led to the establishment of three enclave ADPs in Funtua, Gombe and Gusau between 1976 with joint funding by the Federal Government of Nigeria, the World Bank and the respective State governments. Major innovations introduced by the ADP include:

a. Construction of feeder roads.
b. Provision of portable water through earth dams, boreholes and tube well for human use, livestock use and for small-scale irrigation.
c. Provision of improved seedlings/stems etc.
d. Provision of extension agents to farmers.

All these were designed to increase production, and raise rural income and hence, the standard of living of rural dwellers. The success achieved in these piloting projects and others that followed led to the establishment of the eventual thirty-one state-wide ADPs in the country. The programme is assessed to be a major contributor to the significant growth recorded in the agricultural sector in the late 1980s to early 1990s (CBN, 1993). However, there is fear that the programme may not be able to survive long after the World Bank would have withdrawn their funds.

17.3.5 Operation Feed the Nation (OFN) 1976
The OFN was part of the Third National Development Plan (1975 – 80) which was voted ₦2, 050.738 million. Like the earlier plan, there was no categorical strategy for rural development, except some ₦500 million for rural regrouping (Olayiwola and Adeleye, 2005). The Operation Feed the Nation came into being just at a time the National Accelerated Food Production Programme (NAFPP) is just finding its feet. It was introduced by the Federal Military Government under Rtd. General Olusegun Obasanjo in 1976 with a major objective of creating awareness about the importance of agriculture in national development. To mobilize the people to embrace agriculture, eliminate the traditional disdain for agriculture by the educated, enhance food production on a large scale, create jobs and income and utilize all available land resources in the country. The programme was designed to involve all the segments of the population including students who were engaged during the long vacations. According to Akinbile (2007), the programme was introduced in 1976 as a strategy to increase food production by harnessing the human, material and natural potentials of the country towards substantially increasing food production through inputs supply. The programme, however, had no articulated extension delivery system. The main problems with the

objectives were not specific and therefore not measurable. The programme naturally passed away with the regime that introduced it.

17.3.6 Green Revolution Programme (GR) 1980

GR means a well marked improvement in agricultural production in a short period of time and the sustenance of higher levels of agricultural production over a fairly long period of time. The Green Revolution Programme was created in 1980 by the civilian administration of the Second Republic (Alhaji Shehu Shagari). The programme was meant to accelerate the country's movement towards self-sufficiency in food production in five years. It placed emphasis on inputs supply, improvement of infrastructures and provision of price incentives. With this at the back of their mind, the Shehu Shagari administration in 1980 launched the Green Revolution.

Features of Green Revolution

a. **Package on inputs:** The G.R. evolved a strategy where by farmers were meant to adopt gradually all the inputs needed for facilitating and enhancing productivity which include improved seedlings, fertilizers, plant protection, manures, improved agricultural implements etc.

b. **Greater intensity of cropping:** The G.R was not only concerned with increased yield but with a greater intensity of cropping. Everybody was asked to embrace agriculture as a vocation.

c. **High yield varieties:** Using our street language we say "Gabbage in, Gabbage out" The programme is founded on improve high yield varieties to encourage bumper harvest.

d. **Multiple cropping:** This encourage higher yield per acre or unit of land. Many crops are planted in one piece of land at the same time.

e. **Plant protection measure:** This is the use of insecticides, herbicides etc. in protecting crops in the farm.

f. **Increase in use of fertilizer:** This was made available to farmers to encourage high agricultural yields.

g. **Agricultural research and technology:** This involved the use of implements and machinery in agriculture.

Hence, the approach lacked clear focus and there was diversification of efforts into several activities which could not be sustained, thus, the programme failed. The programme went a step ahead of others by introducing agricultural credit for small-scale farmers. However, the programme was seriously affected by unnecessary political rivalry between State-controlled and Federal-controlled programmes. It was heavily politicized that the real farmers hardly benefited from the activities of the programme; it finally died with the exit of the founding fathers.

Problems of Green Revolution

i.   **Corruption:** The system created many arm chair millionaires. Money was readily and easily diverted. We remember the Minister of Agriculture under Shagari's regime, Alhaji Umaru Dikko, who was the most powerful minister of the administration. And also the most corrupt.

ii.   **Increase in polarization:** The scheme created large term millionaire farmers who had the money to buy inputs and intensive technology, thereby sidelining the small scale farmers who cultivate the food that feeds the nation.

iii. **Income distribution:** Derived from above, the gap between the rich and poor expanded the more the scheme no doubt gave more impetus to millionaire farmers.

iv.   **Labour displacement, unemployment and urban migration:** The arrival of millionaire farmers created what we were called 'absentee farmer's' while also creating the landless peasants. Those who want to farm have no access to land because it has been taken away by absentee millionaire farmers, who may not readily make use of the land.

v.   **Environmental problems:** The irrigation schemes dams and takes constituted some environmental hazards such as water logging and water-borne diseases. The "Tiger" dam disaster of 1989 in Kano State is a pointer.

vi.   **Growth of capitalist farming:** The poor were thrown out of farming since they could not purchase the modern and scientific tools and equipment.

vii. **Expensive in cost:** Because of emphasis on improved implements and technology, it was an expensive project.

17.3.7 Agricultural Credit Guarantee Scheme (ACGS) 1978

Agricultural Credit Guarantee Scheme (ACGS), 1978 till date. Established by Act No. 20 of 1978, this offers a 75 percent guarantee backed by the

Central Bank of Nigeria (CBN) on agricultural credit in default, net the amount realized from the disposal of security for such credit with the primary aim of providing guarantee to Commercial Banks for loans taken by them for agricultural purposes. The scheme included the creation of an Agricultural Credit Guarantee Fund (ACGF) jointly by the Federal Government and the Central Bank of Nigeria. Under the scheme, the Commercial Banks were required to channel a minimum proportion of their loan portfolio into the agricultural sector. The Commercial Banks are made to deposit the shortfall with the Central Bank, which made such fund available to Nigeria Agricultural and Cooperative Bank for its operation. Financing is at market-determined interest rates. The CBN offers a rebate equivalent to 40 percent of the loan interest when loans are duly repaid. This scheme deals with small scale farmers who need small loans to operate. For instance, in 2005, more than 70% of all loans were smaller than fifty thousand naira to each farmer who applied and accounted for 36% of total loan value. Only 11% of all loans were larger than ₦100,000 and accounted for 32% of total loan value. The scheme has, however, suffered bureaucratic and administrative bottlenecks. For instance, the processing of applications and claims has been slow so much so that at the end of 2005, there was an accumulated backlog of 4064 unprocessed claims, the oldest of which dated back to 25 years (IFPRI, 2008). The scheme was not too successful then, in meeting the requirements. This is due to the risk involved in granting loans to small-scale farmers scattered about in the rural areas.

17.3.8 Directorate of Food, Roads, and Rural Infrastructures (DFRRI) 1986

Apparently, not satisfied with the efforts of previous government in rural development, the former President Ibrahim Badamosi Babangida on assumption of office slashed down the River Basin Development Authority programme from 18 to 11. The Directorate of Food, Roads, and Rural Infrastructure was established by the Babangida's government on the 7th February by Decree No. 4 of 1986 with a total allocation of ₦500 million. DFRRI was created with a determined focus on the development of the entire rural areas of Nigeria in order to improve the quality of life of the rural dwellers, consequent upon the realization, the agricultural development was not accompanied by the provision of necessary social, economic and institutional infrastructure will not lead to the desired rural development. It was charged with a mandate of rural infrastructural development in the areas of feeder, roads construction to open up the rural areas. The directorate was to help the rural communities to identify and evolve viable local level projects by using local community organizations and institutions. DFRRI was also to provide the rural communities with the necessary technical and financial support for the projects through the project development stages. Greater community participation is the bane of the DFRRI as a concept.

Activities/Programme Details

Under the provision of infrastructure, areas affected include physical, organizational, institutional and social infrastructure. Under productive activities, areas covered include food and agriculture, rural industrialization, technology and natural resources development and rural manpower development.

Provision of Physical Infrastructure: The major areas affected in the provision of physical infrastructure include the construction of rural feeder roads; the provision of potable water and sanitation facilities; the provision of rural electricity; and the promotion of improved rural housing.

The Construction of Rural Feeder Roads: The construction of the 30,000 km under Phase 1 of the Nation-wide Rural Feeder Roads Programme is almost completed now. Except for a few States, the project went on very satisfactorily throughout the country. As the first and second Reports indicated, Final Comprehensive Inspections (FCI) has been completed in Katsina, Kano, Borno, Bauchi, Kaduna, Niger, Kwara, Plateau, Cross River, Akwa Ibom, Rivers, Imo, Anambra, Delta, Edo, Ondo, Oyo, Ogun and Lagos States. Please refer to Enclosures 1 and 2, namely the first and second Reports. Those States that have been adjudged to have satisfactorily completed Phase 1 had commenced Phase 2. It is expected that another 30.000 km will be constructed. Consolidation would be simultaneously carried out where it was absolutely essential only. Provision was being made for the maintenance of these roads. The Headquarters, the States, the Local Governments and the benefiting communities would all contribute to this effort.

The Rural Water and Sanitation Programme: One hundred million naira has been disbursed to all the States, including the Federal Capital Territory, for each to provide potable water to 250 communities spread equitably between its constituent Local Government Areas. The complementary aspect of this programme was the promotion of improved sanitation facilities in the rural areas. Reports received at this

Headquarters indicate that most aspects of this programme went on satisfactorily in a good number of States.

Rural Electrification: Mr. President in his 1987 Budget Speech directed that Rural Electrification programmes be added. After series of consultations with States, Federal Ministry of Mines, Power and Steel, and NEPA, about 227 communities nation-wide were identified for connection to the national grid. The total cost of this project was ₦70.8 million. The Directorate contributed N55 million of this amount while the States, Local governments and communities contributed the balance of ₦15.8 million. However, ₦1.5 million as initial contribution to the States was disbursed to each State and the Federal Capital Territory. See Annex C for list of communities that benefited. So far about 4 States (Plateau. Sokoto, Borno and Niger) executed about 60% of their project specification. Four more States (Imo, Anambra, Ondo and Oyo) did over 50%. Other States were at various stages of programme execution.

The programme while it lasted was able to record the following successes:
  a. Rural electrification
  b. Provision of portable water in rural areas through sinking of boreholes; which has been the most massive in history of this nation.
  c. Introduction of community development associations.
  d. Massive construction of earth –road.
  e. Aggressive pursuit of increased food production through one of its cardinal sign-post: food first.

As opined by Adeboye and Okuneye (2005) DFRRI, between 1986 and 1993 recorded success in the area of infrastructural development such as feeder roads but eventually collapsed in 1994 due to policy inconsistency and discontinuity of programmes and projects. Emphases were also placed on how to add value to food production, and storage, other post harvest processing facilities were provided. DFRRI recorded successes as the rural areas bubbled back to life with cottage industries springing up on the heels of rural electrification; the rural people could diversify their business venture from mainly turning to rendering services which was able to resolve the human sense of dignity. The Directorate during the active period of its existence (1986-1993) made its presence felt but its failure to evolve an effective community participation strategy has created sustainability problems for its various projects. In early 1994, the DFRRI was merged with the Ministry of Agriculture and became a department in the ministry. Even though, the unit is still overseeing most of its former activities, the prominence which it enjoyed as an autonomous directorate is now more concerned with having its separate vote removed. The unit is now more concerned with monitoring its erstwhile activities than engaging in actual construction of rural infrastructure, thus, ending the days of its flamboyance.

17.3.9 Mass Mobilization for Social and Economic Reconstruction (MAMSER)

The Directorate of Mass Mobilization for Social and Economic Reconstruction was created with the objective of mobilizing Nigerians towards economic recovery and developing a new social and political order. In other words, the fundamental mandate of MAMSER was to facilitate the nation's process for pooling together, harnessing, actualizing and utilizing potential human resources for a self reliant transformation of the economy. Its programmes for the attainment of its objectives included the inculcation in the populace generally political education, social justice, self-reliance, mass literacy, renewed war against indiscipline. With emphasis on promoting leadership by example at all levels, operation service alert for armed forces, promotion of excellence in public services etc. In spite of various difficulties, the Directorate was able to make tremendous impact in its efforts at mobilizing Nigeria to build a good society, characterized by better life, fair distribution of resources, integrity, honesty, peace, progress and genuine development. Since 1993, however, MAMSER lost its autonomous existence and became a Department in the Federal Ministry of Information and Culture. However, the fact that a new National Orientation Agency was set up to continue the work of moral education where MAMSER left off, is a testimony to the fact that the work of national moral rejuvenation was not yet accomplished.

17.3.10 National Orientation Agency

After the dissolution of the board of the Directorate of MAMSER in 1986, it paved way for the inauguration of a new outfit, the National Orientation Agency. The new Agency is a corporate body which emerged from the merger of the Public Enlightenment and War Against Indiscipline and the National Orientation Movement division of the Federal Ministry of Information and Culture. This was necessitated by the need to pool together and consolidates all efforts and resources utilized by the three bodies in their fields of public enlightenment, social mobilization and value reorientation. The agency which was formally established in August 1993 has the following among others as its objectives:

- ✓ Ensuring that governmental programmes and policies are better understood by the general public.
- ✓ Mobilize favourable opinion for such programmes and better.
- ✓ Encourage formal education through public enlightenment activities and publications.
- ✓ Establish feedback channel to government on all aspects of Nigerian national life.
- ✓ Establish appropriate national framework for educating, orientating and indoctrination of Nigerians towards developing socially desirable attitude, values and culture which project individual/national pride and positive national image for Nigeria;
- ✓ Restore and sustain discipline in our national life;
- ✓ Instill in the populace a sense of absolute loyalty to the fatherland;
- ✓ Ensure and uphold leadership by example and
- ✓ Foster respect for constituted authority.

As at date, the activities of the agency are yet to be fully and widely felt by the majority of Nigerians. The multifarious problems faced by the agency might make it to eventually turn out to be an exercise in futility. Various other governmental agencies with similar case histories include the National Directorate of Employment, the moribund Peoples' Bank, the Community Banks, Nigeria Agricultural Insurance Scheme, Better Life for Rural Women, Nation Agricultural Land Development Authority, Family Economic Advancement Programme, etc. with lofty ideals and objectives which were either partially realized or woefully a failure; thereby failing to bring about the desirable rural development in the country to date. What reasons can be adduced for this failure?

17.3.11 Better Life Programme (BLP) 1987

This is yet another programme for rural community development in Nigeria. The programme (BL) was established in 1987 with a view to alleviate poverty and was transformed into Family Support Programme in November 1994, with the same objectives of encouraging rural dwellers especially women to improve their standard of living. Better Life Programme was established in 1987 with a view to empowering women and the development of the rural areas. It was to ensure good environmental condition such as recreational centres for optimum performance. It transformed to Family Support Programme with the same intention or objective of encouraging rural dwellers and especially women to improve their standard of living. Through this programme, the success noticed and desires to improve living standards were plausible. The programme, however, suffered the same fate like others as political powers change from one person to another. The major concern of the Better Life Programme is improving the lives of rural women within the communities which constitute the largest and most exploited group of the total rural population. It is the binding force for most of the ambitious projects and programmes which the administration has set in motion. The Better Life Programme recognized the consensus of the large population of women as rural dwellers which constitute majority of our labour force. These women work as mothers and wives as well as true bread winners engaged in trading and farming. The programme also suffered discontinuance as a result of change of administration.

The objectives of Better Life Programme were:
- To promote the welfare and full utilization of women in human resources development along with the promotion of responsible motherhood.
- To stimulate action aimed at improving the political, cultural, social and economic status of women as well as support non-governmental organizations.
- To provide modern amenities like those enjoyed in the towns, it was hoped that rural communities could be made attractive. The development of small scale industries and introduce new technology. This is to reduce the problem of employment in the rural areas.
- To formulate and propagate the moral values within the family units.
- To promote the interest of women in the social front to ensure that, they are not relegated to the background.
- To improve the home life and general status of women in rural communities.
- To encourage cooperative activities among women while also working towards the total elimination of all social and cultural values which discriminate against and dehumanized womanhood.
- To encourage acquisition of skills, knowledge and positive effect in agriculture, house management, health education, industrial sectors and cooperative societies.

Better Life Programme played important roles in lives of Nigerian's women and economy. As the women started this programme, there were changes in their standard of living and also it raised their social status. Generally, Better Life Programme aimed at human development through the encouragement of optimal resource management and which generally works with women as its audience would seem to have relevance to women's lives.

17.3.12 Family Support Programme (FSP) 1994

FSP was given birth to when the Babangida's administration was toppled by Rtd. General Abacha. The Better Life Programme being the brain child of Mrs. Babangida naturally died and was replaced by FSP, chaired by Mrs. Abacha. The FSP focused on the status and welfare of children especially in rural communities. The programme aimed at improving the experience of women in development programme. This was mainly done by broadening its scope and sharpening its focus. The overall aim of the FSP was to improve and sustain the family cohesion through the promotion of social and economic well-being of the Nigerian family for its maximum contribution to national development and to promote policies/programmes that strengthen the observance and projection of human rights, the advancement of social justice and human dignity. The specific objectives of FSP were:

- ❖ To promote decent health care delivery in reducing maternal and child mortality and morbidity through improved health care system.
- ❖ To eradicate negative social and cultural factors affecting women and children.
- ❖ To assist families identify economically viable enterprises for income generation, and to provide technical and financial support for their implementation.
- ❖ To assist families increase their agricultural productivity as well as improving their internal status.
- ❖ To carry the public enlightenment campaign to sensitize the general public on matters of human decency, civic responsibilities and concern for the welfare of the disadvantaged.
- ❖ To establish a family round-table for promotion of discipline, morality and family cohesion through projects such as girl child scheme; the boy-drop-out and the children in distress.
- ❖ To enhance the capacity of parents to act as role models to their children through various means including guidance and counseling.
- ❖ To help family members learn more about the psychological dynamics of families as units on which more effective social organization and responsibilities can emerge.

❖ To create, arouse and sustain the interest of government, the Nigerian people and international organizations on the activities of FSP.

❖ To sensitize government on the need to provide adequate shelter for all Nigerians.

❖ To promote the maintenance of high moral standards of the nation as well as responsive action against policies and trends, both foreign and local, that may militate against such standards.

❖ To promote and improve on the welfare of the most vulnerable and disadvantageous groups in the community.

❖ To carry the public enlightenment campaigns to sensitize the general public on matters of human decency, civil responsibility and concern for welfare of the disadvantaged.

17.3.13 National Directorate of Employment (NDE) 1987

The NDE was established in 1987 during the military regime of Ibrahim Babaginda to tackle the problem of mass unemployment involving all categories of labour (skilled and unskilled). The directorate focused its attentions on small scale enterprises, especial public works and vocational skills development. The objectives of the scheme include:

➢ The creation of job opportunities for the forming population of jobless Nigerians.

➢ Nurturing the spirit of self-reliance with minds of Nigerians particularly the youths.

➢ To provide the Nigerian youths majority of who were jobless at the time with practical skills that will enable them to be gainfully self-employed and in the process provide employment opportunities to the members of their communities.

To execute the objectives stated above, the directorate introduced four major programmes; these include;

a. Agricultural Sector Employment Programme
b. National Open Apprenticeship Scheme
c. Special Public Work Programme
d. Small Scale Industries And Graduate Programme.

a) **Agricultural Sector Employment Programme:** This programme is aimed at providing self employment to young school leavers and graduates in agriculture and other related fields, who were unemployed.

b) **National Open Apprenticeship Scheme:** This was introduced as a means of providing many Nigerians who are jobless with productive and marketable skills. These would enable them to be gainfully self-employed or to secure paid employment. Other related programmes were re-introduced which include the National Youth Employment and Vocational Skills Development Programme, the waste to wealth scheme, school on the wheel scheme and the disabled work scheme.

c) **The Special Public Work Programme:** This was designed to provide immediate temporary employment to a large number of the unemployed Nigerians. This group was to take part in public work through intensive labour techniques. Some of the work they do included tree planting exercise, environmental sanitation, land clearing, road maintenance etc.

d) **Small Scale Industries Establishment and Graduate Employment Programme:** This was designed to encourage and to aid employed Nigerians to set up small scale business and to run their own business. NDE conducted the entrepreneurship courses in order to assist the beneficiaries of the loan given under this programme through its job creation loans guarantees schemes, beneficiaries were advised to make judicious use of such loans. Also a scheme for the retirees was part of this programme. Besides other basic achievement of this scheme, it has stimulated the generation of employment to many Nigerians and thus, helped in improving the standard of living of the masses and also have promoted community development in Nigeria.

17.3.14　Community Banking Programme 1991 to 2007

The programme provided for the establishment of Community Banks with a focus on rural banking operations. The National Board for Community Banks (NBCB) was the regulator of these banks until 2002 when this function was transferred to the CBN. It was intended to serve communities that were able to establish one based on personal recognition, character and credit worthiness of the borrower. The operation of the People's Bank faced a number of problems like any community development efforts, among which are the unsustainable rate of branch expansion, the dependence on government for funds and weak management as a result of which its effectiveness in alleviating the problems of the poor remains insignificant. Even so, the Peoples' Bank is no more. As a result of government continued effort, the Peoples' Bank was merged with the Nigerian Agricultural and Cooperative Bank (NACB) to form the Nigerian Agricultural Cooperative and Rural Development Bank (NACRDB).

The establishment of Community Banks was intended to inculcate the banking habit in rural areas and providing the needed banking services to members of their community. Although, the Community Banks can be said to have recorded some successes, it will be fool hardy to believe that it has actually improved the living standards of the rural poor who are supposed to be the target group. For instance, most of those who benefited from the Community Banks are businessmen with medium scale business enterprises. The poor with no collateral and adequate deposit base were largely unable to meet their credit needs from these banks. Apart from this, a large number of these banks are located in the urban areas and most of their services are directed to the urban with less credit risks.

17.3.15 National Poverty Eradication Programme (NAPEP) 1999
National Poverty Eradication Programme (NAPEP), 1999 to date. Like FEAP, NAPEP was established by the Federal government. The mode of operation is tailored towards directed (subsidized) credit to farmers. The programme consists of four schemes namely, Youths Empowerment scheme which involves capacity acquisition, mandatory attachment, and credit delivery; Rural Infrastructural Development scheme which involves the provision of potable water, rural electrification, transportation and communication, Social Welfare Services scheme which is involved with qualitative education, primary health care, farmers empowerment and provision of social services, provision of agricultural input and credit delivery to rural farmers; and Natural Resources Development and Conservation scheme which contains programmes for environmental protection through conservation of land and space, development of agricultural resources, solid minerals and water resources.

17.3.16 Poverty Alleviation Programme (PAP) 2001
On 29th May, 1999, loud ovation heralded the return of democracy that was after the evil years of the draconian dictator, the late General Sani Abacha. Nigerians had believed that democracy is a magic wand and will heal all the wounds, especially putting food on their tables. Many years on, the story had changed, poverty had increased, unemployment had multiplied, school fees had risen, hospitals had become more consulting clinics, armed robbery and spate of assassination had doubled, terrorism

in Niger-Delta had become a nightmare resulting in constant kidnap of expatriate oil workers, rise in ease on pump price of petroleum and the cost of living and above all decline in life expectancy of Nigerians to as low as 42 years. Thus, at the inception of the Obasanjo administration in 1999, many Nigerians believed that employment generation and poverty alleviation are the ultimate goals. The Government embarked on the eradication strategy. In the year 1999 Olusegun Obasanjo, the former President of Nigeria, launched a new employment strategy, which was christened "Poverty Eradication Programme (PEP). The Poverty Eradication Programme on inception in the year 1999 attracted a vote of ₦10 Billion. The following year, 2001, the name was changed by the Federal government to "Poverty Alleviation Programme. The government said the change of the name is in recognition of the fact that poverty cannot be eradicated but minimized. In same year, 2001, the Federal government pumped ₦20 billion into the programme. In 2006, the Federal government has earmarked ₦150 billion for the programme. The problem is that as these huge sums were pumped in, no appreciable impact is seen. However, to date, Nigerians are yet to feel the full impact of this programme.

17.3.17 National Economic Empowerment and Development Strategy (NEEDS) 2004

The National Economic Empowerment and Development Strategy (NEEDS) is the response to the development challenges of Nigeria. In 1999, most people grossly underestimated the extent of social, political, and economic decay of the country. NEEDS—the National Economic Empowerment and Development Strategy (2004–07)—is Nigeria's plan for prosperity. It is the people's way of letting the government know what kind of Nigeria they wish to live in, now and in the future. It is the government's way of letting the people knows how it plans to overcome the deep and pervasive obstacles to progress that the government and the people have identified. The goal of NEEDS is to lay a solid foundation for sustainable poverty reduction, employment generation, wealth creation, and value reorientation; mobilize the resources of Nigeria to make a fundamental break with the failures of the past and bequeath a united and prosperous nation to generations to come. It is also a way of letting the international community know where Nigeria stands—in the region and in the world—and how it wishes to be supported. Nigerians have agreed, however, that the major thrusts of NEEDS are what Nigeria needs to move forward.

Features of NEEDS

Nigeria's new reform programme NEEDS, designed to last from 2004 to 2007 has several distinctive features, which distinguishes it from the erstwhile National Rolling Plans that it is replacing, namely:

(i) It is Nigeria's Poverty Reduction Strategy and gains inspiration from the Poverty Reduction Strategy Paper (PRSP) which had been under preparation since 2001.

(ii) It is a reform programme aimed at re-engineering the growth process.

(iii) Its formulation process has been largely participatory.

(iv) The President expressed his commitment to the programme and has set up an economic team to drive it.

(v) The States have also broadly agreed to design the States Economic Development Strategy (SEEDS) to complement the NEEDS. The local governments are also expected to prepare local government components "LEEDS" There is of course no information yet on the degree of compliance, the NEEDS having been launched only on May 29, 2004.

(vi) The NEEDS focuses on strategy and policy directions rather than programmes and projects. It signals a shift in the direction of decentralized project planning and execution.

(vii) Implementation of aspects of the NEEDS began even before the formal launching of the document.

Objective/Policy Thrust

The objective of NEEDS is to enable Nigeria achieve a turn around and grow a broad based market oriented economy that is private sector - led and in which people can be empowered so that they can, as a minimum, afford the basic needs of life. It is therefore, a pro-poor development strategy with sources of economic empowerment being gainful employment and provision of social safety nets for vulnerable groups.

NEEDS at a Glance
The diagram below tells the whole story about NEEDS
Figure 17.1: The NEEDS at a Glance

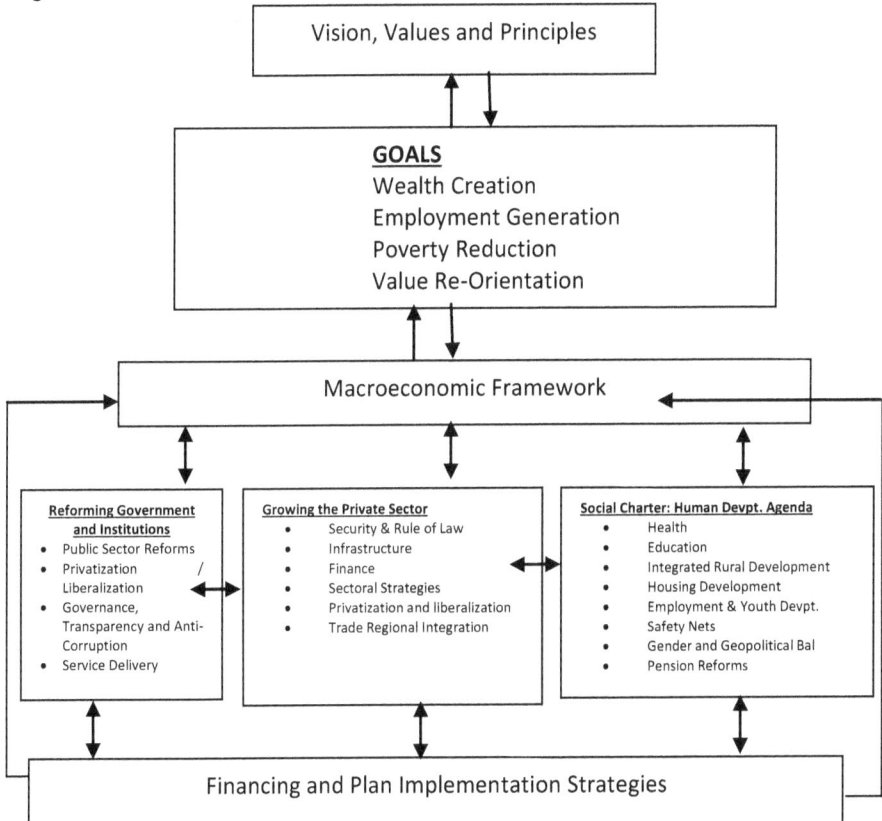

Vision
The Vision and mission of the strategy derives from Nigeria's history, endowments, experience, and aspirations. The visioning process drew inspiration from the views of a cross section of stakeholders and the provisions of the constitution regarding the overall thrust of the directive principles of state. The vision underscores the necessity and urgency of the challenges facing Nigeria. It is therefore drafted as follows: "to build a truly great African democratic country, politically united, integrated and stable, economically prosperous, socially organized, with equal opportunity for all, and responsibility for all, to become the catalyst of African

Renaissance, and making adequate all embracing contributions, sub-regionally, regionally and globally."

Goals
The goals of NEEDS are wealth creation, employment generation, poverty reduction and value – orientation. These goals inform most of the strategies contained in the strategy.

Values
The Strategy stresses the imperative of value re-orientation, society having for long been subjected to the syndrome of getting wealth with little or no effort. That syndrome combined with a "get rich quick" mentality and reliance on government patronage has largely been responsible for the disrespect for efficiency norms. Not only should there be value re-orientation to enthrone the ethics of hard work and transparency, there indeed has to be paradigm shifts in certain aspects of the country's value system. The shift, according to the posture of the strategy, must be towards greater service to Nigeria, wealth creation through productive effort and engagement in government as a service rather than commercial business.

If there is anything like a home-grown reform programme, NEEDS is it. For the first time, Nigerians embarked on an extensive consultative and participatory process, involving major stakeholders in the design of the programme. However, to date, Nigerians are yet to feel the full impact of this programme.

17.4 GENERAL CRITIQUE OF THE PERFORMANCE OF RURAL DEVELOPMENT PROGRAMMES IN NIGERIA
In evaluating the performance of development programmes and the problems associated with their apparent failure, Nweke (2003) poses the problem of political communities. For him, Nigeria is a land of paradoxes: it is a rich country, but its people are poor. The World Bank ranks the country among the 25 poorest countries in the world. Yet as has been depicted above, the country since independence in 1960 and 2003, according to him, there have been 15 ministries charged with the fight against poverty for rapid rural development and about 30 institutions, agencies and programmes, designed to energize the struggle against poverty, ensure rural development and stimulate the process of inclusion. The fundamental question that logically arises is: what strategies should

Nigeria adopt to ensure the efficiency of its programmes against poverty and exclusion?

One major problem has been that since independence, successive governments simply made a rehash of the old strategies for rural development under new names. Not only were these programmes hijacked by the political class, which has never been honest in the formulation and execution of public policy. Then too, the governments, one after the other, hardly ever sought the participation of the political communities (regrouping of the organs of government, pressure groups, the media) and individuals, all this for various reasons. And yet it seems obvious that the political communities have, each of them an interest in every specific political field and try to exert through consultation and partnerships with the political decision makers as they design and implement the policies likely to enhance poverty eradication and ensure rural development.

Another major factor that has contributed to the failure of rural development programmes to achieve their noble goal of poverty eradication in Nigeria today is the policy of the centralized control of the programmes of rural development set up by members of the elite who do not have the data available from the deprived social groups or even from the private sector. If the strategies adopted by government have to succeed, the Nigerian government would have to adopt a policy of efficient consultation and collaboration based on partnership, with the political communities. Such an arrangement would make it possible, on the one side, for the programmes to be mutually controlled by the authorities and the rural dwellers themselves, and, on the other side for the necessary responsibility and transparency. This has been the major preoccupation of many Non-Governmental Organizations and the International Agencies like the International Bank for Reconstruction and Development (the World Bank), the International Finance Corporation (IFC), the International Monetary Fund (IMF) and a host of other United Nations agencies in their position as partners in the poverty reduction programmes and donors as well as lenders to rural development projects in the third world.
Okafor (2003) in contributing to the search for viable solutions to the problem of stunted rural development in the third world opined that the relationship between governance and socio-economic development has become important today, the international community (in particular the multilateral financial institutions) recognizes that the correction of the macro-economic imbalances, market reforms and trade liberalization are

no longer enough to improve economic efficiency and promote sustainable rural development. The reality of today's world demands that the promotion of good government in all its ramifications should be the essential element of the frame in which the economy can prosper. These ramifications embrace for example, respect for the rule of law, enhanced efficiency in and responsibility for the public sector, the reinforcement for the partnership between the private and public sectors and civil society; the enlargement of the mechanisms of decision-making. The analysis of some of the programmes of government since independence in its rural development efforts to date as depicted above highlights their effects, which would explain why over 70 percent of the Nigerian populations still live below the poverty threshold. A survey by Okafor (2003), of 450 Nigerians randomly selected to represent all the strata of the society; revealed that the failure of the old poverty reduction and rural development programmes is mainly attributed to:

> Their weak political base and their personalization;
> The proliferation of projects with little, if any effort to harmonize and/or coordinate their activities.
> The lack of sustainability arising from the abandonment of programmes as soon as the Head of State, often its initiator, leaves office;
> A top-down approach to project formulation, rarely the bottom-up approach;
> Little or no involvement of the Non-Governmental Organizations or other parties concerned in the development projects;
> The inadequate funding of the project. Besides, the performance of the rural development agencies and programmes launched either by the agencies or government are almost always second-rate. The reasons suggested for this by Okafor (2003) include:
> The politicization of the programme by men in power;
> The poor "ownership" of the programme by over half the population (70%) which surely affects its attitude and involvement;
> The allegations that a large share of the fund, committed by the government has been misappropriated and fraudulently ends up in private pockets, etc.

Lastly, the efficient tools of poverty eradication and rural development would be shared governance and a scenario in which all the parties involved (government, private sector, civil society and community development organizations) would take part in the decision-making process, as well as in the execution of the development programmes in all its ramifications should be the essential element of the frame in which the economy can prosper. These ramifications embrace for example respect for the rule of law, enhanced efficiency in and responsibility for the public sector, the reinforcement for the partnership between the private and public sectors and civil society; the enlargement of the mechanisms of decision-making.

Chapter Eighteen

MONITORING AND EVALUATION

18.1 MONITORING

Monitoring is the continuous/periodic assessment of programme/project implementation by stakeholders to ensure that work is progressing according to plan. Monitoring is basically concerned with the delivery process, ensuring that inputs through activities are transformed into outputs while at the same time analyzing their quality and quantity.

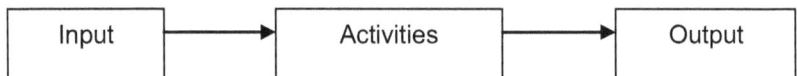

18.1.1 KEY PECULIARITIES OF MONITORING

- Monitoring is continuous
- Monitoring system should be in place before project start up.
- One level of monitoring is done by projects staff.
- Supervisors are responsible for monitoring the staff and tasks under them.
- Project Managers are responsible for monitoring all aspects of the project.
- The other level of monitoring is done by other stake holders through field visits, and routine reports from Project Managers, etc.
- Monitoring assess progress of projects implementation.
- Monitoring tracks inputs.
- During monitoring lots of information is collected and documented.
- Monitoring indicators must be developed prior to commencement of monitoring.
- Such indicators must be known and understood by all that is involved in the monitoring exercise.

18.1.2 HOW TO CARRY OUT MONITORING

- Monitoring could be carried out through field visits, review of service delivery, records/reports, use of information, filed/household inquiries etc.
- Quantify data where possible and qualify data otherwise (events description)

- Use appropriate forms to collect and report data information
- Use data from other sources to verify your data
- Go to the filed yourself.

18.1.3 **MONITORING TOOLS**

Two important monitoring tools are the work plan and the progress review.
(I) THE WORKPLAN
The work plan should provide:

- The expected outputs and activities described in a scheduled sequence.
- Activities planned starting and finishing dates.
- The responsible persons/party for carrying out the activities (see table 1)

(II) THE PROGRESS REVIEW

- The progress review should answer the following questions
- Are inputs being made available as planned?
- Are activities being carried out according to the work plan
- Are outputs being produced as planned?
- What are the constraints
- What remedial actions have been taken/planned?

TABLE 18.1: Frame work for the Work plan

S/N	Activities Description	Preceding Activities	Activities to Follow	Responsible Person/party	Time of Activities		Expected output	Monitoring and evaluation summary
					Start	Finish		

TABLE 18.2: INFORMATION FOR MONITORING PROGRAMME /PROJECTS OPERATIONS

Category of Information	What to monitor	What records to keep	Who collects data	Who uses data	How to use information	What decision can be made
1. Work plan activities	• Timing of activities. Availability of resources	• Work schedule-es. • Monthly quarterly work plans	• Programme Managers All stakeholder-rs are available	• Programme Managers All stakehold-ers are available	• Ensure that staff and other resources are deployed of	be made •Reschedule activities and resour-ces a needed
2. Costs and Expenditur-es	Budgeted amounts and funds on hand and expenditures • Balance in	• Ledger of expendi-tures by budget category. • Receipts	• Financial Officer/Acco-untant	• Project Manager • Auditor • Other stakehold-ers	• Ensure that funds are available to execute activities • Ensure	• Authorized expenditu-re • Making budget and

					compliance with funding regulations if there is fee for service, determine fee structure.	project revisions • Determine need for other funding sources
	Budget by approved cost categories	• Bank transactions • Reports for stakeholders.				
3. Staff and supervision	• Knowledge attitudes & skills of staff. • Educational level of staff salaries and Benefits • Job Performance	Performance reviews. Job Descriptions Personnel Resume of Staff. Feedback from training attended.	• Supervisors Project Managers. Personnel Directors Trainers	• Supervisors Personnel Director	• Motivate staff and resolve employment problems. Advise staff on career.	• Placement . Training needs promotions. Disciplinary action.
4. Commodities	• Stock • Ordering and procurement Status Procurement regulations.	Stock registers. Invoices Field workers reports	• Logistic Manger	Project Manager • Other stakeholders	Ensure availability of commodities in Stock and distribution to field. • Ensure good condition of commodities	• Quantity to order. • When to order. Amount to keep in reserve for emergency
5. Results project	• No and type of services provided commodities dispensed. Characteristics of persons served e.g. Educated	• Clients card forms clinic Registers. • Field Workers reports.	• Field supervisors • Clinic nurse	• Field supervisors • Project Managers • Other Stakeholders	Ensure objectives are realistic. Assess quality of services provided. Access appropriateness of services	• Review objectives. • Restrain staff • Review strategy approach

18.1.4 CONSTRAINTS TO MONITORING
- Failure to pre-develop monitoring indicators
- Crowded activities - Failure to plan
- Absence of baseline data
- Lack of skills to analyze data to generate information
- No clear and consistent unit of measure
- Lack of effective monitoring machine

18.2 WHAT IS EVALUATION?
Evaluation is the process of determining the merit, worth or value of something. It showcases your achievements and helps to make your programme better. It can become one of the most rewarding aspects of

your job, because it is where you see the results of your work. Evaluations can be carried out for a range of reasons and it is important to be clear about exactly why you are undertaking it. Evaluation is the periodic assessment of project performance. It is the review of the relevance, efficiency and effectiveness of the project against pre-stated aims and objectives.Evaluation assesses the impact and effects of the project on the target beneficiaries. Purposes may include one or more of the following:

- To find out how effective the project is.
- Affords stakeholders an opportunity to take stock of achievements and shortcomings, and recommend improvements based on lessons learnt.
- Governments seek to ensure that available funds are directed towards worthwhile projects; evaluation can therefore lay bare the effectiveness of government efforts.
- To see whether developmental objectives have been achieved.
- Evaluation affords an opportunity to assess the successes or failures of the project plan.
- Implementing ministries/parastatal need such information with which to compare the successes or failures of the various projects planned.
- To learn how well things are being done.
- Evaluations provide information on achievements, realization of project objectives and project strengths and weaknesses. Private contributors to the project want to know that their donations are having a positive effect. Thus greater openness about achievements and failures can help build trust and allay criticisms.
- To learn from experience and adopt best practices
- Evaluations can and should be a learning experience which project stakeholders use to improve future planning and implementation skills, analytical capacity and awareness.

An evaluation plan simply sets out the information that you need to determine if your programme's objectives have been met, together with the methods that you are going to use to collect this information. Ideally, your evaluation plan should be prepared when you are establishing your programme, though it is also possible to prepare it later in the process. The importance of having an evaluation plan (or evaluation framework see Figure 17:1) cannot be overstated. Many evaluations fail when, without a plan, they go off track and fail to answer the most important questions.

18.2.1 **WHY EVALUATE?**

There are many good reasons for a community to evaluate its efforts. When done properly, evaluation can improve efforts to promote development at any level from a small local to a statewide or even national effort. Evaluation offers the following advantages for communities:

- Collecting information about how things are done and the results help us understand how community initiatives develop, offering lessons other groups can profit from.
- Providing on-going feedback can improve community work by encouraging continuous adjustments of programmes, policies, and other interventions.
- By involving community members, people who haven't had a voice may gain the opportunity to better understand and improve local efforts.
- Finally, evaluation can help hold leaders accountable to the community and to the supporters, who provide funding.

18.2.2 **PRINCIPLES, ASSUMPTIONS, AND VALUES OF COMMUNITY EVALUATION**

When we look at the process of supporting and evaluating community initiatives, we need to look at what our ideas are based on. The following principles, assumptions, and values serve as the foundation for these processes. You will notice that they reflect the challenges of addressing both of the major aims of evaluation and understanding community initiatives while empowering the community to address its concerns.

1) Community initiatives often function as catalysts for change in which community members and organizations work together to improve the quality of life.
2) Community initiatives are complex and ever-changing, and they must be analysed on multiple levels.
3) Communities initiatives help launch interventions that are planned and implemented by community members.
4) Community evaluation must understand and reflect the issue, and the context in which it is happening.
5) Community evaluation should involve people from the entire community.
6) Community evaluation information should be linked to questions of importance to key stakeholders.
7) Community evaluation should better community member's ability to understand what is going on, improve practices, and increase self-determination.

8) Community evaluation should begin early and be on-going.
9) Community evaluation results, if positive, should be used to help sustain and promote widespread adoption of the community initiative and/or its components.
10) Community evaluation should be coupled with technical assistance to provide total support.

Community initiatives engage community members and organizations as catalysts for change: they transform the community to have a better quality of life. Community evaluation is based on the premise that community initiatives are very complex. To be effective, they need many levels of intervention. Researchers try to understand the issue, the history of the initiative, and the community in which it operates. Ideally, local initiatives are planned and implemented with the involvement of many community members, including those from diverse backgrounds. Because of this, community evaluation is a participatory process involving a lot of collaboration and negotiation among many different people.

Evaluation should take place from the beginning of an initiative. That way, it can offer ongoing information and feedback to better understand and improve the initiative. Evaluation priorities (that is, what to evaluate) should be based on what is of most importance to community members. If done properly, evaluation results should actually help sustain and renew the community initiative. The information gathered in evaluation can be used to obtain resources show how to improve, and offer an opportunity to celebrate accomplishments. If the initiative seems to be effective, information from community evaluation can be used to promote its widespread adoption. Finally, evaluation should be coupled with technical assistance to provide a complete support system for the initiative. Evaluation without support can actually hurt the initiative.

An evaluation process
Evaluation is a process that includes:
- Having a purpose.
- Asking a question.
- Identifying the information needed to answer the question.
- Designing and testing a method for collecting the information.
- Collecting the information
- Analyzing the information.
- Determining the answer to the question.
- Using the answer.

In community development processes and some human service processes the following features exist:

- ❖ Each process is unique - it is not a standardized process.
- ❖ The specific goals to be achieved may not be known at the beginning of the processes - it is an open-ended process not a pre-determined one.
- ❖ Often the goals to be achieved are difficult to precisely define.
- ❖ The steps in the process are often not known in advance; nor are they precisely defined.
- ❖ Different people in the service process may have different values and so make different judgments about the worth of the service process.
- ❖ People in the processes are part of families, friends, neighbourhoods, work teams, communities.
- ❖ Service provides are parts of service networks.
- ❖ There are many causes and many effects and so it is hard to show cause and effect relationships.
- ❖ People in the processes make choices about their commitment and participation.
- ❖ People in the processes may want different things.
- ❖ There are often conflicts between good service practice and good data collection practice.

These characteristics affect the appropriateness of the strategies and tools. For example it is not appropriate to use unit costing in community development processes because unit costing requires standardized processes whereas community development processes are grouped and open-ended.

Evaluation Strategies and Tools
Many different strategies and tools are used in evaluation processes, e.g.

- Interviews,
- Questionnaires,
- Focus groups,
- Assessments,
- Case reviews,
- Peer review,
- Statistical analysis.

HOW TO GO ABOUT EVALUATION

All involved in an evaluation mission should:

Have a clear and common understanding of its purpose and have an opportunity to express views on what the priorities are

- Agree on the approach to be used (e.g. internal, participatory or joint)
- Agree on how findings/reports will be produced and disseminated

18.2.3 SETTING UP MONITORING AND EVALUATION SYSTEM

The Principal components of the system are:

- Indicators
- Data collection mechanism
- Data analysis/interpretation
- Reporting system

INDICATORS

Indicators are principal tools in a monitoring and evaluation system. Project Managers/team should determine the criteria and indicators on which success will be measured.

ASSESSING INDICATORS

The method of assessing indicators depends on the type of indicator. However, experience has shown that Project Managers generally use qualitative information, which are observed and analyzed by comparing two situations and value judgment passed. It should be specified how the indicators will be assessed, who will be responsible for the assessment and when.

MONITORING AND EVALUATION INDICATORS FRAMEWORK
TABLE 18.3: LOG FRAME FOR MONITORING AND EVALUATION

S/N	Planning Parameters	Objectively Verifiable Indicators (OVI)	Means of Verification (MOV)	Risks and assumption	Monitoring and Evaluation Summary
1.	Aim: State the aims of the project	Evidence to show that problem is resolved	Source of information and method of data collection	Factors beyond project control	Impact indicators of change on the lives of the people
2.	Activities what are the planned activities	Evidence of accomplishment of activities	-Do-	External factors affecting accomplishment	OUTCOME Indicators of targets accomplishment
3.	Budget what is	Amount needed	-Do-	Outside factors	OUTPUT

				delaying funding	Input converted to output/results
4.	Budget what is the budget sum	Amounts needed to accomplish individual activities	-Do-	Outside factors delaying funding	Input project resources quantified in measurable terms

18.2.4 **CONSTRAINTS TO EVALUATION**

- lack of proper planning
- Inadequate/improper developed evaluation indicators
- Absence of baseline data/information
- Lack of skill on data analyses to allow for sound judgment
- Poor knowledge of evaluation indicators

18.2.5 **MONITORING AND EVALUATION REPORTING MACHINERY**

All stakeholders in a programme/project need and use information for efficiency and effectiveness. THE PROJECT interface (Staff of DPRS) and other implementers.

a. The staff of DPRS in ministries/parastatals collects and uses information that can meet their monitoring needs of project implementation. The DPRS should regularly feed their ministries/organizations and the office of IGR, Economic Planning and Monitoring with appropriate information about operations in their ministries. The management of ministries/organizations and the State Planning outfit (Office of IGR, Economic Planning and Monitoring) needs to know what is happening for informed decisions.

b. Each level in the project management must access information from the implementing agency in order to produce periodic reports. In addition to furnishing them (management hierarchy) with information on programme/project performance, such reports should highlight constraints /problems requiring immediate management decisions and actions.

c. The office of IGR, Economic Planning and Monitoring should prepare regular reports on programme performance and provide financial documentations of expenditure variance, to the Executive Council and to the Executive Governor, to meet accountability requirements.

18.2.6 **REPORTING FRAMEWORK FOR THE DIFFERENT STAGES OF THE PROJECT**

(a) Implementation Monitoring Report

This report should indicate whether planned activities are proceeding according to schedule.

FRAMEWORK

- Name of Ministry/organization
- Project Title
- Location address
- Period covered
- Progress of Implementation
- Constraints
- Necessary action

(B) EVALUATION REPORT

This report should be based on project objectives, criteria, and indicators in the indicator framework, methodology and time of evaluation.

FRAMEWORK

- Attainment of project objectives with regard to indicators earlier identified.
- Changes in quality of life of the people that can be attributed to the project (positive and negative)
- Constricts and other factors with positive effects on the project
- Suggestions for improving future plans for similar projects

(C) COMPLETION REPORT

A completion report is the avenue through which the Project Manager tells his boss that the project is done. Information in the completion report could be stored in the data base and can also be used in writing other reports, prepare for valuation and write-ups for press briefing

FRAME WORK:

* Basic Project Information
    a. Projects Title
    b. Projects location address
    c. Total cost of project

* REACHING THE PROEJCT OBJECTIVES
    d. What is/are the objectives of the project?
    e. Was/Were they reached
    f. What is/are the result(s) of the project?
    g. How many people/organizations contributed?
    h. How many people will benefit from the project?

* THE ROAD OF IMPLEMENTATION
    i. When did the project start?
    j. When was it completed?
    k. What problems were encountered?
    1. How were they solved?
    m. What specifically went well?

* POST PROJECT ASSESSMENT
    n. How will the project be maintained?
    o. How many people were trained?
    p. On what were they trained
    q. What further training do they need?
    r. Are the proper record keeping systems in place?

* OUTCOME AND IMPACT OF THE PROJECT
    s. What is/are the outcome(s) of the project?
    t. How will this/these outcome(s) contribute to the overall impact on the beneficiaries.
    u. What numbers/evidence do you have?
    v. Will this/these impact(s) be sustained?
    w. How

18.2.7 INTERNAL CONTROLS AND AUDITING
INTERNAL CONTROLS

Internal controls are measures built into programmes/projects to guide and regulate people's behaviour in the process of implementing activities by applying enabling rules, regulations and processes to ensure that resources are properly utilized and accounted for in a manner that will guarantee the achievement of pre-set objectives.

NATURE OF INTERNAL CONTROL

The internal operational measures in the form of
    x. Rules
    y. Regulations

z. Procedures
Activities
Should be clearly stated before project implementation

AUDITING
This is an exercise designed to verify or examine financial accounts to ensure that they are kept in order.
(I) AUDIT REQUIREMENTS
    a Approved /authorized procedures are stated
    b Disbursement of money are as stated in financial budget and other documents
    c Disbursements are adequately authorized
    d The control measures are reliable and correctly maintained stipulated.
    e. All projects should be audited at least once a year.

(II) AUDIT REPORTING FRAMEWORK
The report should be able to say whether:
- Project disbursements are valid and supported by adequate documentation
- An appropriate Internal Control System is maintained
- Project Financial reports are accurate and fairly presented.
- Project Monitoring and evaluation reports are prepared as required.

18.2.8 GENERAL REPORTING FRAMEWORK
1. Summary of findings and recommendations
   This should be an abstract. It should contain among other things, opinions and recommendations based on facts
2. Introduction (including terms of reference)
3. Design
   - Order or sequence of project implementation. According to the work plan
4. Implementation
   - Level of results achieved at the time of reporting. What and what have been done out of the activities scheduled in the work plan.
5. Performance
   - is a kind of evaluation e.g. 20% of the 40% planned have been achieved.
6. Special Concerns
   - e.g. Delays and reasons for it.

- Opinions based on facts
7. Findings, Conclusions and Recommendations
   - Details
8. Lessons learned
   - Extraordinary things/events encountered but which are not contained in work plan.

Chapter Nineteen

CASE STUDIES

The foci of community development are as varied as there are human needs. The term community development has been used to connote at different times, a process, a method, a programme, an institution or even a movement. The examples presented in this book have tried to demonstrate how these varying perceptions of community development are applied in practice.

Again, in order to compare rural development activities elsewhere in the developing nations, few case studies have been reviewed. This is to help in the cross fertilization of ideas, as well as to observe how those countries have failed. It is hoped that as these reviews are done, you will be able to identify strengthes and weaknesses of those countries approaches so that you can explain why your country's system has made the kind of progress being experimented so far.

The over-arching aims are to:
* Involve people on a community basis in the solution of their common problems.
* Teach and insist on the issue of democratic principles in the joint solution of community problems.
* Activate or facilitate the transfer of technology, resources and knowledge to the people of a community for more effective solution to their problem.

19.1 CASE STUDY 1: AKASSA COMMUNITY AND THE STATOIL HYDRO COMPANY IN NIGERIA

The Akassa Model - a Process

Statoil Hydro is supporting a community development project in Akassa in Nigeria to help abolish poverty and build local capacity which started in 1997. Akassa is a remote coastal Ijaw community, Bayelsa State in the extreme South of Nigeria in the outer Niger Delta. The clan's 30,000 members are spread between 19 villages, are of Ijaw origin and speak the Akaha dialect. Mainly fisher folk, most Akaha people live sandwiched between the salt water of the ocean and the brackish water of the world's largest mangrove swamps, on sand barrier islands that lie only 1.5 meters above sea level. There is no road system, no electricity supply and no clean drinking water. Accordingly, Akassa clan was chosen because an Environmental Impact Assessment identified Akassa as the community most likely to be affected by any oil accidentally spilt from exploration wells in Statoil's offshore blocks 128 and 129 (previously OPLs 217 and 218) located in deep water off the coast of Nigeria.

The Akassa model is a process that enables communities to plan together using participatory methodologies to produce a development plan that, in this case, involves all 19 communities. The process began by bringing all the communities together into a corporate community-based organization called the Akassa Development Foundation (ADF). Existing community groups such as youth, women, the Council of Chiefs and others send representatives to sit on the General Assembly of the ADF. Representation on the General Assembly is gender balanced. In this way, all stakeholders in Akassa have a voice and say in the management of the ADF. Additionally, all members of the General Assembly must be resident in Akassa to ensure decisions are made by those who are most marginalized geographically and politically and therefore most affected by poverty in Akassa Development Area. New institutions have also been mobilized to meet the objectives of the development plan, including institutions for education, health, natural resource management and training and capacity building. The ADF also has a Board of Trustees and is registered with the Corporate Affairs Commission, which ensures that the ADF is a legal and accountable institution.

The Development Plan

Each year, the ADF facilitates the adoption of a development plan for the Akassa Development Area, which should be in line with the Millennium Development Goals. The plan ensures a range of projects spread across the development area through a prioritization process. This process brings together representatives (a balance of men and women) from institutions and communities to decide which community projects shall have the highest priority.

It forces community members to think about the whole development area rather than just their own community, removing the potential for powerful so-called benefit captors to allocate funds to projects in their own community. This is an innovative approach to producing development plans for a geographical region. The type of projects that are prioritized depends on the perceived needs in a given year, but projects generally fall into the following categories:

- Health facilities (identified by health institutions in Akassa)
- Educational support (identified by schools and PTAs in Akassa)
- Women in development projects (identified by women)
- Youth in development projects (identified by youth)
- Natural resource management programmes
- Micro credit schemes, capacity building programmes for various institutions including the Council of Chiefs, and infrastructure projects
- The development plan also has a budget attached. The budget includes recurring costs and capital costs to run the ADF secretariat.

Chosen projects are then implemented by the relevant institution affiliated to the ADF. Each institution must submit a technically correct, fundable proposal to the ADF outlining how it will implement the project. The ADF secretariat helps the institution to manage the project through Project Management Committees. In the case of infrastructure, the Project Management Committee will put the work out to tender and assess both financial and technical aspects of the work. The Project Management Committee, with support from the ADF, then monitors the chosen contractor (normally a local artisan) who carries out the work.

Replicating the Akassa Model across the Delta

StatoilHydro believes this innovative approach can be replicated across the Niger Delta by applying the following lessons learned from Akassa:

- Partner with whole communities in line with political-administrative boundaries (in this case, we partnered with all the communities in the Akassa Development Area) rather than with host communities, which are exclusive and which will contribute to conflict.
- Establish a corporate community-based organization (CBO), registered with Local and State Government initially and finally with the Corporate Affairs Commission. This is facilitated by NGOs, which can represent a whole development area in line with political-administrative boundaries. Multiple stakeholder support can then be found for the CBO.
- Promote a long-term process of Participatory Rural Appraisal and Development Planning

- Create a process for Development Plans to fit into Local and State Government planning to support bottom up planning and the Millennium Development Goals.
- Long-term capacity building to ensure communities develop competence in prioritizing, planning, managing and monitoring development projects and programmes
- It is believed believe this process is worth replicating. The process promotes community empowerment and increases local participation in decision-making. It ensures that even the most marginalized people can have a stake in development decisions and not just the powerful members of a community.

The process is transparent: ADF publishes accounts and expenditure reports monthly in the community and quarterly in local newspapers. Accounts are also audited annually by external auditors. Decision-making is also transparent, and this enables community members to understand why certain projects were prioritized and why others were not. It is believed that this would go a long way in reducing conflict in a region where there is much mistrust and little confidence in decision makers. Essentially also, StatoilHydro Nigeria has received considerable praise for the Akassa project. In 2005, the project received the prestigious World Petroleum Congress Excellence Award in the Social Responsibility category and, in 2006; it received the CWC Excellence Award for Sustainable Development.

Key Achievements of the Akassa Development Foundation
Fundraising and advocacy: ADF is now taking further steps towards sustainability by advocating closer partnership with government. When ADF was formed, the communities were completely marginalized in relation to government and decision making processes. Now, through the capacity building programme, ADF and the Akassa community as a whole are more confident in approaching government for support for projects in their development plan. In particular:

- ADF has been successful in advocating support from State Government and its Honourable House of Assembly Member for roads in the Community Development Plan. In particular, the Government has supported the Kongho - Bekekiri Road.
- In addition to roads, the State Government has also supported other CDP projects, including: World Environment Day, the Youth Turtle Club Observation Centre and the Football Team.

- NDDC is supporting the Akassa Clan Women Association in building another school in Minibie. This work commenced in 2007 and was completed in 2008.
- ADF have provided training, through the "living university" for staff of the Ministry of Local Government and Rural Affairs and NDDC Bayelsa Staff.
- The Ministry of Agriculture has made the micro-credit and savings system used by the ADF (the Akassa Savings Scheme) a central part of the Food and Security Programme for Bayelsa State.
- ADF also makes regular visits to government ministries to generate support for the activities identified in the Community Development Plan. The visits have increased in number in 2008. Before, it would not have had the confidence to do this. It takes the Development Plan to meetings as an advocacy tool, and it has built their confidence in negotiations.

ADF has continued to implement projects according to the Development Plan despite restrictions caused by security problems on the waterways. Apart from the road projects, ADF has also completed pit latrines for improved sanitation in remote communities, supported school renovations and even started constructing a Town Hall for the entire area. The Akassa Savings Scheme now has ₦5.4 million in circulation, with loan repayments still very high.

19.2 CASE STUDY 2: ANGOLA THIRD SOCIAL ACTION FUND (FAS III)
CONTEXT
Angola gained independence in 1974 when the rebel Movement for the Popular Liberation of Angola (MPLA) overthrew the Portuguese Colonial Administration. Over the years of resistance against the Portuguese, three rebel groups emerged: MPLA, the National Front for the Liberation of Angola (FNLA), and the Union for the Total Independence of Angola (UNITA). Each group attracted external support according to its political ideology. The United States and Zaire (now Democratic Republic of Congo) supported the FNLA, which was concentrated in the north; South Africa backed UNITA in the south; whereas socialist nations were sympathetic to MPLA. UNITA and the government finally signed a ceasefire in April 2002; an Interim Poverty Reduction Strategy was soon prepared and funded through a transitional support strategy. This new impetus both to address poverty and to make the transition for peace and democratic government will help to lay the foundations for economic

growth. The strategy emphasizes expanded service delivery to war-affected and vulnerable populations and more transparent, efficient, and credible management of public resources.

Policy Environment: Decentralization and Local Governance
During the conflict, economic and political power became concentrated in the central government. The ceasefire agreement and the political developments since its signing have provided favorable conditions for decentralization. The agreement also offered a window of opportunity for the Third Social Action Fund (FAS III), allowing it into previously inaccessible areas and to support the movement toward decentralization and the strengthening of local government. The society faces the triple challenge of transitioning from war to peace, from centralized to democratic government, and from a state-controlled to a market economy—a complex transition, with much being attempted in a short time frame. FAS III is intended as the cornerstone of the lending programme of the Transitional Support Strategy, which was designed for multiple transitions. It builds on two previous phases of the Social Action Fund, FAS I and II, which placed greater emphasis on service delivery and less on social and governance outcomes. FAS III incorporates a more intensive CDD approach, aiming for greater involvement of communities and local government in making decisions about service delivery.

Institutional Environment
By fostering links between municipal administrations and communities, FAS III hopes to encourage a culture of accountability and service delivery from the bottom up. This transparency of resource management is intended to increase confidence in government and contribute to national reconciliation. The limited capacity of the local government to respond to community demands means that it lacks the human resources to run a project like FAS. A governmental department attached to the Ministry of Planning oversees the project and provides financial and technical support. Civil Society Organizations and NGOs implement and facilitate the project at the local level; however, FAS III aims to transfer responsibility for project implementation to local government and to build the capacity of local government officials to fulfill this role. By implementing FAS III through the local government, the emphasis is on strengthening the capacity of local government as a means of preparing for decentralization. FAS III also aims to build social capital at the local level by establishing inclusive community forums and representative links between local government structures and communities. The emphasis on

inclusion and cohesion is intended to contribute to peace building at the local level.

Operational Environment
The CDD project is part of a broader effort to rebuild Angola, reignite development, and alleviate poverty. An important focus is to improve and expand services, which deteriorated during the years of war. The project complements efforts by other donors to raise the standard of service delivery and contribute to a better standard of living. The development objectives are the improvement and expansion of community-based social and economic services through participatory processes involving communities and municipal administrations and a governance system that supports and enhances mutual accountability of communities and municipal administrations.

Community Environment
The forums for community engagement are five-member community committees that work through the CDD process of consultation and participatory decision making, using a fixed menu of choices. The menu includes: construction and rehabilitation of primary schools; rehabilitation and maintenance of health posts; construction and rehabilitation of water and sanitation facilities; repair and maintenance of roads; and construction and rehabilitation of markets. The project documentation acknowledges that little is known about how the conflict has constrained or fostered the building of social capital. Because building social capital is one of the project's key development objectives, more needs to be known about how the conflict has affected people's ability to participate at the local level. This will be done through a Conflict Impact and Vulnerability Assessment that will build knowledge about (i) the nature and scope of vulnerability at the community level, traditional means for assisting vulnerable community members, and the extent to which vulnerable population groups have been able to benefit from structures and services provided under FAS; (ii) the impact of conflict at the community level; (iii) commitment and capacity to negotiate different viewpoints and engage in truly collective action around a common goal; and (iv) the nature and scope of community demand for targeted support to vulnerable groups and peace building efforts (World Bank, 2006).

Lessons Learned
- Bringing resources down, local capacity and partnerships up. Giving greater decision making authority in development to communities

and local government—in other words, matching decentralization with devolution—must be supported by three further processes: (i) institutional and fiscal devolution of resources (to back up deferred decision making with real resources and the means to act on decisions at the local level); (ii) capacity building of staff and institutions at the local level in order to support and manage what is expected of them; (iii) building stronger partnerships among institutions, municipalities, and communities so there are functioning pathways for the gradual transfer of responsibilities.

- Building trust and simplifying participation. Management of this type of project benefits from: (i) transparent and accountable management mechanisms to build trust in the process, and (ii) standardized and simplified project documentation, which makes it easier for communities to participate.

- Better sector-wide coordination and communication. One of the main challenges for FAS at the macro level is a lack of coordination with other sectors. Made up of voluntary members who receive no pay, the FAS board has no decision-making power. More involvement by the relevant ministries is needed. FAS should be included in sector-wide discussions on poverty reduction—at the moment it is not. For example, FAS was not included in discussions surrounding the PRSP. There is a need for coordination between FAS and other poverty alleviation programmes that might take a different development approach. Coordination will ensure that the different approaches are both sustainable and complementary. For example, health centers rebuilt through FAS need to be tied to the health ministry's strategies for the provision of ongoing medical services if the new health centers are to be useful and sustainable.

- Sustaining project committee leadership. The community committees are difficult to sustain. Members have tended to lose their motivation and give up their positions, seeing it as a government responsibility to provide services for the people. FAS is trying to address this by building people's leadership skills as an incentive to stay involved and by including the committee members in the evaluation of the project. At the same time, project staff members are wary of building up a new form of leadership in the community that is entirely connected to and dependent on the FAS project. The ideal would be to build leadership skills that promote the development of the community, rather than leaders who act as cadres for the FAS alone.

19.3 CASE STUDY 3: RWANDA DECENTRALIZATION AND COMMUNITY DEVELOPMENT PROJECT (DCDP)

Context

Since the end of the conflict and establishment of a new government in Rwanda, the major challenges for the country have been poverty reduction, national reconciliation, and the building of a legitimate state. In the years immediately following the genocide the focus was on emergency supplies, resettlement, and rehabilitation. Between 1998 and 2001 the government undertook a broader programme aimed at building good governance for poverty reduction. The emphasis on governance was based on the assessment that poor governance was at the root of the genocide. Rwanda had decades of unsuccessful attempts at community development associated with a top-down approach and lack of consultation with local populations. The Government of National Unity, acting within the framework of the Arusha accords, resolved that democratization was necessary to reconcile the Rwandan people and to fight poverty.

Policy Environment

The Decentralization and Community Development Project (DCDP) combines the processes of decentralization with a move to greater degrees of CDD. The aim is to support communities that are empowered to lead their own development under an effective local government. DCDP builds on the lessons learned and experience consolidated through an earlier Community Reintegration and Development Project, expanding this model from 11 to 39 districts. After the genocide, governance suffered from deficits in institutions and resources. The government has since launched a concerted effort of public sector and administrative reform of which decentralization is a central part. The third phase of the national decentralization programme ends in 2008. Community development, civil society capacity building, advocacy, and fiscal decentralization are key aspects.

Institutional Environment

Efforts to establish a system of CDD streamlined with local government structures are undermined by a lack of coordination of multiple aid and development initiatives. Local government structures must respond to different development agents from the public and private sectors and from civil society, which strains their already weak capacity. The Rwandan government plans to overcome this challenge by developing mechanisms for partnership and coordination. The chronic lack of institutional capacity throughout the local government system is especially true at the district level. There are severe limitations on the availability of qualified and trained people, and needs are greater than can be met through workshop based training or administrative manuals. Capacity is also weak in monitoring budgets and public expenditure. National good governance institutions are not represented at the local level and so are unavailable for the required ongoing support. Delayed disbursements of central government grants also have adverse effects at the local level. If district development plans are not supported in a timely manner, the project could lose credibility in communities and communities could lose faith in local government (World Bank, 2006).

The DCDP offers a new injection of capacity and funding into an existing structure of local government based on historical institutions of the cellule and district that predate the conflict. The project does not propose a new structure of local government, nor does it entail an overhaul of existing representative structures. Using existing structures to promote a new development approach offers a radical, and sometimes problematic, readjustment for personnel who have to adapt to new forms of management. The Restated Strategic Investment Agreement highlighted significant local challenges that affect the ability of communities to engage in the project. These include: acute poverty; citizens' feelings of powerlessness and inability to change or improve their own situation; social support systems strained by internally displaced persons, refugees, orphans, widows, and HIV/AIDS; lack of access to capital; lack of technical knowledge; and fear of persisting civil unrest.

Operational Environment
The project's strong social assessment component and its findings have been incorporated into the project design (e.g., extra measures taken to promote inclusion in the postwar context). It is noteworthy that the DCDP is community driven rather than NGO driven. Although local government capacity is weak, the project proposal rejects working with NGOs as intermediaries for communities. Such an approach is not seen as consistent with the management autonomy the government has assigned to districts. The other danger of such an approach is that the NGO intermediary would be responsible for implementation, disbursement, and procurement, which might separate communities from administrations and erode trust between the government and the people.

DCDP entails a very comprehensive set of structures for CDD. These structures streamline the community forum within local government decision-making structures. The key operational unit for DCDP is the Community Development Committee (CDC), established at four levels of local administration (prefectures, districts, secteurs, and cellules). In 2001 the population elected officials to committees at each level. There were allocations for both women and youths on CDCs. The planning process starts at the cellule CDC. The plans that emerge here are then sent to the secteur and district level for amalgamation with input from technical sector departments. The districts construct five-year strategic plans on this basis, which are transmitted for approval to the Ministry of Community Development and Social Affairs in the Ministry of Local Administration and the Ministry of Finance. The project is unique in that it supports the entire series of institutions along the chain that consolidates plans from cellule to secteur level and integrates this with budget systems.

The project's fund-allocation system gives district officials the final say on which community sub-projects will be funded. Since funding is finite officials will be unable to accommodate all proposals, which might have negative consequences, because poor levels of transparency lead to mistrust of the government. There is also the risk that vulnerable groups could be excluded, promoting adverse social outcomes, although measures are being taken to ensure that the allocation system is monitored and open to scrutiny. The community projects financed through DCDP are in construction and rehabilitation of basic infrastructure, specifically schools, water supplies, access roads, health care clinics; community centers; income generating activities; youth training; and HIV/AIDS prevention.

Lessons Learned
- Differentiated approach to community mobilization. A need exists for a differentiated approach to mobilizing society that reflects the broad spectrum of technical competence, interest, and capacities for social engagement. Evidence of the previous CRDP project in Rwanda is that the introduction of an opportunity for micro projects can galvanize a common vision and goal even within severely disrupted communities. The CRDP allowed Rwandans of all backgrounds and ethnicities to engage in local development around common interests to overcome differences.

- Small-scale goods and services. The CDD potential is greatest for small-scale goods and services. Activities should fall within the management capacity of communities and be financially viable at the local level.
- Participatory monitoring techniques should be mainstreamed into the CDD project by strengthening district capacity to lead a process of planning and consultation with local communities. This should be backed up by participatory creation of indicators of success and inclusion, transferring monitoring responsibility to communities.
- Decentralized funding systems. Developing a matching grants system to finance sub-projects is effective. Responsibility for the system is shared by community, district and external donors. The flow of funds could be decentralized by allowing community committees to open local bank accounts.
- Managing expectations. Clear guidelines and policies should be in place on the ownership, maintenance, and sustainability of completed projects. Communities need clear information about their rights and responsibilities toward the new asset. Clarity will prevent raised expectations and subsequent disappointment.
- Link with top-down planning. The PRSP tackled the issue of a disconnect between local planning and top-down budgeting. The link did not work well at first due to poor capacity and micromanagement from top ministers. It was resolved over time as the PRSC rectified and broadened participation of ministries and donors and improved communications. Officials, including the president, made an effort to explain problems and solutions. Technical staff also came out to talk to communities. For example, there was confusion over district-level procurement, which was resolved by issuing simple manuals and giving communities a chance to manage their own affairs. TV and radio were also important in getting this communication right (World Bank, 2006).

19.4 CASE STUDY 4: NEPAL POVERTY ALLEVIATION FUND
Context

Over the past decade Nepal has experienced continued poverty, slow economic growth, poor governance, social exclusion, and deep inequality. An entrenched rebel insurgency now presents the most serious obstacle to peace. What began in 1996 as a low-intensity and primarily rural campaign to replace the present polity with a "people's republic" has since gained considerable strength by taking advantage of the scanty government presence in many remote areas. Although the insurgency seems to be a political movement at its core, it has been successful in tapping into the grievances caused by deep-seated political, economic, and social exclusion based on class, caste, gender, ethnicity, and geographical isolation.

Poverty in Nepal is pervasive, with about 40 percent of the population living below the poverty line. About 86 percent live in rural areas engaged in subsistence agriculture on small plots of poor land. With limited access to credit, infrastructure, markets, and basic social services, often because of remoteness, the poor rely heavily on seasonal migration and remittances. Ethnic minorities, lower-caste communities in remote areas, and women (especially female-headed households) lag seriously behind the rest of the population in incomes, assets, and most human development indicators.

The breakdown of democratic processes has compounded difficulties. Nepal's deepening crisis, nevertheless, has renewed the drive for reforms over the past several years. Compelled by a sense of urgency, reform-minded leaders have been pushing for changes that could lead to more sustained and equitable economic and social development. One of the main issues identified in Nepal's Poverty Reduction Strategy (PRS) is the plight of marginalized segments of the population—women; Dalits, a group that is the lowest in the caste system; or Janajati, a group (not included in the caste system) that lives in remote areas and receive few public services. The economic handicaps of marginalized groups are multiple. They face social biases, suffer from poor education and health care, and live in areas with extremely poor infrastructure.

Policy Environment
Because of poor security conditions, local elections have not been held since July 2002. This has derailed the government's decentralization programme, which had begun to gain momentum. Most local bodies maintain an administrative structure, but the administrative staff of many village development councils (VDCs) has been forced to relocate to district headquarters, leaving many VDCs virtually void of basic government services. Decentralization is an important enabling factor for CDD approaches. Given current political uncertainties (such as no elections), there is not a strong likelihood of decentralization ensuring project sustainability beyond 2006 (end date of project).

Institutional Environment

The insurgents claim that their objective is to eliminate social exclusion. Following the breakdown of the cease-fire, the insurgency escalated once again from 2003–4, and again in 2006, which has led to a climate of fear and insecurity in rural areas. Although the security situation is extremely fluid, a number of districts are under strong insurgent influence, especially those outside urban centers, while others operate under heightened security threats. The insurgents generally allow development efforts to continue in the districts where they have strong influence, provided that they are supported by local NGOs and local communities. Although more than one third of the country's 3,900 VDC buildings have been damaged or destroyed as symbols of government authority, the insurgency tends to spare community-owned infrastructure from attacks. Nonetheless, increased incidents of extortion against individuals involved in development activities in the field could begin to limit the ability of the government, donor agencies, and NGOs to operate in conflict affected areas.

The Poverty Alleviation Fund (PAF) is a new, targeted instrument for reaching poor and excluded communities. An autonomous poverty-alleviation agency, the PAF is based on a CDD approach that allows the government to test new approaches to reach marginalized and excluded groups. It aims at improving access to income-generation projects and community infrastructure for groups that have been excluded due to gender, ethnicity and caste, as well as for the poorest groups in rural communities. The PAF helps accelerate decentralization and embraces local community participation (World Bank, 2006).

Lessons Learned

- Communities in Nepal have demonstrated during project implementation that they can control funds and investment decisions. They are willing to contribute to investments and operational costs if they are assured transparency and effective service delivery. They are as interested in economic opportunities as they are in social action or mobilization.
- Without clarifying linkages between vulnerable groups and the insurgency, it is difficult to assess the impact of CDD on conflict prevention or reduction. In preparing CDD programmes, the relationship between the rebel insurgency and the endemic poverty of vulnerable groups must be understood.

- Continuous outreach is needed to ensure that those of the lowest social and economic status are included in village decision making.
- Gender-responsiveness in the CDD approach can be improved by studying the impact gender has on the insurgency and by reviewing gender-disaggregated analysis in terms of incomes, assets, and most human development indicators (World Bank, 2006).

Chapter Twenty

PROBLEMS AND PROSPECTS OF RURAL AND COMMUNITY DEVELOPMENT IN NIGERIA

20.1 PROBLEMS OF RURAL AND COMMUNITY DEVELOPMENT IN NIGERIA

Community development has always been directed at the promotion of better living for the whole community, with active participation and if possible, the initiative of the community. Anticipated or unanticipated problems and difficulties can derail community development efforts. The extent to which the drivers of community development can cope with or alleviate these problems represents a major challenge to sustaining the achievements of community development. The problems that can make this unattainable are:

- High degree of corruption.
- Lack of commitment to community development by the community members.
- Poor statistical base for effective planning.
- Shortage of resources to carry out the plans.
- Top-down planning.
- Inadequate understanding of the community.
- Planning without implementation and implementation without planning.
- Lack of monitoring and evaluation.
- Role conflict among the change agents and among some top community leaders.
- Lack of follow up.
- Policy-associated problems.
- Lack of systematic and coordinated implementation of programmes resulting in duplication of efforts.
- Lack of community empowerment.
- Lack of or inadequate feasibility studies before projects are undertaken.

High degree of corruption
This has become a monster that frustrates any meaningful intervention and decimates their benefits since it is so widespread and had permeated the socio-economic fabrics of the Nigerian economy. Effort to combat it

must move from lip services to a responsive and collective determination to wipe it out. Probably it is the most important socio-economic variable militating against development in Nigeria and indeed Africa, it is rarely factored into research equations.

Lack of commitment to community development by the community members

One of the main goals of community development is that its activities be spearheaded by members of the community themselves. Failing this, their participation, in some form is seen as paramount to the success of the project. But in practice, this is often difficult to achieve either because, the members of the community do not fully appreciate the problem that is being addressed or enough time and resources have not been committed or in fact not available for the necessary mobilization requirements before commencing project implementation. Where this problem exists, a foundational threat to project sustainability is already in place. The danger is that even if the project activities were successfully carried out with the initiators forcefully driving the process, as soon as the initiators withdraw, the project begins to degenerate due to lack of steam from community members to keep the project going. To avoid this kind of problem, a number of alternative courses can be taken. These are:

- ✓ Refrain from commencing the programme at all if there are no clear guarantees that community members will support it after the initiation.
- ✓ Spend some quality time explaining the problem, the need for it to be addressed and the fact that it is possible for community members to address it within available resources.
- ✓ Employ community members with vested interests to bear the responsibility for keeping the project alive. As long as their interest is covered in the project, these members of the community will not allow the project to die.

Poor statistical base for effective planning

The absence of data for a proper understanding of the prevailing situation or effectively planning programme implementation is often a big hurdle in community development. Basic assumptions at project initiation may simply be wrong if there are no data to uphold or refute them. Where this happens, community development efforts appear to be "chasing shadows". Where the data available is not enough to take a decision for effective planning, it is often better to spend available resources getting the correct information than to rush head on into project implementation without the right information. Doing this may even worsen the situation as new problems may emerge from removing pillars wrongly assumed to be obstacles.

Shortage of resources to carry out the plans

If the resources to implement a community project are in short supply, the problem of achieving the goals of the plan becomes evident. In this case, a decision needs to be made to scale-down the plan to available resources; seek additional resources through internal or external mobilization or use available resources for alternative purposes. If an attempt is made to proceed with plan implementation without taking one of these three decisions, the shortage of needed resources will starve the project to distortion or death.

Top-down planning

In many cases of community development efforts, few top administrators make decisions for the community members. This top-down planning approach often creates more problems than it sets out to tackle. This is because these administrators sometimes know less about community situations than they care to admit before taken decisions on their behalf. The result is that decisions taking may not address the felt needs of the people, may in fact be the direct opposite of the yearnings of the people or may have only served the vested interest of a few people to the detriment of many others. Getting inputs from the grassroots into development decision may take longer time and require the input of some scarce resources at the outset of a project. However, it is usually worthwhile in the end because the decisions finally taken often address the felt needs of the target group. It also creates the feeling of ownership and inclusion in the decision making process that is particularly valuable in mobilizing community support and sustainability of the project beyond the term of the primary initiators.

Inadequate understanding of the community

This problem is linked to the dearth of information on the situation in the community. Inadequate understanding of the community may include failure to fully appreciate its structure of influence, communication and decision making patterns, existence of factions, norms and values etc. This failure, usually on the part of a person external to the community often results in wrong diagnosis of the problem, failure to comprehend the difficult terrain under which community members operate, proposing solutions that would not be feasible under local conditions and outright infringement on the sensibilities of the local community. To address this problem, there is a need for a period of familiarization, especially for people who are new to the community. During this period, cogent efforts should be committed to appreciation the dynamics of the local community, exploring "how things work" and "what can make things not work". If this period is properly invested, the return in terms of empathy and appreciation from local community members could be social assets that can be exploited in future.

Planning without implementation and implementation without planning

People who have been in the development field long enough will appreciate that several trips to rural communities by researchers, extension officers, social workers and others without visible beneficial action often wear out their reception in these communities. This is because the prevailing feeling of such communities is that too much time is spent planning such that they begin to wonder if any project will be implemented in their community. Also, experiences from politicians visiting communities to make promises on community development projects without fulfilling such promises create similar feeling in community. Conversely, entering communities to implement a project without proper planning creates a prevailing feeling of un-seriousness in the community. In this case, they often adopt the attitude of "siddon dey look" or "wait and see". The import is that when such projects are successful, it does not get the kind of accolade it should and when it fails, it gets more criticisms than it should. It is important, therefore to ensure that an appropriate dose of planning is done before a community project is began and no project should be implemented without adequate planning.

Lack of monitoring and evaluation

Monitoring and evaluation is a system to record and periodically analyze the information that is available in a community development activity to track them and mark progress on a day-to-day and continuous basis. The failure to have a plan monitoring and evaluation component in an activity means there is no systematic way of determining programme accomplishments, facilitating effectiveness and efficiency. The overall purpose of plan evaluation is to provide an avenue to stop and reflect on what has happened in the past in order to make decisions about the future. By evaluating, the community can learn what has worked well and what has not. They then begin to realize why things have or have not worked. Where possible, during on-going evaluation, corrective measures can then be put in place to redirect the project. In ex-post evaluations, the lessons learnt can serve to remove pitfalls from other similar projects in future.

Conflict may arise where the Change Agent is expected to fulfill the Desires of the Sponsoring Agency rather than what the Community wants

Different people participate in community development events for different reasons. These reasons or the individual vested interests may not often be in the same direction or may be in conflict. For instance, a change agent may want the community to have a water system that allows every member of the community access to portable water at short distances, but some community elders may want deep wells located in where compound that other members of the community can come to fetch. This kind of situation can create tension between a change agent and some community leaders. This conflict may be aggravated if some other members of the community become aware of the details of such conflict. This kind of situation tests the expertise of the change agent to achieve a balance between local leaders' vested interest and his or her perception of what is good for the community. The path to take will depend on the specific circumstances of the conflict, the personalities of the change agent and community leaders and the community's perception of the influence and power of both parties in the conflict.

Lack of follow-up

Many community developments efforts have deteriorated or collapsed after some years of completion of the projects due to the problem of lack of follow-up. Follow-up is a deliberate attempt to revisit a completed project to see how well it is faring. It also includes making provisions during project planning to cater for follow-up issues that may arise at the expiration of project implementation phase. This may include mainstreaming project activities into existing community structures, linking the new managers of the project with partners, whose cooperation was taken for granted during the project implementation phase or providing insights or historical antecedents that can further empower the current drivers of the project to sustain the achievements made during and immediately after the active project implementation phase.

Policy-associated problems

Idachaba (2000) provided a critical synthesis of policy related problems including harsh policy environment; design and implementation of workable and desirable agricultural policies for intended beneficiaries and desirable consequences of policies, difficulty of the Nigerian agricultural sector to respond to set of forces in external and domestic environment. High rate of policy instability characterized by frequent reversal of policy is associated with governance and high degree of political instability.

Lack of systematic and coordinated implementation of programmes resulting in duplication of efforts
There are usually streams of interventions from government, international donor agencies and non-governmental organizations to the same target systems but in an uncoordinated manner. In such circumstances, while progress is difficult to be comprehensively monitored and evaluated, more importantly is the fact that interventions grants thus provided are typically balkanized funds with narrow focus tied to donors' priorities.

Lack of community empowerment
Most interventions targeted at rural development rarely affect the lives of the rural folks on a sustainable basis, because they were externally configured and executed with minimal participation of the rural beneficiaries. Meaningful development can only be achieved when beneficiaries determine their principles, participate in planning, implementation and evaluation; and utilize their locally available resources.

Lack of or inadequate feasibility studies before projects are undertaken
It is not an over statement to argue that most rural development programmes fail, because the policy makers did not carry out the necessary feasibility studies on problem situations and their possible remedies. The poor results often recorded are accentuated by apparent definitional problems of the situations on ground. Problem clearly defined is problem half solved, and a good feasibility study conducted at the outset is a sine qua non.

20.2 THE WAY FORWARD
From the foregoing, it is suggested that in order to facilitate rapid, conscious and sustained efforts at rural transformation, the following steps should be taken:
- Rural development problems should be properly identified, demarcated and streamlined to enable the formulation and implementation of possible solutions.

- The national leadership should show enough commitments to rural transformation as a pivot on which the overall nation socio-economic development evolves.
- Enough funds should be made available, and effective monitoring of implementation process made part of the programme package.
- Trained personnel should be recruited and decent accommodations provided for them, to encourage their residing within development areas.
- Requisite infrastructure such as roads, drainage, cottage industries, schools and health facilities, credit and banking institutions should be put in place in the rural communities. This will indeed check the rate of rural-urban migration as well as boost industrial and commercial activities in rural areas.
- Leadership tussle among programme delivering ministries, departments and agencies should be discouraged. This does not augur well for the development of any society. Rather it generates conflicts, violence, loss of property and sometimes loss of lives.
- In order to improve the quality of life of the low income population living in the rural communities on a self-sustaining basis through transforming the socio-spatial structure of their productive activities, the need to set up more microfinance banks in such communities become an imperative. Specifically, rural banking especially through the micro-finance outlets provide financial supports through the extension of such facilities like micro credit, loans advances, overdrafts, and investment in rural based industries to rural dwellers; and involvement in capacity building within the communities; and direct involvement in rural transformation programmes such as sponsoring and financing communal self-help projects within the rural environment.

Bibliography

Abdullahi, S. A., (1982). Historic Role of African Youth and the Contemporary Challenges, Sokoto, Nigeria.

Abdullahi, W. Z., (2007). Evolving of a New Role for Traditional Institutions in the Nigerian Constitution Centre for Local Government Development and Research.

Aborisade, O., (1985). Local Government and the Traditional Rulers in Nigeria. Ile-Ife: University of Ife Press.

Abubakar, S., (1980). The Established Caliphate: Sokoto, the Emirates and their Neighbours. In: Ikime, O. (Ed.), Groundwork of Nigerian History. Heinemann Educational Publishers, Ibadan, pp: 303-326.

Ad hoc Group of Experts on Community Development (1963). Community Development and National Development New York: United Nations.

Adair, J., (1988). Effective Leadership. London: Pan Books. ISBN 978-0330504195

Adams, D. & Sherraden, M., (1997). "Asset-Building as a Community Revitalization Strategy", Social Work; Volume 42, No. 5. September

Adegeye, A. J. and Dittoh, J.S., (1985). Essentials of Agricultural Economics. Ibadan: Duru Press Ltd.

Adesoji, A. O., (2010). Traditional Rulership and Modern Governance in 20th Century, In: Babawale, T., A. Alao and A. Adesoji (Eds.), the Chieftaincy Institution in Nigeria. Concept Publishers for Centre for Black and African Arts and Civilization, Lagos, Nigeria.

Adewumi, J. B. & Egwurube. J., (1985). "Role of Traditional Rulers in Historical Perspective". In Aborisade, Oladimeji (Ed.). Local Government and the Traditional Rulers in Nigeria. Ile-Ife: University of Ife Press.

Afigbo A.E., (1984). Ropes of Sand: Studies in Igbo History and Culture. Nsukka: University of Nigeria Press.

Afigbo, A.E., (1980). Igboland before 1800. In: Ikime, O. (Ed.), Groundwork of Nigerian History. Ibadan, Heinemann Educational Publishers.

Agba, A. M. O. & Ushie, M. A., (2005). Improving the Niger Delta Socio-Economic Status through Active Involvement of Multinational Corporations. Nigerian Journal of Social and Development Issues, Vol. 5 (1).

Agbo, F.U., (2010). Introduction to Cooperative Studies. 45A Okosi Roa Onitsha, Nigeria Kawuriz and Manilas Publishers Ltd.

Aguwa, J. C.U., (1993). "Theocratic Traditions and the Igbo Experience", in: Anyanwu/Aguwa.

Aidelokhai, D.I., (2008). An Evaluation of the Relevance of Traditional Ruler-ship Institution in the Nigerian State. Medwell Journals.

Aina, S., (1992). Personnel Management in Nigeria: A Work Centred Approach. Ikeja: F. Communications.

Ake, C., (2001). Democracy and Development in Africa, Ibadan: Spectrum Books Ltd.

Akpomuvie, B. O., (2010), Self-Help as a Strategy for Rural Development in Nigeria: A Bottom-Up Approach, Journal of Alternative Perspectives in the Social Sciences. Vol 2, No 1.

Akude, I., (1992). Traditional Agencies and Rural Development in Nigeria. In Olisa, M. and Obiakwu, J.I. (eds), Rural Development in Nigeria: Dynamics and Strategies. Awka: Mekslink Publishers.

Alao, A.A., (1990). Military Rule and National Integration. In: Toyin F., (Ed.), Modern Nigeria: A Tribute to G.O Olusanya. Lagos Cargo Compass, Lagos.

Aliyu, A. Y. & P. H. Koehn (1982). Local Autonomy and Inter-governmental Relations in Nigeria, the Case of the Northern States in the Immediate Post Local Government Reform Period (1976-79). Zaria: Department of Local Government Studies, Institute of Administration, Ahmadu Bello University.

Allen, V., (1972). 'Sitting on a Man: Colonialism and the Lost Political Institutions of Igbo Women.' Canadian Journal of African Studies, Vol.6, No. 2.

Altschuler, D., Stangler, G., Berkley, K., & Burton, L. (2009). Supporting Youth in Transition to Adulthood: Lessons Learned from Child Welfare and Juvenile Justice. Washington, D.C.: Center for Juvenile Justice Reform. Available at www.jimcaseyyouth.org Courtney, M. E., Piliavin,

Aminize, B., (2001) Organizations and Community Development Policy and Design, Benin: Unique Publishers.

Amusa, S.B., (2010). Chieftaincy, Festivals and Rituals: The Role of the Ataoja in the Osun Osogbo Festival in Historical Perspective. In: Babawale, T., A. Alao and A. Adesoji (Eds.), the Chieftaincy Institutions in Nigeria. Lagos: Concept Publishers for Centre for Black and African Arts and Civilization, Lagos.

Ankie, H., (1976). The Sociology of Developing Societies London: Macmillan.

Anyanwu J. C., (1997). Poverty in Nigeria: Concepts, Measurement and Determinants. Selected Paper Presented at Nigerian Economic Society.

Anyanwu, C. N., (1992). Community Development: The Nigeria Perspective. Ibadan: Gabesthe Educational Publisher.

Arndt, H.W. (1981). Economic Development: A Semantic History, Economic Development and Culture Change, Vol. 29(3): 45 7-466.

Ashiru, D., (2010). Chieftaincy Institution and Grassroots Development in Nigeria. In Babawale, T., A. Alao and A. Adesoji (Eds.), the Chieftaincy Institution in Nigeria. Lagos Concept Publishers for Centre for Black and African Arts and Civilization.

Asia Development Bank (ADB), (2000). Rural Asia: Beyond the Green Revolution. Manila: ADB.

Aspen Institute (1996). Measuring Community Capacity Building: A Workbook-in- Progress for Rural Communities. The Aspen Institute, Washington D.C.

Asset Based Community Development Institute, (2012). www.sesp.northwestern.edu/abcd The Asset-Based Community Development Institute (ABCD), established in 1995 by the Community Development Programme at Northwestern University's Institute for Policy Research, is built upon three decades of community development research by John Kretzmann and John L. McKnight. Accessed 19 November, 2012.

Atanda, J. A., (1970). The Changing Status of the Alaafin of Oyo under Colonial Rule and Independence. In Crowder, M. and O. Ikime (Eds.), West African Chiefs: Their Changing Status under Colonial Rule and Independence. Ile-Ife University of Ife Press, 17-19.

Atanda, J. A., (1973). The New Oyo Empire: Indirect Rule and Change in Western Nigeria, 1894-1934. London Longman.

Aubut, J., (2004). "The Good Governance Agenda: Who Wins and Who Loses. Some Empirical Evidence for 2001", London: Development Studies Institute, London School of Economics and Politics.

Bagolin, I., Comim, F.. (2004). Human Development Index (HDI) and its Family of Indexes: an Evolving Critical Review. Revista de Economia, Vol. 34, No. 2 (ano 32): 7•]28, maio/ago. (2008). Editora UFPR. Also available at http://ojs.c3sl.ufpr.br/ojs2/index.php/economia/article/view/12293/8511

Bahá'í International Community, (2011). The Meaning of Community. Information Resource of Bahá'í International Community

Bahá'í International Community, (1996). Sustainable Communities in an Integrating World, a Concept Paper Shared at the Second United Nations Conference on Human Settlements (Habitat II), Istanbul, Turkey, 3-14 June 1996.

Baikie, A., (2002). Recurrent Issues in Nigeria Education. Zaria: Tamaza Publishing Company.

Baird, S., McIntosh, B. & Ozler, M., (2009). Targeting in a Community–Driven Development Programme: Applications & Acceptance in Tanzania's TASAF. Washington, DC: World Bank.

Bakardjieva, M., (2008). University of Calgary http://www.ucalgary.ca/~bakardji/community/definition.html (Accessed Jan 11/13)

Baker, B., (1950). The Human Community New York: Harper and Bross.

Baldock, P., (1977). Why Community Action? The Historical Origins of the Radical Trend in British Community Work. *Community Development Journal.* 12(2): 68- 74.

Basu K., (2006). Teacher Truancy in India: The Role of Culture, Norms and Economic Incentives. Working Paper No. 06-03. http://ideas.repec.org/p/ecl/corcae/06-03.html

Batten, T., (1957). Communities and Their Development, London: Oxford University Press.

Beach D. S., (1975/80). Personnel: The Management of People at Work. , New York Macmillan Publishing Co. Inc.

Bealer R. C., Fern K. W. & William P. K., (1965). The Meaning of Rurality in American Society: Some Implications of Alternative Definitions. Rural Sociology 30:255-266.

Bebbington, A., (1991). Sharecropping Agricultural Development: the Potential for GSO-Government Collaboration, Grassroots Development. Vol. 15(2).

Behman, J. N., (1999). International Business and Government: Issues and Institution. South Carolina: University of South Carolina Press.

Bell, C., & H. Newby, (1971). Community Studies. London: Allen & Unwin.

Bello, M., and Roslan, A., (2010). Future of the Millennium Development Goals in Nigeria. Paper Presented at the International Conference on Business and Economic Research (ICBER), 15-16 March 2010, at the Hilton Hotel in Kuching, Sarawak. Organised by the Global Research Agency.

Bello, O. & Bola-Oni, S., (1987). Community Development: Back-Bone for Promoting Socio-Economic Growth. Zaria Oluseyi Boladeji Company & Gaskiya Corporation Ltd.

Berry, R. A., & Cline, W. R., (1979). Agrarian Structure and Productivity in Developing Countries: John Hopkins University Press.

Bertalanffy, L., (1968). General Systems Theory: Foundations Development Applications. New York: George Braziller.

Biddle, W. Biddle, J., (1968). The Community Development Process, the Rediscovery of Local Initiatives. New York Holt Rrichart and Wriston Incorporated.

Biggs, S., & Matsaert, H. (2004). Strengthening Poverty Reduction Programmes Using an Actor-Oriented Approach: Examples from Natural Resources Innovation Systems. Retrieved 16 September, 2012, from http://www.odi.org.uk/networks/agren/papers/agrenpaper_134.pdf

Binswanger–M, H. P., Jacomina P. De Regt, Spector, S., (2010). Local and Community Driven Development, Washington, DC: The World Bank.

Black, A., (1988). State, Community and Human Desire. Brighton: Harvester Wheatsheaf.

Blackwood, D. L. & Lynch, R. G., (1994). the Measurement of Inequality and Poverty: A Policy Maker's Guide to the Literature. World Development Vol. 22(4).

Blastland, M., (2009-07-31). "Just What is Poor?". BBC NEWS. Retrieved 2008-09-25.

Boarman, P. M. & Schollarhammer, H., (1977). Multinational Corporations and Governments New York: Prager Publishers.

Booth, D., (2008). Good Governance, Aid Modalities and Poverty Reduction: From Better Theory to Better Practice. Retrieved 10 September, 2012, from http://www.odi.org.uk/resources/download/1524.pdf

Booth, M., (1891). Labour and life of the peoples 1889, 1891. Vol 2.

Bornat, J., Pereira, C., Pilgrim, D. & Williams, F., (1993). Community Care. Basingstoke: Macmillan.

Braithwaite, B., (2005). "Securing Social Justice in Rural Areas", Carnegie Commission for Rural Community Development

Bratton, M. (1990). Review Articles: Beyond the State, Civil Society and Associational Life in Africa, World Politics, Vol. 41(3)

Brennan, M.A., Barnett, R., & Lesmeister, M., (2006). Enhancing Leadership, Local Capacity, and Youth Involvement in the Community Development Process: Findings from a Survey of Florida Youth, *Journal of the Community Development Society*.

Britannica Concise Encyclopedia: "Culture". Britanica.com. Accessed 7th September, 2012.

Brown, L. D. & Ashman, D. (1996). Participation, Social Capital and Inter-Sectoral Problem-Solving: African and Asian Cases. World Development. Vol. 24(9).

Bruntland, D. (2003). "A Social Science Curriculum for the 21st century". Paper Delivered at the First World Curriculum Studies Conference. East China Normal University, Shanghai. www.comfsm.fm Accessed 13 September, 2012.

Burkey, S., (1993). People first. London: Zed Books Ltd.

Buvinic, M., Margaret, L. A. & William, M., (1987). Women and Poverty in the Third World. USA The Johns Hopkins University Press.

Cahn, E. S., & Gray, C., (2005). Using the Coproduction Principle: No More Throwaway Kids. Putting Youth at the Center of Community Building. *New Directions for Youth Development.* 106: Summer.

Callahan, B., (2004). Development Funding Assistance Programme. African Development Foundation. Retrieved January 30, 2013 from www.adf.gov/applicationenglish.pdf

Carley, M., & Christie, I., (2000). Managing Sustainable Development. London: Earthscan.

Carnegie UK Trust, (2009). What Are Asset-Based Approaches to Community Development?; International Association for Community Development (IACD) November 2009 www.carnegieuktrust.org.uk

Carnegie UK Trust, A Charter for Rural Communities, Dunfermline: Carnegie UK Trust (2007). http://www.carnegieuktrust.org.uk/publications/2007/a-charter-forrural-communities

Carney, D. (1998). Sustainable Rural Livelihoods: What Contribution Can Make? In Carney, D. (Eds) Sustainable Rural Development. London: DFID.

Carney, D., (1999). Introduction to Sustainable Livelihoods: What difference can we make? London: DFID.

Caroline, C. I. Charles, E., (1997). A Practical Approach to Personnel Management. Port Harcourt Nigeria: Gostak Printings and Publishing Co. Ltd.

Carroll, T. F., (1992). Intermediary NGOs: The Supporting Link in Grassroots Development. Hartford, CT: Kumarian Press.

Cartledge, B., (1995). Population and Environment: Women the Neglected Factor in Sustainable Development. New York Oxford University Press.

Cavaye, J., (2000). Understanding Community Development. www.communitydevelopment.com.au/DOC.

Central Bank of Nigeria (1993). Annual Report and Statement of Accounts for the Year Ended 31st December 1992.

Chalofsky, N. E. & Reinhart, C., (1988). Effective Human Resource Development. California: Jossey Bass Inc. Publishers.

Chambers, R. (1997) Whose Reality Counts? Putting the Last First; London: Intermediate Technology Publications

Chambers, R., & Conway, G. (1992). Sustainable Rural Livelihoods: Practical Concepts for the 21st Century: Institute of Development Studies, University of Sussex.

Chambers, R., (1983). Rural Development: Putting the Last First. London: Longman.

Chambers, R., (1987). Sustainable Livelihoods, Environment and Development: Putting Poor Rural People First Discussion Paper no. 240). Brighton: Institute of Development Studies.

Chavez, E.M. (2003). "Increasing Productivity of Rural Work" UN Economic and Social Council (ECOSOC) UN Headquarters, New York.

Chavis, D. M., Hogge, J. H., & McMillan, D. W. (1986). Sense of Community through Brunswick's Lens: A First Look. Journal of Community Psychology, Vol. 14.

Cheam, P. V., (2009). NGO's Approach to Community Development in Rural Cambodia, Cambodian Institute for Cooperation and Peace, (CICP); Cambodia: Phnom Penh, http://www.cicp.org.

Cheney, G. (1995). "Democracy in the Workplace", Journal of Applied Communication, Vol. 23

Chino, T. (2000). Foreword. In Rosegrant, M. W. & Peter, B. R. H. (Eds.) Transforming the Rural Asia Economy: The Unfinished Revolution. Hong Kong: Oxford University Press.

Chitambar, J. B., (1973). Introductory Rural Sociology: A Synopsis of Concepts and Principles. New Delhi: Wiley Eastern Limited.

Christensons, J. A. & Robinson, J. W., (1980) Community Development in America, Amos; Iowa State University Press.

Chukwuezi, B., (1999) Deagrarianization and Rural Employment in Igboland, South-Eastern Nigeria. Deagrarianization and Rural Employment Network. ASC Working Paper 37.

Chukwuezi, B., (2000). Issues in Community Development. Nsukka: Mike Social Press.

Clark, D., (1983). The concept of community education. Journal of Community Education 2(3).

Clark, J., (1999). Democratizing Development: The Role of Voluntary Organizations. West Hartford: Kumarian Press.

Clover, J., (2003). Food Security in Sub-Saharan Africa. African Security Review, 12(1).

Coady International Institute, (2012). Canada http://www.coady.stfx.ca/work/ABCD/ Accessed December 14, 2012

Cohen, R., (1970). Traditional Society in Africa. In: Paden, J.N. and E.W. Soja (Eds.), the African Experience: Essays Northwestern University. Evanston.

Coleman, J.S., (1958). Nigeria: Background to Nationalism. London University of California Press, Berkeley and Los-Angeles, England.

Colonial Office, (1958). Community Development. *A Handbook*, London: HMSO.

Community Development Exchange, (2006) CDX Information Sheet, Sheffield, CDX.

Community Development Foundation for Communities and Local Government, (2009). Community Development Challenge Report". http://www.cdf.org.uk/communitydevelopmentchallenge.pdf. Retrieved 06-03-2011

Conscience International, (1998) 1(12): 45-46.

Cook, J. B., (1994). Community Development Theory. Retrieved from http://extension.missouri.edu/explore/miscpubs/mp0568.htm on November 15, 2012.

Cooke, B. & Kathari, U., (Eds.). (2001). Participation: The New Tyranny? : Zed Books.

Cooke, I. & Shaw, M., (Ed.) (1996). Radical Community Work: Perspectives from Practice in Scotland. Edinburgh: Moray House Institute of Education.

Coombs, P. H. & Ahmed, M., (1974) Attacking Rural Poverty: How Non Formal Education can help, Johnson Hopkins University Press, London.

Cornwall, A., (2002) 'Making Spaces, Changing Places: Situating Participation in Development'. IDS Working Paper 170. Brighton: IDS.

Cornwell, J., (1984) Hard Earned Lives, London: Tavistock.

Cousins, B., & Lahiff, E., (2005). Smallholder Agriculture and Land Reform in South Africa. IDS Bulletin Vol. 36(No 2).

Covey, J. (1995). Accountability and Effectiveness in NGO Policy Alliances, *Journal of International Development.* Vol. 7(6).

Craig, G., (1989). Community work and the state. Community Development Journal Vol. 24(1).

Crowder, M. and O. Ikime, (1970). West African Chiefs: Their Changing Status Under Colonial Rule and Independence. Ile-Ife, New York University of Ife Press.

Curtiers, M. H., (1958) "Community Development: A Democratic Social Process" Adult Leadership, Vol. 6.

Curtin, P.D., (1976). The Atlantic Slave Trade, 1600- 1800. In Ajayi, J.F.A. and M. Crowder (Eds.), History of West Africa. 2nd Edn., Lodon Longman.

Damer, S. (1980). State, Class and Housing: Glasgow 1985-1919. In J. Melling (ed.), Housing, Social Policy and the State. London: Croom Helm.

Dauda, S. (2003) The Crisis of Development in Africa: The Democratic Imperatives. J Dev Soc, 1(4).

Dawarakinth, R., (1967). "Community Development as Means of Organized Social Change" Selected Readings on Community Development, T. P. S. Chowdhari (ed.) National Institute of Community Development: Hyderabad.

De Satge, R., Holloway, A., Mullins, D., Nchabaleng, L., & Ward, P. (2002). Learning About Livelihoods: Insights from Southern Africa. Cape Town: Periperi Publications and Oxfam Publishing.

Department for International Development. (2006). Social Protection in Poor Countries, Social Protection Briefing Note Series no. 1

Desai, V. & Potter R. B., (ed) (2008). The Companion to Development Studies, London: Hodder Education Publishers

DFID (Department For International Development) (1997). Eliminating World Poverty: A Challenge for the 21st Century. London: The Stationery Office.

Dharam, G., Martin G. & Franklyn, L., (1979). Planning for Basic Needs in Kenya, Geneva: ILO.

Dhunpath, R., & Paterson, A., (2004). The Interface Between Research and Policy Dialogue: Substantive or Symbolic? Journal of Education No. 33 Retrieved 21 July, 2009, from http://www.ukzn.ac.za/joe/JoEPDFs/joe%2033%20dhunpath.pdf

Dimock, M. E. & Dimock, G. O., (1970) Public Administration, New Delhi: Oxford and IBH Publishers (Indian Ed.)

Dine, G. U., (1983).Traditional Leadership as Service Among the Igbo of Nigeria: Anthrpotheological Approach. Rome: Pontifical Universita Laterannense.

Direction des Coopératives, Ministère de l'Industrie et du Commerce., (1999). Taux de Survie des Entreprises Coopératives au Québec. Québec: Direction des Communications, Gouvernement du Québec.

Dlamini, P. & Julia, M., (1993). South African Women and the Role of Social Work: Wathint' Abafazi Wathint' Imbokodo (Provoke Women and You've Struck a Rock). International Social Work. Vol. 36, 1993.

Dominelli, L. (1990) Women and Community Action, Birmingham, Venture Press, UK.

Dongier, P., Julie V. D., Elinor O., Andrea R., Wendy W., Bebbington A., Sabine A., Talib E., and Polsky, M. (2003) "Community Driven Development." In Poverty Reduction Strategy, Washington DC: Paper Sourcebook

Doug P., (2008). "Social strife: The birth of the co-op". *Cotton Times, Understanding the Industrial Revolution.* Retrieved 14 November, 2012.

Dreze, J. and Sen, A. (1989). Hunger and Public Action. London: Clarendon Press.

Drucker, P. F., (1999). Management Challenges for the 21st Century, New York: Harper Business.

Earnshaw, A., (2000). Remember Food Co-Ops? Portland's Still Flourishes, *Business Journal-Portland.* 25 August.

Easton, D., (1965). A Framework for Political Analysis, Englewood Cliff: N. J. Prentice Hall.

Edozien, E.C., (1975). Rural Poverty: Case Study of Giwa local Government, Kaduna. Some Issues in Concept and Theory, NES Annual Conference.

Edwards, M. and Hulme, D. (Eds). (1996). Beyond the Magic Bullet. Connecticut: Kumarian Press.

Egonmwan, J. A., (2000). Public Policy Analysis: Concepts and Applications. Benin: Resyin Publishers Company.

Ekanem, E. U. U., (2003). Oil Companies and Security Management in Host Communities, Nigeria Journal of Social and Development Issues. Vol. 3(1).

Ekong, E.E., (1988). An Introduction to Rural Sociology, Ibadan: Jumak Publishers Ltd.

Ekong, E.E., (2003). An Introduction to Rural Sociology, Uyo: Dove Educational Publishers.

Ekpo, A. H., (1989). Manpower Development in Nigeria, In SC Ogbuagu (Ed.) Strategy for National Development in Nigeria Calabar: University of Calabar Press.

Elaigwu, J. I., (1990). The Military and the Democratization of the Polity: the Nigerian Experience, "Paper for the Research Committee on Armed Forces and Society (IPSA) Interim Meeting on the Theme: Democratization and Politicization of the Military, Madrid, Spain July 5-7

Elizur, Y. (1995). Eco-systemic consultation in the kibbutz: Social process and narrative in Two Cases of Community "Epidemic." Contemporary Family Therapy, Vol. 17(4).

Ellis, F. & Biggs, S. (2001). Evolving themes in Rural Development 1950's - 2000s: Development Policy Review, 19(4).

Emmanuel, A. A., (2010). The Effects of Community-Based Organizations' Activities on Local Economic Development in Geographically Contrasting Areas of Ondo State, Nigeria. PhD Thesis. Department of

Urban and Regional Planning, Federal University of Technology, Akure.

Emordi, E.C. and Osiki, O. M., (2008). Traditional Rule in Nigeria: The Crisis of Relevance in Contemporary Politics. Ife J. History, Vol. 4.

Enikanselu, S.A., Akanji, S. O., and Faseyiku, O.I. (2005). Principles and Economics of Co-operative. Lagos: DARTRADE Limited.

Fairtrade Foundation, (2009). International Fair-trade Labeling History, Retrieved 16 September, 2009, from http://www.fairtrade.org.uk/what is fairtrade/history.aspx

FAO, (2004). The State of Food and Agriculture 2003-2004: Agricultural Biotechnology: Meeting the Needs of the Poor? Rome: United Nations.

FAO, (2005). An Approach to Rural Development: Participatory and Negotiated Territorial Development (PNTD). Rural Development Division Food and Agriculture Organization of the United Nations (FAO) April 2005. http://www.fao.org/sd/dim pe2/docs/pe2 050402d1 en.pdf

Farrington, J., Bebbington, A., Wellard, K. & Lewis, D. (1993). Reluctant Partners?: NGOs, the State and Sustainable Agricultural Development, London: Routledge.

Fernando, N. A., (2008). Rural Development Outcomes and Drivers: An Overview and Some Lessons. Manila: Asia Development Bank.

FGN, (1998). National Policy on Education. Lagos: Federal Government Press.

Fiedler, F. E., (1967). A Theory of Leadership Effectiveness: McGraw-Hill: Harper and Row Publishers Inc.

Fields, G. (2007). Dual Economy, ILR Collection: Working Papers, http://digitalcommons.ilr.cornell.edu/cgi/viewcontent.cgi?article=1016& context=workingpapers Retrieved 10 September, 2012.

Fleishman, E. A., (1953). The Description of Supervisory Behaviour, *Journal of Applied Psychology*, Vol. 37(1).

Fleishman, E. A., Mumford, M. D., Zaccaro, S. J., Levin, K. Y., Korotkin, A. L. & Hein, M. B., (1991). Taxonomic Efforts in the Description of Leader Behaviour: A Synthesis and Functional Interpretation. Leadership Quarterly, 2(4).

Flora, C. B. & Flora, J. L., (2004). Rural Communities: Legacy and Change. Boulder, CO: Westview Press.

Flora, J. L., (1998). Social Capital and Communities of Place. Rural Sociology, 63(4).

Forde, D. & Jones, G. I., (1950), "The Ibo-and Ibibio-Speaking Peoples of Southeastern Nigeria", London: International African Institute (reprint 1967).

Fraser, J. (1987) Community: the Private and the Individual, *Journal of Sociological Review Vol* 35 (4).

Friedmann, J. (1992). Empowerment: The Politics of Alternative Development. London: Blackwell.

(FCWTGs) Federation of Community Work Training Groups, (2002). The National Occupational Standards in Community Development. Sheffield: FCWTGs.

Gardella, L. G. (2000) The Group-Centered BSW Curriculum for Community Practice: An Essay. Journal of Community Practice, Vol. 8(2).

Garforth, C., & Harford, N. (1997) Extension Experience in Agriculture and Natural Resource Management in the 1980s and the 1990's. In V. Scarborough, S. Kilough, D. Johnson & J. Farrington (Eds.), Farmer Led Extension: Concepts and Practices. London: Intermediate Technology Publications

Germain, C. B., & Gitterman, A. (1995). Ecological perspective. In R. L. Edwards R. L. (Ed.-in-Chief), Encyclopedia of social work (19th ed). Washington, DC: National Association of Social Workers Press.

Gerth, H. & Mills, C., (1946). From Max Weber: Essays in Sociology. New York: Cambridge University Press.

Gertler, M. (2001). Rural Co-operatives and Sustainable Development, Saskatoon SK: Centre for the Study of Cooperatives, University of Saskatchewan

Gilchrist, A. (2004). Community Development, The Well-Connected Community: A Networking Approach to Community Development: 21-25. Bristol: The Policy Press.

Giltinger, J. P., (1972) Economic Analysis of Agricultural Projects London John Hopkins University Press.

Gofwen, R., (1999). Community Development in Nigeria: What is New and What is Old? Nigerian *Journal of Social Work,* Vol. 3.

Goltzsche, M., (1976), " Gesellschaft und Politik bei den Ibo um 1900. Die Rolle völkerkundlicher Studien als Quellen zur afrikanischen Geschichte", Frankfurt/Main, Peter Lang.

Gough, I. and Thomas, T (1994) "Need Satisfaction and Welfare Outcomes: Theory and Explanations," Social Policy & Administration, 28(1).

Grabowski, R. & Shields, M. (1996) Development Economics, USA: Blackwell Publishers Incorporation.

Grameen Foundation (2009). Microfinance FAQs. Retrieved 16 September, 2012, from http://www.grameenfoundation.org/

Grau, I. M., (1993). "Die Igbo-sprechenden Völker Südostnigerias: Fragmentation und fundamentale Einheit in ihrer Geschichte", Wien, Verband der Wissenschaftlichen Gesellschaften Österreichs.

Green, A. & Matthias, A. (1995). NGOs – A Policy Panacea for the Next Millennium. *Journal of international Development.* Vol. 7(3).

Green, M. M., (1947), "Igbo Village Affairs. Chiefly with Reference to the Village of Umueke Agbaja", London: Sidgwick & Jackson (reprint London, Frank Cass, 1967).

Groves, F (1985): What is Cooperation? The Philosophy of Cooperation and It's Relationship to Cooperative Structure and Operations, Madison: UWCC Occasional Paper No. 6

Gwanya, T. T. (1989). Rural development Planning in Developing Countries. A Fact Paper No. 5, University of Transkei, Bureau of Development Research and Training.

Hackman, J. R., & Wageman, R. (2005). A Theory of Team Coaching. Academy of Management Review, Vol. 30(2).

Hackman, J. R., & Walton, R. E. (1986). Leading Groups in Organizations. In Goodman P. S. (Ed.), Designing Effective Work Groups: 72–119. San Francisco: Jossey-Bass.

Hahn-Waanders, H., (1985). "Traditionale Herrschaft im Wandel: Untersuchungen bei den Igbo Nigerias unter besonderer Berücksichtigung von Nkpologwu", Berlin, Dietrich Reimer.

Hanachor, M. E., (2005). Impact of Voluntary Groups in Community Development, Unpublished Seminar Paper of University of Port Harcourt.

Hanachor, M. E., (2009). Influence of Community Based Organizations in Community Development, Unpublished Ph.D Dissertation, University of Port Harcourt.

Hancock, W. K., (1942). Survey of the British Commonwealth Affairs, Problems of Economic Policy, 1918-1939.

Hannington, W., (1967). "Never on our Knees", London: Lawrence Wishart.

Hannington, W., (1977). "Unemployed Struggles: 1919-1936", London: Croom Helm.

Harbison, F., (1973). Human Resources as the Wealth of Nations. New York: Oxford University Press.

Harper, E. H. and Dunham, A., (1959). Community Organization in Action. *Basic literature and critical comments*, New York: Association Press.

Harris, J. (1982). General Introduction, In Harris, J. (Eds.) Rural Development: Theories of Peasant Economy and Agrarian Change. London: Hutchinson University Library.

Harrison, P., (1981). Inside the Third World, England: Penguin Books.

Hartsock, N., (1998). The Feminist Standpoint Revisited and Other Essays. Boulder, CO: Westview Press.

HDR (1990) Human Development Report. UNPD

Hemphill, J. K., (1949). Situational Factors in Leadership, Columbus: Ohio State University Bureau of Educational Research.

Henkel, H. & R. Stirrat (2001) 'Participation as Spiritual Duty: Empowerment as Secular Subjection'. Chapter 11 in Cooke and Kothari, 2001:168-184.

Hersey, P., Blanchard, K. & Johnson, D., (2008). Management of Organizational Behaviour: Leading Human Resources (9th ed.). Upper Saddle River, NJ: Pearson Education.

Heword, H. & Voorhes, C. V. (1969). The Role of the School in Community Education. Michigan Pendell Publishing Company.

Hillman, A. (1960). Implantation of Sustainability Lesson from Integrated Rural Development, Maxwell School: Syracuse University

HLSP Institute, (2005). Sector Wide Approaches: A Resource Document for UNFPA Staff.

Hobsbawm, E. (1994). "Introduction: Inventing Traditions". In Hobsbawm, E & T Ranger (Eds.). The invention of Tradition. Cambridge: Cambridge University Press.

Hoggett, P. (1997) 'Contested Communities' in P. Hoggett (Ed.) *Contested Communities. Experiences, Struggles, Policies*, Bristol: Policy Press.

Holdcroft, L. E. (1976). The Rise and Fall of Community Development: 1950 - 1965. Retrieved 10 September, 2012, from http://ageconsearch.umn.edu/bitstream/11123/1/pb76ho01.pdf

Homans, G. C. (1974) Social Behaviour: Its Elementary Forms. New York: Harcourt Brace Jovanovich.

House, R. J., (1971). "A Path-Goal Theory of Leader Effectiveness", Administrative Science Quarterly (Johnson Graduate School of Management, Cornell University) 16 (3) doi:10.2307/2391905. JSTOR 2391905.

House, R. J., (1996). "Path-Goal Theory of Leadership: Lessons, Legacy, and a Reformulated Theory". Leadership Quarterly 7 (3). Doi:10.1016/S1048-9843(96)90024-7.

Human Resources, (2006). "Leadership Evaluation Guidelines."

Hunger Project (2000). The African Women Food Farmer Initiative: Exclusion from Development Policy and Programmeming Equation, New York.

Hyde, C. (1996). A Feminist Response to Rothman's "The Interweaving of Community Intervention Approaches." Journal of Community Practice, Vol. 3(3/4).

Ibekwe, O.U. (1984). Modern Business Management: Owerri: New African Publishing Co. Nigeria Ltd.

Idachaba, F. S., (2000). Desirable and Workable Agricultural Policies for Nigeria. Ibadan University Press.

Idode, J.B. (1989). Rural Development and Bureaucracy in Nigeria. Ibadan; Longman Nigeria.

Idowu, E. D. & Dopamu, P. A. (1980). Religion and Culture. Ibadan: Onibanoje Press.

IFAD, (2009a) Revised IFAD Policy for Grant Financing. IFAD, Rome: http://www.ifad.org/gbdocs/eb/98/e/EB-2009-98-R-9.pdf

IFAD, (2009b) "Rural Finance Policy", IFAD, Rome: http://www.ifad.org/pub/basic/finance/eng.pdf

IFAD, (2009c) "Community-Driven Development Decision Tools for Rural Development Programmes", IFAD, Rome. http://www.ifad.org/english/cdd/pub/decisiontools.pdf

IFAD, (2011) "Rural Poverty in Nigeria", http://www.ruralpovertyportal.org/web/guest/country/home/tags/nigeria International Fund for Agricultural Development.

IFAD, (2012) "Matching Grant", International Fund for Agricultural Development Report

Ifemesia, C. C., (1978). "Southeastern Nigeria in the Nineteenth Century. An Introductory Analysis", New York: NOK.

Iheanacho, G.O.S (2012). "Community Development as the Bastion of Sustainable Development in Nigeria" Journal of Educational and Social Research Vol. 2 (9).

Ihimodu, I. I., (1988). Cooperative Economics: A Concise Analysis in Theory and Application, A Bulletin of the Research and Planning Division Nigeria Agricultural Cooperative Bank Ltd, Kaduna.

IICD (2006). ICTs for Agricultural Livelihoods: Impact and Lessons Learned from IICD Supported activities. The Hague: International Institute for Communication and Development.

Ijere, M.O., (1981). The Prospect of Employment Creation Through Cooperatives in Nigeria. *Nigeria Journal of Rural Development and Cooperative studies*, Vol. 2.

Ikotun, A. (2002). Strategies for Promoting Integrated Rural Development in Nigeria: Theory and Practice. Badagry: Matram.

ILO, (2002). The ILO's Recommendation on the Promotion of Cooperatives 2002: (R.193), www.ilo.org/empnet/units/cooperatives/lang--en/index.htm

Imoudu, P. B. (1986) "The Role of Credit in Rural Development in Nigeria", A Paper Presented at Training Course in Administration of Rural Development Programme Organized by the Department of Farm Management and Extension, FUTA and Rural Development Agency of Ondo State, 6th – 9th December.

Isichei, E., (1976). "A History of the Igbo People", London/Basingstoke, Macmillan.

"Indicators of Poverty & Hunger". United Nations. Retrieved 2011-05-27.

Jegede, A. O. (2000). Assessment of Selected Non-Governmental Organizations on Poverty Alleviation Strategies: A Case Study of Countrywomen Association of Nigeria (COWAN). BTech. Thesis. Federal University of Technology, Akure.

Jolliffe, D. (2004). The Impact of Education in Rural Ghana: Examining Household Labor Allocation and Returns on and off the Farm. Journal of Development Economics, Vol. 73.

Jolly, R. (2006) Redistribution with Growth. Retrieved 10 September 2012, from http://www.id21.org/classics/Jolly.html

Jones, D. (1977) 'Community Work in the UK' In Specht H. & Vickery A. (eds.) *Integrating Social Work Methods*, London: George Allen and Unwin.

Jones, G.I. (1957), "Report of the Position, Status, and Influence of Chiefs and Natural Rulers in the Eastern Region of Nigeria", Enugu, Government Printer.

Juhász, P., (2001). The End of the "Agricultural Miracle" and Property Reform in Hungary, In I. Osamu (Ed.), The New Structure of the Rural Economy of Post-Communist Countries. Sapporo: Hokkaido University.

Kaimowitz, D., (1993). Management Consulting in Africa: Utilizing Local Expertise, Hartford, CT: Kumarian Press.

Kanbur, R. (1990), Poverty and the Social Dimensions of Structural Adjustment in Cote d' Ivoire: Social Dimensions of Adjustment in Sub-Saharan Africa. (SDA) Working Paper Series, The World Bank, Washington, D.C.

Karen, A. G. & Miller-Cribbs J. E. (2011). Latino Small Businesses and the American Dream: Community Social *Work* Practice Chicago, IL: Lyceum Books.

Kauffman, S. (1995). At Home in the Universe: The Search for the Laws of Self-Organization and Complexity. New York: Oxford University Press.

Kemp, S. P. (2001) Environment through a Gendered Lens: From Person-In-Environment to Woman-in-Environment. Affilia, 16(1).

Ketilson, L.H., Michael G., Murray F., Roy D., & Leslie P., (1998). The Social and Economic Importance of the Co-operative Sector in Saskatchewan. Research Report Prepared for Saskatchewan Department of Economic and Co-operative Development. Saskatoon: Centre for the Study of Co-operatives.

Kilby, C., (2000). Sovereignty and NGOs, In Stiles, K. (Eds) Global Institutions and Local Empowerment: 59, London: Macmillan Press.

Kim, J. W., & Schweitzer, J., (1996). The Causes of and Perceptions Toward Social Capital in a Neighborhood Community Context. Paper Presented at the Association for Research on Nonprofit Organizations and Voluntary Action, New York, NY.

Kirk-Greene, A.H.M., (1976). Crisis and Conflict in Nigeria: A Documentary Sourcebook. London Oxford University Press.

Konopka, G. (1973). Requirements for the Healthy Development of Adolescent Youth in Adolescence, VIII, 31, Fall.

Koontz, H., O'Donnel C. & Weihrich H., (1980). Management. Japan: McGraw Hill Publishing Company.

Korten, D. C. (1990). Getting to the 21st Century: Voluntary Action and the Global Agenda. Hardford, CT: Kumarian Press.

Korten, D. C., (1995). When Corporations Rule the World. San Francisco: Kumarian Press.

Kouzes, J. M. & Posner, B. Z. (2002). *The Leadership Challenge.* San Francisco: Jossey-Bass.

Kretzmann, J. P. & McKnight, J. (1993). Building Communities from the Inside Out: A Path Toward Finding and Mobilizing a Community's Assets. Center for Urban Affairs and Policy Research, Neighborhood Innovations Network. Evanston, Ill: Northwestern University.

Kretzmann, J. P. & McKnight, J., (1996). Asset-Based Community Development, National Civic Review: Vol. 85, Issue 4. Winter

Krugman, P. R., (1996). The Self-Organization Economy, Cambridge MA: Blackwell Publishers.

Kubisch, A. C. (2005). Comprehensive Community Building Initiatives--Ten Years Later: What We Have Learned About the Principles Guiding the Ork. Putting Youth at the Center of Community Building. *New Directions for Youth Development.* No.106: Summer 2005.

Kuper, A., & Kuper, J. (Eds.). (1999). The Social Science Encyclopedia (2nd ed.). London: Routledge.

Laidlaw, A.F (1974): The Cooperative Sector, Columbia: University of Missouri

Lamb, S. (1991) An Analysis of Linguistic Avoidance in Journal Articles on Men Who Batter Women. American Journal of Orthopsychiatry, Vol. 61(2).

Larson, A. M., & Ribot, J. C. (2005) Democratic Decentralization through a Natural Resource Lens: An Introduction. In Larson A. M. & Ribot J. C. (Eds.), Democratic Decentralization through a Natural Resource Lens. Oxford: Routledge.

Lawal, M. M. (2006) Manpower Management: A Hand Book for Personnel Managers and Students of Administration. Abuja: Roots Books and Journals Nigeria Limited

Ledwith, M. (2005) Community Development (1-55). Portland: Policy

Lele, U. (1975) The Design of Rural Development: Lessons from Africa. London: John Hopkins University Press.

Lengermann, P. M., & Niebrugge-Brantley, J. (1990) Feminist Sociological Theory: The Near Future prospects. In Ritzer G. (Ed.), Frontiers of Social Theory (316–344). New York: Columbia University Press.

Lewis, D., (2007). Management of Non-governmental Development Organizations. NGOs and Development: Analysing NGO Roles: Implementers, Catalysts and Partners. London: Routledge.

Lightelm, A. A. & Wilsenach, A. (1993). Development, Poverty and the Environment with Particular Reference to the Eastern Transvaal Region. Development Southern Africa, 10 (1).

Long, J. R., (1998). Economic Planning and Development. Uyo: Inyang-Umoh Publishers

Lotz, J. (1970) Training in Community Development. Journal of the Community Development Society. Vol. 1 (1).

Lowe, P. M. J. & Ward, N. (1995). 'Networks in Rural Development: Beyond Exogenous and Endogenous Models' In Beyond Modernisation, (Eds) Van der Ploeg, J D and Van Dijk C. 87-105, Assen, The Netherlands: Van Gorcum.

Lynn, A. (2005). Youth Using Research: Learning Through Social Practice, Community Building, and Social Change. Putting Youth at the Center of Community Building. New Directions for Youth Development, No. 106: Summer 2005.

Macmillan Dictionary, (1981). For Students Macmillan, Pan Ltd. Retrieved 28, December, 2012 http://en.wikipedia.org/wiki/Adolescence

Maghsoudi, A., (2010). The Role of Cooperatives in Developing and Sustaining Local and Regional Communities – a Success Story of Female Breaded Households' Cooperative Societies in BAM. Review of International Cooperation, Vol. 99, No. 1

Marshall, J., (1997). Renewing Hope in Urban Areas, Christian Science Monitor. Volume 90, Issue 24. December 30.

Mathie, A & Cunningham, G. (2005) "Who is Driving Development? Reflections on the Transformative Potential of Asset-based Community Development", Canadian Journal of Development Studies. Vol. 26 (1).

Mathie, A. & Cunningham, G. (2003) From Clients to Citizens: Asset based Community Development as a Strategy for Community-Driven Development, Development in Practice 13 (5).

Mayo, M. (1975) 'Community development: A Radical Alternative?' in Bailey R. and Brake M. (eds.) *Radical Social Work*, London: Edward Arnold.

Mbaku J.M. (1994), Africa After More Than Thirty Years of Independence: Still Poor and Deprived. Journal of Third World Studies Vol. 11(2).

McArthur, S. (2008). Global Governance and the Rise of NGOs. Asian Journal of Public Affairs 2 (1).

McGrath, J. E. (1962). Leadership Behaviour: Some Requirements for Leadership Training, Washington, DC: U.S. Civil Service Commission.

McIntosh, A. & Friedman, M. 1989. Women's Producer Groups in Rural Kwazulu: Limits and possibilities. Development Southern Africa, 6(4).

McIntyre, B. D., Herren, H. R., Wakhungu, J., & Watson, R. T. (Eds.). (2009). International Assessment of Agricultural Knowledge, Science and Technology for Development: Global report: Island Press.

Meek, C. k., (1937). Law and Authority in a Nigerian Tribe. London: University Press, p.201.

Meziro, J. D., (1967). Dynamics of Community Development, New York: Scarecrow Press

Microsoft Encarta Dictionary (2009): ©1993-2008 Microsoft Corporation. All right Reserved

Midgley, J. with Hall, A., Hardiman, M. and Narine, D., (1986). *Community Participation, Social Development and the State*, London: Methuen.

Miniclier L. M. (1957) "Introduction" Community Development Review, Vol. IV, March 1957.

Muchinsky, P. M. (2000) Psychology Applied to Work. USA: Wadsworth/Thomson Learning.

Mukul, D., (2007-12-02). "When a dollar a day means 25 cents". bbcnews.com. Retrieved 2011-05-28.

Murry, R. (1966): Case Histories in Community Organization. New York: Harper and Bross.

Musgrave, P. & Feber, R., (1976). Finding the Poor: On the Identification of Poverty Households in Latin America. Brookings Institution, Washington. D.C.

Naoroji, D. (1901), Poverty and Un-British Rule in India. New Delhi. Nigerian Economic Society (NES). (1975). Poverty In Nigeria. Proceedings of the 1975 Annual Conference, Ibadan University Press.

Naples, N. A. & Sachs, C., (2000). Standpoint Epistemology and the Use of Self-Reflection in Feminist Ethnography: Lessons for Rural Sociology. Rural Sociology, 65(2).

National Youth Agency, NYA (1999). Developing Youth Work for Young People. Dept. of Education and Employment, London: Oxford University Press.

Ndebbio, J. E. U., (2002). The Role of Multinational Companies in the Economic Backwardness of the Niger Delta, Nigerian Journal of Social and Development Issue. Vol. 2(1).

Nemes, G. (2005) Integrated Rural Development: The Concept and its Operation. Retrieved 10 September, 2012, from http://www.policy.hu/nemes/publikaciok/muhelytaulmany2005_6.pdf

Nicolis, G. & Prigogine, I., (1977). Self-Organization in Non-Equilibrium Systems, New York: Wiley Inter-Science.

Nigerian National Bureau of Statistics (NBS), (2005). Poverty Profile for Nigeria, Abuja.

Nigerian National Bureau of Statistics (NBS). (2011) Harmonized Living Standards Survey 2010. Abuja.

Nitzberg, J., (2005). The Meshing of Youth Development and Community Building. Putting Youth at the Center of Community Building. *New Directions for Youth Development,* No. 106: Summer.

Nongo, S. (2005). Fundamental of Management. Makurdi: Aboki Publishing Company.

Nweke, E.N. (2003). Policy Communities Consultation and Partnership: A Strategy for Poverty Reduction in Nigeria. Paper Presented at the Second Regional International Conference of the International Institute of Administrative Sciences, Yaounde, Cameroon.

Nweze, C. (1988). Perspective on Community and Rural Development in Nigeria. Jos: Centre for Development Studies.

Nzimiro, I., (1972). "Studies in Ibo Political Systems. Chieftaincy and Politics in Four Niger States", London, Frank Cass.

O'Brien J. & Green M., Moore H. (2006). When People Care Enough to Act: Asset-Based Community Development, Toronto-Canada: Inclusion Press

Obikeze, O. S., (2006) Issues in Community Development. Onitsha: Book Point Ltd.

Obisi C., (1996). Personnel Management. Ibadan: Freeman Publications.

Obodoechi, O. B., (2006) The Theory Jungles of Community and Rural Development: An Introductory Text. Enugu: Chimex Publications.

Odekunle, F., (2002) Youth as Vanguards of Democracy Guest Lecture, 2nd Annual Lecture and Award Giving Ceremony National Association of Democratic Youths, Arewa House Kaduna).

Odumosu, O., (1963). The Nigerian Constitution: History and Development. Sweet and Marx Well, London, pp: 43-44.

Odusanya, J. A., (1972). Career Exploration and Job Opportunities for Youth in Agriculture. Young Farmers Club, Western State, Nigeria.

Ogbuozobe, J. E., (2000). Community-Based Organisations (CBOs) in the Provision of Social Services in Ibadan Metropolitan Area. Nigerian Institute of Social and Economic Research (NISER) Monograph Series No.1, Ibadan: NISER.

Ogbuozobe, J.E. (2000). Community-Based Organizations (CBOs) in the Provision of Social Services in the Ibadan Metropolitan Area. Nigerian Institute of Social and Economic Research (NISER) Monograph Series No.1. Ibadan: NISER.

Ogili, E. E. (2004). Community Development for New Africa. Enugu: Adels Publishers

Ogunlela, Y. I. & Mukhtar, A. A. (2009). "Gender Issues in Agricultural and Rural Development in Nigeria: The Role of Women". *Humanity and Social Sciences Journal,* Vol. 4 (1).

Ojha, P. D., (1970). A Configuration of Indian Poverty. Reserve Bank of India Bulletin, January, 16-27.

Okafor, A. O., (2003). Roles, Strategies and Instrument for Government and Public Bodies. Paper presented at the Second Regional International Conference of the International Institute of Administrative Sciences, Yaounde, Cameroon.

Okojie, C.E.E., (2002). Gender and Education as Determinants of Household Poverty in Nigeria. UNUWIDER, Discussion Paper No. 37. World Institute for Development Economic Research.

Okoli, F.C., (1985). Western Ideology and Community Development. Benin; University of Benin Press.

Okonkwo, J. N. P., (1980). Introduction to the Study of Cooperative. Enugu: Cooperatives Publishers, Ltd.

Oku, O., (2003). The Universal Basic Education (UBE) Programme: Issues and Problems of Policy Implementation. Journal of Nigeria Languages & Culture, Vol. 5(1).

Olajide, S. O., (1980). Nigerian Small Farmers: Problems and Prospects in Integrated Rural Development; CARD, Nigeria: University of Ibadan

Olawoye, J. E., (1987). Degree of Rurality: Questioning the Empirical Existence of the Typical Village. The Rural Sociologist, Vol.4(4).

Olayide, S.O. et al., (1981). Elements of Rural Economics. Ibadan: University Press Publishers

Olayiwola, L. M. & Adeleye, O. A., (2005). Rural Infrastructural Development in Nigeria: Between 1960 and 1990 – Problems and Challenges; *Journal of Social Sciences*, Vol. 11(2): 91-96

Olise P (2007), Primary Health Care for Sustainable Development, Abuja, Ozege Publications

Oloko, O. (1976) Nigeria 20 Basic Problems Yet Unsolved. Lagos: Apapa Printing Press.

Olopoenia, R. A., (1983). "On the Meaning of Economic Development" In Osayimwense I. Z. (Ed.) Development Economics ands Planning, Nigeria Ibadan: University of Ibadan Publishing Consults.

Omodia, S., (2004). The Family as a Vehicle for Sustainable Democracy in Nigeria. J Fam Dev, 1(1): 83.

Omodia, S., (2005). Poverty Alleviation in a Deregulated Economy. Challenges and Prospects For Sustainable Democracy in Nigeria. J Adm, 2(1): 118 – 124.

Onoja, A., (2007). Redefining Tradition: The Chieftaincy Institution in Nigeria. Ife J. Hist., 4(2): 227-243.

Onuekwusi G. C. & Effiong E. O., (2002): Youth Empowerment in Rural Areas through   Participation in Rabbit Production; A Case of Akwa Ibom State, Nigeria." *Nigerian   Journal of Rural Sociology*, Vol. 4.

Onwuejeogwu, M. A., (1980), "Nri Kingdom and Hegemony. An Outline of an Igbo Civilization. A.D. 994 to Present", Nri: Tabansi Press.

Onwuejeogwu, M. A., (1981). "An Igbo Civilization: Nri Kingdom and Hegemony", London: Ethnographica.

Onwuzulike, P. N., (1987). Community Development in Adazi-Nnukwu, Unpublished N.C.E. Project.

Orji, K. E. & Olali, S. T., (2010). Traditional Institutions and their Dwindling Roles in Contemporary Nigeria: The Rivers State Example. In: Babawale, T., A. Alao & A. Adesoji (Eds.), The Chieftaincy Institution in Nigeria. Concept Publishers for Centre for Black and African Arts and Civilization, Lagos, pp: 401-414.

Ortíz, M. J. L., (1994). "Desorrollo Sustentable y Paricipacíon Movimiento Cooperativo: Una Visíon." Horizontes (Revista del Centro de Estudios y Capacitacion Cooperativa, San José, C.R.) 6: 87–95.

Osegbue, C. (2003) "Ife Eji Abu Onicha": Rethiking Strategies for a Sustainable Community – Driven Development. Onitsha: Book Point Ltd.

Pahl, R. E., (1966). The rural-urban continuum. Sociologia Ruralis 6:299-329.

Pardeck, J. T. (1996). An Ecological Approach for Social Work Intervention. Family Therapy, 23(3), 189–198.

Parry, N., & Parry, J., (1979). Social Work, Professionalism and the State. In N. Parry, M. Rustin, & C. Satyamurti (Eds.), Social Work, Welfare and the State. London: Edward Arnold.

Patel, R., Holt-Gimenez, E., & Shattuck, A. (2009). Ending Africa's Hunger. The Nation, 21 September

Patrick, R., (1995). "Four Variations on Drucke's Active Learning Paradigm", Research Strategies 13 Winter, 1995:40-50.

Peppiatt, D., Mitchell, J., & Holzmann, P. (2001). Cash transfers in emergencies: evaluating benefits and assessing risks: Humanitarian Practice Network: Overseas Development Institute.

Perkins, D.D., & Zimmerman, M.A. (1995). Empowerment theory, research, and application. American Journal of Community Psychology, Vol. 23.

Phillips, R. & Pitman, R. H., (2009). An Introduction to Community Development. New York: Routledge.

Phuhlisani & PLAAS. (2008). Guidelines for Delivering Effective Settlement and Implementation Support for Land Reform in the Western Cape: Department of Local Government and Housing, South Africa: Phuhlisani Solutions.

Phuhlisani and PLAAS, (2009). International and Local Approaches to Rural Development Key Issues and Questions: A Review of the Literature for the Drakenstein Municipality, South Africa: Phuhlisani Solutions

Pieterse, J. N. (2001). My Paradigm or Yours: NGOs. In Development Theory: Deconstructions/Reconstructions. London: Sage Publications: 84-85, 93.

Piffner, J. M. & Presthus R. V. (1960) Public Administration. New York: The Ronald Press Co.

Portes, A., & Sensenbrenner, J. (1993) Embeddedness and immigration: Notes on the social determinants of economic action. The American Journal of Sociology, Vol. 98(6).

Poston, M., Conway, T. & Christiansen, K. (2004) The Millennium Development Goals and the IDC: Driving and Framing the Committee's Work. London: ODI.

Potter, R. B., (2002) "Theories, Strategies and Ideologies of Development", In Desai V. & Potter R. B. (Eds.), The Companion to Development Studies. London: Arnold.

Pradip, K. G., (1984). Population, Environment, Resources and Third World development. Washington, D. C.: Greenwood Press.

Pretty, J. & Hine, R., (2001). Reducing Food Poverty with Sustainable Agriculture: A Summary of New Evidence. Final report from the 'SAFT_World' (The Potential of Sustainable Agriculture to Feed the World) Research Project. London: University of Essex's Centre for Environment and Society. Retrieved from http://www2.essex.ac.uk/ces/ on 22 December, 2012.

Pretty, J. & Ward, H. (2001). Social Capital and the Environment. World Development, 29(2): 209-227.

Prigogine, I. & Stengers, I. (1985). Order Out of Chaos, New York: Bantam.

Profit, N. J. (2000). Survivors of Woman Abuse: Compassionate Fires Inspire Collective Action for Social Change. Journal of Progressive Human Services, Vol. 11(2).

Putnam, R. D. (1993). Making Democracy Work: Civic Traditions in Modern Italy, Princeton, NJ: Princeton University Press.

Ravallion, M. & Huppi, M. (1991). Measuring Changes in Poverty: A Methodological Case Study of Indonesia During an Adjustment Period. The World Bank Economic Review 5(1): 57-84.

Raymond Hickey. "Motives for Language Change". Cambridge University Press. Retrieved 19 July 2012.

RBCDS (1995): What Are Cooperatives? Washington: Cooperative Information Report.

Report of The Political Bureau, (1987). Abuja: Directorate for Social Mobilization, March, 1987.

Reulinger, S. & Selowsky. M, (1976). Malnutrition and Poverty. John Hopkins University Press. Baltimore.

Rheingold, H., (2008). *The Virtual Community* http://www.rheingold.com/vc/book/intro.html (accessed Jan. 11/13)

Robb, C. M., (2002) Can the Poor Influence Policy? USA: World Bank.

Roberts, F. O. N., (2004). Traditional Rulers, Governance and the Post Colonial State. In Vaughan O. (Ed.). Indigenous Political Structures and Governance in Nigeria. Ibadan: Book Craft Ltd.

Rooy, A. V., (1997). Civil Society and the Aid Industry. London: Earthscan.

Rowlands, J., (1995). Empowerment Examined, Development in Practice. 15(29): 101-7.

Rowntree, S., (1901). Poverty: A Study of Town Life. London: Macmillan.

Ryan, B., (1992). Feminism and the Women's Movement: Dynamics of Change in Social Movement Ideology and Activism. New York: Routledge.

Rycroft, R. W. & Kash, D. E., (1999). The Complexity Challenges: Technological Innovation for the 21st Century. London and New York: Pinter.

Ryder, A.F.C., (1980). The Trans-Atlantic Slave Trade. In Ikime, O. (Ed.), Groundwork of Nigerian History. Heinemann Educational Books, Ibadan, 242.

Saith, A., (2007). 'From universal values to MDGs: lost in translation', Development and Change, 37 (6): 1167–1199. Sanders, I. T. (1958) Theories of Community Development, Rural Sociology, Vol. 23 (Spring).

Sanders, I. T., (1958). Frontiers of Community Research and Action, Madison: Wisconsin University

Scoones, I., (2009). Livelihoods Perspectives and Rural Development. Journal of Peasant Studies, Vol. 36 (1).

Scouller, J. (2011). The Three Levels of Leadership: How to Develop Your Leadership Presence, Knowhow and Skill. Cirencester: Management Books 2000.

Seer, D., (1981). The Meaning of Development. In Crounch, B. & Chamala, S. (Eds), Extension Education and Rural Development. John Wiley and Sons, New York.

Seibel, H. D., (2004). Upgrading Indigenous Microfinance Institutions in Nigeria: Trials and Errors. Research Paper, Development Research Centre, Germany: University of Cologne.

Sen, A. (1990). Gender and Cooperative Conflicts. In Tinker, I. (Ed) Persistent Inequalities. New York: Oxford University Press.

Sen, A. (1995). Gender Inequality and Theories of Justice. In Glover, J. & Nussbaum, M. (Eds). Women, Culture and Development. London: Oxford University Press.

Sen, A., (1976). Poverty: An Ordinal Approach to Measurement, Econometrics, March, 219-231

Sen, A., (1983), "Voice of the Poor. Can Anyone Hear Us". "Poor Relatively Speaking." Oxford: Economic Paper 36:153–69.

Sen, A., (1984). Resources, Values and Development. Cambridge, Massachusetts: Harvard University Press.

Sen, A., (1999). Development as Freedom. New York: Anchor Books.

Shar, A. (2003). Non-Governmental Organizations on Developmental Issues. Retrieved January 31, 2013, from www.globalissues.org/TradeRelated/Poverty/NGOs.asp-67k

Shumpeter, J., (1911). The Theory of Economic Development: An Inquiry into Profits, Capital, Credit, Interest and the Business Cycle (original title in German).

SIL International, (2011). "Community Development", www@sil.org

Silverberg, G., Dosi, G., & Orsenigo, L. (1988). Innovation, Diversity, and Diffusion: a Self-Organization Model. Economic Journal, Vol. (98).

Skeat, W., (2005). *An Etymological Dictionary of the English Language.* Dover Publications.

Smith, A. & Frank, F., (1999). The Community Development Handbook – A Tool to Build Community Capacity, Canada: Human Resources Department.

Smith, B. (1987). An Agenda of Future Tasks for International and Indigenous NGOs: Views from the North. World Development. 15(supplement): 87-93.

Smith, R. E., Smoll, F. L., & Curtis, B., (1979). Coach Effectiveness Training: A Cognitive-Behavioural Approach to Enhancing Relationship Skills in Youth Sport Coaches. *Journal of Sport Psychology*, Vol. 1.

Spencer, H., (1841). The Study of Sociology, New York: D. A. Appleton.

Stacey, M., (1969). The myth of community studies. British Journal of Sociology Vol. 20.

Staples, H. L., (1990). Powerful Ideas about Empowerment. Administration in Social Work, 14(2): 29-42.

Staples, L. H. (1998). "Insider/Outsider Upsides and Downsides." Keynote Lecture: Symposium on Community Work, Joint World Congress, International Federation of Social Work, Jerusalem, Israel, July 5.

Staudt, K., Rai, S. M., & Parpart, J. L. (2002). Concluding Thoughts on Empowerment, Gender and Development. In Rethinking Empowerment. London: Routledge.

Stirrat, R.L. (1996) 'The New Orthodoxy and Old Truth: Participation, Empowerment and Other Buzz Words'. Chapter 3 in Bastian and Bastian (1996).

Streeten, P. (1979). "Development Ideas in Historical Perspective," in Rothko Chapel Colloquium (ed.), Toward a New Strategy for Development. New York: Pergamon Press.

Streeten, P., (1984) "Basic Needs: Some Unanswered Questions," World Development 12(9): 973-978

Streeten, P., (1984). The Distinctive Features of a Basic Needs Approach to Development. In Ghosh P. K. (Ed.), Third World development: A Basic Needs Approach: International Development Resource Books.

Strickland, C. F., (1934). Report on the Introduction of Cooperative Societies into Nigeria. Lagos: Federal Government Printer.

Suleiman, S. (2002) "Geographical and Community Targeting as an Alternative Approach to Poverty Alleviation in Nigeria". A Paper Presented at the Conference on Economic Strategy for Northern Nigeria in the 21st Century held at Daula Hotel, Kano.

Taimni, K.K. (1997): Cooperatives in the New Environments: A study of the Role of the Registrar of Cooperative Societies in Selected Countries in Asia, Rome: FAOUN

Tangenberg, K. (2000). Marginalized Epistemologies: A Feminist Approach to Understanding the Experiences of Mothers with HIV. Affilia, 15(1), 31–48.

The Nigerian *Newswatch* Newspaper, 1988: 16

The Nigerian Tribune Newspaper, (1966). *Nigerian Tribune Online* (African Newspapers of Nigeria Plc.)1966: 6-7.

The Rochdale Pioneers Museum (2002) – web page accessed on: http://www.manchester.com/tourist/rochdale/ on 15 April. ^ "The Shore Porters' Society: About Us – Our History". 2007. Retrieved 6 May 2008

The Working Together Project. www.librariesincommunities.ca/?page_id=3 (accessed Feb. 23, 2013)

Thomas, A. (1992). NGOs and the Limits to Empowerment. In Wuyts, M., Mackintosh, M. and Hewitt, T. (Eds) Development Action and Public Policy. London: Oxford University Press.

Thompson, D., (1994). "Cooperative Principles Then and Now". *Cooperative Grocer* (National Cooperative Grocers Association, Minneapolis). Retrieved, 26-01-2013.

Thorns, D. C., (1976). The Quest for Community: Social Aspects of Residential Growth. London: George Allen & Unwin.

Tong, R., (1992) Feminine and Feminist Thinking: A Critical and Creative Explosion of Ideas. Anima: The Journal for Human Experience, Vol. 18(2), 30–77.

U. S. Census Bureau (2000) Women in the United States: March 2000 (PPL-121). Retrieved October 20, 2012 from: www.census.gov/population/www/socdemo/ppl- 121.html.

Uchendu, V. C., (1965). "The Igbo of Southeast Nigeria", New York: Holt, Rinehart & Winston.

Ugwu, C.E, (2009). "The Dynamics of Community Development Programmes in Enugu State: Reflections on the Role of Ekete Local Government Council 2005-2007" in Egbo, E.A et al (Ed) Rural and Community Development: Critical Issues and Challenges. Onitsha: Austino Publishing Company.

Ujo, A. A. (1994). Development Administration in Nigeria, Kaduna: Solmora Ventures Ltd.

Umobi, A., (2008). Domestic Violence Against Women in Nigeria: A Legal Anatomy, Nigeria: Folmech Publishing Ltd.

UN, (1956). The Cambridge Summer Conference on African Administration, London: Oxford University Press.

UNDP (2001). Human Development Indicators. Human Development Report. 2001 New York: University Press.

UNDP Nigeria. (2011) Human Development Report Nigeria, 2008-9. UNDP, Abuja.

UNDP, (1990) Human Development Report 1990. New York: Oxford University Press

UNDP, (2007). The Millennium Development Goals Report 2007, Sales No. E. 07. I. 15. Also available from http://www.un.org/millenniumgoals/pdf/mdg2007.pdf

UNDP, (2010) The Real Wealth of Nations: Pathways to Human Development. Human Development Report 2010. http://hdr.undp.org/en/media/HDR_2010_EN_Complete_reprint.pdf

United Nations (1955) "Report of the Ashbridge Conference on Social Development": United Nations Miscellaneous Publication 523. (February)

United Nations (1955) *Social Progress through Community Development*, New York: United Nations.

United Nations (1995). Report of the World Summit for Social Development, Copenhagen, 6-12 March 1995. Sales No. E. 96.IV.8. Also available from http://www.un.org/esa/socdev/wssd/index.html.

United Nations Development Fund for Women (UNIFEM). (2000). Women and Economic Empowerment, New York.

United Nations Development Programme, (1998). Human Development Report 1998: Consumption for Human Development. New York and Oxford: Oxford University Press.

United Nations Development Programme. (1996). Human Development Report. Windhoek: UNDP.

United Nations, (1978) National Experience in Promoting the Cooperative Movement: Report of the Secretary General (New York: Economic and Social Council Report No. E/1978115)

United Nations, (2000) United Nations Millennium Declaration. Resolution adopted by the General Assembly. 8th Plenary Meeting, 8 September 2000. http://www.un.org/millennium/declaration/ares552e.htm Accessed November, 2012.

USAID. (2009) Country Health Statistical Report, Nigeria. December 2009.

USAID/Armenia (2005) Integrated Rural Development: Lessons Learned. USAID. Retrieved on 15 September 2008 from USAID/Armenia at http://pdf.usaid.gov/pdf_docs/PNADF432.pdf

UWCC (2002): Cooperatives, University of Wisconsin Centre for Cooperative, at www.uwcc.com

Van der Ploeg, J., Renting, H., Brunori, G., Karlheinz, K., Mannion, J., & Marsden, T., (2000). Rural development: From practices and policies towards theory. Sociologia Ruralis, 40(4), 391-408.

Van Domelen, J. (2007). "Reaching the Poor and Vulnerable: Targeting Strategies for Social Funds and Other Community–Driven Programmes", Social Protection. Discussion Paper 0711, Washington DC: World Bank.

Van Rooyen, J., Vink, N. & Malatsi, M., (1993). Agricultural Change, the Farm Sector and the Land Issue in South Africa: View point. Development Southern Africa, 10(1): 127-130.

Vaughan, O., (2000). Nigerian Chiefs: Traditional Power in Modern Politics, 1890 to 1990s. University of Rochester Press, Rochester, 6-99.

Von Braun, J., & Meinzen-Dick, R. (2009). "Land Grabbing" by Foreign Investors in Developing Countries: Risks and Opportunities: IFPRI Policy Brief 13 April 2009.

Warren, C. B., & Stokes, M. T., (1985). Investing in Development: Lessons of World Bank Experience. O.U.P: 473

Weber, M (1947) Theory of Social and Economic Organization Trans. A. Henderson and T Parsons. (Glencoe III: Free Press).

Weed, E. & Shor, N., (Eds.). (1997). Feminism Meets Queer Theory. Bloomington: Indiana University Press.

Westerinen. A. (2003) What is Policy and What can it be? Document retrieved from www.dmtf.org on 15 December, 2012.

White, T., (2011). Leadership Development, http://www.whitestag.org/index.html. Assessed 17th February, 2013.

Whitener, L. A., Gibbs, R., & Kusmin, L. (2003). Rural Welfare Reform: Lessons Learned. Amber Waves, 1(3), 38-44.

WHO, (1978). Primary Health Care Report of the International Conference on Primary Health Care Alma-Ata USSR, 6 -12 September, 1978 Switzerland

Wikipedia, (2007). Conflict Process, Wikipedia: http://en.wikipedia.org/wiki/conflict process Accessed November, 03, 2012

Wikipedia, (2008). http://en.wikipedia.org/wiki/Virtual community (Accessed Jan 11/13)

Wikipedia, (2009). Community Development. Wikipedia: Wikimedia Foundation, Inc. http://en.wikipedia.org/wiki/community_development Accessed December 15, 2012

Wikipedia, (2009). Non-Governmental Organization, Retrieved June 15, 2012, from http://en.wikipedia.org/wiki/Non-governmental_organization

Wikipedia, (2011). Department for International Development (DFID). Retrieved July 17, 2012 from http://en.wikipedia.org/wiki/DFID.

Wikipedia, (2011). United States Agency for International Development. Retrieved July 27, 2012 from http://en.wikipedia.org/wiki/United_States_Agency_for_International_D evelopment

Wikipedia, (2012). Conflict Resolution, Wikipedia: http://en.wikipedia.org/wiki/conflict_resolution Accessed November, 16, 2012

Wikipedia, (2012). Women, Wikipedia: http://en.wikipedia.org/wiki/women Accessed November, 16, 2012

Wilcox, C. & Shepherd W. G. (1975). Public Politics Towards Business, Home-word: Richard D. Irusin Inc.

Wilkinson, K. P. (1979). "Social Well-being and community", Journal of the Community Development Society. Vol.10(1).

Willetts, P. (2002). What is a Non-Governmental Organisation. Output from the Research Project on Civil Society Networks in Global Governance. Centre for International Politics, School of Social Science, City University, Northampton Square, London. Retrieved June 5, 2012, from http://www.globalpolicy.org/ngos/intro/general/2000/anal00.htm

Williams, G., (1976) Nigeria Economy and History, London: Rex Collins

Williams, S. K. T. et al., (1984). A Manual for Agricultural Extension Workers in Nigeria. Ibadan: Les Shyraden.

Willmot, P., (1989). Community Initiatives: Patterns and Prospects. London: Policy Studies Institute.

World Bank (1975). Rural Development: Sector Policy Paper: Washington DC. World Bank

World Bank (2006). Empowerment in Practice. From Analysis to Implementation. World Bank, Washington DC.

World Bank Development Indicators (Nigeria) 2000/2001 Report.

World Bank, (1991). World Development Report. New York: Oxford University Press.

World Bank, (1996a). Nigeria: Poverty in the Midst of Plenty. The Challenge of Growth with Inclusion. A World Bank Poverty Assessment, May 31, The World Bank, Washington, D.C.

World Bank, (1996c). Taking Action for Poverty Reduction in Sub-Saharan Africa. Report of an African Region Task Force, May, 1, World Bank, Washington, D.C.

World Bank, (1997). Rural Development: From Vision to Action: Washington DC. World Bank

World Bank, (2007). Poverty Net. Retrieved April 26, 2012 from: http://web.worldbank.org/WBSITE/EXTERNAL/TOPICS/EXTPOVERT Y/"The World Bank, 2007, Understanding Poverty". Web.worldbank.org. 2005-04-19. Retrieved 2010-10-24.

World Bank. (1995). Status Report on Poverty in Sub-Saharan Africa: Incidence and Trends of Poverty. Human Resources and Poverty Division, African Technical Department, Washington. World Bank.

World Bank. (1996b). Pursuing Common Goals: Strengthening Relations Between Government and NGOs in Bangladesh. Dhaka: World Bank.

World Bank. (2008). Nigeria – A Review of the Costs and Financing of Public Education. Vol. II., Main Report. The World Bank, Washington.

World Bank. (2009). An Assessment of the Investment Climate in Nigeria. Washington: The World Bank.

World Bank. (2011). Operationalizing the 2011 World Development Report: Conflict, Security and Development. Washington: The World Bank.

World Development, (2000). Community Driven Development in Africa: A Vision of Poverty Reduction Through Empowerment, The World Bank African Region

World Employment Conference, (1997). Employment, Growth and Basic Needs: A One-World Problem, New York: Praeger Publishers.

World Employment Conference, (1997). Meeting Basic Needs: Strategies for Eradicating Mass Poverty and Unemployment (Geneva: ILO).

World Health Organization (WHO). (2007). Bulletin, Vol. 85, No. 10, October.

Wu, B., (2003). Farmer Innovation and Self-Organization in Marginal Areas, Sustainable Development in Rural China. London & New York: Routledge.

Yalokwu, P. O., (2000). Management: Concept and Techniques. Lagos: Peak Publishers.

Zaccaro, S. J., Rittman, A. L., & Marks, M. A. (2001). Team leadership. Leadership Quarterly, 12(4), 451-483.

Zastrow, C., (2006). The Practice of Social Work: A Comprehensive Work-text, California: Wadsworth Pub Co.

Zeldin, S. (2002). Sense of Community and Positive Adult Beliefs Toward Adolescents and Youth Policy in Urban Neighborhoods and Small Cities. *Journal of Youth and Adolescence,* Vol. 31(5).

Index